PARA·DOXA
STUDIES IN WORLD LITERARY GENRES

CONTENTS Number 15

Native American Literature: Boundaries and Sovereignties

Kathryn W. Shanley	"Born from the Need to Say": Boundaries and Sovereignties in Native American Literary and Cultural Studies	3
James Welch	*Paradoxa* Interview with James Welch	17
Valerie Adamcyk	Revising the Captivity Narrative: *Lost Bird of Wounded Knee*	38
Ellen L. Arnold	Maps Over the Face of God: Remapping Epistemologies in Linda Hogan's *Solar Storms*	49
Celia Naylor-Ojurongbe	Contested Common Ground: Cherokee Freedpeople's National Identity and Land Ownership in the Cherokee Nation, Indian Territory	61
Duane Niatum	The Transformational Tracks of a Marginalized Life	75
Simona Fojtová	Forging the Discursive Presence in Gerald Vizenor's *Manifest Manners: Postindian Warriors of Survivance*	86
Peter Alan Froehlich & Joy Harris Philpott	Leslie Marmon Silko's *Ceremony*: A Different Kind of Captivity Narrative	98
Jane Haladay	Solemn Laughter: Humor as Subversion and Resistance in Simon Ortiz and Carter Revard	114
Mark Ingram	Envisioning Anthropology: David MacDougall and the Next Culture	132
Jennifer Lei Jenkins	Hearths and Minds: Violence and Domesticity in a Hopi Life	146
Roger Dunsmore	The Power of Kinship	158
Louis Owens	As If an Indian Were Really an Indian: Uramericans, Euramericans, and Postcolonial Theory	170
Jesse Peters	A Multitude of Routes, Roads and Paths: Transcultural Healing in A.A. Carr's *Eye Killers*	184

Beth Hege Piatote	Bodies of Memory and Forgetting: "Putting on Weight" in Leslie Marmon Silko's *Almanac of the Dead*	198
Malea Powell	Imagining a New Indian: Listening to the Rhetoric of Survivance in Charles Eastman's *From the Deep Woods to Civilization*	211
Linda Palen Ruzich	"Sacred Thresholds": Transformation and Liminality in the Novels of Linda Hogan	227
Elvira Pulitano	Travelling the Hyperreality of Indian Simulations: Gerald Vizenor's *Darkness in Saint Louis Bearheart*	241
Kimberly Roppolo	Towards a Tribal-Centered Reading of Native Literature: Using Indigenous Rhetoric(s) Instead of Literary Analysis	263
Kimberly Roppolo	Wisdom of the Elders	275
Geary Hobson	Indian Academics Must Speak for Themselves	279
P. Jane Hafen	More than Intellectual Exploration	280
Jeane Breinig	To Native Scholars, Just Starting Out	281
Clifford E. Trafzer	Sharing with Native Communities and Elders	282
Carol Miller	Academe as Indian Country	283
Louis Owens	Part and Whole: Dangerous Bifurcations	286
Vine Deloria	No More Free Rides	287
Martha Barter	Review of *The Insistence of the Indian: Race and Nationalism in 19th Centiry American Culture*	288
Susan Bernardin	Review of *Leslie Marmon Silko: A Collection of Critical Essays*	292
Andrew Denson	Review of *The Voice of the Dawn: An Autohistory of the Abenaki Nation*	297
Robert F. Gish	Review of *The Rock Island Hiking Club: Poems by Ray A. Young Bear*	300
Carol Miller	Review of *Louise Erdrich, A Critical Companion*	306
Jace Weaver	Review of *Coyote Kills John Wayne*	310

Paradoxa is listed in the Modern Language Association's *Directory of Periodicals* and in the *American Humanities Index*.

"Born from the Need to Say": Boundaries and Sovereignties in Native American Literary and Cultural Studies

Kathryn W. Shanley
University of Montana, Missoula

> *Touch home.* I'm driving my car up the switchbacks so familiar I close my eyes. *Touch home.* Your hands on that piano almost too large for the room. *Touch home.* My best friend passed out next to the dumpster outside the Trading Post. *Touch home.* Your house older than the trees that surround it. *Touch home.* Blue Creek, Turtle Lake, so close to our uranium mine the water drives a Geiger counter crazy. *Touch home.* Your mirrors that don't hold my reflection. *Touch home.* My family portraits that don't carry a white face. *Touch home.* We don't have keys for the same doors.
>
> Sherman Alexie, "Red Blues"

Nothing defines indigenous peoples more than belonging to a place, a homeland. No single political issue has been more important to indigenous peoples than the effort to retain land bases, recover lost territories, and hang on to hunting, water, mineral, and other rights associated with living in a particular place. Yet "home" also functions metaphorically to refer to a future place of self-esteem (on the individual level), and self-governance, cultural maintenance, revitalization, and sovereignty (on the collective level). "Home" may not be a "place" indigenous people have ever been before—the global economic structure requires new forms of culture and governance. The drive to go "there" nevertheless urgently continues.[1]

For example, on March 3, 2001, thousands of Mexican Indians[2] gathered in Nurio, Mexico, to demand that the Mexican government pass the Indigenous Rights Bill, an amendment to the Constitution; then they continued their march north to Mexico City. According to Associated Press

---

[1] William Bevis' article, "American Indian Novels: Homing In," captures the metaphorical use and sense of the term well, although he is careful to disavow any efforts to be "proscriptive [or] exhaustive" in discussing American Indian novels (581).

[2] Throughout this essay I will use the terms "Indian," "American Indian," "Native American," "Native," and "indigenous" fairly interchangeably, depending on the context. "Indian" is a term reservation people often use in referring to themselves, and do so, I would argue, as a gesture of reclaiming the term for their own uses. "American Indian" may be less riddled with the negative uses to which "Indian" has been put ("dirty Indian," "drunken Indian," etc.), but to the unaware hardly strikes a

reporter Mark Stevenson, the Indians and their supporters attending the National Indigenous Congress "are united in their belief that the accord would help them preserve their diverse cultures, their languages and their land" (*Missoulian* A10). As a practical strategy, the Mexican National Indigenous Congress unites diverse groups of indigenous peoples, following a centuries-old imperative to cross borders and blur boundaries—literal and figurative—for political survival. In instances where such border-crossing alliances occur, the particularities of tribal identities take a back seat to the need for constructing a united front against oppressions that threaten indigenous cultures and peoples.

Paradoxically, pan-Indian movements preserve the sovereignties that keep the peoples distinct from one another. In other words, threats to cultural distinction and to self-determination drive pan-Indian movements and alliances that, in turn, tend to generalize identities and issues. Perhaps sorting out such issues necessitates a period of somewhat unproblematized unity.

Such terms as "border-" or "boundary-crossing" extend to other aspects of identification as well—who is that small collective of people that is confronting their government? Within their ranks, their own ethnic boundaries are blurred. For example, the Zapatista leadership is itself peculiar. The charismatic, indeed enigmatic, leader of the Zapatistas movement, Subcommandante Marcos, who is non-indigenous, said a curious thing to the media about his place among the traditionalists and dissidents. He said that the "village elders had told him: 'You are no longer you. You are one of us'" (*Missoulian* A10).[3] His service to and identification with indigenous peoples and their causes has earned him an indigenous identity of sorts, a place within the community. So what does that signify about cultural boundaries? about identities?

American Indian literatures figure in both the politics and the aesthetics of such boundary-crossings—the messages and the mediums—and they also embody such paradoxes as pan-Indian defenses of cultural distinctions. Identity, however, is only one of the many threads in the tangle of issues accompanying emergent literatures. As the body of writing grows and older works are rediscovered, that literature spins out theories of its reasons for being—fuller versions of the how, the what, the why. Native North American literatures and the attendant literary criticism movement are at such a juncture.

---

new chord; legally the term refers to the indigenous peoples of the lower forty-eight states. "Native American" refers legally to indigenous peoples of the lower forty-eight states as well as Alaskan Natives and Native Hawaiians. "Native" and "indigenous" seem to capture the more dignified implication of being first in a particular geographical region. "First Nations," a term that originated in Canada, claims sovereign status with other nation-states, and therefore, most aptly represents political relations between nations. Being tribally specific whenever possible also fosters the sense of the distinctiveness of tribal groups, both politically and culturally.

[3]Marcos calls himself "Subcommandante" instead of "Commandante" to make the point that he serves the elders.

The people(s) whose voices have begun to mount in significant numbers, representing various perspectives, tribal affiliations, and experience, comprise that emergent literature, and early writings merit reexamination in light of these new voices and new perspectives. As Elizabeth Cook-Lynn notes:

> The emergence of the indigenous voice in academia in the last several decades has been recognized as a huge breakthrough for the right to speak for oneself and one's people. It is as fundamental as food and decent housing. It is a common acknowledgment that men and women do not live by bread alone; they live by the creative arts, by storytelling, and the intellect, all of which give vibrancy to culture and politics. (80)

Celebrating the recognition of the right of formerly subjugated peoples to speak requires coming to terms with history, with the "bread and butter" of contemporary tribal existence, and with the political and social issues around (post)colonial recovery.[4]

Intellectual traditions persist despite the absence of recognition by mainstream society, but the openness of the contemporary literary movement sets it apart from movements of the past. In 1915, Arthur C. Parker, early twentieth-century Seneca scholar, forthrightly denounced the injustices meted out to American Indians, when he wrote: "The people of the United States through their governmental agencies, and through the aggression of their citizens have ... [r]obbed a race of men—the American Indian—of their intellectual life ..." (97). To that charge, Parker adds a list of things robbed: "his social organization," "his native freedom," "his economic independence," "his moral standards" and "racial ideals," "his good name among the peoples of the earth," and "a definite civil status" (97). That the intellectual credibility of American Indians rates first among the many losses Parker identifies presages the truth of Cook-Lynn's idea that expressive aspects of cultures are as essential as bread and butter to a people.

In order for the vibrancy of the creative arts of which Cook-Lynn speaks to persist, without their becoming separated or disconnected from the politics of liberation and social justice, they must be accompanied by an appropriately cogent and visionary criticism. That criticism must also be historically grounded, just as the literature itself often must explain its cultural terms if it hopes to be published and understood by a non-indigenous readership that makes publication profitable in a capitalist economy. More importantly, grounding the literature in history matters to the integrity of the art as well

---

[4] Given the latest scandal (Cobelle v. Bureau of Indian Affairs and Secretary of the Department of Interior), surrounding a century-long mismanagement by the Bureau of Indian Affairs of American Indian individual accounts, American Indians can hardly be seen as "formerly subjugated," in the absolute sense of the phrase. Here I refer to the tribal nations' move from colonial subjugation to a state of quasi-sovereignty.

as to the politics it reflects and furthers. At every turn in the growth process, an emergent literature's critical arm must take account of its continued connection to the peoples whose struggles gave it life to begin with.

We must ask ourselves, who speaks for whom, and out of what sort of indigenous experience arise the most useful questions to guide the periodic self-checks in the field of American Indian literary study? Furthermore, can such critical perspectives be offered by non-indigenous thinkers and writers also and as well? These are *authenticity questions* at base. They are questions that bear the great weight of poignancy when the underlying goal is to preserve Native cultures and languages in the context of larger struggles to protect indigenous lands and resources. Granted, prevalent notions of culture as static often inhibit or deny nuanced readings of social realities; nonetheless, the "authenticity" of the "message" can matter almost as much as the right of indigenous people to speak on their own behalf, when ethnic distinctions are flattened in order to reach a broader audience. Or so it would seem, as in the case of Subcommandante Marcos becoming "one of us" to the Mexican indigenous people. Yet, empowering Native peoples to speak, to publish, to hold academic positions—in short, to reclaim the intellectual place lost through institutional racism, assimilationist practices and policies, cannot be ignored.[5] Intellectual honesty about the complexities of issues must guide us, as must a recognition of the stakes for tribal nations in the debates.

Although we all know in a commonsensical way that such a thing as *authenticity* exists, locating and defining that thing is not simple or easy, especially when it comes to written works. Authenticity might refer to an ontology or epistemology, and should not be confused with a generalization based on a notion of the "typical" individual of a particular group, such as, "the Lakota woman." Contemporary postcolonial theories begin to enable us to sort out the questions and, thereby, to configure the implications. Amritjit Singh and Peter Schmidt, in their introduction to a collection of essays entitled *Postcolonial Theory and the United States*, divide authenticity debates into two different camps: "Our thesis is that recent U.S. race and ethnicity studies split into two groups with rather different premises, the 'borders' schools and the 'postethnicity' school …" (xi). In the former, individuals move through and around categories to express themselves and to advance their causes; in the latter, categories themselves melt away in an effort to allow for all philosophically possible perspectives. Singh and Schmidt pose the

---

[5] Formal university education by no means constitutes all that we might term American Indian intellectualism. Traditional knowledges may, in fact, best be preserved in the oral tradition, as far away from publication and academic institutions as possible. While knowledge as representation in the modernist sense, "mind as mirror reflecting reality," has been replaced by "knowledge as action, a political and social tool," in American pragmatist thought (McCarthy 8), non-indigenous readers often expect American Indian representation to be transparent—a mirrored reflection of American Indian life.

question: "[T]o what degree may the necessity of borders and transnational emphases be confirmed—especially when debates about 'authenticity' and identity and who may speak on behalf of tribal communities have such huge consequences?" (42). Regardless of whether a particular critic may fall readily into one camp or the other (as if the two were mutually exclusive!), he or she must nevertheless acknowledge the political implications of his or her position relative to the "huge consequences" that the representations of indigenous or American Indian lives can have on the people(s) themselves. Policy decisions are based on the public attitudes and information about them that these critics influence and inform. Perhaps saying so makes a greater claim for the power of intellectual work than it deserves, but I do not think so.

In many ways, the late twentieth and early twenty-first centuries find North American Indian intellectualism on the rise as if for the first time, and this happens when indigenous peoples around the globe face challenges that North American Indians have faced for centuries.[6] That is not to say America's indigenous peoples have been without intellectualism; as Parker indicates, they have been robbed—denied recognition, suffered denigration and distortion—of their ontologically different intellectual authority and beauty, both as indigenous nations and as tribal individuals who developed sophisticated bicultural intellectual expression and achievements. U.S. indigenous struggles, however, are positioned differently than are those of other groups, even within the western hemisphere. For example, Phillip Wearne, author of *Return of the Indian: Conquest and Revival in the Americas*, focuses on the indigenous populations and movements north and south of the United States. He explains the differences briefly by saying,

> Indian peoples coming out of the English colonial experience have fought for treaty rights and sovereignty as a priority, whereas indigenous groups in Latin America have more traditionally demanded their rights as subjects of Latin American nation states. Such historical differences can produce chasms of misunderstanding when indigenous peoples from north and south America meet. (18)

Following Wearne's reasoning, U.S. and Canadian indigenous groups base their demands on the terms that treaty-making has allowed them, terms they inherited through the British system of controlling the sale and transfer of

---

[6] Robert Warrior argues, in *Tribal Secrets: Recovering American Indian Intellectual Traditions*, "An intellectual and critical praxis in which we focus on such tensions, differences, and process confronts us with the material reality American Indian people face in the struggle for self-determination. For if we are to build American Indian nations (or whatever other project of self-determination Indians engage in), experience tells us what problems we must confront and resources we will utilize to reach our goals" (118).

lands by the crown, and later by the central governments of the U.S. and Canada. Over time that system has shaped the nature of Native American dealings with the American and Canadian governments. While this observation may be accurate, I would argue that such a reading of the different situations of north and south American indigenous groups (south beginning sat the Mexican—U.S. border) eclipses an oppressive binarism under which all indigenous peoples struggle—the idea of "primitive" and "civilized." Viewed as a vanishing race for almost two centuries, American Indians continue to struggle against the notion of Progress and Manifest Destiny.

Writing against the grain of such binaries as savage/civilized and orality/literacy often draws indigenous writers—north and south—together in theme and focus. Simona Fojtová (in this collection) quoting Gerald Vizenor on the subject of binary thinking, stresses the importance of dissolving such dualisms: "the manifold anxieties and desires that arise from the tension announced in the binary of savagism and civilization are other simulations in the literature of dominance." While it may be difficult to dismantle all binary thinking (Vizenor himself creates the binary pair, survivance/dominance), being conscious of cultural and historical complexities implied in such pairings is a start. Just as generalizing all indigenous groups into one lump is not desirable, the historical bases for the differences among indigenous groups in the Western hemisphere does not preclude the possibility of identifying common intellectual concerns. The tendency for people outside the cultures to see indigenous peoples through the lens of the savagism/civilization binary persists in subtle and not-so-subtle ways. Embedded within that paradigm resides an implicit devaluing of oral literatures (and the least literate cultures) by viewing them as if on a continuum—a historical trajectory on which advance is represented as a movement away from orality, and toward literacy. Ironically, literate indigenous cultures can also be seen as no longer "authentic."

Craig S. Womack, Creek writer and literary critic, identifies what he calls "a 'pure versus tainted' framework" in reference to linguistic translations that can be extended to other realms as well. On the "pure side" reside oral tradition, performance, original language, precontact, Indian religion, and Indian culture; on the "tainted side" we find writing, print, translation, postcontact, Indian Christians, and Indian politics (65). The role of critics of Native American literatures involves restoring Indian perspectives to older texts—texts which have not had the critical attention they deserve—and insisting upon readings of old and new texts that complicate the human realities depicted beyond mere identification of binaries. Womack states, "Critics create literary theory in relation to literature, and one would expect nothing less from national literatures—that the oral tradition would generate vital approaches for examining Native literatures. Oral tradition, then, becomes central to Native political analysis and the development of Native literary theory rather than fodder for backing up critics' pet theses..." (66-7).

Womack's solution to the problem of keeping the literature tied to its political roots, at least in part, involves seeing how oral traditions are inextricably bound to contemporary writing—a point with which this introduction began.

The idea for this collection came about before I was asked to serve as editor. An initial discussion occurred among several respected American Indians about possible hot-button topics; various Native Americans were consulted about ideas; and the initial participants narrowed the focus to "Sovereignties and Boundaries." I took part in that narrowing, because I had hoped to elude somewhat the current border studies approach by insisting upon recognition of the political base from which Native American literature springs—sovereignty struggles. The project was announced, and papers were invited from a wide spectrum of Native American scholars, writers, and poets. Many expressed interest who were regrettably not able to contribute. Over time, the project evolved organically from the more than seventy submissions received; as new books came out, reviews were added. The idea for the email conversation that Kim Roppolo conducted came toward the end. While we expected to produce something more narrowly focused, the final form ranges over many different views of sovereignty and borders. We have all learned a great deal about the logistics of shuttling paper back and forth across the continent, and more importantly about negotiating understanding, negotiating feedback, negotiating positive criticism, about how to offer and receive helpful suggestions, generous and trusting responses. We have learned a great deal about the variety, the multiplicity, the wonderful diversity with the Native way, all of which we hope will contribute toward a broader and more nuanced appreciation of the richness of Native history and wisdom.

The interview with author James Welch (*Riding the Earthboy 40*, *Winter in the Blood*, *Death of Jim Loney*, *Fools Crow*, *Indian Lawyer*, *Killing Custer*, and *Heartsong of Charging Elk*) was, for me, years in the coming. His first novel, *Winter in the Blood*, inspired my pursuit of a Ph.D. in American Indian literature during the 1980s, offering as it does a view of American Indian life in the part of the country I call home. Much as Welch has said of his own realization that he, too, could be a writer, I accepted the challenge of writing about what I know. Welch speaks, in our conversation, in ways that illustrate a splendidly complex, subtle, nuanced Native way of negotiating subjects with generosity, with respect, with humor. We hoped for fluency, mutuality, reciprocity, and, ultimately, a level of comprehension of the issues involved in Indian writing that would be useful to students and writers of Native literature—a conversation that would be honest and engaged, without pretending to be the last word. The reader will be the best judge of whether or not we achieved our goal.

It is fitting that the essays themselves begin with Valerie Adamcyk's "Revising the Captivity Narrative: *Lost Bird of Wounded Knee*," an essay in which the genre of the captivity narrative is discussed as it applies to the lifestory of a Native woman, Zintkala Nuni, Lost Bird. Adamcyk discusses Rebee Sansom Flood's biography of Zintkala Nuni who was an object of contestation from the time she was an infant, snatched from her dead mother's arms four days after the Wounded Knee Massacre. As the "ultimate boundary situation," Zintkala Nuni's short, tragic life involved child abuse, exploitation as a "trophy of war," and, ultimately, rejection by both white and Lakota peoples. Although she did not find the "home" where they always have to take you in, her place within the history of her people, the Lakota, has since been secured.

The often clichéd expression of "living in two worlds" takes on new and expanded meaning in Ellen Arnold's essay on Linda Hogan's novel *Solar Storms,* new meaning with *poignancy* restored. In "Maps Over the Face of God: Remapping Epistemologies in Linda Hogan's *Solar Storms*," Arnold speaks of Hogan's second novel as one that "negotiates the divided world [in which humans separate themselves from nature, where individuals and peoples suffer racial divides] with multiple ways of knowing and being, and thus participates in the healing of its divisions." Mapping, in the context of Hogan's writing, Arnold argues, blurs the boundaries of land (and its inhabitants) that colonialist endeavors would parcel and price for exploitation. At the same time, Hogan illuminates the complex identity issues of a young woman seeking the home within her. As the question is posed by one of the novel's characters—"how do conquered people get back their lives"?—the seamless whole of how seeking social justice connects with seeking personal and familial healing becomes clear.

Whereas Arnold takes up the war being fought for the besieged earth, Celia E. Naylor-Ojurongbe, focuses on the WPA narratives of Cherokee freedmen who returned to the Cherokee Nation, Indian Territory, to make their home after the devastations of the Civil War. Contradictions and ironies abound as Naylor-Ojurongbe reads the historical groundings of "race" relations involving Cherokee slavemasters, African/Native American slaves, and other players in post-war Indian Territory.

Duane Niatum (Klallum) offers a reading of American Indian poets and poetry since the outpouring of writing in the 1960s and 1970s, the time when N. Scott Momaday and Niatum himself led young Indian writers to find their voices in the genre. Honoring young poets Elizabeth Woody, Sherman Alexie, Deborah A. Miranda, Arthur Tulee, Tiffany Midge, and Mary Lockwood, Niatum constructs his essay around the theme of home. In responding to Alexie's poem, "Where the Indian never loses," Niatum muses, "These lines ... could almost launch Crazy Horse into a sit-up position from his secret grave and spur him to ride for the Milky Way, if he was not already riding somewhere along the black slopes of Paha Sapa, singing for a way to get this poet home before the fire burns out." The journey described suggests links between writing and surviving (or Vizenor's term, "survivance"), and singing in the traditional way, for centering and healing.

Simona Fojtová offers a close reading of "the discursive presence" in Gerald Vizenor's text on representation and postmodernism, *Manifest Manners: Postindian Warriors of Survivance*. The language game Vizenor constructs takes issue with the cultural perspectives that diminish and distort American Indian voices and views through scientific or romantic impositions. Fojtova writes, "In order to battle the extermination of tribal cultures in representations, strategies for surviving the invention become central to Vizenor's writing. When Vizenor contrasts academic invention with tribal imagination, when he compensates for the absence of the real with the presence of humor and tribal memory, he avoids representing images no matter how 'native' they are." Without ways of imagining ourselves out of representations in which we find ourselves trapped, we would merely duplicate the static and essentialist images and assumptions of dominant discourses.

While much has been written about Leslie Marmon Silko's *Ceremony*, Peter Alan Froehlich and Joy Harris Philpott add new dimensions to the study of that important novel by focussing on the ways in which it functions as "a different kind of captivity narrative." Tayo's "capture" takes place because he does not understand the ideological terms of his position in the world as an in-between person, a person suffering from post-traumatic shock. As Froehlich and Philpott argue, "Tayo cannot return to a separate and distinct natal culture," as would be the case with a traditional Euro-American captivity narrative, "because he has always occupied what Richard White calls a 'middle ground.' This model represents the frontier as contested space, a region occupied by a hybrid culture that is part of, yet distinct and set apart from, the two or more cultures that contribute to the combination." Shunning regenerative violence as a means to resolve his hybrid nature, Tayo fashions a whole self out by forging a connection to the deeply rooted belief of harmony with the natural world. Like Lost Bird, Tayo must struggle to understand himself in relation to a much larger politic and history.

In a way that reflects upon the double consciousness American Indian writers must employ to write from their own experiences while at the same time communicating with non-tribal readers, Jane Haladay examines the mediating power of humor in her study of the works of Simon Ortiz and Carter Revard. Haladay writes, "[W]hile the profound biases, distortions, misunderstandings, assumptions, condescensions and outright hatred in colonial and post-colonial literary representations of Native American peoples are centuries old, it has not been until relatively recently—within the last one hundred years—that Native people have had opportunities to represent themselves to a significant degree in mainstream texts." Putting to good use the humor so prevalent in Indian communities, Ortiz and Revard "tease and invert the highly prized white creation of 'Indian' as artifact, dress-up doll, and passive consumer commodity." Native peoples have used humor to explain and deconstruct threatening Others perhaps since first contact, and humorous writing dates back at least a century. These authors aptly illustrate how the traditional expressions of satire and irony continue to function.

Mark Ingram, in his essay-review of David MacDougall's collected essays, *Transcultural Cinema*, tackles the difficulties surrounding the use of the term "culture," as it may or may not be applied to "a new global context." Moreover, MacDougall's essays reflect the filmmaker anthropologist's thirty-two year career and twenty-two ethnographic films. Ingram claims that MacDougall "both speaks to anthropological debates, and seeks to recast documentary film as a dynamic and creative genre," despite disastrous portraitures of indigenous peoples in films such as *The Gods Must Be Crazy*. Taking apart the descriptive phrase, "participant observer," Ingram presents an analysis of documentary film and locates MacDougall as one who uses the media as "reciprocal observation and exchange." Harkening back to Womack's liberation of oral tradition from its static location in binary opposition to writing, I find MacDougall's position, as presented by Ingram, of the potential in documentary film refreshing: "Visual images ultimately undermine the totalizing qualities of writing through their presentation of excess, i.e., that which is not reducible to analysis and interpretation." Vizenor should read MacDougall, if he hasn't already, for Vizenor's effort to keep language fluid and images turning resembles MacDougall's insistence on using film "as a kind of 'visual communion.'"

Jennifer Lei Jenkins explores the painful period in Hopi history when the division of the people into "hostiles" and "friendlies" threatened the basic premise of ceremonial and social life—harmony and balance. Reading Helen Sekaquaptewa's autobiography, *Me and Mine*, through the Hopi creation story as well as how it is informed by the historical events of Sekaquaptewa's time, Jenkins illuminates Hopi cultural truths regarding violence and discord. The boundaries set up by the people themselves reflect the dominant culture's pressures to assimilate Hopis into mainstream education, economics, and social fabric. The response to those external pressures illustrate strategies for adapting to change, particularly in Sekaquaptewa's own life choices, and for responding to tragedies discussed by others in the collection, most notably the struggles of Lost Bird. Roger Dunsmore also discusses the importance and power of kinship in indigenous thought and life, and he explicitly aims "to show how this deep expression of kinship, or relatedness, was used to heal wounds within the tribe, how it extended to other species, and what the implications of this might be." Education figures into both Jenkins' and Dunsmore's essays, implicitly and explicitly arguing for culturally appropriate learning settings and knowledges.

Speaking from the position of teacher and writer, Louis Owens (Choctaw/ Cherokee) broaches the subject of the "complete erasure of Native American voices in post-colonial theory" and how there is "no symmetry of expectation" among scholars when it comes to understanding the subfields within the study of literature. Knowing about American Indian cultures and contemporary concerns does not seem to be an imperative for literature scholars or theorists, Owens argues:

> [C]ritics and teachers of Native American literature are . . . very properly expected to have and exhibit a crucial knowledge of canonical European and Euramerican literature; if we fail to be familiar with Shakespeare, Chaucer, Proust, Flaubert, Dickinson, Faulkner, Eliot, Joyce, Pound, Yeats, Keats, Woolf, Tolstoy, Tennyson, and so forth—not to mention the latest poststructuralist theory—we are simply not taken seriously and probably will not have earned a university degree in the first place.

Beyond speaking of erasures, Owens cites Leela Gandhi, in arguing that the "relationship of reciprocal antagonism and desire between coloniser and colonised" require boundary blurring without losing the voice that speaks.

Such gestures, strategies, and tactics for healing the rifts and recovering the voice are the subject of Jesse Peters' discussion of A.A. Carr's *Eye Killers*. Within the novel, Peters asserts, "transcultural contact is a positive space in which positive growth and change occur." Religious choices, like other decisions that contemporary people make, often reflect the syncretic nature of the world, exposed as we are to influences as wide ranging as technological wonders and new awarenesses and knowledges of the natural world. Drawing on the writings of Bakhtin and Gerald Vizenor, Peters offers a reading of Carr's novel as a sort of unwriting of stereotypes. Carr fittingly chooses a vampire named Falke as a symbolic equalizer of humankind, a predator to whom blood-quantum wars have no meaning. Boundaries created within our minds regarding one another, like borders we create across space to label one thing "mine," sometimes require that they be imagined dialogically in order to be dispelled.

Beth Hege Piatote (Nez Perce) discusses Leslie Silko's *Almanac of the Dead* in relation to "the role of boundary-crossing that is necessary for indigenous people to reclaim a relationship that has been fractured through colonization." She also illuminates the text's theme of "seeing," another form of boundary-crossing that enables a recovery of prophetic powers and (re-)humanization of colonized subjectivities. The subjugation of indigeneity is born on the body, just as potentially liberating "spirits" move through the body, reclaiming the self from domination. The author asserts that "The success of colonization relies upon a constantly imposed fracture of memory, place and culture in a way that paralyzes the colonial subject in the present moment. This is precisely the reason why Native Americans must 'acknowledge no borders' if they are to survive." Laying claim to our own history requires fluidity of movement through time, space, and memory, as Piatote so expertly illustrates in her analysis of characters in *Almanac* who chose opposite survival strategies for themselves.

Malea Powell (Miami) complicates the portrait of Charles Eastman who is so frequently seen as a self-deluded man "caught between two worlds" wishing he were white, and she does so by reading Eastman's presentation of himself instead as a "tactical authenticity." To view Eastman as a person of bi-cultural vision and strategies to the extent that Powell does, allows us to understand the growth of American Indian intellectualism in the past century and a half. Powell's insightful discussion of Eastman enables us also to see the limitations that sometimes plague American Indian writers in their own lifetimes, when the discourse for resisting readings (and writings) has not been adequately put into place.

The mythic structure in Linda Hogan's *Mean Spirit* and *Solar Storms,* according to Linda Palen Ruzich, requires re-tellings of ancient stories in tandem with contemporary stories of struggle, unbounded returns to truth, and a belief in balance. Such purposive circularity imitates life cycles more than it dead-ends in teleological conclusions about cultural and historical particulars. Thus it is that Hogan creates "tribes" as she does characters to depict the larger struggle to preserve the integrity of the natural environment of which humans are but one part. Hogan's characters find themselves in liminal states in terms of personal growth, just as the environment works to right itself. As Ruzich says of Hogan's fiction,

> The sense of perimeters of life pervades the novels of Linda Hogan. It is in the interstices of places and events where conflict occurs and damage is done; it is also the site of healing, growth and change…. Renewal occurs when the earth is valued, when people spend time to listen to the terrestrial call of God, best heard in those marginal places on the edge of human activity.

While those "marginal places" require borders for definition, they also can contain great potential, the possibility of breaking down borders and bounded consciousness. Spiritual at their core, such depictions and representations rely upon the reader to complete them, which can be tricky if Hogan's representations strike those all-too-familiar chords in popular American culture's repertoire of ways of understanding "Indianness."

Representation takes on at least two meanings in this collection: first, the democratic idea of having a voice representative of an American Indian point of view; second, the idea of discursive and visual representation as they do or do not reflect the real lives of American Indian peoples. Elvira Pulitano, in her essay "Travelling in Hyperreality," utilizes the views of Gerald Vizenor and Umberto Eco to locate conceptual constructs that can be used to combat the dominant discourse that consistently distorts representations of American Indians and, thereby, that alter and inhibit genuine democratic representation.

Pulitano takes up the task of showing "how Vizenor's trickster discourse reconstructs and *re-imagines* the 'real,' causing the liberation of the signifier 'Indian' from the absolute fake of hyperreality." The political significance of humor, in the context of Vizenor's work, becomes clear as Pulitano walks us through the constituting metaphors of his writings.

Kimberly Roppolo (Cherokee/Choctaw/Creek) also grapples with the boundaries between differing epistemologies and ontologies—Native and non-Native, intertribal—to assert that a "tribal-centered reading" of Native American literatures can illuminate the literary roots of those writings in the oral tradition. She sees a necessity to read stories "appropriately" and to avoid "cutting away, and a "splaying" of the writing in a Western style of criticism that is linear and analytical. Following her essay, she introduces a series of statements—from respected Native American scholars Geary Hobson, P. Jane Hafen, Jeane Breinig, Clifford E. Trafzer, Carol Miller, Louis Owens and Vine Deloria–in response to questions she posed about intergenerational responsibilities and imperatives toward American Indian communities.

We have included reviews of six important new additions to the field of Native American literature and literary study. Robert Gish's (Cherokee) review of *The Rock Island Hiking Club, Poems by Ray A. Young Bear*, pays tribute to Young Bear's fine achievement as one of America's most accomplished poets. Andrew Denson's review of Frederick Wiseman's *The Voice of the Dawn: An Autohistory of the Abenaki Nation* fits perfectly with our theme: Who is an Indian? Wiseman's book navigates two spheres: that of popular culture—that is, what "casino Indians" mean to the average person who picks up the newspaper—and that where legal issues get decided and a people's fate determined—defining Indians in law for the purpose of determining whether they qualify for the "special status" of sovereignty. It is difficult to imagine a more timely scholarly discussion, one that interests American Indians as well as others, academics as well as neighbors to tribes and other U.S. citizens who ponder the meaning of contemporary American Indian existence. Two reviews—Martha Bartter's review of *The Insistence of the Indian: Race and Nationalism in 19th Century American Culture* and Jace Weaver's (Cherokee) review of *Coyote Kills John Wayne*—particularly center on representation in ways relevant to our theme of boundaries and sovereignties. Two others—Susan Bernardin's review of *Leslie Marmon Silko: A Collection of Critical Essays* and Carol Miller's (Cherokee) review of *Louise Erdrich, A Critical Companion*—provide useful perspectives on how these two texts further the conversations on these two extraordinary American Indian writers as well as how the texts function as resources for teachers. We are grateful for the insights these pieces lend us in assessing new works in our field.

When read as a whole, these essays, reviews, the Welch interview, take up similar issues, however different and significant the groundings of their particular subjects. Similarly, as we in the North observe what is happening to the indigenous peoples of Chiapas and other Mexican states, with populations of over ten million indigenous people, we recognize the urgent necessity of border-crossings—we see their struggles for social justice, their efforts to recover and continue intellectual traditions, as very much related to our efforts. The imperative to connect politics and aesthetics in writing continues. I concur with Ernesto Galeano, who states, "I only believe in words that are born from the need to say" (NPR, 3/11/01). The fact that Leslie Marmon Silko's *Almanac of the Dead* predicts the march north of recent days speaks to the interrelatedness of our times and places and purposes.

Works Cited

Alexie, Sherman. "Red Blues." In *Old Shirts & New Skins*. Los Angeles: University of California, American Indian Studies Center, 1993. 85-87.

William Bevis. "American Indian Novels: Homing In." *Recovering the Word: Essays on Native American Literature*. Eds. Brian Swann and Arnold Krupat. Berkeley: University of California Press, 1987. 580-620.

Cook-Lynn, Elizabeth. "How Scholarship Defames the Native Voice . . . and Why." *Wicazo sa Review*. Minneapolis: University of Minnesota Press, 2000. (Fall 2000). 79-92.

Galeano, Edwardo. "Interview with Michael Silverblatt." *Bookworm*, NPR, March 11, 2001.

McCarthy, Doyle. *Knowledge as Culture: The New Sociology of Knowledge*. London and New York: Routledge, 1996.

Parker, Arthur C. "Arthur C. Parker Indicts the Government for Its Actions." In *Talking Back to Civilization: Indian Voices from the Progressive Era*. Edited by Frederick E. Hoxie. Boston: Bedford/St. Martin's, 2001. 95-102.

Singh, Amritjit, and Peter Schmidt. *Postcolonial Theory and the United States*. Jackson: University Press of Mississippi, 2000.

Stevenson, Mark. "Indigenous Congress calls for rights legislation in Mexico." *Missoulian*. Sunday, March 4, 2001. A10.

Vizenor, Gerald. *Manifest Manners: Postindian Warriors of Survivance*. Hanover and London: University Press of New England, 1994.

Robert Warrior. *Tribal Secrets: Recovering American Indian Intellectual Traditions*. Minneapolis: University of Minnesota Press, 1995.

Wearne, Phillip. *Return of the Indian: Conquest and Revival in the Americas*. Philadelphia: Temple University Press, 1996.

Womack, Craig S. *Red on Red: Native American Literary Separatism*. Minneapolis: University of Minnesota Press, 1999.

Paradoxa Interview with James Welch

Kathryn W. Shanley
University of Montana, Missoula

The following interview was conducted at the home of James and Lois Welch, on July 12, 2000.

Kate Shanley: Thank you for being willing to do this.
James Welch: My pleasure.
KS: In an interview with Joe Bruchac published in Survival this Way, *you said, "[G]rowing up around the reservations, I just kept my eyes and ears open, listening to a lot of stories. You might say my senses were really brought alive by that culture. I learned more about it than I really knew. It was only after I began writing about it that I realized what I had learned. I knew quite a bit, in certain ways, about the Blackfeet and Gros Ventre ways of life, even though I wasn't raised in a traditional way. It made sense to me and I tried hard to understand those small parts." Can you elaborate on what "made sense" to you about Blackfeet and Gros Ventre ways in your growing up years?*
JW: Well, I think like most northern reservation cultures, you know, there's lots of full-bloods and mixed-bloods and government people and so on and there's just an amalgamation. I mean it's not just traditional Indian culture. And so I was part of that kind of non-traditional Indian culture. But I did keep my ears open and I listened to a lot of stories told by full blooded people who were more traditional. I also got a sense of the dynamics of the people living on the reservation. How they all worked together so that I think that my work might reflect that kind of diversity of experience rather than being about traditional Indians or about, say, a mixed blood, trying to decide whether he fits in or not. I mean, those elements are there. I think growing up on the reservations helped me to just understand how they came together.
KS: And how the bureaucracy worked within that environment, as well?
JW: Yeah, you know I just reading the *Missoulian*. Did you read that article about the "Blackfeet politics"? That was fantastic. But that's the way it is. All the families and loyalties to certain families and then they kick the whole business council out and they put new people in and that's kind of hard for other people to understand. They don't know that that's the way politics works on reservations. But I think if you spend some time on a reservation you would know that and you would know how eccentric it is but how natural it is at the same time.
Lois Welch: Can I ask, where did you hear the traditional stories? I mean, under what circumstances? In the kitchen?
JW: Well, yeah, when my relatives got together, they would be telling stories. And other people would come and tell stories. You know a lot of them were just gossip and that kind of thing. But every now and then stories would enter in.

LW: But it was basically at home that you heard them?
JW: Or at somebody else's house. Somebody else's parents' for instance. When I was a kid I might have been eating dinner with them or whatever.
LW: But it wasn't a formal story telling setting?
JW: No.
LW: I think us honkies often think that there must have been magical storytelling moments.
JW: Well, since I don't understand Blackfeet or Gros Ventre I don't think I would, or could have heard them in the real traditional sense.
KS: It seems to me that the tiyospaye, *which is what they call it in Lakota, "the family circle," was how you decided on representation, so the article on "Blackfeet politics" eclipsed that ...*
JW: Yeah. Right.
KS: I have to confess that the first time I read Winter in the Blood, *I found it sad and depressing. The second time, I laughed, well, chuckled, all the way through. It seems to me that the strength of that book is the balancing act it does between absurdity and tragedy, despair and hope. Would you talk about how you think Indian humor works in American Indian oral traditions and in American Indian writing, particularly in your work?*
JW: Well, there's two parts there. I always give an example when I talk about Indian humor of, uh, once when I was at the University of North Dakota, doing a two or three day kind of thing and Jim Crumley was there and it was kind of a literary festival. But I hooked up with some Indian people and one night, I guess after my reading, we went out to this trailer way out in the middle of nowhere. You know, just a caravan of cars. I was getting kind of worried because it was way out there and I didn't know about those Sioux. We got out there and, you know, in about 15 minutes I just felt completely at home and I laughed for about 3 or 4 hours straight. I mean it, the humor, the wit that was going around that room. You just don't hear that kind of humor and wit in other groups of people. I mean, they have their own humor. But that kind, that teasing, it just made me feel really kind of dumb because I don't have the quickness that a lot of Indian people have. I think that Indian humor is really a part of Indian life and it should be a part of the literature, too, written about Indians or by Indians. Having said that, as they say ... my books have gotten increasingly somber. You know, there's a little bit of humor here and there, but in *Winter in the Blood* I felt like I was really on top of things in terms of humor. The absurdity. I really loved the absurdity and the idea of juxtaposing things that don't seem to be quite put together. You know, like in the bar scene where the two suits are there and then one has the film out, and they're arguing about whether there are fish here or there or wherever. I've always liked that kind of humor. I don't know that that's particularly Indian humor but it's absurd. So when I could I've tried to combine some of that kind of contemporary Indian humor which, I'm sure, was done in traditional times, too. That teasing and putting people down if they get a big

head, you know. Making fun of them. I think that probably has gone on all the time. And I tried to capture a little of that.

KS: *I remember once, describing to a colleague of mine at the University of Washington, the way in which Indian people like to laugh. They make something to laugh about out of the smallest things. You couldn't have a literary critic necessarily analyze it. You could, I suppose, and I actually could talk about it, but it does seem like Indians like to laugh and most people in the mainstream society don't seem to know that.*

JW: Yeah, absolutely. I mean, it's really funny. Like, up in Browning one of the jokes was, you know, somebody pulled away, and someone else yelled at them, "Hey, you're draggin' a dog." For some reason, that's very humorous to think of this car dragging a dog.

One of the areas up in Browning is called 'Death Row,' you know (laughter). So-and-so lived on Death Row. Where does that all come from?

KS: *In Poplar we have a place that we call Chinatown.*

JW: Yeah, there's a Chinatown in Browning.

KS: *Because the people there are yellow from cirrhosis.*

LW: Your Chinatown, that was architectural, wasn't it? In Browning?

JW: I don't remember what it was but there was a Chinatown, for sure. But, yeah, as you say, I mean even the smallest things people can find something to laugh about. They're so inventive. They can think up things to call a certain place that's totally appropriate only totally humorous.

LW: Ken Lincoln in his book on Indian humor talks about it as post-apocalyptic humor. He includes you in this, Jim. In which these people who have just been through hell use humor as a way of surviving and, you know, I think feeling their humanity. It's not satire. It's a way of common bonding.

JW: Yeah. That's true.

KS: *I think so, too. I think it's common bonding, but as Jim mentioned, in order to remain in a group, one person can't think he or she is that much better than the other person. So there is a lot of self-deprecating humor and other-deprecating. And if you can't take the teasing you're in tough shape, because they're gonna go after you.*

JW: Yeah. That's right. They'll nail you if you can't take the humor or laugh at yourself.

KS: *Well, I have written about your depiction of the men in the bar and in* The Death of Jim Loney. *Not in the bar, in the café, and they're talking about going into business. And then the character named Pepion can't take a joke. And he's so dead serious about it that it becomes funny. And you'd almost have to be Indian to understand why that's funny. Because certainly in kindergarten and grade school and mainstream educational teaching, you're not supposed to make fun of anyone. And so, it has a different ring.*

JW: Uh-huh.

LW: And we think of children as cruel when, on the playground, they make fun of each other, but it is scornful then, nya-nya-nya. It's not teasing, it's alienating.

KS: Interesting questions about humor.
LW: You didn't talk about tragedy and humor,... to keep you on track.
JW: Um, well, I always think I'm telling it like it is. You know, when I write about Indian people and reservation life and so on. A lot of people have been depressed by *Winter in the Blood* and *The Death of Jim Loney*. Or, they think it's really sad and tragic what's happening here on the reservation. But, in a way, that's kind of just life with Indian people, you know. Gosh, all you have to do is look at the statistics about everything. Drinking, poverty, unemployment, and so on. And, you know, it's hard for people to try to look on the bright side, or look at their situation rationally. And so I think, in one way, that part of Indian humor is almost a gallows humor. Because their situation's so bad they can almost make sport of it. Again I just try to capture the way I have seen Indian people. I've seen young men thirty years old, thirty-two years old who just have a hell of a time making it. They end up becoming alcoholics and get in a car wreck and die or something like that. So when I write about Jim Loney or the narrator in *Winter in the Blood* I'm just kind of writing about the kind of person I have seen on the reservation. And known.
LW: Well, and your nicknames, too. I mean, "Pus Guts." That wasn't a secret name that people had, that's what they called him, right?
JW: Yeah, the head of the reservation cops up at Ft Belknap was named Plumage. I went to school with 2 of his kids. He was a big, fat guy who could barely sit behind the wheel of his cruiser. And everybody called him Pus Guts. Which I thought, now, man, that's Indian, you know. That's really demonstrative and describes him absolutely perfectly in a real humorous, kind of ugly light.
LW: Well, and in your family, Toodles and Fat. Fat, it turns out, was enormously skinny. Those are nicknames.
KS: *Better that than the two who were not skinny.*
JW: Yeah. That would have been cruel.
KS: *Well, talking about cruelty, I've never had a nickname because people see my sensitivity and I think they don't want to hurt my feelings.*
JW: Uh-huh.
KS: *So, even though I live in Indian communities and have all my life, it's been interesting how a gentleness can come out in humor as well. That you don't just call just anybody Pus Guts.*
JW: No, that's true.
KS: *Because a lot of Indian people are overweight. There's lots of reasons for that. Commodities, for one.*
JW: Yeah, right. I think that that nickname probably happened a long time ago and, uh, I mean, just read the *Glacier Reporter,* the Browning newspaper. It's full of all kinds of nicknames. And some of them sound a little cruel but they're probably not. That's just what they call that person and that person accepts it and probably calls the others something else.

KS: I've been thinking that we need to find some way to archive these local newspapers locally, and that future generations of researchers will find a richness in them that will come out in all these small ways. I remember one from Poplar where these parents are wishing their child a happy birthday. The child is probably about 18 and they say, "Happy Birthday to our Number One Poop-face" (laughter). Not the sort of thing you would print in the Missoulian.

JW: No. That's right.

KS: Well, that topic could constitute an interview in itself. In your first four novels, you depict male protagonists who are, in one way or another, coming to terms with their identities as American Indian or Pikuni men. Winter in the Blood *is the only one of your novels presented in the first-person voice, however. Would you talk about why using a central male protagonist seems to work best for you?*

JW: Well, I suppose the obvious answer is that I'm male and, you know, it's easy. It's a lot easier for me to look at the world through male eyes because that's what I do all the time. So, I guess, in a way, it's uh, natural. But that does raise a good point because I have thought of using a female point of view. I've used it, partially, in alternating chapters in some books. But I've never consistently used a female point of view. I think it's basically just because I find it easier through the male eyes. I haven't quite accepted the challenge of looking at the world through female eyes like Jim Harrison did in *Dalva* and, I think, the sequel to *Dalva*. Other male writers have done that but it's just not been something I've been comfortable doing so far. Although it would be a challenge and I'd be happy to do it if I could think of the right situation, a right novel to have a female protagonist. That's what you call it, I guess. And look at the world through her eyes. I think I'd like to try that.

KS: Well, that leads to the next question. Would you talk a little about how your depiction of female characters has changed from book to book?

JW: Well, in *Winter in the Blood* I'm not so sure that any women come off, actually, very well. You know, they all have ...

KS: Neither do the men.

JW: No, that's true. Maybe that's what people found kind of bleak about it was the characters. In *The Death of Jim Loney* I think the character of Rhea and his sister Kate both exhibited certain strengths. Especially Kate, obviously. She was quite a go-getter. I always tell people when they ask me about the character of Kate, that I've seen her so often, you know, because in contemporary Indian society, quite often, it's the women who kind of run it. Who have the responsible jobs. Who are very important in education. They're in health or whatever. And, so, Kate to me is quite a natural character. Kind of an amalgam of some very strong Indian women I have known. And I think I tried to make the women characters after *Winter in the Blood* more ... I tried to understand them better, maybe. *Winter in the Blood* was my first novel, and I didn't know quite what I was doing. I didn't know how to juggle

all the balls. So I may have given the shorter shrift to the women characters in that book. But I think in subsequent books I've tried to make them more rounded. Whether they're strong people or not, at least they're rounded and they're more sympathetic. I think I'm trying to empathize with them so that I can present them as real people. I think that's what I've pretty much done in this new book (*Heartsong of Charging Elk*). There are women characters that are very strong and rounded and then there's one that's not. I mean she's weak, in a way, because she's an ignorant country girl working in a house of prostitution. And she's insecure because if she isn't a prostitute she has to be a washer woman or something, so the house of prostitution is better than her alternatives. So in a sense she's weak. But I think she's sympathetic. You can understand why she thinks the way she does and feels the way she does.
KS: So women are circumstantially different from men in a society that doesn't give them jobs or that discriminates against them because they are women, basically. But what you're saying is that what you try to do is to depict them in a real way.
JW: Yeah, given the times that they lived in, you know. In my historical novels, the women had different, I wouldn't say roles, but maybe in *Fools Crow* they had a different role from the men. But in this latest one, I'm not so sure that the women had different roles, but they were looked down upon for the most part unless they were of the upper classes. But a woman like Marie, the prostitute, people just looked at women like her as servants in a lot of ways.
KS: The Death of Jim Loney *and* Indian Lawyer *take up very different sides of prison life—Jim Loney would rather die than go to prison and Sylvester Yellow Calf struggles with the politics involved in being an Indian lawyer on the parole board. I'm curious why you did not write about prison life itself. And this question raises the issue of Who owns the story? In other words, would it be a violation of another person's right to his or her own story to write about some of the things you learned through your ten years on the parole board?*
JW: Well, I think Sylvester Yellow Calf was a pretty natural choice. When you're on the parole board you go over to the prison once a month, and you go to the youth camp, and you go to the life skills centers. There's one in Billings and one in Great Falls as well as one in Missoula, you're there very briefly to interview people and decide whether they should have parole. You get all kinds of prison reports, and psychological reports, and rap sheets, and all that kind of stuff. You've got a lot of material before you so that you can make a pretty informed decision. But you don't really get into the inner workings of the prison. You're still pretty much a visitor. We've had tours of the prison, you know, to all the units: max, and the low side of security, and so on. I could write a novel about an inmate set completely in prison based on my knowledge of Deer Lodge, but so far an idea hasn't come to me. What would I write about? Who would the characters be, what would be the conflict, and so on. Just because you don't write about something that you

may have had some experience with doesn't mean that you don't want to or you can't. It's just that you find other things at any given time more important, more interesting to write about. Who knows, I'm not done yet. My next novel might be about an inmate in Deer Lodge. Or a woman.

KS: Yeah.

JW: That's nice about being a writer, you know, there's lots of things you can write. Ways you can challenge yourself. Because I always try to write something different each time out. I don't want to write the same sort of thing. I like Louise Erdrich a lot but I think she has a tendency to write about the same kinds of things, book after book. Just a different take on it. I think she really needs to step back, come at things from a whole different point of view. So I've made a conscious effort to write about something different each time.

KS: Since you mentioned Louise Erdrich, I'd like to ask you a question about her work. Do you feel she is formulaic in the way in which she depicts people's foibles? Or do feel like what she's trying to do is to present a community in almost, not meaning it in a derogatory way, a soap opera style?

JW: Well, she certainly has investigated many areas of the community she writes about. You know Jim Burke, the mystery writer? In his first couple of mystery novels with Dave Robicheau, I really liked, you know, being down there in Louisiana, exotic country and great characters and so on. Then the third one, I couldn't even finish. I had no desire to read because he kept mining the same territory. That is formulaic. That's mystery writing stuff.

LW: And you don't just mean geography. You mean situation, relation to situation, and all that.

JW: Yeah. And the same formula for violence, you know. He's always got to get beat up at least twice. And he's got to beat up people three times. And they all have to shoot each other. And there's got to be a big, menacing guy, you know. Louise Erdrich, I mean, she is really exploring the community that she writes about, different characters and so on. It's just that, you know, maybe you should take a rest once in a while from that particular community and go on to something else. You could even relate to that community but just a point of view that would be kind of unexpected. And so I think that's kind of what I miss in her succeeding work. Louise is a wonderful woman. I would really like her to knock my socks off next time. And she is more than capable of it.

LW: And *From Columbus* wasn't the excursion.

JW: No. That was a big money-making venture.

KS: Well, my favorite Erdrich work is Tracks *and I think the reason it's my favorite is because it covers the early reservation years and presents, in Nanapush, a character who attempts to intersect with tribal politics and bureaucracy in a meaningful way for Indian people. And the rest of it fits with it: the depiction of Fleur, certainly the lake, the levels of spirituality in the Catholic church, and all that. But I like the backward reach of that book. That's the book I most frequently teach.*

JW: Is that right?
KS: Uh-huh.... *One way of looking at the trajectory of your work, at least as far as themes are concerned, is to watch you coming to terms with the force of history—both written history and the oral history of Native peoples.* Killing Custer, *in fact, represents a sort of culmination of historical inquiry about what happened in the mid-nineteenth century to Plains Indian people. Would you comment on how history and historically based events figure in your development as a writer?*
JW: Well, let's see. I got to go back and say that after *Winter in the Blood* and *The Death of Jim Loney* and my book of poems, my editor said, "You have written about these guys, they're in their 30's, they're at loose ends, and both books," he said, "were very downers." And he said, "You've got to write about something different." And I said I been thinking about the historical Blackfeet. A novel about them. He said, "Great. That's great. Why don't you do that?" And so that's how that book kind of came about. I had been thinking about it, really, but not too seriously that soon. And so when I wrote it I felt that it just really opened my eyes to where these people came from? These contemporary people that I was writing about. Where did they come from? What was the difference between that old tribal, traditional culture and where they are now? So it really was kind of an eye opener for me. And it made me think that, you know, the history really is every bit as interesting as contemporary life. Because to me, back then, I thought that you had to write about contemporary life if you were to depict the Indian accurately. And so, when I started writing about the traditional life I realized that, boy, this really feeds into where they are, what they lost, and what kind of life was so natural to them. And then they lost it and this is what happened. And so, yeah, I've become interested in Indian history with *Killing Custer* and now with, um, uh, I can't remember the name of my new one (*Heartsong of Charging Elk*). But, at any rate, you know they are all historical. And I love to write about historical situations. It just makes them more plausible by today's society's standards. You know what I mean? The Lakota people were really trying hard to live. You know, Sitting Bull and Crazy Horse, the Hunkpapas, the Oglalas. They weren't making trouble. In fact, they were avoiding trouble. They wanted never to see a white man as long as they lived. They just wanted to go out into the hunting areas of Montana and so on. But, of course, the soldiers came for them and, in a way, people seemed to put the shoe on the other foot. That the soldiers were after them because they were such troublemakers and, you know, just raising hell and killing people and everything. They weren't. So in a way, when you write about history like that you can almost correct perceptions about Indians from long ago.
KS: *Well, that's worth doing.*
JW: I think it is.
KS: *You have spoken elsewhere about your use of real names, how they carry power, and I understand some Indian people do not like seeing their names*

used in fiction. Have you taken any flack for using the names of living American Indian families? Have your thoughts changed about this over the years?
JW: Um, I took flack once for one of the characters in *Fools Crow* which is a family name. And I understood that the family didn't like my fictional depiction of their ancestor. That was Yellow Kidney, you know, who fornicates with the girl dying of small pox. And they catch him and cut off his fingers and so on. They didn't like that depiction of one of their ancestors, and I can't blame them. I guess that that was insensitive. If I had it to do over again I would create a totally fictional name for that character. But I've found that most Indian people are kind of thrilled by having their names in my books. *Earthboy*, you know, writing *Earthboy* I had a young woman come up and say I'm an Earthbo, (laughter), and I've had people from Browning mention their songs and so their names were in my book. And so, I think they're kind of innocent and naïve enough to be kind of pleased that their names were being used. Maybe they think it's a history book instead of a novel. But I find that very touching and I really haven't had any flack except in that one instance.
KS: *What about Lame Bull in* Winter in the Blood?
JW: Well, um, I had no flack, as far as I know. There was a guy who used to work for my Dad named Charlie Lame Bull and he was quite a character. And, uh, he and I used to do a lot of fence building and stuff like that. He had the Indian humor that we talked about earlier. And, so, when I thought about it, I thought the name was terrific. And, you know, I just used it.
KS: *Lame Bull was the first person among Gros Ventre people to sign the treaty and to welcome the whites. That didn't figure into your choosing the name?*
JW: No. No.
KS: *Because the character does actually kind of seem like he wants to adopt white ways.*
JW: Yeah, he wants to get ahead. You know, he wants to be a successful rancher and so on. Yeah, um, and Charlie Lame Bull had a little spread of his own and he would have liked to have acquired some more cattle and, uh, and gotten ahead. You know, I think it's natural that Indian people would, just like any other rancher up in that country, want to get a little more land, a little more hay land, a few more cattle and buy a new pickup. Stuff like that.
KS: *Sure.*
JW: So, Charlie Lame Bull actually was just this guy that I liked a lot so I used his name.
KS: *Looking back on your own writing, can you identify pieces or whole works that you most enjoyed writing and re-reading? And there's a more delicate question related to this, and you certainly don't have to answer it, Is there anything you have written that you would take back if you could? You just mentioned changing Yellow Kidney's name. Is there anything else you would take back? and What have you liked about what you have done?*
JW: Well, again, I've tried to write about something different in each book,

take a different situation and, uh, maybe a different type of Indian. *Indian Lawyer* was a very successful Indian: what kind of things did he face being a successful Indian? A lot of people ask, "Which one of your books is your favorite?" and it's really hard to say, you know, because each one of them was trying something different. So for that reason, each one has a good spot in my heart. Some were more successful than others. For instance, I think in *Indian Lawyer* I kind of missed the ending. I think now if I was going to rewrite it, I could write a much stronger ending. As for what would I take out? I don't think I'd take out anything because, uh, you know,... once I was signing out at a mall and this Indian woman came by. It was for *The Death of Jim Loney* and she read the back, you know, and I can't remember what the jacket said on it but it was about an Indian who has a problem with alcohol and whatever. She looked at that and she kind of threw the book down on the table and said, "I wish they'd stop writing about Indians being alcoholics." And I was stunned because I thought she might be gonna buy it but just the opposite. I've always said that, well, you really have to be totally honest when you're writing. I mean, if you start thinking, "Oh, boy, I don't know if I should do that because a certain group of people are not gonna like it. They're gonna be offended."... I guess I like all parts of my books because I think they've been honest. I've never once pulled my punches. And I have had so many Indian people come up to me and say that *Winter in the Blood* was just, you know, just like it is on their reservation. Not only northern plains reservations but in the southwest or midwest or whatever. So, I think as long as you can write truthfully people will recognize the truth of what you are writing. Indian people will. And, uh, they'll say, "We do have a problem with alcohol." And, "Some of our young men are very aimless. You know, they don't have a direction in life." So, I've had good responses and I don't think I'd take anything out except maybe to change that name.

KS: *Well, you've kind of answered my next question already. Which of your works do you think has been most successful with readers and why?*

JW: Well, I would say it's between *Winter in the Blood* and *Fools Crow*. *Winter in the Blood*, I think because it's first person, very simple, a picaresque kind of novel about a guy walking around. There's humor in it. For some reason, it just appeals to people. They can almost immediately identify with that guy. Even if they're white. And *Fools Crow* is just, it's almost like magic. It has a magic spell on people. You know, they read the first 20 pages and they're into it. They're just totally into it. I've had whole high school classes write to me about how they just became interested so quickly and the whole book just kept them right there. And it's taught quite a lot in colleges and they're the same way. So I feel that that book struck a chord. So many books of that nature are written from the outside looking in on the Indian culture. This book is from the inside as the Indians look out at the rest of the world. And I think that kind of viewpoint was kind of missing in virtually all of the historical fiction written about Indians. So, it really was good in the sense that it allowed people to enter in, and people were very willing to enter that world. They didn't want to become observers in that world, they wanted to enter that world. And so I think that was what that book did for a lot of people.

KS: What are your thoughts about the censorship of Fools Crow?

JW: That is so weird. I don't know. It's uh, you know, it's just the Christian right. Just one person, basically, in each community. But, I mean, obviously backed by the rest of the Christians who raised objections in Laurel (MT) and then in Bozeman (MT). And, unfortunately, if only one person objects to a book, you know, it just throws everything into pandemonium and then the school board's involved, fighting over whether this should be part of the curriculum, or what. And in Laurel they buckled. They said it was too hot to handle. In Bozeman they didn't. The school board—I think they have nine members— voted like nine to nothing to keep the book. So I was really pleased about that, but then I ran into a woman here in Missoula who was here for summer school. She's a teacher in Three Forks. She started talking to Lois and then she kind of included me into the conversation. She said that she just loved *Fools Crow* and she wanted to teach it this past year, but she brought it up with her principal, I guess, and he said, "No, you'd better not." So I'm worried that that business in Laurel and Bozeman could have a chilling effect on other small schools around the state. Never had a problem anywhere else in this country or in Europe, where it's taught all over the place. It's just these two schools in Montana. But what it's saying is that here in Montana other teachers now are having misgivings about teaching it because of all the controversy that could happen.

KS: This is more of a comment than a question. It seems to me that Montanans might not want it taught because it does what you say it does, it depicts the internal reality of native peoples. The Blackfeet in the mid-nineteenth century. And many other Montanans need to know that and, in fact, want to know that.

JW: I think so, yeah.

KS: So it seems important that way. Early on in your career, from Riding the Earthboy 40 *through your first two novels, your work determinedly refuses to back away from the harshest sides of Indian life—though it is by no means only a depiction of harshness. With* Fools Crow *you shift to another kind of depiction and toughness, and with* Indian Lawyer, *yet another. Reservation life continues to be hard today, although American Indian people have made great gains in taking charge of their own lives. What do you see now as the most serious and difficult problems and challenges facing American Indian people?*

JW: Actually, you know, I've said this for a long time and I know a lot of Indian people feel this way, but you very seldom hear about this because people are worried about the social problems, and so on. Actually I think economic development is the cure all for reservations. I mean, if they can attract industry and a lot of people can go to work for industry on the reservations, I think a lot of the social problems would take care of themselves. Because having a job, making good money, and going to it everyday, really builds a sense of self-worth. And, consequently, I think you wouldn't need to feel you had to retreat into alcohol or drugs or wife beating or whatever. I think that if by magic suddenly some big industries located on every reservation in America, a lot of the problems would go away. Not only the economic problems but a lot of the social problems would be no more prevalent than in the rest of society, at least.

KS: *Will you ever go back to writing about reservation life?*

JW: Yeah, I would. I've got another novel that I'm writing now. I've got a draft written and I'm sort of going to revise it intensively. It's set in France. But, yeah, I would hope, really, to set one on the reservation again. But I guess it would depend a lot upon if I had a different enough take on the material. Because I wouldn't want to go back and rewrite *Winter in the Blood* or *The Death of Jim Loney* again. I would like to have a whole, fresh look at the reservation. And the reservation is changing, too, you know, from those days 'til now. I mean, the Tribal Colleges on all the reservations out here in the West are just a great thing. So, I mean, that's a huge step in conquering a lot of problems Indians have. I mean, they're being trained. They're being educated. They can get better jobs. So, I mean, that's happening and that wasn't happening back then, back in the 60s and early 70s. So, the reservation is changing and if I could find a way to write about the changes in and on the reservation, I would certainly like to do it.

KS: *Do you think that the revival of religious practice would enter in then?*

JW: Yeah, I think so. On the revival of the language, you know, I don't know how that's gonna turn out yet. But at least people on reservations are trying to teach the kids, like Daryl Kipp and Dorothy Still smoking up at Browning with their Immersion Schools. Getting those kids at a very early age—when they walk onto those school grounds they can no longer speak English. They have to speak Blackfeet. So, this is happening on reservations. But I read an essay by this guy who wrote that a learned language doesn't carry the cultural weight of the language that comes naturally. But I think that Indian people are combining learning the language with the language as the carrier of tradition, of culture. So, I mean, it's not like they're just teaching Blackfeet (the language), for instance, up at Browning, but they're teaching the whole culture that the language represents. So I really hope this guy is wrong. And, you know, the language is going to go, among some Indian people for sure, like in California tribes. Because they're so small and they're so surrounded by the dominant culture, but I think that in Montana and the Dakotas and, of course, obviously in the Southwest, there's a good chance that the language will be retained and the culture will be retained as a result.

KS: *Louis Owens, Choctaw writer and literary critic, describes what you attempt in* Fools Crow *as "the nearly impossible feat of conveying a feeling of one language through another while simultaneously avoiding the clichéd formal pidgin of Hollywood Indians." Students in my classes again and again*

Interview with James Welch

have been moved and persuaded by the language of the novel, so I would say that you have succeeded at that "nearly impossible feat." Can you talk about the process of thinking that you had to engage in to create the special language of the novel? The importance of knowing the native language of a culture takes on special meaning in your latest novel, Heartsong *of Charging Elk. Do you see this novel as an extension of* Fools Crow *in regard to language? And can you describe your own process of acquiring enough knowledge of French and Lakota to write the book?*

JW: I'm not so sure it's an extension of *Fools Crow*. I think it's kind of a counter to *Fools Crow* because Fools Crow was within his own culture and everybody around him was of that culture. And so the language was just like any language. Everybody spoke it. But in *Heartsong* this guy is in an absolutely foreign culture and he can't speak. He can't communicate because nobody in France can speak Lakota. He can't speak French or English and, so, in a way it's just the opposite of *Fools Crow* in terms of language. He can't communicate. Eventually—the book covers 16 years—he learns rudimentary French. And, then, by the end of the period he can talk fairly well. Although he has kind of an Indian accent, you know, so the French people have a hard time understanding him. But he can understand them and if they try hard, they can understand him. So, it's kind of an evolving from no language at all to being able to communicate in a difficult way. Lois knows French and I worked very closely with my French editor and my French translator. They're really good about it. If I have questions, I can fax them and they can fax back the answers about certain phrases in French. Like I might know the proper French phrase but then there's the more vernacular phrase that would be used in French. So, you know, between Lois and those people I've gotten a lot of help with French. The Lakota, um, I have a Lakota dictionary up there in my study. And I've talked to Lakota people and I have learned some phrases and so on. So basically the Lakota is in there to give the guy, Charging Elk, a kind of reality because he looks at this one guy, who he ends up killing in the novel, who is a *siyoko*, which is a witch, a bad spirit. And something happens in the book and Charging Elk ends up killing him. He doesn't feel bad about it at all because he rid the world of a bad spirit. I just used both the French and the Lakota to try to give the sense of reality, the sense of place, so that the reader doesn't think that it's just a story, because it's about culture, too. And language is a part of the culture.

KS: *So it wasn't really the language that interested you in this novel as much as the situation of the character?*

JW: Yeah, right. You know, in a sense, I kind of used language as a sort of a logistic ... so that the reader would always be aware of these two other cultures. If an American reader just read it without, say, these particular references to Lakota culture and French culture, including language, they might think they were just reading a story, and I wanted it to be more than a story. More about the old trite phrase of "clashing cultures." But that's pretty much true.

KS: *The novel also has a sense of the mystery of* Indian Lawyer. *First, there's the question of what's going to happen to Charging Elk. And then his entanglements with the law, his love affairs, his desiring of women who are not Lakota. So there's that mystery with a small 'm.' But then there also seems to be Mystery in the larger sense. Are you interested in writing a novel in the mystery genre?*

JW: No. No. In *Indian Lawyer* I kind of used a lot of elements of mystery. But, you know, in the end, it wasn't really a mystery. There was no suspenseful kind of thing leading to something surprising, no act of violence or whatever. I always feel like I write about normal life and to write in the mystery genre never seems, to me, to be real life. It's all fantasy and sort of ... maybe it's just escapist literature, basically. So, in this book, if there is any mystery it's because, you know, I want the reader to kind of follow him, to follow his adventures and think, "What's going to happen to him?" Right from the start when he wakes up in the hospital bed in Marseilles. All the way to the end, it's him learning to survive and he has ups and downs. Sometimes he's up when he thinks the young prostitute's in love with him and he's thinking about asking her to come live with him. This is a great joy to him. Then, of course, just when things start looking up—Bam!—you know, something else happens. And then he gets to another point where things are starting to look good and then something else happens. And it's kind of discouraging to him that just when it looks like he's going to pull out of things, something happens. So, I guess, if there's any mystery, it's just what's going to happen next to him.

KS: *How did you get the idea for your latest novel,* Heartsong of Charging Elk? *and can you talk about how it changed from conception to execution as others responded to readings of it as a work in progress?*

JW: OK, the first part..., I was on a book signing tour in France when *Fools Crow* came out. Of course, you always start in Paris and then there's the book festival which is the largest of France on the Britany Coast in a little walled city called St. Mâlo. We went there next. Then we started touring various cities around France. One of the places was Marseilles. I was signing books up in this stifling mezzanine of the bookstore and it was really hot. It was in late May and really hot. So I was anxious to get out of there. Business wasn't all that good, but this guy kept hanging around. He was kind of a tall, thin guy and he had blue jeans and a kind of cowboy type shirt that had embroidery on it and the blue jeans were bell-bottoms, and his boots had a kind of buckle on the side, and he wore a vest. So he looked like he was trying to be dressed like a cowboy, French style. And he just kept hanging around. Not saying a word. We went to an outdoor café to have something cold to drink. And actually it was amazing. About 12 people sort of materialized and they were all writers. You know, just kind of the writing scene in Marseilles. I was there with Lois and my editor. He speaks really good English. But this guy was sitting on the other side of Francis. They were talking away and I was listening to people talk over here and, finally,

Francis says that this guy says he's part Lakota and that his grandmother came over with Buffalo Bill's Wild West Show in 1905. She was a Lakota woman and fell in with a Frenchman and stayed. And so he was the grandson of that union. And Francis says, "I don't believe him. I think he's a wannabe." So we kind of dismissed him. Lois and I came back to Missoula. And that summer, when I was out mowing the lawn, I was thinking of this— when you're riding a lawn tractor you think of a lot of stuff— and I thought about that guy and what he said. I thought, wow, that's pretty incredible, you know, whether you believe it or not. It's sort of an interesting idea. So then it just kind of evolved and I started to think about an Indian from the Wild West Show who got sick in Marseilles and had to stay and the show moved on. So that was it.

KS: And so you transformed the person into a man who was easier to get ...
JW: Yeah. Yeah.
KS: It's easier as a man.
JW: Mm-hmm. And I allowed him to be a young performer who had lived the old way before going to France instead of living at the agency with all the other Indians. He and a group of people had been at the Stronghold which later became famous as the Ghost Dance site. But they were kind of renegades. They didn't want to come in and be bossed around by the white people. So he lived that way from his childhood. He and his friend ran away from school. They were 12 years old and in the second grade, or something. And, so that's the way he lived, by his wits, by hunting and stealing things from the miners in the Black Hills. So when he went to France he was really just a babe in the woods. Most of the other young men had been at the agencies for a number of years by then and could speak English. But he hadn't been, and he couldn't. So that's why I chose him. I wanted him to be just totally in a foreign culture with absolutely no idea of what was going on.

KS: The Missoulian *ran an article in the spring about the French people conferring upon you an aristocrat's title, "Sir Welch," and quoted you as saying that the French like your "stuff," meaning books. Would you talk a little about how it is a European audience has grown over the years for your work? Do you think they read your work differently than Americans do?*
JW: Well, most of my experience is in France and Italy. I seem to go to those two countries quite a lot and for various reasons. So I talked to a lot of people and, you know, they really do like my work. The French, especially, are very interested in Indians. Even contemporary Indians. I mean when I've been there, there have been petitions, you know, almost constant petitions to free Leonard Peltier. They know all about AIM. They are really quite knowledgeable. They're not really too knowledgeable about historical Indians, though. They kind of live in the present. I think my books help them to kind of understand historical Indians and sort of weigh the two. Like how the character in *Winter in the Blood* has evolved from those traditional people of the nineteenth century in *Fools Crow*. So, I think, in a way, they kind of get the whole package of Indian culture—all aspects—at

least the Blackfeet. I don't know about all Indian cultures but, so yeah, it's been that way. And then I've been to Holland and to Sweden and England, places like that. Germany. I've had people say they enjoyed my work a lot. But I haven't traveled in those countries very much.

KS: *Does it affect the way you write to know that they are your audience, too?*

JW: In a sense, this last book, *Heartsong of Charging Elk*, I think it is pretty understandable that a French audience might have influenced my writing of it because I kept thinking, "What would they think? They know their culture. Is this right? Could this happen?" So, in a way, I kind of had a French audience in mind. But, on the other hand, when you're writing historical stuff, even, you know, something just at the turn of the last century, a hundred years ago, you become almost the expert, in a way. Not many people can really gainsay what you are writing about as long as you work hard to make it as accurate as possible. And I've never had anybody say, "No, that's not right," or whatever. So most people I think, say, OK this is fiction so they kind of give you the benefit of the doubt, even if they did have some doubt.

KS: *The details in* Heartsong *struck me. Certain things like corkscrews, like the ones we know today, or rolled cigarettes—when did they actually become a commodity that the average person used? Did you research details like that?*

JW: Yeah, I did. I sure didn't want anything to be anachronistic, so little things like that stiletto knife was there then, and then larger issues like electricity. At one point I had this family, this Soulas family listening to a gramophone-type thing after dinner in the evening. Then I got to thinking, "Wait a minute." So I went and looked in this encyclopedia and it was invented a few years later than I had it, so I took it out. So I tried to be as accurate as I could in those kinds of things. The telephone was just becoming a thing and it was very tinny and during the daytime it was hard to talk without static and stuff like that. Things like that, I think, helped give the book a kind of particularity. I hope that readers will kind of react like you did about some of these little things and say, "Well, I wonder when custom cigarettes came into being?" So I hope it kind of elicits that curiosity.

KS: *It certainly has marvelous detail. I really enjoyed it.* Heartsong *is dedicated to your wife who is one of your biggest fans. I remember once after you read the passage from* Fools Crow *at Cornell, Lois had tears in her eyes and she explained how moved she is by hearing you read your work. Would you care to talk about how Lois has influenced your life and work?*

JW: Well, she certainly has influenced my life a lot. We've been married 32 years now and I've just always admired her incredibly for her career, the things she's done, and the battles she's had to fight. You know, this English Department has really been a male chauvinist department for many, many years. Sometimes she was the only woman. Sometimes she was one of two women. And so she just had to battle, you know, for everything. Other than that we just had great fun and she reads my work and she's not my best critic. Because if she finds things wrong, she'll tell me but I think, overall, she's gonna like it. And I need somebody to say, "No, you can't do that," or "This is really boring," or whatever. But she is my first reader and she's really valuable in many, many ways. It's just that I have to realize that she's going to like my work. And also I have to realize that I'm gonna become defensive when she criticizes a passage that I really like and says it doesn't make sense or something, then I will try to explain the passage and so on. But she either wins or we compromise or whatever. So we've had a good life together and she's really been valuable to me in my writing. I mean, she speaks French very well and in this last book, and in all the times we've been to France she's been a terrific go-between. I kind of hide behind her skirts while she communicates.

KS: *When you began writing, there were so few Indians writing and being published—N. Scott Momaday and Duane Niatum, for example, are the only two who come to mind.*

JW: Leslie Silko just a little while later.

KS: *Yes, and Leslie Silko and Simon Ortiz. American Indian writing has exploded since then as has American Indian literary criticism; it's so hard to keep up. Who do you read these days, and what do you think of the contemporary Indian writing scene?*

JW: Well, I think it is evolving and certainly in a very good way. People are finding other things to write about. I remember that *House Made of Dawn* and *Ceremony* both dealt with men coming back to the reservation and would they be accepted back. Would they like to be back? And what forces are at work? You know, for instance, as Leslie says, that there have to be ceremonies to cleanse you of that outside world so that you can become back with your own people again in your own culture. So, that was kind of a theme about Indians coming home. "Can you come home again?" Others were Indians going out into the world and what kind of experiences did they have? How did they react? I think now people are—well, Sherman Alexie, for instance, has introduced a great element of humor and irreverence into Indian writing. I like that. I think it was time for that to come along and he does a good job of it. He's a really good writer. But it's interesting to me that even with the young people a lot of the themes are still things like fitting in. You know? Who's an Indian? Who's not an Indian? If you go out into that outside world, you remain an Indian. How do people accept you back. It's interesting that that notion seems to be such a strong feeling amongst Indian people still. So maybe the culture in the last 25 or 30 years still has those concerns. Reservation Indians versus urban Indians and that kind of thing. Those are still big concerns. In *The Surrounded*, D'Arcy McNickle's novel, Archilde comes home from the big city and just has a hell of a time up here on the Flathead Reservation. So these themes are still going. It's interesting to me.

KS: *It is interesting. There are quite a few writers writing about gay/lesbian experiences among Indians. And there are some writers, like Rex Jim, who writes in Navajo, and Ophelia Zapata who writes in Papago and English.*

So there's some growth in terms of Native language use and writing. So I agree with you, it's diversifying, too.
JW: Yeah, boy, I didn't know Rex Jim wrote in Navajo.
KS: He wrote a book and published it only in Navajo. It was Princeton, I think, University Press. It would be interesting if one were a Navajo speaker to study how many Navajos read the poetry because the closest equivalent in the oral tradition is song, I suppose. So, it would be interesting to study it in that sense.
JW: It would be interesting to find out how many people actually read it.
KS: And how big the print run was, and if it sold out.
JW: Right. Exactly.
KS: Recently, many more non-Indian writers have been writing about American Indian life or developing American Indian characters. Can you comment on how you view the work of, say, Craig Lesley, Ian Frazier, Frank Kinsella, Tony Hillerman and others? In another generation it would have been D. H. Lawrence.
JW: Right. Yeah. I kind of have a different response to each of them. Kinsella I think I don't respect what he has done in his writing about Indian people in that they're foolish and they speak a strange kind of language. I don't think he portrays a very rounded picture of Indians and I guess that's what I would really ask of any writer. Certainly those people exist but then there are a lot of people who aren't like them. So I think focusing on one group in a kind of semi-derogatory way ... like *Stay Away, Joe*. The Indians decide to celebrate. They've just gotten a small herd of cattle, a bull and some cows—and when they celebrate they kill the bull and eat it. I mean it makes them sound really dumb and so on.
KS: When they would probably know that better than any other.
JW: Oh, absolutely.
KS: Breeding animals and horses.
JW: Ian Frazier's (Sandy's a friend of mine) I thought his latest book was really quite interesting. I liked *The Great Plains*, too, which dealt with Indian people as well. But *On the Rez* I thought was really well done. And I've been to Pine Ridge 3 or 4 times, you know, reading at Tribal Colleges and doing this and that. I've gone to trailers and here and there and I've enjoyed it. It's been a good experience because I've been pretty well accepted. Not by everybody, I'm sure, but in certain circles who are interested in writing or maybe in the Blackfeet culture and so on. I think Sandy's book is very balanced. It might have a few instances of, you know..., when his Indian pal, Le War Lance comes to Missoula to visit him along with some people and they've been drinking all the way and he, essentially, is very inhospitable to them. They have been hospitable to him on the reservation although he always gives them money. And so he feels bad about his inhospitality to them. And, you know, I think that's a good, honest response. It's too bad that he was inhospitable but to write about himself being that way, I think, is a very truthful way to write.

KS: *The ugly side of each of us.*
JW: Yeah. Exactly. Right. And really an ungenerous thing on his part and he should have felt bad about it. Craig Lesley, I've always enjoyed his work. You know, I think he's carved out a niche for himself in his writing. Who was the other person?
KS: *Tony Hillerman.*
JW: Yeah. Now he's a very problematic kind of person because he has always written about Indians. That series is just really immensely popular. It hits the best seller list, every book. But he is such a nice man, personally. He is just a fantastically nice man and the Navajo people really like him. And so it's almost like they've given him a dispensation to write about their culture in the way he does. You know, with the spiritual and mystical things going on and just basically the Navajo culture. So I think some people can write about Indians in a very gracious way. And other people, I think, when they write about them, they present them in a very negative light. They sort of focus on the foibles of Indian people and not the rest of it.
KS: *Well,* Stay Away, Joe *was made into a movie with Elvis Presley so those images of Indians matter in popular culture. And it does seem to me that a non-Indian writer has an easier time becoming your best seller than many Indian writers do.*
JW: Oh, yeah. I think it's really right about Indians and white writers. Like the guy who wrote the novel, *Dances with Wolves.* He had a white hero. Although it was set in the Indian culture, it made a great movie because Kevin Costner could play the white hero and he could fall in love with the only white woman in the whole Indian country.
KS: *Even though she did hack off her hair ...*
JW: Yeah. Right.
KS: *Well, it is a touchy subject I think among Indian writers, and my position would be that each writer has to be taken on his own terms. Certainly the French people will be critical of how you present French people. And women will be critical how male writers present them. So there's always that question and you can't have a novel that doesn't have a mixed presentation of humankind these days.*
JW: Right. Yeah, that's true. You know its almost like you wrote the book and then it went out into the world and then it's fair game for anybody. And then some of these newer critical theories even take you out of the equation. So suddenly the book is just there. It has no background. It has no future or anything. It's just there. And I always find that pretty incredible.
KS: *What advice would you give to both Indian and non-Indian readers of American Indian literature? Do they need to do some homework before or after reading? What should they be careful not to assume?*
JW: Well, boy, that's a tough question. I would suggest that they read different people. Not just focus on one group of writers or another. But just kind of shop around in a sense and then get an idea of how different tribal groups

are, how various cultures are. So you don't say that, OK, the Plains Indians really represent Indians, because you know that West Coast Indians and Eastern Indians, Southern Indians, Southwestern Indians, they're just totally different. So I think that one assumption a lot of people make is that Indians are basically all alike and they've seen all the movies about the Sioux and kind of think that, OK, those are the real Indians. Or the new movie, *The Last of the Mohicans*, not new but fairly recent, that they are representative and they are really a cruel lot. So you have to balance all these various depictions of Indians in order to get a kind of understanding of how different Indians are and how similar they are in certain ways.

KS: *What advice do you have for American Indian young people who want to become writers?*

JW: Well, boy, I just hope it continues ... this sort of burgeoning group of Indian writers. I think one thing that they have to do is to learn the English language well. Very well. Because they're not gonna be given any favors. You know, their novels are gonna have to be just as good as any other novels out there. And, so, I think young Indian people need to learn the English language well. They need to experience things. They need to reflect upon those experiences. Reflect upon their culture, their relatives and families and so on because basically that's what happens after you become a mature writer. You are using those experiences and observations from way back. So, you know, you need to keep your eyes and ears open, learn English really well, learn forms, poetry, fiction, novels, short stories, plays. They just need to learn as much as they can and find which form seems most comfortable for them to write in. I know a lot of Indian people feel quite comfortable writing poetry. And that's good because I think that's very close to a lot of the elements of their own culture. Poetry seems to be very close. I know in the Southwest, what's that? ... the Institute of American Indian Art. They've produced a lot of poets. Navajos and Pueblos and people from Oklahoma who have gone there. You know, go to a school like that or to a school that will encourage you to write and find a teacher, whoever, and just go with it.

KS: *Are going to write poems again.*

JW: I keep thinking that I will. You know, like when I finish this book. Every time I finish something I think, boy, it'd be nice to try to get back into poetry. At least write some poems. Then a new project rears its head and I start thinking about that and that window of opportunity kind of goes by. Because I don't think I could just go upstairs and write a poem right now. I think I would have to get into thinking like a poet. Kind of get into using language like a poet. One of the things I found when I was trying to balance poetry and prose was that my prose was very jumbled up, very thick, and my poetry was kind of losing the lyric quality and losing its elasticity. So I was not satisfied with the language in either one. That's why I had to drop poetry and concentrate on the fiction.

KS: You mentioned that you have a manuscript set in France. Where are you going from here with your work?
JW: Well I'm not quite sure. I just know where I'm going with this next novel which is going to be a contemporary situation basically set in France but involving an American professor. He's a professor now. I don't know if I'll keep him a professor, but he meets a young woman who is the great-great-granddaughter of Charging Elk at a conference in France. An American Studies conference. She's a graduate student in Aix-en-Provence, which is near Marseilles. And they have a literature program. She convinces him to come with her to Marseilles after the conference. So he goes down there and gets a motel room. Then he visits the family and becomes more and more involved with the family. Charging Elk is dead by now and his great-great-granddaughter is the young woman. And so, it's about these generations and what they remember of Charging Elk and so on. So it's kind of a look back at Charging Elk and what happened to him after 1905.
KS: At various times, you have described yourself as "lucky." How do you understand that term as an American Indian man and as a writer?
JW: Well, boy, I don't know. Just the fact that I am sitting here talking with you about my work is just absolutely incredible to me, still. You know, I just uh, I think I'm a good writer. I think I've worked hard to be a good writer. But, on the other hand, I know of so many good writers who just haven't had the luck that I've had. For one thing, I've chosen to write about a subject that is really interesting to a lot of people. So if you can write about that well, then you'll have a good readership. If I had decided that I didn't want to write about Indians I don't know what would have happened to me. If I hadn't married Lois or if she hadn't said, "Well, go ahead, write your poetry." You know, she didn't hound me to go out and get a job or to go for my PhD or whatever. So, just that simple act of saying, "Go ahead, do it. I earn money. I'm a professor." She was an assistant professor, I guess. She just kind of gave me this freedom and that doesn't happen in a lot of cases. Most people have to worry about things. And now that my novels and works are selling quite well I'm making a good living, but most people have to hold down a whole career or job while they try to write on the side. It's very discouraging. You can't concentrate as much as you should. Besides, I've just been extremely lucky and I consider myself lucky having been born up there on the Blackfeet Reservation and spent time on the Ft Belknap Reservation. My parents worked with the Indian Service so we lived in Indian communities like Chemawa, Oregon and Mt Edgecombe, Alaska which was an island and had hospitals and boarding schools and a tuberculosis sanitorium. My Dad worked there at the tuberculosis sanitorium. So I just got to meet so many different Indian people and hear so many stories from various tribal groups. So all of that I think is just kind of the luck of the draw that I was there then and listened to those stories. And later on, maybe they didn't exactly enter my writing verbatim but they would have influenced my writing.

Revising the Captivity Narrative: *Lost Bird of Wounded Knee*

Valerie Adamcyk
Binghamton University

Renee Sansom Flood began to research the life of Zintkala Nuni, or Lost Bird, when she came upon an 1891 photograph of an Indian child in the arms of a white general in full dress uniform. The photograph presents an interesting study in contrasts. The man, in epaulettes and tasseled sash, towers over the infant, swathed in a white robe. He clutches the child possessively at his side, but maintains the impression of formal distance between them. His studied, arrogant glare challenges the camera, while the child's face registers a baby's bemusement. The man's European-American features contrast startlingly with the Indian features of the child, yet the two appear clearly bound to each other in the roles of helpless dependant and authoritarian protector.

In her biography of Zintkala Nuni, *Lost Bird of Wounded Knee: Spirit of the Lakota*, Flood narrates the life of the Lakota child found at the site of the Wounded Knee massacre and adopted into the Colby family of Nebraska. Separated from her Lakota family, Lost Bird grew up in a culture constructed in the spaces forcibly vacated by Indian peoples. She was regarded primarily as a curiosity by the community that sought to assimilate her and was subsequently rejected by members of her Lakota tribe, leaving Lost Bird stranded between cultures, without a clearly-defined cultural identity. Lost Bird became the casualty of a conflict that in 1890 had all but ended, with the victors continuing in their expansion across the country, while Indians became culturally segregated and geographically isolated. But though she remains a little-known figure in American history, Lost Bird's experience stands as a vivid illustration of a residual cultural clash that lingered after the battles had ended, in the uneasy co-habitation of conquerors with the conquered in an unevenly divided land.

In relating the story of a child deliberately taken from her community and assimilated into an alien culture, Flood describes a situation similar to that of early white settlers who were captured by Indians. In fact, Lost Bird's story bears an ironic resemblance in form and content to the traditional Indian captivity narrative. While Indian captivity narratives ordinarily recount conflicts in which Indians are the threatening force, Lost Bird's story demonstrates an inversion in the power structure of America's occupants, in which Indians play the subordinate role, captive instead of captor.

Traditional captivity narratives incorporated specific structural elements to give meaning to the captivity, presenting an "ultimate boundary situation" as a means of reflecting upon larger social issues (Ebersole 9). Captives crossed the border between distinct cultures, and their removal into a community dramatically different from their own provided them with the distance necessary for a thorough examination of their own social structures and values. While some captives, such as Mary Jemison, ultimately rejected their original culture and chose to become assimilated into the society of their captors, the majority of captives who produced narratives of their captivity used their experiences as a means of reinforcing the foundational values of their original culture. Mary Rowlandson, for example, composed a narrative of her experiences with the Wampanoag Indians which incorporates and promotes her original Puritan values and theology. She narrates her captivity through a framework provided by the Bible, attributing her experiences to the will of God. Her immensely popular narrative was read as a spiritual allegory of trials set by God for human beings to overcome.

Flood likewise presents Lost Bird's history as a means of addressing larger social issues, but from an historical vantage point dramatically different from the time when whites were newcomers to the land. Flood focuses upon the marginalization of Indians and their culture in the face of the encroaching white society, using Lost Bird as an example of the challenge to identity experienced by Indians as they lost their claims to the land that formed the basis of their culture. Though Flood's use of a captivity narrative's archetypal elements seems an unintentional aspect of her biography's design, these elements are nevertheless implied, as part of the story of Lost Bird's life. By including in the biography a traditional captivity narrative's stages of capture, initiation, and release or redemption of the captive, Flood demonstrates in literary terms the culmination of white conquest in America. The transfer of possession of the land from Indians to whites appears complete when the whites have appropriated even the Indian role in the captivity narrative.

The captivity narrative incorporates broad themes and ideas, which have opened the genre to different interpretations and revisions from contemporary critics. Christopher Castiglia argues that captivity narratives "refuse to be static texts endorsing essential, unchanging identities and hence fixed social hierarchies of race and gender," adding that the narratives "persistently explore generic and cultural changes, divisions, and differences occasioned by the captives' cultural crossings"; he situates Patty Hearst's autobiography in the framework of captivity narrative (Castiglia 4). Colin Ramsey traces elements of captivity narratives in "contemporary legends" such as those that demonize outsider social groups, such as hippies, as threats to the dominant culture. Michelle Burnham suggests that Harriet Beecher Stowe drew from captivity narratives in depicting the abuses of slavery in *Uncle Tom's Cabin*, using them as a source for the "affective logic of her antislavery argument" (Burnham 123).

Critical responses to Flood's work in book reviews applaud the thoroughness of Flood's research, but also question her presentation and motives. As Zintkala Nuni did not leave much in her own voice to tell of her experiences, Flood reconstructs Lost Bird's life in a narrative that reflects her own perspective on issues raised in the telling. "Historians," writes Sherry L. Smith, "will raise an eyebrow at Flood's willingness to assert motives and behaviors without sufficient evidence and at her unusual language regarding Lakota holy men" (Smith 240). Marilyn Jean Englander comments that

> "The author introduces her subject in a prologue in which she rails against prejudice toward Indians, mistreatment of Indian mothers by ignorant white social workers, non-Indian adoptions of Native children, sexual harassment in the work place, and more. The author is obviously emotionally involved with her subject matter, and she inappropriately attempts to mold the biography of Zintkala Nuni to address the issues that concern her. This threatens to obscure the genuine power of the life stories she has to tell" (Englander 86).

The criticism of Flood for advancing personal objectives through the life story of Zintkala Nuni offers another parallel to the production of captivity narratives, for, as Castiglia notes, "almost without exception an interpretive 'frame' was provided for the captivity narratives by someone other than the captives themselves" (Castiglia 8). The Mathers are frequently cited as influential in shaping captivity narratives, by situating them within religious frameworks that represented the captivity experience as divine punishment or trial. "In the majority of captivity narratives," writes Castiglia, "editors obscure and revise the captives' stories in order to strengthen flagging religious devotion, to justify westward expansion and the extermination of Indians, and to create the illusion of a stable and paternal nation" (Castiglia 20). Castiglia wonders, in cases where captives "received editorial 'assistance' of some sort, how one can speak of the 'captive's voice' in the narratives?" (Castiglia 80). In the case of Lost Bird, the answer seems to be that we can not speak of the captive's voice at all; an interpretation of *Lost Bird of Wounded Knee* as captivity narrative must rely on the reported events and details of Lost Bird's life, without speculating upon her own responses to her extraordinary experiences.

Flood begins her narration of Lost Bird's story with a thorough description of the archetypal first stage of captivity: the attack and capture. Mary Rowlandson's narrative, which many critics consider the "first and best example of the genre" (Kestler xxiii) begins with a description of being "butchered by those merciless heathen, standing amazed, with the blood running down to our heels," as the Wampanoag Indians attacked and burned the Lancaster settlement of the Massachusetts Bay Colony on February 10,, 1675 (Rowlandson 11). Flood cites eyewitness accounts from both soldiers and Lakota of the massacre at Wounded Knee on December 29, 1890, presenting a similarly horrific record of an attack on a defenseless community of people, including this description from Dewey Beard, a Lakota: "When I saw these women, girls and little girls and boys coming up, I saw soldiers on both sides of the ravine shoot at them until they had killed every one of them" (Flood 42). A captivity narrative invites the reader to identify with the captive, with gruesome details that illustrate the brutality of the attackers and demonstrate the treacherous nature of the environment the captive will soon be entering. These details emphasize the relatively helpless position of a captive in the possession of an antagonistic force.

Four days after the Wounded Knee massacre and a blizzard that followed, a burial party came upon the frozen corpse of a woman who had died clutching an infant girl, who was frostbitten but still alive. No one could identify the child, who immediately became a focus of intense interest and curiosity to some of the white men who had come to Pine Ridge after the massacre, seeking attention and opportunity. Though few records for verification exist, Flood believes that Lost Bird was originally promised to Major John Burke, Buffalo Bill Cody's press agent, who wanted the child either as a curiosity for Cody's Wild West show, or possibly to give to childless friends of Cody. However, Lost Bird's history presents an unusual, ironic spin to the conventional act of capture. Instead of being taken immediately by her captors, Lost Bird nearly escaped capture when the Lakota removed her into a hostile camp to protect her from Leonard Colby, the white commander of the Nebraska National Guard who had apparently bargained with Burke for possession of the baby. But despite the Lakotan efforts to keep the child hidden, Colby eventually accomplished the capture through an act of deceit. Posing as a Seneca Indian, he pursued the child into the camp and convinced the Lakota to grant him her custody. His Indian disguise stands as one of the more ironic elements of Lost Bird's capture: as an imposter, misrepresenting his intentions, he effectively stole the child from the Lakota. Theft and deception are behaviors commonly attributed to Indians in captivity narratives. Colby embodied the stereotype of the ruthless Indian in his pursuit of Lost Bird and succeeded in capturing the Indian child only when he assumed the role of the traditional captor, evoking the stereotype of an Indian in physical appearance as well as in cunning behavior.

The underlying motives for capture demonstrate further similarities between captivity narratives and the story of Lost Bird. Indians had earlier taken white captives for a variety of reasons, such as revenge for white appropriation of their land, ransom from the settlements, or replacement for deceased tribal members. Mary Rowlandson, for example, was taken for ransom: the Indians eventually exchanged her for £20 worth of goods after holding her for nearly twelve weeks. The motive commonly involved in the capture of children was that of replacement, as children were considered more "culturally malleable" and adaptable to change, thus making suitable candidates for successful adoption and assimilation into the tribe (Derounian-Stodola and Levernier 5). Mary Jemison, for example, was captured by Shawnee Indians when she was fifteen years old; the Shawnee then traded her to a tribe of Seneca, who adopted her, in her words, to "supply [the] loss" of a tribal member killed in war (Kestler 127).

Flood indicates replacement, combined with personal aggrandizement, as a possible motive for Lost Bird's capture as well. Colby sought fame and admiration for adopting a survivor of Wounded Knee; he believed that saving this "Child of the Battlefield" would make him a hero, and he wished to emulate Andrew Jackson, who had won public esteem as well as political power when he adopted a Creek orphan during the Creek Wars (Flood 70). However, Colby also persevered in his pursuit of the child in part to remedy his "keen disappointment" over the Colbys' only other child, an adopted son named Clarence labeled by Flood as "developmentally slow," who remained below the mental age of thirteen throughout his life (Flood 113). Flood demonstrates that the idea of finding a replacement for a "flawed" child was not entirely inconsistent with Colby's nature. In 1893, when Colby had lost interest in his Indian daughter, considering her a burden just two years after adopting her, he had another child in an extramarital affair and eventually deserted his family to form a new alliance with his mistress and their illegitimate son. Thus, in his pursuit and capture of Lost Bird, Colby may have been motivated by the desire to replace Clarence, a child he rejected, just as he would later reject Lost Bird and replace her with another child.

With Lost Bird's capture a success, Flood's narrative moves into the second stage of traditional captivity narratives, which details the transformation or initiation and adoption of the captive. Even captives held only for ransom, who were not candidates for adoption into the tribe, experienced what Richard VanDerBeets calls "transformation by immersion into an alien culture," accompanied by rituals of initiation (VanDerBeets 43). In many cases of white captives, this initiation involved ritual acts of exposure such as running the gauntlet, in which the captors came into direct contact with their captive. Surrounded by Indians, captives were physically and psychologically engulfed by their captors and plunged into their captors' culture.

Lost Bird's process of initiation began on January 19, 1891, when Leonard Colby formally adopted her, just five days after removing her from the Lakota camp. The adoption process legally established Colby's claim to the child and officially separated her from the community of her origins: Colby, in fact, hurried to finalize the adoption to ward off any future Lakotan attempts to regain custody of Lost Bird.[1] Though she was not subjected to actual physical threats upon her entry into the white community, Lost Bird's experiences shortly after her adoption offer an interesting parallel to the gauntlet ritual. On the journey back to Nebraska from South Dakota, Colby displayed his newly-adopted daughter to crowds of curious people. The manager of a Lincoln hotel reported that in the dining room, the "little heroine

[1] Colby apparently also feared that the child was related to Sitting Bull, and perhaps was even his daughter.

of Wounded Knee ... received for three hours the attention and caresses of hosts of ladies and gentlemen" (Flood 82). Upon their arrival in the Colbys' hometown of Beatrice, Nebraska, Colby celebrated with an open house in which at least five hundred people visited Lost Bird. The following evening, the town held a reception for Colby, and nearly a thousand people jammed the Beatrice Auditorium to view the child.

In these ritualized welcoming ceremonies, the white community crowded around its newest member. Lost Bird was passed from person to person, an object of constant attention. People lined up to pass her crib and touch her as she slept. Though apparently well-intentioned, this gauntlet of onlookers posed an invisible threat to Lost Bird: the day after the Beatrice reception, she developed pneumonia, which Flood claims was the "first virus she had known" (Flood 85). Sudden exposure to different people in a new environment brought the risk of disease, a consequence of introduction into an alien community that was as life-threatening to an infant as the gauntlet's physical attacks were to white captives. Though unintentionally transmitted, Lost Bird's illness demonstrates the potential dangers of initiation. As means for altering identity, initiation rituals invariably involved a threat to a captive vulnerable to unfamiliar influences. The bodily harm sustained by the captive emphasized the severity of the transformation from his or her original culture and reinforced the assignment of a new identity as captive.

As captives are transformed under pressure from their captors, their bodies become sites for inscriptions of their captivity. "In captivity (as in war)," asserts Gary Ebersole, "one's body is experienced in more fundamental ways than previously" (Ebersole 7). Hunger, thirst, and forced physical labor mark the captive's body as indelibly as ritual scarring, and the captive perceives his or her body, often for the first time, as fragile, vulnerable, and subject to exploitation. Though Mary Rowlandson, for example, struggles to preserve her Christian identity through prayer and Bible reading, her body's reactions to physical strain and deprivation force her to acknowledge her new identity as captive. She writes of being "cold and wet, ... and hungry, and weary," and remarks continually upon her physically weakened state (Rowlandson 19). She summarizes her captivity as a time of "sickness and wounds, and death, ... and affliction," focusing on the effects her experiences had upon her body (Rowlandson 57). Captivity removes a captive's sense of bodily autonomy: captors are free to manipulate the body of a captive through actions such as deliberate wounding, sexual assault, and deprivation of food and water.

Throughout the transformation stage of her captivity, but especially in her infancy, Lost Bird's body likewise proved susceptible to exploitation by her captors. This mark of her captivity was symbolic rather than literal, but powerful nonetheless in determining her new identity. As in traditional captivity narratives, the captors, in this case her adoptive parents, controlled the captive's body and used it for their own purposes. (Admittedly, the power was easy to exercise, since the captive in question was an infant at the time and unable to resist.) The Colbys, both Leonard and his wife Clara, saw their adopted daughter as a potent symbol. Her identity not only as an Indian, but also as a survivor of the Wounded Knee massacre, was rich with potential meaning, and each parent chose to use Lost Bird to advance personal goals.

Leonard Colby considered Lost Bird a "most interesting Indian relic," symbolic of white conquest in America (Flood 71). Lost Bird was his "trophy of war," and he claimed absolute ownership: his declaration that the child belonged to the "Nebraska National Guard, its commander and to the citizens of Beatrice," is tellingly self-referential (Flood 63, 84). Not only was he a member of the Nebraska National Guard, he was also its commander, and a noted citizen of Beatrice, as well. Leonard Colby made effective use of Lost Bird's body in displaying her to increase his own standing in the community. His fellow citizens had formerly considered him dishonest and underhanded: in his early years as a lawyer in Beatrice he had tricked many people into signing their property over to him (Flood 84). However, when he arrived home in 1891 brandishing Lost Bird, his past sins were forgiven, and the citizens of Beatrice gave him a hero's welcome. He had correctly calculated Lost Bird's value as a symbol: the living body of this Indian orphan brought him attention, fame, respect, and a permanent association with military victory and conquest.

Like her husband, Clara Colby also saw symbolic potential in Lost Bird: however, the cause she sought to promote was not so obviously herself, as was the case with Leonard. Rather, Clara used Lost Bird to advance the cause of women's suffrage, a movement that claimed her steadfast devotion. Clara quickly discovered the symbolic attraction of Lost Bird, who continued to receive an extraordinary amount of attention as a living example, ironically, of white beneficence in attempting to "civilize" the Indians. Shortly after Clara announced the adoption in the suffrage newspaper she edited, the *Women's Tribune*, she was inundated with inquiries about the child. Seizing the opportunity to increase circulation, Clara offered a picture of Lost Bird for every new subscription. The child's popularity brought a tremendous audience directly to Clara's door, and she took advantage of this unusual opportunity to promote suffrage to her adopted daughter's admirers. At one gathering, Clara wrote that "interest or curiosity impelled at least ten thousand persons to seek to see [Lost Bird] ... which splendid opportunity the writer made good use of by distributing suffrage literature to all who came" (Flood 124). Though her cause seems somewhat more exalted than Leonard's self-interest, Clara similarly used Lost Bird's body as an instrument to achieve her personal goals: their Indian daughter proved quite profitable for the Colbys. As in traditional captivity narratives, the captive's body became an object for the captor's use. In Lost Bird's case, the symbolic value of her body overshadowed her identity as an individual, securing her an undesirable position in her new culture, as a curiosity made interesting only by her status as "other."

Additional details of transformation and initiation comprise most of Flood's narrative of Lost Bird's life. Lost Bird never achieved full acceptance into her new culture. The initiation process continued throughout her life, transforming her with additional ordeals, but never erasing her Indian ancestry, which proved an insurmountable barrier to adoption by the white community. The Colbys had worked at eradicating all traces of her original culture when she was a baby, replacing her Lakota clothing with baby clothes of (predictably) "suffrage white," and changing her Lakota name (Flood 125).[2] However, despite these surface alterations, Lost Bird's physical appearance marked her as an outsider, and no amount of training in white cultural behaviors could remove the stigma an Indian identity posed in white society.

As Lost Bird progressed through the rituals of her new culture, learning English and attending white children's schools, she lost her appeal as a novelty. Her heritage had intrigued people when she was an infant and the Wounded Knee massacre still gnawed at the public conscience. As she grew older, however, the memory of Wounded Knee lost its sharpness as the event retreated into the past, and Lost Bird's Indian ancestry became a liability in white society. When she emerged from her parents' protection to face the general public, Lost Bird was targeted for racial attacks directed against minorities in general. White people's reactions to her physical appearance left Lost Bird uncertain about her identity; though she had been raised as a white child, she was called "'chinee,' 'tar baby,' 'squaw.' [and] 'nigger'" (Flood 180). Her mother would not allow her to have any non-white friends, but white children would not speak to her except to shout insults. This rejection illuminates an interesting distinction between white and Indian cultures. Though there are accounts of Indians who accepted white children, such as Mary Jemison, into their community after rituals of adoption, white society's behavior toward Lost Bird demonstrates that racial prejudice superseded Lost Bird's position as legal daughter of the Colbys.

In another feature common to captivity narratives, Flood repeatedly describes Lost Bird's desire for escape. Captivity narratives resonate with the captives' ardent yearning for release: Mary Rowlandson continually longs for her "house and home and all [her] comforts" (Rowlandson 13). Lost Bird similarly sought to return to her Lakota culture, though she had no knowledge or memory of it. She badgered her adoptive mother until she was allowed to attend Indian boarding schools, in which she encountered other Indian children for the first time. Ironically, these boarding schools, which served as instruments of captivity for so many other Indian children, were seen as a haven by Lost Bird, who was desperate for any contact with her

---

[2] Leonard Colby initially removed the child's Indian name altogether, baptizing her as Marguerite Elizabeth. Clara Colby partially restored Lost Bird's Lakota name, but altered it from Zintkala Nuni to the more easily pronounced Zinkta.

Lakota culture.[3] Never accepted into the white community, Lost Bird craved acceptance back into Lakota society. However, despite the fact that Clara Colby had managed to enroll Lost Bird in the Lakota tribe, the Lakota would not claim her. Her adoption by the Colbys seemed to have erased her from tribal memory, and though she repeatedly returned to Lakota reservations, she could not find a Lakota who would acknowledge her as a relative. Lost Bird actively sought escape, but her biological family never emerged to aid her.

Perhaps more damaging to Lost Bird's fragmented sense of identity, the Lakota also would not accept Lost Bird as an Indian at all. Though Lost Bird's transformation in white culture was insufficient for the white community to accept her, it was sufficient for the Indian community to reject her; she was a "nonwhite physically but a nonIndian socially" (Flood 246). Raised by an ardent suffragist, Lost Bird learned to be assertive, especially around men. However, according to Flood, Lakotan women behaved differently, taught to "[turn] their eyes away from men," and be quiet and modest (Flood 248). When Lost Bird visited the reservation seeking entry back into her tribe, her aggressive behavior marked her as an outsider, and the Lakota shunned her. Until recently, the only memory of Lost Bird's visits to the reservation that survived among the Lakota told of her inability to pronounce her own Lakotan name.

Lakotan rejection prevented Lost Bird from progressing in her lifetime to the stage that concludes the archetypal captivity narrative: the rescue or release of the captive back into his or her former culture. This post-captivity phase generally presents the captive's return as a form of redemption in rebirth or renewal: the captive reenters his or her original culture enlightened by the captivity experience. Mary Rowlandson concludes her narrative by describing the changes in her self wrought by her captivity, declaring a new understanding of the "awful dispensation of the Lord towards [the community], ... [and] His wonderful power and might." Her captivity had validated an idea that had formerly been an untested belief, that "when God calls a person to anything, and through never so many difficulties, yet He is fully able to carry them through and make them see, and say they have been gainers thereby" (Rowlandson 57). In the final section of her narrative, Rowlandson explores the meaning of her captivity. Her return home completes the captivity experience and allows her to evaluate its significance in reaffirming her identity, beliefs, and the values of her own culture.

Flood demonstrates that Lost Bird never achieved the satisfying closure of return and renewal. After a brief, tumultuous, and unpredictable life, Lost Bird died in California in 1920 at age 30 and was buried with her white

---

[3] According to Flood, Lost Bird was happy at the first boarding school she attended, with Lakota children, but she ran away when she was moved to a different school with children from other Indian nations.

husband's family. Though she had continued to return to Lakota reservations until her death, Lost Bird could not achieve acceptance or even recognition as a tribal member. She remained on the social and economic fringes of white American society, performing as an Indian in Wild West shows and silent films, though only as an extra, as all central Indian roles were played by white actresses in body paint. Thus, Lost Bird's captivity experience never ended: she remained against her will in her captors' society for her entire life. Even in narratives of captives who did not return to their original culture, the captivity experience comes to an end when the captive chooses to stay with the Indians, exercising a freedom that transforms him or her from captive to willing participant in the cultural community. This transition and release from the role of captive eluded Lost Bird.

Lost Bird, however, achieved a posthumous return to the community of her origins, when Flood discovered her California grave in 1991 and brought her to the attention of the Lakota. The new generation of Lakota finally embraced Lost Bird as a member of their tribe and reinterred her remains at the Wounded Knee site with a sacred burial ceremony. In reclaiming Lost Bird, the Lakotan Arvol Looking Horse acknowledged a need to "understand where we came from ... to put everything back in place, in balance with nature," yet seventy-one years after her death, Lost Bird still retained more value as a symbol than as an individual (Flood 22). Her burial attracted media attention and curious onlookers, and the Lakota sought to memorialize her as "a symbol for all people ... who had been violently deprived of their heritage" (Flood 16). Though she was finally accepted as a Lakota, Lost Bird's life regained significance mainly as an example of cultural oppression. In death as in life, Lost Bird gains recognition only through her symbolic value, illustrated in the photograph of the baby and Colby that emphasizes cultural contrasts. Her posthumous return to the Lakota granted her an identity, but she can not be rescued from her enduring captivity in cultural symbolism.

Works Cited

Burnham, Michelle. *Captivity and Sentiment: Cultural Exchange in American Literature, 1682-1861*. Hanover, NH: University Press of New England, 1997.

Castiglia, Christopher. *Bound and Determined: Captivity, Culture-Crossing, and White Womanhood from Mary Rowlandson to Patty Hearst*. Chicago: The University of Chicago Press, 1996.

Derounian-Stodola, Kathryn Zabelle, and James Arthur Levernier. *The Indian Captivity Narrative, 1550-1900*. New York: Twayne Publishers, 1993.

Ebersole, Gary L. *Captured by Texts: Puritan to Postmodern Images of Indian Captivity*. Charlottesville: The University Press of Virginia, 1995.

Englander, Marilyn Jean. Rev. of *Lost Bird of Wounded Knee: Spirit of the Lakota*, by Renee Sansom Flood. *Western Historical Quarterly* 27.1 (Spring 1996): 86-87.

Flood, Renee Sansom. *Lost Bird of Wounded Knee: Spirit of the Lakota*. New York: Scribner, 1995.

Kestler, Frances Roe. *The Indian Captivity Narrative: A Woman's View*. New York: Garland Publishing, 1990.

Ramsey, Colin. "Cannibalism and Infant Killing: A System of 'Demonizing' Motifs in Indian Captivity Narratives." *CLIO* 24.1 (Fall 1994): 55-69.

Rowlandson, Mary. *The Captive: The True Story of the Captivity of Mrs. Mary Rowlandson Among the Indians and God's Faithfulness to Her in Her Time of Trial*. Show Low, AZ: American Eagle Publications, 1996.

Smith, Sherry L. Rev. of *Lost Bird of Wounded Knee: Spirit of the Lakota*, by Renee Sansom Flood. *The Journal of American History* 83.1 (June 1996): 239-40.

VanDerBeets, Richard. *The Indian Captivity Narrative: An American Genre*. Lanham, MD: University Press of America, 1984.

Valerie Adamcyk is completing her Ph.D. dissertation on domestic ideology in women's literature of the American west.

Maps Over the Face of God: Remapping Epistemologies in Linda Hogan's *Solar Storms*

Ellen L. Arnold
East Carolina University

Maps are only masks over the face of God. (*Solar Storms*, 138, 346)

Chickasaw writer Linda Hogan's first novel, *Mean Spirit* (1990), set during the Oklahoma oil boom of the 1920s, depicts a world divided, one in which both Natives and nature are under attack by the mean spirit of White capitalist greed. This violent split is mirrored in the novel's setting, a town with two competing names; called Watona, "the gathering place" (*Mean* 53), by the native Osages, the town is renamed Talbert by White newcomers. In a world where "things are flying apart" (70), the remnants of the Osage people, fleeing dispossession and murder for their oil wealth, retreat at the end of the novel to the village of the Hill Indians, who maintain traditional lifeways hidden from the outside world. In contrast, Hogan's second novel, *Solar Storms* (1995), maps out a different kind of survival that does not necessitate withdrawal, but rather negotiates the divided world with multiple ways of knowing and being, and thus participates in the healing of its divisions.

Both *Mean Spirit* and *Solar Storms* are, in Hogan's words, "about people and the land and what happens to each when one is destroyed" (McAdams 134). Inspired by the protests against the James Bay HydroQuebec Project in the early 1970s,[1] *Solar Storms* is set in the Great Lakes boundary waters

---

[1] The James Bay hydroelectric project, announced in 1970 by Quebec Premier Robert Bourassa, planned the damming of three major rivers that drain into James Bay, in order to provide jobs for Canadians and power primarily for export to the U.S. Construction of Phase I began in 1972, and by 1984 two dams had been completed on the La Grande River, at immense cost in both dollars and environmental destruction. When Phase II was announced in 1984, to include the completion of two more dams on the La Grande and sixteen additional dams on other rivers, protests mounted by the Cree and Inuit of the area gained international support. According to Jace Weaver, "James Bay I had rendered the La Grande River and its tributaries a series of stagnant lakes incapable of supporting most life" (100). Twelve thousand square kilometers of land were inundated, and high concentrations of mercury in the water poisoned fish, wildlife, and caused widespread permanent neurological damage among the Cree. Animal and bird migration routes were disrupted, and in 1984, 10,000 caribou drowned in a single attempt to cross a flooded river. In 1994 Phase II was cancelled. For more detailed accounts, see Weaver (99-106), Churchill (*Struggle* 333-52).

region between the United States and Canada, an area inhabited by indigenous Crees and Anishnabeg, and the descendants of other Native and European immigrants brought there by the fur trade, including an invented tribe Hogan names "The Fat-Eaters." Hogan explains that she deliberately fictionalizes this novel "in a way that would make it impossible for anyone to pinpoint a location or tribe," in hopes of subverting the tendency of critics to keep Native writers "in our literary place, not as fiction writers, not as creative people, but only as voices responding to the oppression of history" (123).

While *Solar Storms* vigorously responds to the oppressions of history, it does so within a wider matrix of relationships that locates that history in the context of the evolution of earth and universe, and resituates issues of tribal and mixedblood identities within broader issues of *human* identity, in particular the shifting boundaries between humans and the natural world. Building on complementarities between traditional Native American cosmologies and the worldview emerging from postmodern science,[2] Hogan brings Western discourses into intimate conversation with silenced Native histories, cosmologies, and epistemologies. As she rewrites EuroAmerican history to include the perspectives of the colonized (women, Natives, animals, land), she also writes the voices of the colonized into the discourses of Western science and claims the language of science in the interests of indigenous sovereignty.

"[H]ow do conquered people get back their lives?" wonders *Solar Storms*' Dora-Rouge (226). Hogan's novel is the reply: by reclaiming the power to self-define, individually and collectively, and thus, to write a new reality into existence. *Solar Storms* maps out an indigenous resistance to the forces of destruction that bonds individual and national identities intimately with the sovereign identities of specific places and their constituent non-human life forms, and with the universal processes that bring place and life into being. From that collective site of resistance, Hogan's text reaches out to rewrite dominant discourses that separate science from history and spirituality, humans from nature, and mind from body, ultimately enfolding these Western narratives within a re-imagined indigenous worldview of interconnectedness and participation that recognizes the interdependence of Native and Western epistemologies and the necessity of their integration for human survival.

---

[2] At a 1995 Colloquium at Emory University, Hogan stated that biology and quantum physics are among the most important influences on her work. She mentioned specifically the work of David Bohm, and commented that her understanding of the new sciences is that they are moving toward a worldview very similar to traditional Native American worldviews.

Entering the Between

[S]omething wonderful lived there, in that span we call "between." (*Solar Storms* 31)

In her essay collection, *Dwellings* (1995), Hogan observes that "the drive towards knowledge has brought ruin to our Eden. Knowledge without wisdom, compassion, or understanding has damned us as we have been stirring about in the origins of life, breaking apart the miniature worlds of atoms just to see where that breaking will take us" (141). *Solar Storms* restores wisdom to knowledge by remaking in language the "covenant" between humans and the world that was broken by the practices of objectivism, materialism, and reductionism long before science split the atom. In oral traditions, Hogan writes, "an object and its name were not separated. One equalled the other." She continues (quoting Octavio Paz): "as soon as man acquired consciousness of himself, he broke away from the natural world and made himself another world inside himself" (*Dwellings* 52-3). *Solar Storms* traces the origin of the destruction humans have visited upon the earth in the name of science, industrialization, and colonization, to that "broken connection" between "inner and outer worlds" (53), and reweaves those worlds in the narrative of seventeen-year-old Angela Jensen's homecoming.

Angela returns to border country in search of the mother who abandoned her, and the secrets of the history written on her body in a map of scars and self-inflicted "tattoos" (*Solar* 26). Arriving at Adam's Rib, home of her great-grandmother Agnes and great-great-grandmother Dora-Rouge, she steps into the "place that holds her life" (23) and into her birth name, Angel. Before, she says, "Scars had shaped my life" (25), a life defined by anger, fear, internal emptiness, and escape. Her body records the history of two cultures in conflict; the scars that divide her face into halves—one "hated," the other "perfect" and "beautiful" (34)—and the red hair and dark skin that mark her as a mixedblood divide Angel against herself. Asked the "forbidden question" about the origin of her scars, Angel strikes out at the mirror that reflects her split image and shatters it. Afterwards she cries, "Me, the girl who never cried." That same night, Angel has a dream that foreshadows her coming passage through chaos into wholeness, a dream she recalls in the mixed languages of science and ancient myth:

> I fell over the edge of land, fell out of order and knowing into a world dark and primal, seething, and alive as creation, like the beginning of life.... I began to feel that if we had no separate words for inside and out and there were no boundaries between them, no walls, no skin, you would see me. What would meet your eyes would not be the mask of what had happened to me, not the evidence of

violence, not even how I closed the doors to the rooms of anger and fear. Some days you would see fire; other days, water. Or earth. You would see how I am like the night sky with its stars that fall through time and space and arrive here as wolves and fish and people, all of us fed by them. You would see the dust of sun, the turning of creation taking place. But the night I broke my face there were still boundaries and I didn't yet know I was beautiful as the wolf, or that I was a new order of atoms. (54)

Having broken through the mask of alienation that separates her inner emptiness from the world, Angel allows her fear and anger to give way to grief, and that grief opens her to be filled by creation.

Angel's passage through the mirror plunges her into the wilderness that lives within and outside her, so that the skeleton of her personal history, which Agnes, Dora-Rouge, and her surrogate grandmother, Bush, have helped her piece back together, can be clothed in the flesh of the world. On the difficult canoe journey north with her grandmothers to join protesters at the dam that threatens the land and the indigenous lifeways that depend on it, Angel seeks her mother Hannah and an "unbroken line between me and the past" to hold together the "fragments and pieces left behind by fur traders, soldiers, priests and schools" (77). However, as Agnes' partner Husk tells Angel, "Einstein believed time would bend and circle back to itself, maybe in the way that planets orbit," and Angel finds herself "traveling backward in time toward myself at the same time I journeyed forward, like the new star astronomers found that traveled in two directions at once" (64). As science's reductionist attempt to understand creation by splitting the atom opened onto a new vision of a quantum universe, so Angel's quest for a linear path to her origins brings about a complex revisioning of her internal and external realities.

The journey of the four women through the wilderness "unravels time," and they enter "a kind of timelessness" (170) that allows them to experience "a place between worlds," an older world alive in the present one. "[W]earing the face of the world," the four women become "like one animal," hear "inside each other in a tribal way" (177). In their shared embodied merger with the world, they communicate with each other through the circulation of breath and blood and become "articulate in the languages of land, water, animal" (193). They are "articulated" by the world—given shape, written and spoken into being in the multiple languages of the natural world—at the same time they hear and speak the languages of this boundary world with and through their bodies. Their journey maps the "between" of mingled worlds, and the passage of their bodies tells a new/old story that includes the voices of the non-human world. At the same time, the women's journey reverses the historical path of the French fur traders and the destruction they brought with them south into lake country, and participates in the growing vigor of the pan-Indian movement of the 1970s—the formation of AIM and the creation of a pan-tribal identity that brought traditional ways to the demands of contemporary politics. As Angel puts it, the four women "journey out from the narrowed circle of our history the way rays of light grow from the sun" (93); they are participating in the unfolding creation of a new world.

Balancing the Equation

> We are what is missing from the equation of wholeness. ("Department of the Interior" 168)

As Angel begins to sense an "older world lost to me" which "only [her] body remembered," she comes to realize that she is "part of the same equation as birds and rain" (79), an equation that includes the world's perceptions and thoughts about humans. "We are seen, our measure taken, not only by the animals and spiders but even by the alive galaxy in deep space" (80), she says; "We [are] only one of the many dreams of earth" (170). Angel enters that dreaming to speak with the land and learn the uses of medicinal plants, a healing art that Hogan describes elsewhere as "an intricate science reconnecting and restoring the human body with earth, cosmos" ("Department" 166). Angel merges with plants in the same way that, according to Bush, "Two parts hydrogen, one part oxygen ... married" to become ocean (*Solar* 179). Hogan's choice of the word "equation" evokes the formulas of physics and chemistry, making the interconnections visible in dreams comparable to the bonding transformations described by such equations. The languages that translate across the gap in the equation that separates humans from the world include both the language of dreams (the language of bodies and earth) and the language of science (the language of words, empiricism, reason, analysis). Both dreaming and the creation of a third substance occur in the "between," in the space of the equals sign, the space in which this novel is written.

Angel's entrance into the dreaming of earth, her baptism in the wilderness river that carries the women north, are both described in terms of this equation: "[T]he roots of dreaming ... are like the seeds of hydrogen and the seeds of oxygen that together create ocean, lake, and ice. In this way, the plants and I joined each other" (171); "I made my way to water and dived.... I thought of Bush ... saying, 'Two parts hydrogen, one part oxygen,' in her dreamy way. When I was inside water, I understood how these simple elements married and became a third thing" (179). Yet equations can also represent an equivalence that is static and dead, as well as conversions that are dynamic and creative. The space of the equals sign may be a gap that separates, a mask of alienation, an "abyss" between signifier and signified; it may also constitute the skin that contains life, the word that articulates meaning out of the flux, the boundary that divides land from water and gives rise to creation. As Husk teaches Angel, the language of science, like the language of dreams, can translate across this space, can "prove" what was taken for granted in the "older world"—that "everything [is] alive" (35), that "insects are intelligent" (91), that "we are made from stars" (120). The language of science offers another of many ways to restore the "broken covenant" between humans and world.

Hogan's choice of the word "marry" to describe the union of hydrogen and oxygen is also significant, bestowing desire and agency on the chemical elements of life. For Hogan, it is hunger, desire, and longing that open the gaps—the words, the skins, the surfaces—that create and hold life and also destroy and consume it. Angel reflects, "People say that in the beginning was the word. But they have forgotten the loneliness of God, the yearning for something that shaped itself into the words. Let there be. Out of that loneliness, light was conceived, water opened across a new world, and people rose up from clay" (94). New science tells a similar creation story: the vast flowing wholeness that David Bohm (a physicist with whose work Hogan is familiar) calls "holomovement" contains an "implicate order" which gives birth to explicate reality. Yet this wholeness cannot be the perfect wholeness of undifferentiation, for in perfect equilibrium, no movement or life is possible. For creation to occur, something, some other, must be desired, taken apart, consumed. Out of imbalance and the hunger it creates, life and history are born.

Embodied, the hunger for union and reunion also finds expression in the literal hunger of the body for food. According to Hogan, humans repress the wildness that lives inside them and project it onto nature's others in an attempt to kill it in them, because "they mirror back to us the predators we pretend not to be" (*Dwellings* 71). She makes it clear that humans help to maintain the alienation between themselves and the world by refusing to acknowledge our dependence on the sacrifice of other living beings, an acknowledgement that allows us to shift perspectives and to experience our own embeddedness in the processes of the natural world. In "Department of the Interior," Hogan writes, "The experience of the wild is inside us, beyond our mental control, and it lies alongside the deep memory of wilderness, and it has rules and laws that do not obey our human will" (167). *Solar Storms* suggests that in order to re-experience the unity lost to objectivity and objectivism, humans must open their skins of denial to the pain and grief that are the inevitable consequences of destroying and consuming other lives as intelligent and sentient as our own.

This theme is actualized in Angel's journey and reiterated in the experience of LaRue Marks Time, the Metis storekeeper whose education Angel takes on in an effort to make him a worthy suitor for Bush. His name tells his complex story: "LaRue Marks Time" inscribes the split the character has fallen into, the divisions opened up between his inheritance of the French fur trade (symbolized by his French given name) and his indigenous history and connection to place (suggested by his surname). In the language of surface inscriptions, the language of the antique colonial maps he collects, his name translates as "the street marks time," naming the processes of mapping and abstraction that freeze time and stop life in order to commodify and possess both space and bodies.[3] Translated into the languages of earth, of body and emotion, "rue" suggests both the sorrow that "marks time" inside LaRue's body and the medicinal plant rue. LaRue's healing lies in his grief. Only after LaRue grants value, feeling, and consciousness to the animals he hunts is he able to be fully himself. In his distress over the death of an animal that is the last of its kind, he cries,

> ... for the animal, for us, our lives, and for the war he'd endured and never told about. He changed after that, inch by inch. Another person might not have noticed, but I saw it. And so did Bush. She was moved by his new openness, his lack of skin. Tears have a purpose. They are what we carry of ocean, and perhaps we must become sea, give ourselves to it, if we are to be transformed. (340)

LaRue's willingness to open himself finally to pain and loss restores him to the world, and the novel draws to a close with his vision of his own face reflected in windowglass as a wolverine, which he comically rushes to shoot, laughing with Angel later that he "thought it was too ugly for a wolverine" (350). Wolverine is a "mask" (321) reflecting back the "human gone wild" (84), the knowledge and experience of interconnectedness overlayed by the "ugliness" of our destructiveness, which in the end can only reflect back on us in self-destruction. Humans are the agents of our own destruction, but our salvation lies in our equivalence with and to the wild. We are, like Wolverine—Mondi "who'd made the world" (321)—co-participants in the world's ongoing creation.

Andrea Musher, in her interpretation of *Mean Spirit*, observes that the Indians who have lived in the White world, in order to reconnect with ancient traditional tribal life and spirituality, must first journey through Sorrow Cave, must pass through the sorrow of their terrible history and "out the other side"; "penetrating the depths of sorrow," she says, "provides the way out of sorrow" (34-5). When Agnes speaks in the prologue to the novel of "the mourning [that] was our common ground" (15), she refers specifically to the Native and mixedblood people of Adam's Rib, whose lives have been torn apart by the violent history of colonization, genocide, and theft. Hogan understands that grief to be part of a larger one, the denial of human identity

---

[3] The relationship between the possession of land and bodies is powerfully suggested by one of the old maps that LaRue lends Bush, which depicts mudflats with "paintings of sinking things," including "a boat with Indian people chained together as slaves for the far continent" (131).

with the world, a denial that breaks our covenant with life and prevents the healing of the divisions wrought by violent histories. To be created anew, restored to full humanity in awareness that our "bod[ies] and the land are the same things," as Hogan puts it in an interview (McAdams 128), we must pass through the barriers of objectivity, not turn away from them. Healing cannot be a smoothing over of scars, a wiping away of divisions and wounds; healing must include the conscious understanding of the wound's function, of the necessity of resistance for survival, of the interdependence of life and death, creation and destruction. For Hogan, healing lies in the process of seeing doubly, the ability to see and experience the gap of separation and the scars that close it as both wound and the fullness of connectivity, to live in the between of joy and pain, reason and emotion, matter and spirit.

The Map of the World = The Map of the Mind

This is what I know from science:
that a grain of dust dwells at the center
of every flake of snow,
that ice can have its way with land,
that wolves live inside a circle
of their own beginning.
This is what I know from blood:
the first language is not our own.
There are names each thing has for itself,
and beneath us the other order already moves.
(*The Book of Medicines* 37-38)

Two-Town Post, the center of indigenous resistance to the dam project, also serves as an outpost to both Holy String Town, a town dominated by the Catholic Church and laid out in "a long thin line, a single road" like a string of rosary beads, and the town of the Fat Eaters, which is "laid out like a cross along two roads, with smaller, more narrow roads in between" (221). Compared to the town with two names that is the focal setting of *Mean Spirit*, this arrangement of side-by-side towns, one commanded by the Church and arranged linearly, the other laid out like a spider's web according to the four directions, provides a visual image that crystallizes Hogan's different project in *Solar Storms*. *Solar Storms*' two towns and the two ways of life and epistemologies they represent are complementary; they are a twinned structure, and their juxtaposition mirrors their differences yet holds them together as a whole. And both towns are threatened equally by the machinery of greed that would consume them to provide electricity for faraway urban centers. Angel herself mirrors the two towns, "part one thing and part another" (273), but she travels freely between them and the worlds they signify, uniting them in a new equation. On the other hand, Angel's icy-hearted mother Hannah, the woman who mutilated and abandoned her, lives in another town with two names, Ohete and New Hardy (121); Hannah fell into the gap between indigenous and EuroAmerican worlds that Angel, with the help of her grandmothers and her non-human kin, learns to navigate.

Unlike Hannah or Hannah's lover and killer Eron, who was raised in the old ways but was taught in school that the old beliefs were wrong, and "got lost" between these "two knowings" (246), Angel acquires from her teachers the ability to negotiate these different epistemologies. Within her they are "married," which enables her to find the way to the older world of participation and respect by "mak[ing] a new way through the world" (*Book* 49). Bush obsessively charts their canoe trip north with the old maps of conquest, studying them "with the precision of a mathematician" (*Solar* 121), struggling to comprehend their discrepancies. Dora-Rouge, on the other hand, understands that "earth has more than one dimension. The one we see is only the first layer" (123); she navigates the wilderness world of shifting boundaries with the memories that live in her body, intuitive and sensory, like the internal maps that guide the migrations of birds. "Maps are only masks on the face of God," says Dora-Rouge; "There are other ways around the world" (138). Dora-Rouge's intuitive maps, growing out of both her personal memory and the collective memory of genetic inheritance (like the instinct to migrate), add to Bush's two-dimensional maps the ability to maneuver systems that are dynamic and unpredictable. With her grandmothers, Angel learns to read the surfaces that are mapped by sight and to understand how those maps both participate in the construction of the world and limit one's vision. At the same time she learns to "feel and hear where the faraway and ancient began" (93), to "see [in the dark] with my skin, touch with my eyes" (120), to map the depths with other senses. She acquires the skill to enter and find her way through the dreams of earth to locate healing plants, like the traditional hunters of the north who followed the "dreams they called hunger maps [to find] their prey" (170).[4]

Angel receives a different kind of education from Agnes's partner Husk, who "love[s] science" and introduces Angel to his "stacks of magazines and books that divulged the secret worlds of atoms and galaxies, of particles and quarks" (35). Husk knows that science will prove "the world [is] alive" and teaches Angel to watch "the magazines for hard evidence" (139). In the interplay of these different knowings, the layering of two kinds of mapping, two epistemologies (like the "words of war, obituaries, stories of carnage and misery" that merge with the scars on Hannah's body when she is laid out on newspaper in death [253]), Hogan makes it evident that scars, maps,

---

[4] At the same 1995 Colloquium Hogan acknowledged that Hugh Brody's ethnographic work among Ojibway hunters influenced *Solar Storms*. See Brody, "Maps of Dreams." As is typical of this novel, she strives to keep what even Angel realizes "others might call the superstitions of primitive people" (189) grounded in science.

and language itself are all masks on the face of God; they can inscribe histories of abuse and murder on body and earth, can fragment, objectify, and possess; at the same time they can heal by making visible the hidden histories of violence that threaten individual, communal and tribal identities, and can open into the timeless realm of the holomovement and help chart paths to a restored wholeness.

According to Mark Warhus' *Another America*, a study of Native American mapping practices at the time of contact, the maps made by Native Americans were not meant to be permanent documents, but were "transitory illustrations for the oral documents" that related geography to "history, traditions, and kin, in relationships with the animal and natural resources that one depended upon, and in union with the spirits, ancestors, and religious forces with whom one shared existence" (3). In contrast, Carolyn Merchant notes that the "The mapping of space by explorers ... began the process of its devaluation from an active place of power to a fixed, inert, geometric surface. Mapped space distances the observer, breaking down participation through the imposition of perspective.... [T]he land is seen as a bounded object. A spatial perspective leads to its management and control" (51). Hogan turns the maps of conquest against the forces of colonization, demonstrating that the topographical map not only has it uses in the interests of resistance, but can also lead to revelation. Layered, these static maps reveal unfolding changes; in them Bush can read the secrets of creation, how the beavers, "the true makers of land" (123), reordered relationships between land and water to make new worlds. "Names," says Husk, are "like layers of time" (65), and so are maps; the reiteration of their two-dimensional patterns moves toward a third dimension, opening on a realm of interdimensionality where times and worlds mingle. Finally, on the journey north, the oldest map falls apart into fragments in Bush's hands, like the mirror that Angel breaks, marking the emergence of the older world into the present.

The progressive alteration of Angel's name throughout the narrative—from Angela Jensen (her "White" name) to Angel Iron (the name she takes when she arrives at the end of her journey through water) to Angel Wing (which she takes after her mother's death)—reflects a similar layering process. The first name that appears in the text, Angela Jensen, "holds" her original name Angel within it, but also joins it with her European paternal ancestry. The surnames Iron and Wing link her to her maternal forbears and to a more "tribal" form of naming that reflects Angel's passage through and acceptance by the natural world. At the same time, the names Iron and Wing unite earth and sky and mirror the blood and breath that link humans most intimately to each other and to the earth. Angel's evolution toward wholeness reflects a complex systematic exchange that understands all parts to also hold the whole, like a hologram. The subject/object split is healed—but not erased or merged—through the recognition that, as the self comes into being in relationship with all others, simultaneously the universe comes into being in this same space, in interaction with all its parts, recreating itself anew in each individual self. Angel is herself the remade covenant, the restored pact between human and animal, land and water. At the end of her canoe journey through the wilderness, Angel emerges naked from water to meet her mother for the first time; this final act of self re-creation also reenacts the old story of the creation of humans by beaver, "who rose out from the darkness beneath waters" of the flood that covered earth to remake land and create humans out of it in a pact that "They would help each other" (238-39).

Like the old native man who "rid his people of the outsiders" by making them a map that would lose them in the interior waterways of the continent, Hogan maps a way into the future that "loses" the dominant culture within an older world. *Solar Storms* layers the linear and abstract with/in the spatial map of the four directions, the cycles of the seasons and of time moving in two directions and folding back on itself, which structure the novel. The abstracted, dismembering, commodifying perspective of Enlightenment science cannot be rejected; it is part of reality, co-participant in its unfolding evolution. The fatal error is to "take the map for the territory," to forget that objectivity, like skin or water, is a another mask on the face of God, a surface that emerges in the intersection of differences that also holds and connects and can open onto that "older order" that moves beneath us. Like the pictographs written on cliff faces or the figures of ancient myth, drawn on the oldest colonial map, the two-dimensional mappings of an objectivist epistemology may also provide the surfaces that make the spirit world, the infinite potentialities of creation, manifest in the material world. Read with both mind and body, kinesthetically, sensorially, and emotionally, the maps of conquest become living signs of survival and healing, evidence of the ongoing creation inherent in destruction, of the world's wholeness. Or as Angel puts it, "[I]t is not that the old ways are lost from us but that we are lost from them. But the ways are patient and await our return" (346). By joining what we "know from science" with what we "know from blood," we may find our way to them.

Works Cited

Bohm, David. *Wholeness and the Implicate Order*. Boston: Ark, 1983.
Brody, Hugh. "Maps of Dreams." *Out of the Background: Readings on Canadian Native History*. Eds. Robin Fisher and Kenneth Coates, Toronto: Copp Clark Pitman, 1988. 256-66.
Churchill, Ward. *Struggle for the Land: Indigenous Resistance to Genocide, Ecocide, and Expropriation in Contemporary North America*. Monroe, Maine: Common Courage, 1993.
Hogan, Linda. *The Book of Medicines*. Minneapolis: Coffee House P, 1993.
—. Colloquium. Emory University. Atlanta. 20 March 1995.

Hogan, Linda. "Department of the Interior." *Minding the Body: Women Writers on Body and Soul.* Ed. Patricia Foster. New York: Doubleday, 1994. 159-74.

—. *Dwellings: A Spiritual History of the Living World.* New York: W.W. Norton, 1995.

—. *Mean Spirit.* New York: Ivy Books, 1990.

—. *Solar Storms.* New York: Scribner, 1995.

McAdams, Janet. "An Interview with Linda Hogan." In *This Blood Is a Map: Voice and Cartography in Contemporary Native American Poetry.* Emory University dissertation, 1996.

Merchant, Carolyn. *Ecological Revolutions: Nature, Gender, and Science in New England.* Chapel Hill: U of North Carolina P, 1989.

Musher, Andrea. "Showdown at Sorrow Cave: Bat Medicine and the Spirit of Resistance in *Mean Spirit*." In *Studies in American Indian Literatures* 6.3 (1994): 23-36.

Warhus, Mark. *Another America: Native American Maps and the History of Our Land.* New York: St. Martin's P, 1997.

Weaver, Jace, ed. *Defending Mother Earth: Native American Perspectives on Environmental Justice.* Maryknoll, New York: Orbis Books, 1996.

Ellen L. Arnold has published essays and reviews on literature, film, and web media by and about Native Americans in *Studies in American Indian Literatures, Modern Fiction Studies,* and *National Women's Studies Association Journal,* and in the anthologies *American Indian Studies: An Interdisciplinary Approach to Contemporary Issues* (Ed. Dane Morrison, Peter Lang, 1999) and *Web.Studies: Rewiring Media for the Digital Age* (Ed. David Gauntlett, Arnold, forthcoming). She edited a collection of interviews with Leslie Marmon Silko titled *Conversations With Leslie Marmon Silko* (UP of Mississippi). She is currently studying the ways in which contemporary Native American writers of fiction and poetry blur the boundaries between science and nature.

Contested Common Ground: Cherokee Freedpeople's National Identity and Land Ownership in the Cherokee Nation, Indian Territory

Celia E. Naylor-Ojurongbe
Duke University

How do we comprehend the "meaning of freedom" for previously enslaved people of African descent and those defined as "free people of color" or "free Negroes"?[1] What kinds of experiences during the post-Civil War/ Reconstruction period influenced freedpeople's overall sense of themselves as "free" citizens? How do we capture the various facets of freedpeople's lives that are not readily accessible from solely reviewing census records and other official government documents? By utilizing the Works Progress Administration (WPA) Oklahoma interviews conducted in the 1930s,[2] I explore how ex-slaves in Indian Territory reconstructed their identities as

[1] See McGlynn and Drescher, eds., *The Meaning of Freedom: Economics, Politics and Culture After Slavery*. See also Foner, *Nothing But Freedom*; Richardson, ed., *Abolition and Its Aftermath: The Historical Context, 1790-1916*; and Scott, "Exploring the Meaning of Freedom: Postemancipation Societies in Comparative Perspective," 407-428.

[2] See Rawick, ed., *Oklahoma and Mississippi Narratives*, vol. 7 of *The American Slave: A Composite Autobiography* and *Oklahoma Narratives*, vol. 12, Supplement Series 1 of *The American Slave: A Composite Autobiography*. Volume 7 of Rawick's collection includes the interviews of seventy-five ex-slaves and/or children of ex-slaves. Of these seventy-five interviewees, a total of fourteen self-identified as ex-slaves or children of ex-slaves of Native Americans in Indian Territory—six Cherokee ex-slaves, four Creek ex-slaves, two Choctaw ex-slaves and two Chickasaw ex-slaves. Volume 12 of Rawick's collection includes the interviews of sixty-seven ex-slaves and/or children of ex-slaves. Of these sixty-seven interviewees, a total of thirty-four identified themselves as ex-slaves or children of ex-slaves of Native Americans in Indian Territory—sixteen Cherokee ex-slaves, nine Choctaw ex-slaves, eight Creek ex-slaves and one Chickasaw ex-slave.

The American Slave series edited by Rawick represents the most thorough collection of WPA interviews of ex-slaves, including the interviews of freedpeople residing in Oklahoma. However, in 1996, T. Lindsay Baker and Julie P. Baker published a collection of interviews of one hundred and thirty ex-slaves, including several that had not been previously published. Baker and Baker's publication created renewed interest in the Oklahoma slave narratives; however, the majority of the newly published interviews are of former slaves from other parts of the United States who relocated to Oklahoma as freedpeople during the western migration in the late 1800s and early 1900s.

freedpeople by identifying and exhibiting multiple connections with particular Native American nations. These interviewees provide evidence of their lives in bondage and in freedom within the context of nineteenth-century Indian Territory.[3] In this article I highlight Cherokee freedpeople's expressed sentiments regarding their connection to the Cherokee Nation, as well as their notions of a Cherokee national identity.

Journey Back Home

During the Civil War, many European-American masters in the southern United States, as well as Native American slaveowners in Indian Territory, forced their slaves to leave with them as a result of actual warfare or the threat of warfare. Some Cherokee slaveowners wanted to remain within the limits of Indian Territory and thus chose to move to areas in the Choctaw and Chickasaw nations. Other Cherokee slaveowners left their homes and belongings and temporarily relocated their families, including their African-American slaves, to Kansas, Arkansas and Texas.[4] For many slaves, especially those born and raised in Indian Territory, this journey to surrounding areas was the first time they had traveled out of Indian Territory.

Leaving Indian Territory before and during the Civil War was a decision that owners made for their slaves; however, after the Civil War, the desire to return to Indian Territory was a decision many Cherokee freedpeople made for themselves. Although the disruption of the War provided opportunities for some slaves to leave their owners' farms and plantations, either of their

---

[3] Even though the usefulness of these interviews remains debatable, they contain invaluable material pertaining to the experiences of African-American slaves. Particularly insightful works on the uses and misuses of slave narratives, autobiographies and oral interviews are Blassingame, "Using the Testimony of Ex-Slaves: Approaches and Problems," 473-492; Cade, "Out of the Mouths of Ex-Slaves," 294-337; Bailey, "A Divided Prism: Two Sources of Black Testimony on Slavery," 381-404; Escott, *Slavery Remembered: A Record of Twentieth-Century Slave Narratives*; Woodward, "History from Slave Sources," 470-481; and Yetman," Ex-Slave Interviews and the Historiography of Slavery," 181-210.

[4] While only a child during the Civil War, one of the most vivid memories for ex-slave Sarah Wilson centered on the journey during the war from the Cherokee Nation to an area "way down across the Red [R]iver in Texas ... close to Shawneetown of the Choctaw Nation but just across the river on the other side in Texas bottoms." Her master, Ben Johnson, moved them "in covered wagons when the Yankee soldiers got too close by in the first part of the War" (Rawick, vol. 7:350-351). Shawneetown was located in the southeastern corner of the Choctaw Nation, approximately five miles north of the Red River. As Sarah Wilson explained, once they crossed the Red River, they entered the state of Texas. Once in Texas Ben Johnson, and other masters who had left the Cherokee Nation, continued to profit from their slaves' labor. Johnson obliged his slaves to live in camps during this time, and he "hired the slaves out to Texas people because he didn't make any crops down there" (351).

own volition or as a result of their masters' orders, in their interviews a number of ex-slaves focused on their desire to return to Indian Territory after the War came to an end.[5] After the Civil War, such individuals, like other freedpeople throughout the United States, began searching for close kin. The separation of family members during slavery continued throughout the Reconstruction Era, and often left little record behind, so families had to pursue any slim clues to the whereabouts of lost or sold family members. Many of the Cherokee freedpeople who had been relocated outside Indian Territory made their way back in an effort to find lost relatives. Other Cherokee freedpeople returned to Indian Territory because Indian Territory represented the only home they knew—the only place they identified as home.

This desire to return to the Cherokee Nation reverberates throughout the WPA interviews of Cherokee ex-slaves. Charley Nave was born and raised in Tahlequah (the capital of the Cherokee Nation) and his master Cherokee Henry Nave was also his father. Charley Nave's son, Cornelius Neely Nave, born in 1868, recalled his father's need to return to Indian Territory after the war. Cornelius Nave identified the place where he and his father were both raised as "home"; it was "that home after the war [that] brought my pappa back home" (Rawick, vol. 12: 236). After completing his service in the Union Army, Nave recalled that his father, Charley Nave, initially "took all the family and moved to Fort Scott, Kansas, but I guess he feel more at home with the Indians for pretty soon we all move back, this time to a farm near Fort Gibson," within the boundaries of the Cherokee Nation, Indian Territory (Rawick, vol. 12:236).

Although Charley Nave successfully relocated his family to the Cherokee Nation, other freedpeople were not as fortunate and were forced to rely on the generosity of their previous owners for their return to the Nation. Freedwoman Patsy Taylor Perryman and her mother had been relocated to Texas with their owner Cherokee Judy Taylor. However, after the war, their mistress decided that she "wasn't going to take us with her." Patsy Taylor Perryman distinctly recalled how, upon hearing of their mistress' decision to leave them behind, her mother "cried so hard she [her mistress] couldn't stand it and told us to get ready" (Rawick, vol. 12: 252). As a result of her mother's pleas they did in fact return to the Cherokee Nation with their former owner.

Even though there were slaveowners who were willing to aid in their ex-slaves' return to Indian Territory, not all ex-slaves accepted their previous masters' assistance. Ben Johnson and his Cherokee wife Annie Johnson had relocated their family and slaves, including Sarah Wilson and her mother, to Texas during the Civil War. Some time after the war ended, Ben Johnson

---

[5] During the Civil War, slaves often deserted the farms and plantations they had worked on for years, some for a lifetime, and joined a nearby Union camp, in search of freedom, refuge and food. For descriptions of this return home to Indian Territory, see the WPA interviews of Matilda Poe, Jack Campbell, John Harrison, Moses Lonian, Chaney McNair, R.C. Smith and Lucinda Vann.

offered to help his ex-slaves "all get back home" if they "wanted to come." In response to his offer, Sarah Wilson's mother told him "she could bear her own expenses" (Rawick, vol. 7:351-352). Determined to be independent, Sarah Wilson's mother may also have had other reasons for refusing support from Ben and Annie Johnson. For, her former owners' son, Ned Johnson, was the father of her daughter Sarah (Rawick, vol. 7:351-352).[6]

From Sarah Wilson's interview it is unclear if she knew exactly what transpired between her mother and Ned Johnson. What is clear from Wilson's interview is that her mother did not want to be indebted to the Johnson family in any way. Indeed, because her mother refused Johnson's offer, Sarah and her mother had to "straggle back the best way we could, and me and mammy just got along one way and another till we got to a ferry over the Red River and into Arkansas. Then we got some rides and walked some until we got to Fort Smith" (Rawick, vol. 7:352). They rested for some time in refugee camps along the way and then headed for Fort Gibson, located in the Illinois District of the Cherokee Nation. Wilson described the trip "as hell on earth. Nobody let us ride and it took us nearly two weeks to walk all that ways, and we nearly starved all the time. We was skin and bones and feet all bloody when we got to the Fort" (Rawick, vol. 7:352).[7] Instead of creating a new life for herself and her daughter in Texas or even in another state, Sarah Wilson's mother was determined to return to the Cherokee Nation no matter what the cost. Although she did indeed make the journey back, soon after arriving at Four Mile Branch in the Cherokee Nation, Sarah Wilson's mother died.

As many Cherokee ex-slaves made their way back to Indian Territory, they returned with hopes for a new life in the Cherokee Nation. It is hard to imagine that freedpeople like Sarah Wilson's mother would have made the long journey back to Indian Territory from surrounding states without good reason. It could have been the need to reunite with family members in Indian Territory that compelled them to make the journey—a need enhanced by a significant cultural connection to the Cherokees. Perhaps their return to the Cherokee Nation signaled their personal recognition that the Nation was indeed their homeland. To the Cherokee freedpeople, freedom meant on some level that their previous association with the Cherokees, that is as their slaves, had been changed forever. Now, they believed they were free to, and had a right to, rebuild their lives in the Cherokee Nation.

[6] When she was eight years old, Sarah Wilson's maternal grandmother had informed her that her young master, Ned Johnson, was indeed her father. Sarah Wilson also recalled Ned Johnson's flippant remarks about his blood connection to her. When her mistress, Annie Johnson, was abusing her as a little girl, Sarah remembered that Ned Johnson sometimes laughed and stated to his mother, "Let her alone, she got big, big blood in her" (Rawick, vol. 7:347).

[7] Daniel Littlefield explained that "when the freedmen had begun to return to the Cherokee Nation, the federal troops had offered a source of refuge to them. Fort Gibson was the hub of activity, and most of the main routes of travel into the Nation ended there." Littlefield, *Cherokee Freedmen*, 28.

Rebuilding Free Lives on Forty Acres and Maybe More

After the Civil War, residents in the United States and Indian Territory started the business of reconstructing their lives. It was a challenge even to think about rebuilding in some areas given the extensive devastation, the human losses, and the persistent animosities. According to one report, the war had "thrown them back, so that in a great measure they [had] to do over again the work of years in building up their homes and fortunes" (*Report on Indian Affairs by the Acting Commissionrt for the Year 1867,* 22). J.W. Dunn, U.S. Indian Agent for the Creeks, described 1867 as "a time of severe and necessary labor—a struggle for existence—and every energy of the people was directed to the cultivation of crops and the building of houses" (*Report on Indian Affairs for the Year 1867,* 321).[8] The Cherokee Nation also suffered in the summer of 1867 due to an epidemic of cholera throughout the Nation.[9]

For the Cherokee freedpeople, resettling in the Nation initially meant finding an available area to build homes and plant crops. Depending on the region in which they settled, the majority of freedmen planted crops that were suitable for that location; they also chose crops they were familiar with harvesting and useful in nourishing their families, particularly wheat, corn and various fruits and vegetables. As far as the freedpeople were concerned they had a right to make improvements upon land in the Cherokee Nation by virtue of Cherokee laws regarding the "public domain" (Cherokee Nation, vol. 6: 75-6). Cherokee freedpeople worked the land as did freedpeople in the southern United States; however, unlike southern freedmen, they were only limited to tenant farming or sharecropping during the first few years of Reconstruction. Moreover, the Cherokee freedpeople, unlike others, did not benefit greatly from the variety of services offered by the Bureau of Refugees, Freedmen and Abandoned Lands, more commonly referred to as the Freedmen's Bureau.[10] Without the services of this bureau, Cherokee freedpeople could only rely on the laws and treaties of the Cherokee Nation for some assistance during the post-Civil War period.

Although the issue of slavery within the Cherokee Nation was finally laid to rest by the Treaty of 1866, this treaty engendered new questions in the era of Reconstruction related to the status, rights and citizenship of Cherokee

---

[8] In addition to the effects of the war, the summer of 1866 proved to be a particularly harsh one for the Creeks, when an onslaught of grasshoppers destroyed a great deal of their fruit and vegetable crops.

[9] The cholera epidemic also severely affected the Seminole Nation.

[10] Created in 1865, the Freedmen's Bureau provided medical assistance for freedpeople, helped with the relocation of freedpeople to areas with more opportunities particularly in the agricultural sector, funded schools specifically for freedpeople and created opportunities for freedpeople to lease and even to purchase abandoned lands.

freepeople.[11] Proclaimed on 11 August 1866, the Treaty of 1866 specifically approved the Cherokee freedpeople's inclusion as citizens of the Cherokee Nation, their access to land in the Cherokee Nation, and their legitimate claim to "all the rights of native Cherokees" (Kappler, 944).[12] No matter what the Cherokee freedpeople might have construed as their connection to the Cherokee Nation, their right to claim the Cherokee Nation as their home, and even the Cherokees as their people, would remain debatable within the Nation for several decades.

Only three months after the Treaty of 1866 had been approved and adopted, the Cherokee freedpeople's claims to Cherokee citizenship including land settlement became severely limited by the Cherokee Nation. In November 1866, the articles specifically related to Cherokee citizenship were included in the Cherokee Constitution as amendments. One of the significant changes to the Cherokee Constitution included the delineation of who would be considered part of the Cherokee citizenry. The amendment to Article 3, Section 5 of the Cherokee Constitution stated: "All native born Cherokees, all Indians, and whites legally members of the Nation by adoption, and all freedmen who have been liberated by voluntary action of their former owners or by law, as well as free colored persons who were in the country at the commencement of the rebellion, and are now residents therein, or who may return within six months from the 19th day of July, 1866, and their descendants, who reside within the limits of the Cherokee Nation, shall be taken, and deemed to be, citizens of the Cherokee Nation" (Cherokee Nation, vol. 7:25). This and other related amendments were presented, approved and adopted at a general convention of the people of the Cherokee Nation in Tahlequah on 28 November 1866; the next day, the Cherokee National Council ratified these amendments (Cherokee Nation, vol. 7:25).

In the first months following the Civil War, many Cherokee freedpeople returned to the Cherokee Nation; however, for some their return to the Nation

[11] In February 1863, three years before the ratification of the Treaty of 1866, Thomas Pegg, serving as Acting Principal Chief of the Cherokee Nation, convened the Cherokee National Council for an unexpected session to discuss the status of the Cherokee Nation's treaty with the Confederacy, as well as the status of slaves in the Cherokee Nation. On 21 February 1863, the Cherokee National Council passed an act declaring "that all Negro and other slaves within the limits of the Cherokee Nation, be, and they are hereby Emancipated from Slavery. And any person or persons who may have been held in slavery, are hereby declared to be forever free." The National Council proclaimed that this act would not be effective until 25 June 1863. Although this act declared the emancipation of all slaves in the Cherokee Nation, it did not address the incorporation of freedpeople within the Nation. See "An Act Emancipating the Slaves in the Cherokee Nation," *Cherokee Nation Papers*.

[12] The 1866 treaties between each of the so-called Five Civilized Tribes and the United States are reprinted in their entirety in Kappler's *Indian Treaties 1778-1883*: Treaty with the Seminoles, 910-915; Treaty with the Choctaws and Chickasaws, 918-931; Treaty with the Creeks, 931-937; and Treaty with the Cherokees, 942-950.

took several years. There were others who never made the journey back home at all due to limited resources, illness and other circumstances. Not all Cherokee freedpeople had heard of the six-month limitation for their return to the Cherokee Nation stipulated by the amendment to the Cherokee Constitution. For those who returned after the six-month deadline, oftentimes referred to as the "too lates," they became involved in a lengthy legal process not only with the Cherokee Nation, but also with the United States government. Beginning immediately following the Civil War and continuing into the next century, this time requirement would become a point of contention in determining which Cherokee freedpeople would be recognized officially by the Cherokee government as Cherokee citizens. Embedded within the question of Cherokee citizenship was the issue of land ownership.[13]

The mythical promise of "forty acres and a mule" popularized during Reconstruction still resonates throughout scholarly analyses of the Reconstruction Era; however, due to the work of the Dawes Commission, land ownership for Cherokee freedpeople was not a myth.[14] After being enrolled by the Dawes Commission, by proving they were indeed Cherokee citizens, a significant number of Cherokee freedpeople received land

[13] The Cherokee freedmen's fight for equal rights, included not only the right to own land in the Cherokee Nation, but also a right to a percentage of the annuities made by the United States government to the Cherokee Nation. Yet, the Cherokee government was not the only entity making decisions regarding the status of the Cherokee freedpeople; the United States government also became actively involved in the negotiations between the Cherokee freedpeople and the Cherokee government. Indeed, the intrusion of the United States government in the affairs of the Cherokee Nation during the Reconstruction period further exacerbated the relationship between the Cherokee freedpeople and the Cherokee government. Cherokee freedpeople attempted to navigate institutional systems of the Cherokee Nation and the United States in order to procure their rights as Cherokee citizens. Ongoing resistance from the Cherokee Nation in regard to the status and rights of Cherokee freedpeople resulted in appeals by the freedpeople to the Cherokee Nation and the U. S. government.

[14] The General Allotment Act of 8 February 1887, also known as the Dawes Act, empowered the President of the United States with discretionary powers so that Native American reservations could be divided into allotments of land in severalty. Although the so-called Five Civilized Tribes were initially excluded from the provisions of the Dawes Act, in March 1893, the U.S. Congress approved the establishment of a commission to negotiate agreements with the Five Tribes that would involve the dismantling of their national governments and the allotment of their lands to individual citizens of their respective nations. Even though the Cherokees, Chickasaws, Choctaws, Creeks and Seminoles refused to negotiate with the Dawes Commission, the U.S. Government continued exerting pressure on these nations. In 1895, Congress endorsed a survey of the lands in Indian Territory owned by the Five Tribes; in 1896, Congress passed an act authorizing the Dawes Commission to ascertain which individuals had a rightful claim to citizenship within the Five Tribes and to create what was to be the definitive roll of citizens of each of the Five Tribes. Even as

allotments in the Cherokee Nation.[15] On 4 March 1907, the date the Dawes Rolls were closed, 53,724 applications had been received for enrollment in the Cherokee Nation. In the end there were 41,798 enrolled citizens of the Cherokee Nation; of the total enrolled, 4,924 freedpeople were officially enrolled as part of the Cherokee Nation.[16] By the end of June 1907, 4,208 Cherokee freedpeople had received land allotments totaling 409,500.26 acres, an average of 97 acres per freedperson.[17] For some freedpeople, owning land in the Cherokee Nation represented the only way of declaring their rightful position as members of the Nation. For other freedpeople, land ownership signified only part of their struggle to be recognized as legitimate members of the Cherokee Nation.

During their WPA interviews, Cherokee freedpeople noted the importance of receiving their land allotments.[18] Although her mother died shortly after their return to the Cherokee Nation, Sarah Wilson resettled in Four Mile

---

members of the Five Tribes continued to resist the dissolution of their nations, the U.S. Congress maintained its resolve to dismantle the sovereignty of the Five Tribes. On 28 June 1898, Congress passed the Curtis Act which eliminated tribal rule without Native Americans' compliance and endorsed the allotment of lands in severalty. By the spring of 1900, the Dawes Commission began advertising appointments for the enrollment of citizens of the Cherokee Nation.

[15] Even though one of the significant aspects of Article 4 of the Treaty of 1866 concerned the right of Cherokee freedpeople, recognized as such by the Cherokee Nation, to settle on land in the Nation, Cherokee freedpeople were not officially granted land allotments until they were enrolled as citizens of the Cherokee Nation by the Dawes Commission.

[16] *Reports of the Department of Interior for the Fiscal Year Ended June 30, 1907*, vol. II, 296. Also see *Reports of the Department of Interior for the Fiscal Year Ended June 30, 1908*, vol. II, 195. In 1914, adjustments were made to the rolls by an act of Congress; as a result, there were 41,835 officially enrolled citizens of the Cherokee Nation, including 4,919 Cherokee freedmen. For a thorough examination of the creation and utilization of the Dawes Rolls within the Cherokee Nation, see Littlefield, *Cherokee Freedmen*, 214-248. Also see Carter, "Deciding Who Can Be Cherokee: Enrollment Records of the Dawes Commission," 174-205.

[17] *Reports of the Department of Interior for the Fiscal Year Ended June 30, 1907*, vol. II , 305. Littlefield, *Cherokee Freedmen*, 238.

[18] Although the WPA interviews highlighted in this section relate to the Cherokee Nation specifically, there are interviews of freedpeople from other nations who mentioned owning land in their respective nations. See interviews of Choctaw freedwomen Frances Banks, Polly Colbert, and Kiziah Love and Creek freedwomen Lucinda Davis, Mary Grayson and Nellie Johnson.

The original Land Allotment Records for Indian Territory are housed at the National Archives, Southwest Region in Fort Worth, Texas. The National Archives in Fort Worth, Texas also houses the original Cherokee Freedmen Enrollment Applications and the Cherokee Freedmen Census Cards. The Cherokee Freedmen Enrollment Applications and the Cherokee Freedmen Census Cards are also available on microfilm in the Archives and Manuscripts Division, Oklahoma Historical Society, Oklahoma City.

Branch in the Tahlequah District and married Oliver Wilson, another Cherokee freedman. Wilson explained that she and her husband participated in the Cherokee enrollment process, claiming that they "both got [their] land on [their] Cherokee freedman blood" (Rawick, vol. 7:353). The Land Allotment records for Cherokee Freedmen indicate that Sarah Wilson, with the assistance of her husband, was allotted at least one hundred acres of land.[19] In her interview, Sarah Wilson indicated that she received her allotment not only because of her position as a former slave of Cherokee Annie Johnson and Ben Johnson, but also because of her "blood" connection to the Cherokee Nation by virtue of the fact that her father was Cherokee Ned Johnson.

Wilson's reference to blood serves to heighten her identity as Cherokee. Moreover, her phrase, "Cherokee freedman blood," blends two separate yet often interrelated identities—the first identity being a Cherokee freedwoman and the second being a person of mixed racial heritage, specifically a person of African and Cherokee descent. Wilson's blended notion perhaps represents the creation of a distinct identity separate from the Cherokees generally and from Cherokee freedpeople who were not of Cherokee descent. It is possible that Sarah Wilson and other "mixed" Cherokee freedpeople conceived of their identity in these terms—a blended identity comprised of status, blood and nation.

Even though Sarah Wilson emphasized the role of her Cherokee "blood" in her enrollment as a Cherokee citizen and her acquisition of land, the Treaty of 1866, and the subsequent amendments to the Cherokee Constitution in 1866, did not require freedpeople to prove a direct "blood" connection in order to be enrolled in the Cherokee Nation. The requirement centered around freedpeople proving that they had been formerly owned by Cherokees residing in the Cherokee Nation and had conformed to the six-month restriction previously discussed. As a result, freedwoman Betty Robertson, who did not identify any "blood" connection to the Cherokee Nation, stated that she "got [her] allotment as a Cherokee Freedman, and so did Cal [her husband]" (Rawick, vol. 7:269). Since she was able to prove her status as a former slave of Cherokee Joe Vann, as well as her residence in the Cherokee Nation during and after the war, Betty Robertson was readily enrolled as a Cherokee freedwoman and received a land allotment within the Cherokee Nation.[20]

---

[19] Sarah Wilson and her children were enrolled by the Dawes Commission. See Cherokee Freedmen Census Card Number 60 for Sarah Wilson and her five children (Lelia, Thomas, Bertha, Allie and Robert). The enrollment application for Sarah Wilson and her children to the Dawes Commission was dated 3 April 1901. Their citizenship certificate was issued on 6 March 1905. National Archives, Southwest Region in Fort Worth, Texas. Also see Land Allotment Record Numbers 182-187, for Sarah Wilson and her children. National Archives, Southwest Region in Fort Worth, Texas.

[20] Betty Robertson was enrolled as a Cherokee freedwoman by the Dawes Commission as Belle Roberson with her husband Calvin and their children. See Cherokee Freedmen Census Card Number 117 and Land Allotment Record Numbers 356-360 and 3076-3077, for Calvin, Belle, Bertha, Watie, Amanda, Arthur Roberson and Minnie Ivory. National Archives, Southwest Region in Fort Worth, Texas.

Although neither Sarah Wilson nor Betty Robertson spoke of the formal process of enrolling as Cherokee freedpeople in their WPA interviews, Patsy Taylor Perryman offered some indication of the application process, which included, for many freedpeople, the presentation of several detailed and lengthy written testimonies. At her home in Muskogee, Oklahoma, Patsy Perryman recalled that as a result of her writing skills, "all the writing about allotments had to be done by me." She had "written many letters to Washington when they gave the Indian lands to the native Indians and their negroes" (Rawick, vol. 12:251-252).[21] Even after writing letters regarding her family's right to land allotments, no evidence exists indicating that Perryman received land in the Cherokee Nation. Since her owner, Cherokee Judy Taylor, relocated Perryman and other members of her family to Texas during the Civil War, it is possible that they returned too late to claim a right to Cherokee citizenship and thus to any Cherokee land. Even though she had been born and raised in the Cherokee Nation, her connection to the Nation was denied and as a result her name was not listed on the final Dawes Rolls of Cherokee freedmen. Perryman's situation was not exceptional; this was the case for over 1,400 freedpeople, whose applications as Cherokee freedpeople had been rejected by the Dawes Commission.

Certain ex-slaves who were not Cherokee freedmen benefited from their familial association to someone who was recognized as a Cherokee freedperson. Born a slave in Arkansas, Katie Rowe married Cherokee freedman Billy Rowe in Little Rock, Arkansas. After they got married they moved to an area near Tahlequah because as Katie Rowe explained "he had land in de Cherokee Nation" (Rawick, vol. 12:283). After her husband died, Katie Rowe continued to reside in the area and later moved in with one of her daughters who lived in Tulsa, Oklahoma (Rawick, vol. 12:283). Katie Rowe was only one of numerous African-Americans from the United States who would become part of the growing communities of new migrants to Indian Territory and Oklahoma Territory. During the post-Reconstruction Era exodus, significant numbers of African-Americans moved from the southern states to the North and to the West, leading to the creation of "black towns."[22] For Katie Rowe and other African-Americans who had been raised

[21] I have been unable to find any enrollment card or application testimony stating that Patsy Perryman was enrolled as a Cherokee freedwoman or received an allotment from the Cherokee Nation. However, Patsy Perryman's third husband, Randolph Perryman, was enrolled as a Creek freedman by the Dawes Commission. See Creek Freedmen Census Card Number 863 for Randolph Perryman. At the time of the interview, Patsy Perryman was living in Muskogee, Oklahoma (previously part of the Creek Nation). National Archives, Southwest Region in Fort Worth, Texas.

[22] Beginning in the 1880s, the influx of African-Americans into Oklahoma Territory would drastically affect the racial dynamics within this area. For more information on this westward migration and Oklahoma's Black towns, see Hill, "The All-Negro Communities of Oklahoma: The Natural History of a Social Movement," 254-268; Chapman, "Freedmen and the Oklahoma Lands," 150-159; Littlefield and Underhill,

on plantations in the southern United States, Indian Territory represented a place of new beginnings, without the overwhelming prevalence of racial violence. For the Cherokee freedpeople who were born and raised in Indian Territory, the Cherokee Nation still represented the only home they knew and for many the only home they would ever know. Having been born and raised as slaves, the reality of owning land became one of the important symbols of a "free" life.

Conclusion

It is not surprising that many ex-slaves explained in their WPA interviews that they decided to remain in Indian Territory following the Civil War, and they fought to become officially enrolled as citizens of the Native American nations with which they had been associated. In their reflections on the post-Civil War period, ex-slaves claimed that they had received their land allotments and recalled the importance of land ownership in Indian Territory. Even those who had been forced to leave Indian Territory during the Civil War, by their slaveowners seeking a means of escape, chose to return to Indian Territory after the war had ended. During their interviews, when speaking about the post-Civil War/Reconstruction Era, ex-slaves expressed notions of national identity and nationalism, as well as a multifaceted connection to their homes and communities in Indian Territory. Their connection to Indian Territory had not been eliminated with their emancipation. Instead, they felt a renewed affinity to their homeland in Indian Territory.

Ex-slaves who had been born and raised in the Cherokee Nation, Indian Territory described themselves as close to, rather than separate from, Cherokees with whom they had lived for most of their lives. In the WPA Oklahoma interviews, ex-slaves of African descent identified areas in Indian Territory as the familiar places of their birth and Native American cultural ways as their own ways. The extent of their cultural interactions, oftentimes intensified by their blood relations, established a group of persons of African descent whose cultural and social ties were with Native Americans. Without disregarding or discrediting the fact that these persons were indeed previously enslaved by Native Americans, one can still talk about the strong cultural connection and identification between freedpeople of African descent and the community of Native Americans with whom they lived in Indian Territory.

"Black Dreams and 'Free' Homes: The Oklahoma Territory, 1891-1894," 342-357; Crockett, *The Black Towns*; Carney, "Historic Resources of Oklahoma's All-Black Towns," 116-133; and Bogle, "On Our Way to the Promised Land: Black Migration from Arkansas to Oklahoma, 1889-1893," 160-177.

On 24 August 1876, in the Delaware District, Cherokee Nation, a group of Cherokee freedpeople organized one of their annual celebrations in recognition and remembrance of emancipation and freedom.[23] The speakers addressed a number of pressing issues during this celebration; they focused primarily on the importance of education, their ongoing concerns with the citizenship requirements within the amended Cherokee Constitution, their legal struggle to be recognized as rightful Cherokee citizens, and the necessity of participating in Cherokee national electoral politics. One speaker, Joseph Rogers, specifically focused on how the six-month limitation had prevented him from being rightfully recognized as part of the Cherokee citizenry. As one of the "too lates," he discussed his frustration at not being officially acknowledged by the Cherokee Nation as a Cherokee freedman. Rogers attested,

> Born and raised among these people, I don't want to know any other. The green hills and blooming prairies of this Nation look like home to me. The rippling of its pebbly bottom brooks made a music that delighted my infancy, and in my ear it has not lost its sweetness. I look around and I see Cherokees who in the early days of my life were my playmates in youth and early manhood, my companions, and now as the decrepitude of age steals upon me, will you not let me lie down and die, your fellow citizen? (*Cherokee Advocate*, 9 September, 1876)

As Joseph Rogers passionately articulated, freedpeople who had been born and raised among Native Americans had developed a keen understanding of their rootedness to specific Native American communities in Indian Territory. Although their affiliation with these communities, specifically their position as slaves, had been previously assumed, their construction of their lives among Native Americans had resulted in tangible and appreciable blood/familial, cultural and national connections with Native Americans. For them Indian Territory did not simply represent a place where they had been enslaved, it represented a place where they belonged. Ex-slaves experienced a dual sense of belonging; they were previously slaves who were owned by, and belonged to, Native Americans, but they were also persons who believed that they were part of, and belonged to, Native American communities in Indian Territory. Thus, after emancipation these ex-slaves chose to live and to settle—at home in Indian Territory.

---

[23] Information regarding this particular celebration was included in an editorial article in the Cherokee Nation's newspaper, *Cherokee Advocate*, 9 September 1876.

Works Cited

"An Act Emancipating the Slaves in the Cherokee Nation." *Cherokee Nation Papers.* Box 155, Folder 6361, Western History Collections, University of Oklahoma, Norman, Oklahoma.

Bailey, David Thomas. "A Divided Prism: Two Sources of Black Testimony on Slavery." *The Journal of Southern History* 46 (August 1980): 381-404.

Baker, T. Lindsay, and Julie P. Baker. *The WPA Oklahoma Slave Narratives.* Norman: University of Oklahoma Press, 1996.

Blassingame, John W. "Using the Testimony of Ex-Slaves: Approaches and Problems." *The Journal of Southern History* 41 (November 1975): 473-492.

Bogle, Lori. "On Our Way to the Promised Land: Black Migration from Arkansas to Oklahoma, 1889-1893." *Chronicles of Oklahoma* 72, no. 2 (summer 1994): 160-177.

Cade, John B. "Out of the Mouths of Ex-Slaves." *Journal of Negro History* 20 (January 1935): 294-337.

Carney, George O. "Historic Resources of Oklahoma's All-Black Towns." *Chronicles of Oklahoma* 69, no. 2 (summer 1991): 116-133.

Carter, Kent. "Deciding Who Can Be Cherokee: Enrollment Records of the Dawes Commission." *Chronicles of Oklahoma* 69, no. 2 (summer 1991): 174-205.

Chapman, Berlin B. "Freedmen and the Oklahoma Lands." *Southwestern Social Science Quarterly* 29, no. 2 (September 1948): 150-159.

Cherokee Nation. *Laws of the Cherokee Nation Passed During the Years 1839-1867,* vol. 6 of *The Constitutions and Laws of the American Indian Tribes.* Wilmington: Scholarly Resources, 1973.

Cherokee Nation. *Constitution and Laws of the Cherokee Nation Published by Authority of the National Council,* vol. 7 of the *Constitutions and Laws of the American Indian Tribes.* Wilmington: Scholarly Resources, 1973.

Crockett, Norman L. *The Black Towns.* Lawrence: The Regents Press of Kansas, 1979.

Escott, Paul David. *Slavery Remembered: A Record of Twentieth-Century Slave Narratives.* Chapel Hill: University of North Carolina Press, 1979.

Foner, Eric. *Nothing But Freedom.* Baton Rouge: Louisiana State University Press, 1983.

Hill, Mozell C. "The All-Negro Communities of Oklahoma: The Natural History of a Social Movement." *Journal of Negro History* 31, no. 3 (July 1946): 254-268.

Kappler, Charles J., ed. *Indian Treaties 1778-1883*. New York: Interland Publishing Inc., 1972.

Littlefield, Daniel F. Jr. *The Cherokee Freedmen: From Emancipation to American Citizenship*. Westport: Greenwood Press, 1978.

Littlefield, Daniel F. Jr. and Lonnie E. Underhill. "Black Dreams and 'Free' Homes: The Oklahoma Territory, 1891-1894." *Phylon* 34 (December 1973): 342-357.

McGlynn, Frank, and Seymour Drescher, eds. *The Meaning of Freedom: Economics, Politics and Culture After Slavery*. Pittsburgh: University of Pittsburgh Press, 1992.

Rawick, George P. ed. *Oklahoma and Mississippi Narratives*, vol. 7 of *The American Slave: A Composite Autobiography*. Westport: Greenwood Press, 1973.

—. *Oklahoma Narratives*, vol. 12, Supplement Series 1 of *The American Slave: A Composite Autobiography*. Westport: Greenwood Press, 1977.

Richardson, David, ed. *Abolition and Its Aftermath: The Historical Context, 1790-1916*. London: Frank Cass, 1985.

Scott, Rebecca J. "Exploring the Meaning of Freedom: Postemancipation Societies in Comparative Perspective." *Hispanic American Historical Review* 68 (1988): 407-428.

U.S. Department of the Interior. *Report on Indian Affairs by the Acting Commissioner for the Year 1867*. Washington, D.C.: Government Printing Office, 1868.

U.S. Department of the Interior. *Reports of the Department of Interior for the Fiscal Year Ended June 30, 1907*, vol. II. Washington, D.C.: Government Printing Office, 1907.

U.S. Department of the Interior. *Reports of the Department of Interior for the Fiscal Year Ended June 30, 1908*, vol. II. Washington, D.C.: Government Printing Office, 1908.

Woodward, C. Vann. "History from Slave Sources." *American Historical Review* 79 (April 1974): 470-481.

Yetman, Norman R. "Ex-Slave Interviews and the Historiography of Slavery." *American Quarterly* 36 (summer 1984): 181-210.

Celia E. Naylor-Ojurongbe recently received her Ph.D. in History from Duke University in Durham, North Carolina. Her dissertation is entitled *"More at Home with the Indians": African-American Slaves and Freedpeople in the Cherokee Nation, Indian Territory, 1838-1907*. Her interests include African-American/Caribbean and Native American history, as well as women's history and literature in the African Diaspora.

The Transformational Tracks of the Marginalized Life

Duane Niatum
Western Washington University

Part One – An Overview: The Path of Internal Exile

    This small gathering of new voices from native North America poets brings into focus the fact that the arts, like life, show the necessity for each of us to resist as best we can the feeling of exile. This has always been a major challenge for the young, since it takes rather a long time for any of us to recognize that the alienating force that is the strongest and most lethal often centers in the psyche. Eventually many learn how to accept this as a part of life's experiences; otherwise, the real world forever eludes us. These poets in their own ways have learned that such alienation severs one from the fabric of creation. They must do everything in their power to find the road that leads back to the physical universe, the home of the senses and the haven of the human spirit. Their poems reveal in unique ways how situations occur in our lives that suggest how crucial it is to write in order to justify one's existence, establish an identity, and confirm our interdependence with the natural world as well as with the human family. And if they have no place they can call home, they wander in a labyrinth and have no sense of a center, a center that their psyches crave.

    These situations are often acute, however, and sometimes extremely painful. Their explosive nature derives from the fact that they expose the degree to which the artist and writer remain outside the mainstream of American society, if not outside every society in the world. Yet, the Indian self that exists in our natures does not enjoy the idea or feeling of being only a marginal person in the American community or landscape, especially the landscape that tells the story of his or her people. For we are taught from birth that we are just one strand in the basket of the universe, and a tiny one at that. And without that connection, we are darker than night and far, far colder. What is equally absurd, however, is for American Indian artists and writers to deny the truth of this internal exile, and by doing so, play into some trap, the double-binds of the self that would inspire mocking guffaws from Raven, Coyote, and Crow, not to mention Blue Jay and Otter. The stories of these characters that we heard so often in our childhood make clear that it is better to face the smashed mirror, the broken hoop, the perfume of death in our dreams, the ambiguity and constant erosion of human relationships, and each new life-storm, than to pretend that what is experienced awake or asleep is only another illusive joke of Trickster. These poets make the effort to come to terms with the interweaving of their inner and outer worlds and must accept the path of internal exile while remembering how frequently their ideas and feelings are contradicted by life's experiences. All the more reason, they think, to resist as best they can the imbalance of living on the edge, split off from the family like a leper.

A falsehood is also challenged by these poets, and that is the claim which was developed in the early part of the last century, that the continuity among generations of American Indians had been broken and that their life and cultures had become so fragmented as to soon vanish from the planet. Yet the continued growth and blossoming in art and literature and ceremonial exchanges among the peoples of native North America prove that this is just not the case. A rebirth of these activities across the land counters this negative view. On the contrary, there is every indication that it will continue to add new branches to that sacred tree. The evidence suggests that these poets and other young artists do indeed have a home and place to return to now and forever.

First Nations people have known for a long, long time that non-Indians need to quit sentimentalizing them. And until non-Indians do this, they will never understand or appreciate that Indian people have a separate but equal community in this country. This attitude simply keeps native North Americans safely tucked away in the far corner of the past of American history and culture. Of course, to freeze Indians in a distant past, and deny them any place in the contemporary world, or any humanity or future, is the way the American government and the established order have dealt with the existence of Indians from colonial times to the present. We should, therefore, not be surprised if the general public follows suit. Yet this attitude is in the process of eroding. With luck and a little help from Raven, a genuine dialogue between the two cultures may one day take place. And that will add several red notes to America's loony tune.

A central theme in the work of these poets is the movement between loss and gain, leaving home and returning to it. Since the land of their ancestors is still under constant threat and shrinking in size minute by minute in many parts of North America, this is an important issue in their writing. The countless pollutions we are faced with today, including the water we drink and the air we breathe, are addressed in these poems as well as the destruction of the remaining forests as the machinery of urban sprawl reaches Indian homelands. These concerns are critical subjects and themes in their work. Now that urban development controls and manipulates most of the world's land base, these poets have no illusions about how this affects their lives or will affect the lives of their children and grandchildren and great grandchildren

Nevertheless, American Indian poets deal with the subjects common to most poets writing today: life and death, growth and decay, love and grief, nature and the social world, but they also have their fingers and toes deeply placed in the soil of their red earth, in their exploration of art as a mirror of tribal religion, family, and rebirth. Furthermore, since these poets live and work in a very precarious relationship with the dominant social order in North America, politics and history will have some impact on their art. Given the circumstances of their existence, how could we expect anything different from them?

The words that fill their poems declare in subtle ways to the reader that the poets keep within them the spirit and home of a common cultural heritage that has been continuous for twelve thousand years from Alaska to the tip of South America. Although there is no uniformity of subject, metaphor, image, or style, these poets show the American community at large how one segment of its ever-expanding pluralistic society sings of its strength and desire to remain one voice for the North American circle of tribes.

But what may not appear so obvious to a reader outside the tribal community is the fact that the works of these authors can never be a part of the dominant culture's literature until its own values achieve or approach social ascendancy. Poems such as these, however, suggest that that door may actually be opening. A broad spectrum of the American Indian vision reflects the need to believe that the future will remain a feast for the imagination and a tree of life that will nourish the heart of our children's children.

These poems imply that the place of the tribe in the natural world and in spirit is more valuable to the protagonist or persona in an American Indian poem than is the individual's ego. Identity is witnessed as fragmented and defeated whenever it is kept locked in to the ego-centric self, rather than embraced in the center of the family, tribe, and earth. A sense of wholeness will be missing until this paradox is accepted and absorbed into the heart. William Bevis calls this type of identity "not a matter of finding one's 'self,' but of finding a 'self' that is transpersonal and includes a society, a past, and a place," (585). In this regard, being an Indian is not only being a member of an Indian family, but a member of a clan, a tribe, a community, and a participant in ceremonial exchanges. To move away from this center of the spirit is to move straight out of the communal circle and into the realm of identity loss and social and spiritual chaos. When Indians cannot relate to one another they cannot relate to anything. Thus, readers will learn that to be in Indian country is to hold to four sacred bundles of tribal culture: its historical past, its present, its future, and its specific place on the earth. This view is the alpha and omega of consciousness for the tribal artist. This frame of reference links him or her to tribal solidarity, uniqueness, the path to the mountaintop. The reader can call it love or law or faith, it defines the very fabric of the North American Indian character and being, what literature, art, and life give meaning to.

These new voices from native North America have added new dimensions to the development of the art over the last thirty years. Many of the poems start from the red earth of our continent, and from the history and dreams of the first Americans, and finish by speaking of the present moment in specific, personal terms. The primary impulse arises from the act of coming home to a past where one has lived before in imagination, if not in fact. And the attempt to regain significant connections to tribal pasts and current events is a theme evident in much of the work here. It is predominantly the voice of the half-breed or mixed blood, dislocated for one reason or another from the lifelines of ancestors. Many of them raised in towns or cities off the reservations, these poets still recognize that the physical home of their people offers the essential knowledge, aesthetic view, and the elemental good—if they are to be known at all. The action and ideas of each poem move into focus the closer the poem reaches the inner circle of the poet's tribe, its homeland, dreams and song.

The poems are in their own way highly individualistic. Yet these personal expressions imply that what really counts for them is that they manifest what the specific tribe experiences in relation to man, woman and child, sea, animal, bird and fish, history and politics. We need only compare the work of Adrian Louis, Gail Tremblay, Anita Endrezze, and Simon Ortiz to see firsthand how these poets write from the ashes and ruins of their personal lives and that of their tribal heritages in an effort to re-join the whole ceremony of that life thread.

Each poem gives something back to the ancient voices, whether of man or woman, animal or mountain, tree or frog. The words will not form themselves without the support of these voices and the land that has always nourished such words. Their elders have passed on to them the belief that every poem worth its echo and breathline is a miniature quest of one sort or another. The old songs are the keepers of the story and these poets have listened to those voices. They and their poems come alive and pull themselves back from the margins of history and society by finding and taking the path home. Such aims are what have directed their contemporary vision quests.

In order to fully experience these poems, the reader's ear and third-eye need to see them fly from the page into the air and into his or her imagination. This is required because most of these poets have stressed and fully integrated into their work the oral tradition. As N. Scott Momaday states in his introduction to *Carriers of the Dream Wheel*:

> In order to understand the true impetus of contemporary Native American poetry, it is necessary to understand the nature of the oral tradition. Until quite recently, the songs, charms and prayers of the Native American—those embodied exclusively within the oral tradition; that is, their existence was wholly independent of writing.

Therefore, if we read and listen closely to these contemporary authors as they celebrate the art of an imagination on the wing, then we will recognize certain fundamental beliefs and attitudes about the nature and spirit of language, the Native North American's continued reverence for the sacred power of words. We can then see from these poems how the authors heard the songs of their ancestors before it was too late: if you reject the external world as a complementary force at every phase of artistic creation, then the inner well of the imagination will run dry. We are thus given the opportunity to experience with them their embrace of the world beyond the self, and share in the way they connect to the family of earth, sea, sky, bird, animal, river and fish, plant and stone, snowflake, turtle and bumblebee.

Part Two – Young Poets Journey Home

As Linda Hogan so eloquently states in *I Tell You Now*, "Telling our lives is important, for those who come after us, for those who will see our experience as part of their own historical struggle. I think of my work as part of the history of our tribe and as part of the history of colonization everywhere" (233). Other poets, like Hogan, are perfectly aware that it is not just flowers, trees, birds, fish, animals and insects that are endangered, but they themselves. What future they can offer their children runs through the poems like a herd of deer or buffalo. Too many neighboring tribes that exist only in name remind them of the vulnerability of their heritage, the possible loss of the oral tradition, and therefore, the extinction of their entire community. To paraphrase Momaday's words in *House Made of Dawn*, those who are the carriers and keepers of the oral tradition are forever one step from extinction. To face and survive such odds will take more than the pounding of drums, the keening of chants, and participation at Pow Wows, to keep the sacred hoop in the center of creation and their lives. The imagination of native North Americans will be from this day forward asked to perform things it never imagined was needed or remotely possible until the final sunset of this century alerted them to the reality of this predicament.

There are several voices from older generations that undoubtedly inspired these younger poets. A few names that immediately come to mind are Roberta Hill, Jim Barnes, Ray Young Bear, Linda Hogan, Joy Harjo, Maurice Kenny, Simon Ortiz, and Wendy Rose. But the younger generation will, after all, soon be responsible for whatever poetry bursts forth from seed to flower from native North America.

What is evident from reading these poems is how necessary it is to write in order to justify one's existence, so that we might survive the emotional bombs we throw mostly at ourselves. These writers have discovered in different ways that the major challenge facing them is the ability to break through the skin that keeps one a prisoner of oneself. Elizabeth Woody, in "The Invisible Dress," pulls all the different strands of her ancestry into a single image, fabric, and form. We learn that the women from Umatilla in Oregon make their dresses from dreams. As she says,

> This is given in Dream.
> The tones focused luminous depiction of story.
> Neither flesh nor labor are empty of reflection.
> Think of the deer. It is appropriate
> to cover with the handiwork of survival.
>
> *(Luminaries of the Humble* 105)

The poem casts light on the belief that was discussed in the first section—that the tribal self plays the most important role in the life of the artist from native North America when it reflects concrete links to the essential truths and beliefs of the people. Until the artist fully integrates these symbols and values into his or her unconscious, so that they surface on their own without any prodding, the art piece will remain a fragment, a shell without spirit.

Sherman Alexie, a Spokane/Couer D'Alene, writes about the family in a way that was rarely seen in poetry before the 1990s, a gut-level directness that shatters stereotypes of First Americans. The honesty and candor of the following lines from "House Fires," his first collection of poetry and prose, *The Business of Fancydancing*, redeems the violence and deliberate confrontational point of view:

> The night my father broke
> the furniture and used the pieces
> to build a fire, my mother tore me
> from my bed at 3a.m.

In another poem of Alexie's that further demonstrates the power of this poet's vision, we see a different side to this complex father figure. The path of survival for the father has been one dictated by *Hard Love*:

> Your father always knew how to love hard;
> you tell me, crawling over broken glass, surviving
> house fires and car wrecks, gathering ash
> for your garden, Hookum, and for the old stories
>
> Where the Indian never loses...
>
> *(The Business of Fancydancing* 31)

The reader is shown how the path can cut and draw blood and pound through the body and soul like a torrent of pain, but it also offers nourishment and a way to live with the pieces in your shaking hands and the memory woven into the dark recesses of your mind. These lines and those preceding could almost launch Crazy Horse into a sit-up position from his secret grave and spur him to ride for the Milky Way, if he was not already riding somewhere along the black slopes of Paha Sapa, singing for a way to get this poet home before the fire burns out.

Deborah A. Miranda's, "For My Other Grandmother," from *Indian Cartography*, takes a new direction in back-tracking to her tribal roots. She talks to the ancestors to find her way to family and wholeness:

> Four sons, Marquesa: one was my father.
> Because you died so young, the only way I know you
> is by the wide square palms of my hands, the long
> "Indian teeth," of my bite, the widow's peak
> of black hair with the stubborn silver streak
> that stands straight up like feathers... (*Indian Cartography* 85)

With these lines we see the path one woman followed in an effort to neutralize the horrible sense of incompleteness and identity blur; we experience her struggle to locate her reflection in the ancestral mirror. This particular struggle heightens the reader's sense of how much the speaker is cut off from the songlines of her Native family. She has said in a biographical note that the forces of colonization that were the most destructive to California Indians were the Gold Rush and the evil of the Catholic missions. The strength of this poem stems in part from the way it shows Miranda countering these destructive forces in her life and the life and early history of her family, by playing detective until those vital and essential roots are found and literally dug out of the earth, the graves and homeland of her ancestors.

Arthur Tulee reaches the shores of his origins the way a salmon does in these two poems honoring Chewana, the river that churns in his blood and speaks to his spirit. Whites named the river the Columbia. These poems illuminate how Chewana's story has been passed down to him in a sacred narrative. His Yakima ancestors have lived along its banks, or along one of its tributaries for a few thousand years. And just as he nearly drowned when he was a young boy and was swept away in its currents, the reader learns the degree to which the river has come to represent his own nature and path. These are the opening lines to "On the Chewana, 1969,":

> I dream of water, how with its own tongues
> carves its path through sky, through ground, through dreams.
> I think of Chewana's edge and of the time
> it carried my cold, blue-lipped, 5 year old body
> a mile downstream while my teenage brothers
> dove to the brown bottom again and again.
> ("On the Chewana, 1969")

In a second poem with the same title, but in 1994 instead, we experience the irony and grief of his relationship to the river. He has survived but the river has been continuously transformed and has had several other dams added to the first one. In the poem he alludes to Celio Falls, a very sacred fishing site to the Yakima and other tribes from the region, a place that was completely submerged when the first dam was constructed decades earlier. These are the first five lines:

> I dream of water and the sound of it: electricity
> and I wonder what these currents of love follow,
> the way of salmon or turbine turbulence?
> My eye follows a barge loaded with everything.
> Everything except Celio Falls and visions.
> ("On the Chewana, 1994")

These excerpts from the two poems show the strength of this river even with the radical transformation of its body and voice by the white man's idea of progress. Nevertheless, we still witness how this river transformed itself into the strength of a boy as he grew into manhood. His Yakima elder, David Sohappy, a steadfast son of Chewana, supports him in his quest by passing on this great legacy of the river to the poet. David Sohappy was a fishing rights activist for his tribe who was imprisoned at Walla Walla because of his demonstrations on the banks of Chewana. And the poems give us two contrasting images of the river, and in the process, we see it flow through the mind of Tulee, the poet, like the powerful force that it is physically and spiritually for all Indian people of the Pacific Northwest, particularly those tribes that live along its shores. The river has enhanced his perspective about himself and his relationship to it and his people and given him an identity he will carry to the grave. He has found a small clearing where courage becomes more than a mask or a pose. It becomes the core of his being.

Another young poet, who recently published an award-winning manuscript in the same North American Authors First Book Series that Deborah A. Miranda also won, is a welcome voice at the close of the twentieth century. Tiffany Midge, a mixed-blood Lakota woman, displays special gifts in her poems that expand and invigorate the range of these authors. She offers us her style of Indian humor that is as exuberant as the whiplash lines of Sherman Alexie or Adrian Louis. The healing power of laughter is frequently found in the stories and novels from native North America, but has been regretfully missing from the poetry. This generation may change all that. These specific poets are re-discovering the potency and creative potential in humor and its positive influence on the spirit of their people. It is a healthy sign since humor has played a role in the lives of their ancestors for thousands of years. Painters and sculptors from Indian country have used it as an important element of their art for a long time. In fact, some of the best art produced in our age is based upon an aspect of the culture that humor throws new light onto. We still dance with chaos and pain but with a smile instead of a sneer.

The sense of how ridiculous and absurd things can become in our everyday world corresponds surprisingly with the high points in our lives. This poet exploits those occasions with good success. Midge is in top form in a delightful series that opens, *Outlaws, Renegades and Saints*. The poems show us the world of her Grandpa Dick. For example:

> 4.
>
> Our grandfather
> never failed
>   each day
>   &
> every day to rise
> like the sun.
> To rise
> like a claimed promise
> &
> wind his way to the corner
> tavern
> spilling out memories of old & stale dreams,
>   pouring out years
>   of accumulated sorrows,
> drinking up, drinking up, drinking up
>   generations of regret.
>   &
> whatever change he had left
> whatever change he had left
> he never failed to deliver
> his promise of chocolate
>   bars & tavern
>   popcorn. ("Spare Change")

Anger is not shoved in your face like a bloody coup-stick, but is directed by a wit that personalizes acts that she has witnessed up close. Thus the words resonate in such a way that we cannot help feeling we have been there once or twice ourselves.

These experiences with parents, friends, relatives, are situations that we can easily relate to on several levels below appearances, where real art almost always holds council. The series "Spare Change," a group of eight poems which includes the preceding section, has the energy and expressive qualities of a passage three times its length. The play of irony alone is so well compressed that double and triple meanings build wildly through the work until the last promise echoes in the air. Let us look at one more passage from this series to confirm this assertion:

Oh why does every lost-looking-old man I see
sitting broken on the city sidewalk have to look at me with
my grandfather's eyes? Why is it that when I looked up the
word *pathos* in my Random House College Dictionary, it
said—see Grandpa Dick. ("Spare Change")

Tiffany Midge is a rare songbird that we are lucky to have in our world. If she continues to grow and expand her special perspective on both our singular and communal lives and world, she may become a favorite word magician the community cannot live without.

Mary Lockwood's poem, "Last," succinctly discloses the group's humble yet tenacious reason for being. It expresses while never stating directly the values and ways of seeing and acting that are at the core of this art regardless of the genre.

> know
> some people
> they're the last
>   I've
>   seen a river
> It's one
> of the last
>   I felt the wool
>   of a musk ox
>   the last
>   time
> I
> saw
> Her
> I held
> my kinfolk...
> one
> last time   ("Durable Breath" 95)

Works Cited

Alexie, Sherman. *The Business of Fancydancing*. Brooklyn: Hanging Loose Press, 1992.
Bevis, William. *Recovering the Word*. Berkeley and Los Angeles: University of California Press, 1987.
Hogan, Linda. *I Tell You Know*. Lincoln, Neb: University of Nebraska Press, 1987.
Lockwood, Mary. *Durable Breath*. Anchorage, Alaska: Salmon Run Press, 1994.
Midge, Tiffany. *Outlaws, Renegades and Saints*. Greenfield Center, NY: The Greenfield Review Press, 1996.
Miranda, Deborah. *Indian Cartography*. Greenfield Center, NY: The Greenfield Review Press, 1999.
Momaday, N. Scott. *Carriers of the Dream Wheel*. New York: Harper & Row, 1975.
—. *House Made of Dawn*. New York: Harper & Row, 1968.
Tulee, Arthur. "On the Chewana, 1969" and "On the Chewana, 1994," unpublished mss.
Woody, Elizabeth. *Luminaries of the Humble*. Tucson and London: The University of Arizona Press, 1994.

Duane Niatum has published several essays on American Indian literature and art, and his sixth book of poems, *The Crooked Beak of Love*, was published by West End Press, Winter, 2000. A collection of sixteen stories based upon his Klallam peoples' myths and legends is making the rounds of publishers.

Forging the Discursive Presence in Gerald Vizenor's *Manifest Manners*: *Postindian Warriors of Survivance*

Simona Fojtová
University of New Mexico

Language is not a neutral medium that passes freely and easily into the private property of the speaker's intentions; it is populated—overpopulated—with the intentions of others. Expropriating it, forcing it to submit to one's own intentions and accents, is a difficult and complicated process.... (Bakhtin 77)

In his book, *Manifest Manners: Postindian Warriors of Survivance* (hereafter *MM*), Gerald Vizenor reappropriates words for his own writing which he populates with his own agendas and expressive intentions similar to the way Mikhail Bakhtin theorizes this process in *The Dialogic Imagination*. Through textual revisioning and re-imagining, Vizenor contests the dominance of the authoritative word of Western civilization with its claims of representation, its hierarchical rules, and its colonial epistemology grounded in the logic of binarism. Vizenor uses the Bakhtinian conception of the discursive battle to oppose and undermine the discourse of the dominant culture.

However, this textual battlefield does not represent a traditional space governed by the binary opposition of winners and losers since the "weapons" Vizenor deploys—such as imagination, humor, and language games—do not strive to assume the last word but rather to complexify the embedded singularity of meanings. Relying on the power of stories, humor, wit, and imagination to create, Vizenor fights with words in order to present his own perspective and assert his right to create new self-imaginings. Thus Vizenor's text explores vital new interpretations and generates its own power to name and unname.

Vizenor's writing demonstrates an awareness of the word's power to create and shape. As he constructs texts, Vizenor examines how language names us, creates us, controls us, lives (in) us; in effect Vizenor explores how meanings produced in language define who we are. If reality, then, is discursively produced, validated, and defined through language, Vizenor, along with many other postmodern critics and thinkers, is interested in exploring how reality can be reimagined and how we can liberate ourselves in the process.

In an interview with Joseph Bruchac, "Follow the Trickroutes," Vizenor talks about such liberatory practices: "A comic spirit demands that we break from formula, break out of program, and there are some familiar ways to do it and then some radical or unknown ways" (290). Formulas, programs, and categories produced by the dominant culture have created vehicles by which what Vizenor calls the "literature of dominance" and "social science monologue" establish their authority and silence the discourses of others. Vizenor's writing strives to transgress and deconstruct the limitations imposed by the dominant culture.

Vizenor's writing opposes the notion of reducing language to pure instrumentality and illuminates the ways in which power has always inscribed itself in and through language. Outlining almost a philosophy of deconstructing language, Vizenor attempts to subvert the power of language by reimagining it. He compares his textual endeavor to "breaking out of boxes" (Bruchac 293). On a metaphorical level, these boxes—which can also be conceived of as social paradigms—represent the limitations imposed on our minds by the dominant culture. In order to break out of these confined and compartmentalized views filled with predetermined meanings, Vizenor suggests we stretch our mental spaces by liberating our imagination. This liberation, resulting in defamiliarized meanings, offers infinite proliferation of possibility for further cognitive creations. Vizenor claims again and again throughout his text that the vehicle of humor possesses not only the power to create new meanings but also possesses the ability to heal; tribal experience, therefore, includes humor as a strategy of survivance:

> The tribes have seldom been honored for their trickster stories and rich humor. The resistance to tribal humor is a tragic flaw. Laughter over that comic touch in tribal stories would not steal the breath of destitute children; rather, children would be healed with humor, and manifest manners would be undermined at the same time. (*MM* 83)

In the same way that he exploits the subversive possibilities of humor, Vizenor also undermines the historical and cultural definitions of language. In her book, *Gerald Vizenor: Writing in the Oral Tradition* (hereafter *GV*), Kimberly Blaeser argues that "Vizenor's struggle with the written involves dissatisfaction with both the underlying philosophies and structures of language use in contemporary society" (72). Thus Vizenor coins new words and phrases,[1] subverts the conventions of language, dissolves grammar with its restrictive rules and linear unfolding, invests in connotations instead of denotations, and creates tropes and metaphors rather than explanations. Such linguistic liberation is for Vizenor deeply rooted in imagination: "I like to imagine words, imagine metaphors not theories, so that the ideas and images are not stereotyped.... So, some of the words I imagine or invent or combine

---

[1] The very title of Vizenor's book, *Manifest Manners: Postindian Warriors of Survivance,* embodies such a neologic use of language.

are ways to avoid the traps, the historical traps" (Bruchac 292). The textual landscape Vizenor creates is populated with paradox, irony, and language games. It is a space in which, through the liberatory possibilities of language, he vitalizes other meanings and multiple ways for interpreting. It is a space which resists clarity and simplification and makes a plea for imagination. The imaginative hermeneutics Vizenor employs complicates the precise, evokes the ambiguous, and embraces the paradoxical.

The English language, Vizenor claims, embodies one of the infinite circles of paradoxes in which we are immersed. It has become both the language of oppression and coercion, as well as the language of liberation which "has carried some of the best stories of endurance" (*MM* 106). Calling attention to its oxymoronic nature, Vizenor says that:

> The English language has been the linear tongue of colonial discoveries, racial cruelties, invented names, the simulations of tribal cultures, manifest manners, and the unheard literature of dominance in tribal communities; at the same time, this mother tongue of paracolonialism has been a language of invincible imagination and liberation for many tribal people in the postindian word. (*MM* 105)

Even though Vizenor writes in English (instead of his tribal language, Anishinaabemowin), he does not merely transmit the meanings the colonizer has constructed in the language. Rather, Vizenor creates possibilities for new meanings since his writing defies entrapping meaning in singularity. Thinking through complexity and ambiguity, celebrating the plurality of consciousness and multiplicity of meanings, Vizenor's fluid language resists firm positioning. The multi-discursive, polysemous, and interrogative quality of Vizenor's writing resists rigid interpretations. Vizenor's deconstructing technique aims to question/erode/shake/undo the effects of the implied totality of meaning, crafting a waterfall of elusiveness which looms behind every interpretation aspiring to claim control over others.

Critiquing dominant, embedded meanings, Vizenor's writing honors the plurality, porousness, and mobility of discourses. Dialogically subversive, the elusive meanings in *Manifest Manners* do not create a universe where final interpretations become worshipped *ad nauseum*. The polysemous space of *Manifest Manners* generates the power to transform, create, and vitalize other meanings. Because they are no longer presumed to be ideologically innocent, epistemologies and interpretations are subject to the effects of imaginative hermeneutics and language games which possess the power to undermine the authority of the dominant discourses:

> The classical notion that thoughts were representations of content, or the coherent meaning of words, is not the same as the nature of shadows in tribal names and stories. Shadows tease and

loosen the bonds of representation in stories. The meaning of words are determined by the nature of language games. (*MM* 72)

Rather than taking refuge in absolute and final answers and the notion of stable definitions, categories, and boundaries, Vizenor's texts examine how to transgress and dissolve the boundaries of categories as well as fixed notions of identity. If one wishes to avoid being confined by limping logic grounded in a claustrophobic understanding of rigid boundaries, one must subscribe to uncertainty and incompleteness, since they represent possibility.

Similar to Vizenor's attempts at undermining dominant narratives, Trinh T. Minh-ha strives to de-center dominant normativity as the marker by which everything else is defined either as complicit with, or abjected from, the colonial norm. In her book, *Woman, Native, Other: Writing Postcoloniality and Feminism*, Trinh examines the possibilities of trespassing the enshrined boundaries of categories, and maintains that "[d]espite our desperate, eternal attempt to separate, contain, and mend, categories always leak" (94). Vizenor's writing provides textual space for an exploration of such leakages and interstices. Vizenor theorizes a notion of shadows that not only examine the seams of categories and the confining nature of social paradigms, but also function as important devices for the subversion of culturally dominant forms. According to Blaeser, Vizenor uses the metaphor of a shadow "to explain multiple referents of imaginative language performance" (77). Vizenor explores the idea of shadows which possess and present liberatory potential due to their multivalent quality because, as he claims, "shadows are that silence and sense of motion in memories; shadows are not the burdens of conceptual references" (*MM* 70). It is precisely the openness of conceptual space that makes room for memory and imagination. As Vizenor says, the shadow is "the unsaid presence in names, the memories in silence, and the imagination of tribal experiences" (*MM* 73).

Vizenor's notion of shadows escapes the established hierarchy of binary oppositions. The image of fleeting shadows becomes emblematic of Vizenor's creative strategy, conveyed through humor, irony, and satire, which aims to challenge readers trained in a more traditional discourse grounded in binary logic. Unlearning the dichotomous consciousness so endemic to Western culture entails unlearning the consequent binary oppositions grounded in the notion of fixed categories: colonizer/colonized, culture/nature, self/other. As Vizenor claims, "the manifold anxieties and desires that arise from the tension announced in the binary of savagism and civilization are other simulations in the literature of dominance" (*MM* 59). Vizenor deliberately endeavors to evoke discomfort in (traditional) readers not simply by advocating a reversal of binary oppositions in order to advantage the currently disadvantaged, but by dissolving dualism itself. As Trinh maintains:

> If it is a question of fragmenting so as to decentralize instead of dividing so as to conquer, then what is needed is perhaps not a clean erasure but rather a constant displacement of the two-by-two system of division to which analytical thinking is often subjected. (39)

Similarly to Trinh's textual decentralization, Vizenor also strives to displace dominant narratives. Even though Vizenor's mocking and satirizing strategy grounded in language games undercuts our expectations (if we are trapped in the comfortable binary oppositions with its established stereotypes), erodes our frame of reference, and thus de-constructs the (familiar) chain of significations, his "languagequake" technique does not construct other centers—and thus other margins—within the text. By replacing the absence of tribal experience in dominant representations with a discursive presence through imagination, humor, and language games, Vizenor's text avoids prioritizing tribal culture over other cultures. It therefore also avoids positing a new center, a center which would necessitate the construction of new margins. Thus Vizenor escapes falling into a trap in which he needs to construct another binary opposition with its hierarchizing qualities because Vizenor's text neither subjugates nor obliterates but, rather, parodies, deconstructs, and resists the way dominant (master) narratives have too often been used.

Escaping the danger of reversing the center and thus creating new margins, Vizenor's text does not posit any cultural superiority/inferiority binary relationship. Instead, in his writing the act of narration becomes an inclusive rather than exclusive endeavor when Vizenor suggests that there are many different ways to create meanings and narrate stories. Throughout *Manifest Manners,* Vizenor critiques dominant culture and its rules of recognition. By employing language games and humor, he decenters any single authoritative perspective. Vizenor writes again and again that there is not one meaning but many meanings, there is not one story but many stories. By refusing to posit a center, Vizenor's polysemic text offers a new way of thinking, interpreting, perceiving, and knowing.

In *Manifest Manners,* Vizenor not only struggles against established literary and linguistic structures but his strategies of liberation also strive to subvert claims of representations, whether scriptual or visual, constructed by the dominant culture. In his writing, Vizenor undermines the institutional and academic stereotypes invented for Native Americans by Euro-American culture. Borrowing the word *simulation* from Jean Baudrillard, Vizenor claims that Indians have become the simulations of the "absolute fakes"[2] in the ruins of representations. In Baudrillard's terms, simulation implies models of a real without actual origin or reality —a hyperreal (*Simulations* 2). Critiquing the absence of the tribal real and the consequent unreal simulations grounded in the image of the invented Indian, Vizenor claims that the "Indian

---

[2] Vizenor borrows the phrase "absolute fake" from Umberto Eco who theorized the term and uses it throughout his book, *Travels in Hyperreality.*

never existed in reality and the word has no referent in tribal languages or cultures" (*MM* 11). Vizenor further argues that tribal cultures, in this sense, "have been invented as 'absolute fakes' and consumed in social science monologues" (*Narrative Chance: Postmodern Discourse on Native American Literatures* 5, hereafter *NC*). Opening the epistemological baggage of Western culture and literature about Native Americans, Vizenor claims that the "various translations, interpretations, and representations of the absence of tribal realities have been posed as the verities of certain cultural traditions" (*MM* 17).

Challenging the self-proclaimed authority of the totalizing master narratives of civilization, Vizenor subverts the authoritative discourses of the culture of dominance. Vizenor strives to re-write the signifier "Indian"[3] and liberate it from the confinement of the static and unchanging domain of words. Disclosing the distorted images and claims of representations imposed by the dominant culture on marginalized groups, Vizenor provides (textual) space for envisioning new possibilities for "self-imaginings." However, such liberation necessarily poses questions about representations and self-representations. When undoing the mental amnesia of Western culture and ascribing the presence of tribal experience into the silence produced by the dominant culture, the question arises whether Vizenor, through his writing, believes that we can replace sets of representations constructed by the dominant culture with sets of representations created by insiders/natives. Are such substitutions in the field of (self)representation possible?

In my reading of the textual landscape which Vizenor creates, I see him deconstructing claims of representations invented by the "social science monologue" and the "literature of dominance" without producing new, corrected or even "right" sets of representations through his writing. Not only does Vizenor in his writing resist the compulsion to reproduce exactly, but he goes even further and problematizes the very production of representations. In *Manifest Manners,* Vizenor argues that claims of representation, grounded in the crippling effects on cognition based on historical *mis*representations, constructed a very different reality from tribal experience: "What has been published and seen is not heard or remembered in oral stories" (*MM* 70). Vizenor goes even further in his critique and argues that the "once bankable simulations of the savage as an impediment to developmental civilization, the simulations that audiences would consume in Western literature and motion pictures, protracted the extermination of tribal cultures" (*MM* 6)

[3] Vizenor's textual effort can be applied at both metaphorical and literal levels. In terms of the latter, Vizenor says about the word *indian:* "I try to avoid it in almost all of my writing. Where I've used *indian,* I've identified it as a problem word in some writing or italicized it in others. I think it ought to be lower-case italicized everywhere. It is one of those troublesome words. It doesn't mean anything, it is a historical blunder, and has negative associations. So I try to avoid the word in writing by referring the reader to the tribal people or 'tribal histories' rather than *indian* histories to try to avoid some of the problems" (Bruchac 292).

In order to battle the extermination of tribal cultures in representations, strategies for surviving the invention become central to Vizenor's writing. When Vizenor contrasts academic invention with tribal imagination, when he compensates the absence of the real with the presence of humor and tribal memory, he avoids representing images no matter how "native" they are. Representations for Vizenor freeze "reality" and static images enslave tribal experience; imagination, on the other hand, expands and liberates the possibilities of experience.

In his writing, Vizenor problematizes the mimetic quality of the act of representation and image production designed for consumption. Drawing on postmodern theory with its shift from image to discourse and its emphasis on process rather than product, Vizenor is not interested in reflecting but *narrating*. Borrowing Stephen Tyler's words, Vizenor considers discourse as the "maker of the world, not its mirror.... The world is what we say it is and what we speak of is the world" (*NC* 4). The discursive space and the act of narration become prominent when Vizenor extends the notion of discourse to tribal culture and views tribal narratives as discourses rather than representations: "Tribal narratives are discourse and in this sense tribal literatures are the world rather than representation" (*NC* 4).

In the discursive space that Vizenor creates, the notion of *temporary poses* strategically replaces static and essentialistic positionality. As Vizenor claims, "postindian narratives are poses, and the poses are neither representations nor the terminal sources of aesthetic modernism (*MM* 70). Vizenor re-utilizes the liberatory potential he sees in postmodern theory and claims that the "postmodern pose is a noetic mediation that denies historicism and representation" (*NC* 4). The postmodern condition for Vizenor offers an "invitation to narrative chance in a new language game and an overture to amend the formal interpretations and transubstantiation of tribal literatures" (*NC* 4).

Vizenor materializes the narrative chance in language games in order to escape the conceptual inventions that trap tribal experience in dominant representations. Commenting on Vizenor's theoretical shift from the static to the dynamic, Blaeser concurs that although "we cannot have 'Indian,' we can have 'postindian,' which replaces the Indian invention. The postindian 'ousts the invention' through 'humor, new stories, and the simulations of survivance'" (*GV* 5). If "Indian" for Vizenor represents invention and simulation, Vizenor's playful coinage "postindian" presents the liberating end of these dominanting practices:

> The Indian was an occidental invention that became a bankable simulation; the word has no referent in tribal languages or cultures. The postindian is the absence of invention, and the end of representation in literature; the closure of that evasive melancholy of dominance. (*MM* 11)

Recognizing the disasterous consequences of Manifest Destiny on tribal peoples, Vizenor defines the dominant culture's historically hegemonic practices as "manifest manners." Blaeser claims that by coining the phrase "manifest manners," Vizenor "demands recognition of the 'cultural legacy' and contemporary manifestations of the theory and policies of manifest destiny, which surface in such places as universities, the various branches of government, our legal system, and our popular media" (*GV* 55). Vizenor critiques the representations of tribal cultures through colonial inventions and simulations in the literature of dominance and claims that manifest manners are the "absence of the real in the ruins of tribal representations" (*MM* 8). Highlighting the elimination of the realities of tribal cultures and the erasure of the discursive presence of tribal experience, Vizenor argues that:

> ... the simulations of manifest manners are treacherous and elusive in histories; how ironic that the most secure simulations are unreal sensations, and become the real without a referent to an actual tribal remembrance. Tribal realities are superseded by those simulation of the unreal, and tribal wisdom is weakened by those imitations, however sincere. (*MM* 8)

Vizenor contends that the claims of dominant representations which assert themselves as real and authentic must be challenged. He stresses creating a discursive presence of tribal experience through narrating new stories which counter the manifest manners of dominance and its colonial representations. Vizenor celebrates warriors of survivance who upset the simulations in the literature of dominance grounded in romantic views of tribal cultures:

> ... postindian warriors of postmodern simulations would undermine and surmount, with imagination and the performance of new stories, the manifest manners of scriptual simulations and "authentic" representations of the tribes in the literature of dominance. (*MM* 17)

Striving to undermine existing social and cultural paradigms and the dominance of colonial representations, Vizenor's ideas are inseparable from his style. In his writing, Vizenor not only subverts acceptable literary forms and challenges the rules of writing, he also resists any compulsion to become static. As Blaeser, borrowing Robert Lee's words, points out, "Vizenor ... has positioned himself as postindian, an ongoing pursuer of all simulations that essentialize and ossify tribal people" (*GV* 57). Because Vizenor argues that "social science theories constrain tribal landscape to institutional values, representationalism and the politics of academic determination," he constantly searches for that which has been left out of dominant narratives (*NC* 5).

Even though Vizenor complicates meanings and established epistemological frameworks, his writing does not attempt to erect coherent systems of truth and meaning. Vizenor's writing does not present itself as mimetic, but evocative; his writing serves as a warning to readers not to seek a single meaning. Vizenor defies lucid explanations and through deconstructive moves he illustrates the allusiveness of writing and the indeterminacy of meanings. Referring to Chris Anderson's analysis, Blaeser calls Vizenor's deliberately ambiguous and elliptic style with its consequent lack of closure the "rhetoric of gaps." She claims that such gaps and interstices "can involve implied absence, suggestion of a connection to something beyond the text, or an obvious allusion to another level of meaning" (*GV* 170). The spirit of imagination, humor, paradox, irony, and language games offers multiple possibilities for interpretation and multiple visions of reality.

Vizenor's writing not only strives to develop a dialogue with the reader, but also to challenge the reader's established epistemological frameworks. Vizenor's writing demands more than a consumption of the text. Insisting on the relational and unfixed nature of meaning,[4] Vizenor's elliptic and allusive writing requires the active imagination of the reader. Blaeser argues that convoluted meanings are "deliberate attempts by the author to 'work against readability,' thus forcing the reader to contemplate the 'surface of language' and the 'complexity of the experience it seeks to describe'" (*GV* 168). Throughout the text, Vizenor creates openings in the meanings in order to deconstruct the binary opposition between the writer and the reader. Blaeser describes Vizenor's employment of silence as one of many textual stategies which open up meanings, and she claims that "Vizenor does more than employ silence dramatically or philosophically in story; it also becomes a dialogic device to engage the reader" (*GV* 22).

Not seeking the authority of the writer, not even seeking the authority of the writing, Vizenor deconstructs his own authoritative position as he gives up narrative control of the story and entrusts his control to multiple possibilities of meaning. Deliberate escape from the historically dominating position of an author produces fluid positionality of the writing/speaking subject; this subject is then liberated from participating in a conventional writer/reader binary and can travel through other subject positions which are involved in producing/reading/interpreting the text. Not positing himself as the sole authority, Vizenor thus attempts to construct an anti-authoritarian ethics where the porous text and interstices opened by humor, language games, and irony allow for the interpretation of interpretations and present an antithesis to dominant values.

---

[4] "The interplay of significations" and the deferral of meaning in Derridean deconstruction come to mind. "Freeplay is the disruption of presence. The presence of an element is always a signifying and substitutive reference inscribed in a system of differences and the movement of a chain. Freeplay is always an interplay of absence and presence, but if it is to be radically conceived, freeplay must be conceived of before the alternative of presence and absence" (Derrida 969-70).

In order to subvert the historical role of the western author and thereby destabilize predetermined definitions, Vizenor claims that the reader must take an active role in his or her engagement with the text. As Blaeser points out, "the liberation of the narrative is achieved only through participation" (*GV* 82). In order to understand a story, we can either create meaning or, unfortunately, meaning can be imposed on us. We find it difficult to perform the "creating" kind of understanding, because, unlike the "imposing" kind, "creating" is not a widespread practice within Western discourse. As Vizenor claims, however, "performance and human silence are strategies of survivance" (*MM* 16). If we find ourselves comfortably lulled to sleep instead of feeling we are in the "labor" of creation, we risk losing our agency in the creation of meaning. As Trinh reminds us:

> ...the story depends upon every one of us to come into being. It needs us all, needs our remembering, understanding, and creating what we have heard together to keep on coming into being. (119)

When we create we do not simply "give birth" to our one and only beloved child—the single interpretation of meaning—which we then raise, pamper, and defend for the rest of our lives. Rather, when we create we let our imagination run loose; in effect, we make sense of words with sacrifice. Our mind and imagination have to step into a seemingly empty territory between ourselves and the other, which requires giving up the previous place, position, or structure and risks losing the familiar for the sake of the unknown. The fear of this risk is the fear of difference. The idea of differences and opposites is precisely the "pampered child" of the Western world.

Within Vizenor's writing, newly coined/imagined words, humor, and tricksters represent those who transgress/trespass and liberate the rigidly defined and enshrined boundaries within dominant/colonial hegemonic narratives. Constituting a challenge to an ideology based upon maintaining the inviolability of categorical boundaries and pointing out strategies of disruption, tricksters become central to Vizenor's work. Due to their paradoxical nature, tricksters represent both liberation and resistance. In his essay, "Trickster Discourse," Vizenor claims that the trickster "is a comic liberator in a narrative and the sign with the most resistance to social science monologues" (196). Suspicious, to say the least, of social science theories, Vizenor finds semantic theories more usable. The trickster for Vizenor is a sign, not an essence easily defined by anthropologists. Opening the possibilities for endless interpretations of meanings, Vizenor believes:

> ... the trickster narrative situates the participant audience, the listeners and readers, in agonistic imagination: there, in comic discourse, the trickster is being, nothingness and liberation; a loose seam in

consciousness; that wild space over and between grounds, words, sentences and narrative; and, at last, the trickster is comic shit. (*NC* 196)

It is no wonder then that Vizenor, the progenitor of possibilities, plays the trickster as he resists closure in the text. As Louis Owens states in *Other Destinies:*

> The key to reconciling, or at least containing, this apparent dialectic lies once again in Vizenor's trickster pose. Embodying contradictions, all possibilities, trickster ceaselessly dismantles those imaginative constructions that limit human possibility and freedom, allowing signifier and signified to participate in a process of "continually breaking apart and re-attaching in new combinations." (235)

Vizenor in his text does not present signification as an unproblematic correspondence between the signifier and the signified but views it as a process through which meaning is continuously recreated instead of assigned by dominant discourse. For Vizenor, the word is born out of imagination under the watchful eye of a trickster who, through humor, reverses the meanings we have labored to create. Vizenor's word is a word in the making which holds the possibilites to liberate our mind from the "straitjacket of a fixed, authoritative discourse" (*Other Destinies* 235).

Works Cited

Bakhtin, Mikhail. *The Dialogic Imagination. Four Essays by M. Bakhtin*, ed. M. Holquist, translated by C. Emerson and M. Holquist. Austin: University of Texas Press, 1981.

Baudrillard, Jean. *Simulations*. New York: Semiotext(e), 1983.

Blaeser, Kimberly. *Gerald Vizenor: Writing in the Oral Tradition*. Norman and London: University of Oklahoma Press, 1996.

Bruchac, Joseph. "Follow the Trickroutes: An Interview with Gerald Vizenor." In *Survival This Way; Interviews with American Indian Poets.* Tucson: University of Arizona Press, 1987. Pp. 287-310.

Derrida, Jacques. "Structure, Sign, and Play in the Discourses of the Human Sciences." In *The Critical Tradition,* ed. David Richter. New York: St. Martin's, 1989.

Owens, Louis. *Other Destinies; Understanding the American Indian Novel.* Norman and London: Univerity of Oklahoma Press, 1992.

Trinh, Minh-ha T. *Woman, Native, Other: Writing Postcoloniality and Feminism.* Bloomington and Indianapolis: Indiana University Press, 1989.

Vizenor, Gerald. *Manifest Manners: Postindian Warriors of Survivance.*
Hanover and London: University Press of New England, 1994.
—, Ed. *Narrative Chance: Postmodern Discourse on Native American Literatures.* Albuquerque: University of New Mexico Press, 1989.

Simona Fojtová, originally from the Czech Republic, is a Ph.D. student in American Studies at the University of New Mexico. She is a co-founder of Medúza, a gender studies center, in Brno, the Czech Republic. She is currently teaching a Gender Studies class at the University of New Mexico.

Leslie Marmon Silko's *Ceremony*: A Different Kind of Captivity Narrative

Peter Alan Froehlich and Joy Harris Philpott
University of Mississippi

> Distances and days existed in themselves, then; they all had a story. They were not barriers. If a person wanted to get to the moon, there was a way; it all depended on whether you knew the directions—exactly which way to go and what to do to get there; it depended on whether you knew the story of how others before you had gone. (Silko 19)

Leslie Marmon Silko's *Ceremony* dramatizes contemporary America's struggle to come to terms with the legacy of frontier. In traditional American mythology, the frontier is where acculturation takes place, transforming different races and cultures into a single, homogenous, Euro-American identity. Increasingly, Americans recognize that our nation contains not one culture but many and that this traditional myth does not have the story quite correct. *Ceremony* follows Tayo as he searches for a new myth, one that explains his identity and experience as a multi-ethnic person in a multi-cultural milieu. With this subject, it is not surprising that Silko's novel contains mythic structures drawn from several different cultures: traditional Laguna and Navajo stories are embedded in the text and the plot follows patterns established in both Native and European myth.[1] While critics have done a tremendous amount of work tracing the novel's mythic appropriations, one source that has been left unexamined is the captivity narrative, a genre intimately connected with the Euro-American mythology of frontier. The novel contains elements appropriated from the traditional captivity narrative—plot line, tropes, and themes—but Silko is actually signifying on the genre: revising the meaning of captivity and offering a new myth of the frontier. Only by freeing himself from the destructive ideology of colonialism can Tayo—and by extension, all Americans—live peacefully and ethically in the multi-cultural nation created by frontier.

Captivity Narratives and Colonialist Ideology

The captivity narrative is an instrument of colonialism, encoding in textual rhetoric Euro-American culture's ambivalent attitude toward the frontier experience. With the resurgent interest in narratives such as Mary Rowlandson's

---

[1] For Silko's use of native mythology see Allen, Bell, Mitchell, Swan, and Peacock. For Silko's borrowing of Euro-American paradigms, see Getz, Ronnow, and Wald.

The Sovereignty and Goodness of God, the story of captivity is familiar: Euro-Americans, usually women, were taken from home in the settlements and brought unwillingly into the frightening, unknown wilderness.[2] They were brought into contact with, immersed in, and usually—often in spite of their resistance—acculturated into a Native American society. This acculturation often manifest on the body of the captive: exposure to the elements tanned and toughened skin; work and travel toned muscles; tongues adopted to new language and digestive systems to new foodways; changes in clothing, hairstyles, tattooing, and body piercing signaled incorporation into native society. The captive body—combining elements of both native and European cultures—came to represent the mixed and contested condition of frontier (Harris 11-21).

Just as their bodies came to occupy a middle space between European and native cultures, so too did the captives' minds. Given access to another group's world view, captives were able to gain a critical perspective on their natal culture and adopt a transgressive or counter-cultural perspective. Mary Rowlandson, for example, criticizes the Puritans' military capabilities (response time, transport, and logistics) in a manner that would not have been possible for a woman in a patriarchal society without the intervention of an extravagant experience (Slotkin, *Regeneration* 112).

From the perspective of the Euro-American settlements, the captive was grotesque: a transgressive image that calls ideology into question by combining things normally thought to be separate and incompatible.[3] The ideology of colonialism that drove expansion across America's frontiers divided space into "settlement" (cultural inside) and "wilderness" (outside of culture), divided societies into "civilization" (those possessing European culture) and "savagery" (those possessing no culture), and divided people into "self" and "Other" (Pearce). In denying positive identity to the savage Other, this binary logic assigns all value to the civilized self. In order to preserve the integrity and value of that self, this ideology requires a frontier that operates as an exlusionary boundary (like the Great Wall of China), designed to keep the barbarians outside and civilization safe within. In reality, however, the expansion of culture along the frontier encouraged—and required—the sort of cross-cultural contact and mixing that captivity narratives describe.[4] By showing that contact and acculturation were possible and beneficial, captivity called into question the assumptions about cultural difference, incompatibility, and superiority that supported the hegemony of Euro-American culture.

[2]For a discussion of why women were more often taken captive, see Castiglia and Namias.

[3]This concept of the grotesque draws on the work of Harpham and Stallybrass and White.

[4]For more on the frontier as a locus of cross-cultural exchange, see Crosby, Jr. and Calloway. The distinction between an exclusionary boundary and a permeable border can be found in Michaelson and Johnson.

The transgressive nature of their experience made it difficult for captives to return to their natal cultures. In addition to reverse culture shock and post-traumatic stress, returned captives faced the curiosity and distrust of neighbors who worried that they had "gone native" or become "white Indians." In order to facilitate their re-integration into society, captives undid the grotesquery of their situation by denying, repressing, or explaining away the alterity of their lives during and after captivity. In their narratives, captives such as Mary Rowlandson emphasize their resistance to enculturation, insisting that their participation in native culture was unwilling and that they were able to maintain crucial aspects of their natal culture, especially their gender roles and religious practices (Harris 23-26). They also maintain, often in the face of contradictory evidence in the narrative, that native cultures are inferior, that native people are incomprehensible and "savage." Mary Rowlandson re-Others her captors by denying them agency, representing Native Americans as demons or as instruments of God (Slotkin, *Regeneration* 99). She also retreats from the understanding of native culture that she achieved during her captivity, reverting to calling native foodstuffs "trash" even though she admits to finding certain foods savory and sustaining. By filtering their extravagant experiences through the lens of colonialist ideology, Mary Rowlandson and other captives re-located themselves—body and mind—within the safety and comfort of their natal culture.

So while the traditional captivity narrative contains a *story* of extravagance, of contact with the strange and Other world of native America, its *discourse* works to contain and control the (perceived) threat produced by this contact. As Richard Slotkin points out, one of the powers of cultural myth lies in its ability to motivate future social action (*Regeneration* 96). Many captivity narratives explicitly function as propaganda for colonialism, advocating the destruction of the grotesque and threatening frontier by means of territorial expansion, Indian removal, or even (as in the case of Mary Rowlandson) genocide. The rhetoric of the captivity narrative opens the way for what Slotkin calls "regeneration through violence," an ethnic and cultural cleansing of the frontier that leaves Euro-American culture untainted by contact and in possession of additional territory. In reinforcing colonial America's resistance to diversity, in defining violence as the only acceptable means of acculturation (Slotkin, *Regeneration* 102), and in establishing a hostile relationship to the environment (Slotkin, *Regeneration* 105), the captivity narrative contributes to the frontier's legacy of individualism, isolationism, racism, and environmental degradation—all of the social problems that Tayo faces in Silko's novel.

Extravagance, Contact, and Captivity in Ceremony

In Silko's novel, Tayo undergoes an extravagant experience not unlike that of white colonists taken captive by Native Americans. Tayo leaves his home on the Laguna reservation and travels west to California, where he makes contact with Euro-American culture. While not wholly unknown, this culture is represented as "Other" even by the Army recruiter: "'Anyone can fight for America,' he began, giving special emphasis to 'America,' 'even you boys. In a time of need anyone can fight for her.... Now I know you boys love America as much as we do, but this is your big chance to *show* it!'" (64).Tayo signals his acceptance of a place within Euro-American society by adopting the "General Issue" crewcut and uniform.

During the war Tayo serves as both captor and captive. Unlike the other American soldiers, whose perceptions are influenced by military training and wartime propaganda, Tayo does not dehumanize his enemy and therefore he cannot participate in his unit's massacre of Japanese prisoners.[5] Instead, through contact the Japanese cease to appear "Other." Tayo's sense of connection with his enemy is confirmed when he sees his uncle Josiah's face on the body of a Japanese soldier and again, after the war, when he sees Rocky's face on a Japanese-American child. This illicit relationship between captor and captive also manifests during his own captivity, in the sympathy that one of the prison guards feels for Tayo following Rocky's death during the Bataan Death March.

After the war, Tayo returns to the United States apparently suffering from mental illness, characterized as battle fatigue and malarial hallucinations. While not inaccurate—we might add that Tayo suffers from depression as well as PTSD—these diagnoses ignore the fact that Tayo's problems were not caused but only exacerbated by his wartime experience. It is more accurate to describe Tayo's condition as a form of cognitive dissonance, common among returned captives, produced by his inability to make sense of his experience using available cultural paradigms. The captivity paradigm suggests that cultural mixing occurs when individuals cross the boundaries that keep cultures separate and distinct; on their return to the natal culture, captives purge themselves of the hybrid identity by separating themselves from the "Other," reducing their alterity by filtering their extravagant experience through the lens of their natal ideology. Tayo's experience does not fit this paradigm, and his attempt to force a fit only makes things worse.

Tayo cannot return to a separate and distinct natal culture because he has always occupied what Richard White calls a "middle ground." This model represents the frontier as contested space, a region occupied by a hybrid culture that is part of, yet distinct and set apart from, the two or more cultures

---

[5]The Philippines setting is extremely well chosen both for the exigency of plot and for symbolic valences. While the character of the fighting is well known, as is the history of the Bataan Death March, it is worth reminding readers that the Philippines was the site of colonialist aggression long before the Japanese invaded during World War II. America's most infamous involvement in the islands came during the "Philippines Insurrection" of 1898-1902, in which American soldiers slaughtered relatively primitive villagers in an action closely paralleling so called "savage wars" against Native American groups. See Slotkin, *Gunfighter Nation* (106-11) and Drinnon (307-32).

that contribute to the combination. Tayo's home—the Laguna reservation and the towns along Interstate 40 in New Mexico—is just such a place, with Mexican, Anglo-American, and various Native cultures in constant, interactive contact. Rather than leaving the area "settled"—dominated by a stable, monolithic, Euro-American society—the frontier left a mixed and contested middle ground.[6]

With his bi-racial identity manifest on his body, Tayo functions as a symbol for the cultural condition of his home region. Tayo's world view contains elements of both native and Euro-American ideology, but he is unable to occupy either perspective comfortably or for long. He remembers a time in his childhood when he spent an afternoon killing flies in the kitchen, in part for fun and in part because his teacher told him that flies "are bad and carry sickness" (101). His uncle Josiah tells him a story about how the greenbottle fly delivered the Laguna people from starvation and death, suggesting that Tayo should be grateful and honor the flies rather than kill them. Tayo cannot wholly discount either point of view:

> He knew what white people thought about the stories. In school the science teacher had explained what superstition was, and then held the science textbook up for the class to see the true source of explanations. He had studied those books, and he had no reasons to believe the stories any more.... But old Grandma used to say, "Back in time immemorial, things were different, the animals could talk to human beings and many magical things still happened." He never lost the feeling he had in his chest when she spoke those words, as she did each time she told them stories; and he still felt it as true, despite all they had taught him in school—that long ago things *had* been different.... (94-5)

His inability to reconcile these incompatible perspectives leaves Tayo's mind in the mixed and contested condition associated with the middle ground.

Tayo's illness is caused by his attempt to interpret his life—his identity, his relationships, and his experiences—through two incompatible perspectives at once:

> He could get no rest as long as the memories were tangled with the present.... He could feel it inside his skull—the tension of little threads being pulled apart and how it was with tangled things, things tied together, and as he tried to pull them apart and wind them into their places, they snagged and tangled even more. So Tayo had to sweat through those nights when thoughts became entangled; he had to sweat to think of something that wasn't unraveled or tied in knots to the past.... (6-7)

[6] For more discussion of the world of the novel as multi-cultural and post-colonial space, see Aldama and Wald.

From Laguna culture, Tayo learned an ethic of relationship and responsibility. Ku'oosh, a Laguna medicine man, explains:

> "But you know, grandson, this world is fragile."
> The word he chose to express "fragile" was filled with the intricacies of a continuing process, and with the strength inherent in spider webs woven across paths in sand hills where early in the morning the sun becomes entangled in each filament of web. (35)

Tayo understands the responsibility that this interconnectedness brings: "It only took one person to tear away the delicate strands of the web, spilling the rays of sun into the sand, and the fragile world would be injured" (38). This sense of communal responsibility is also reflected in Laguna's reaction to Tayo's mother: "For the people, it was that simple, and when they failed, the humiliation fell on all of them; what happened to the girl did not happen to her alone, it happened to all of them" (69). Euro-American society, on the other hand, provides Tayo with an ethical system based on individual identity and personal responsibility: "Christianity separated people from themselves; it tried to crush the single clan name, encouraging each person to stand alone, because Jesus Christ would save only the individual soul" (68). This religious tenet forms one of the bases for colonialism's desire to maintain cultural difference and purity.

When Tayo uses these competing ethics to evaluate his own situation, the result is a muddle. Following his Laguna ethic, he recognizes himself as a product of and symbol for the cultural mixture produced by his region's colonial history; under the influence of colonialist ideology, he can only interpret such contact and mixture as degradation.[7] Tayo acknowledges complicity in his mother's exile and death and in the environmental degradation at Gallup and the uranium mines. He also feels directly responsible for several forms of destruction associated with his extravagant experience. He promised to stay at home and help Josiah raise the spotted cattle; he didn't, and now he blames himself for the death of Josiah and the theft of the herd. He promised to bring Rocky home safely; he didn't, and now he regrets that he, rather than Rocky, survived. While carrying Rocky toward the prison camp, Tayo cursed the rain; he now believes that his curse caused the drought that scorches the reservation. Tayo's ethical dilemma is part of a larger pattern that appears throughout the novel in which Laguna characters (especially Tayo's Aunt Thelma and Emo) struggle to evaluate

---

[7] Sociologist Mary Douglas, in her study of the concepts of purity and pollution in various cultures, suggests that most cultures define purity and degradation as inappropriate mixture of one sort or another: "Holiness means keeping distinct the categories of creation" (53), while dirt is defined as "matter out of place" (35). Thus "our pollution behavior is the reaction which condemns any object or idea likely to confuse or contradict cherished classifications" (36).

cultural contact and mixture. Recognizing the Laguna ethic of mutual responsibility, these characters have also internalized Euro-America's devaluation of the hybrid. Repressing their own complicity, they reject people like Tayo and his mother in order to protect themselves from the shame associated with cultural mixture.

In the first half of the novel, Tayo makes two attempts to relieve his mental suffering—to allay the feelings of loss, guilt, and shame produced by these contradictory ethical systems—by aligning himself with only one cultural perspective. His first attempt comes in the V. A. hospital, where he tries to position himself within the matrix of Euro-American culture. Tayo recognizes that colonial ideology insists that persons fit within a single racial or ethnic category, leaving no space for a person like himself. In order to fit that matrix, Tayo creates an identity that denies the presence of his hybrid body, consciousness, and identity—without which things he can feel neither relationship nor responsibility: "For a long time he had been white smoke. He did not realize that until he left the hospital, because white smoke had no consciousness of itself. It faded into the white world of their bed sheets and walls; it was sucked away by the words of the doctors who tried to talk to the invisible scattered smoke" (14). This retreat into a white world brings no solution to Tayo's problem, however, because Euro-American ideology insists on individuation and categorization. Led back to self-consciousness by an Army psychiatrist, Tayo is identified as an Indian and sent back to his "rightful" place on the reservation.

Without Rocky and Josiah, who made him feel a welcome part of his family and tribe, Tayo cannot feel at home in the Laguna community: "He lay there with the feeling that there was no place left for him" (32). The community does make an effort to claim Tayo, in the Scalp Ceremony that Ku'oosh performs. But that ritual, designed to restore warriors who have killed or touched dead bodies to a peace-centered culture (Allen 10), does not help the Laguna veterans to re-orient their minds to a Laguna perspective or to cleanse them of hybridity:

> The Scalp Ceremony lay to rest the Japanese souls.... But there was something else now ... it was everything they had seen—the cities, the tall building, the noise and the lights, the power of their weapons and their machines. They were never the same after that: they had seen what the white people had made from the stolen land.... Every day they had to look at the land, from horizon to horizon, and every day the loss was with them; it was the dead unburied and the mourning of the lost going on forever. So they tried to sink the loss in booze, and silence their grief with war stories about their courage, defending the land they had already lost. (169)

A Different Kind of Captivity Narrative 105

Tayo then tries to find community with the other Laguna veterans, who seem to share his feeling of isolation and rootlessness after their own extravagant experiences. What he comes to realize, however, is that the Laguna veterans do not desire a peaceful return to their natal community. Their stories are a strange inversion of the captivity paradigm, representing extravagance as an experience of freedom and power and their return as an unwilling separation and captivity. Even after their betrayal by Euro-American society, they continue to reveal the impression of its ideology on their minds: in their still-vehement hatred of the Japanese, in their lust for white women (especially blondes) and other Euro-American symbols of cultural power, and in their devaluation of Laguna culture and the land. As we mention above, Emo and the other veterans reject Tayo out of a desire to distance themselves from the taint of cultural contact and mixing. Emo tells Tayo: "You drink like an Indian, and you're crazy like one too—but you aren't shit, white trash. You love Japs the way your mother loved to screw white men" (63). His statement reveals how thoroughly he has internalized Euro-American ideology, which ties together racist stereotypes (drunken and crazy Indians), classist assumptions (white trash), hate-mongering wartime propaganda, and misogyny. Emo lashes out at Tayo as a representative of white America's betrayal of Native Americans and specifically its refusal to accept native people as full and equal members—a betrayal that Emo feels more keenly than any.

Im part because of this rejection, Tayo is more successful than the other veterans in re-orienting himself according to a nativist perspective. Tayo slowly distances himself from Euro-American society and eventually rejects it in strikingly critical terms:

> If the white people never looked beyond the lie, to see that theirs was a nation built on stolen land, then they would never be able to understand how they had been used by the witchery ... white thievery and injustice boiling up the anger and hatred that would destroy the world: the starving against the fat, the colored against the white. (191)

Tayo's attempt to kill Emo with a beer bottle represents his second attempt to heal himself, in this case by rejecting Euro-American ideology and embracing a nativist perspective. Tayo is profoundly affected by the grotesquery of the image of Emo playing with teeth he removed from the skull of a Japanese officer. For a Laguna—especially one who has experienced the Scalp Ceremony—to show such callous disregard for body parts disgusts Tayo, as it links Emo through white racism to the history of ethnic cleansing during colonialism. In attempting to kill Emo, he is striking out against an image of mixture—a Laguna acculturated (though not accepted) into a society that oppresses his own people. What Tayo does not realize at the time of this attack is that his desire to erase a disturbing, hybrid image through an act of regenerative violence only ties him more closely to the history and ideology of Euro-American colonialism.

Immersing in native culture is no more successful for Tayo than becoming white smoke—both fail because they ignore the claims of the middle ground. There can be no healing for Tayo and the other veterans—and no re-integration into the community—as long as they perceive and evaluate their hybrid condition through the ideology of Euro-American colonialism. That ideology demands that Tayo accept a single identity and a fixed perspective, shoring up categories of difference that ultimately serve the needs of the dominant Euro-American culture. As Scott Michaelson and David E. Johnson argue, Americans can achieve a positive multiculturalism only by deconstructing racial hierarchies, not merely by shuffling their contents.[8] Reversing the directionality of the captivity paradigm toward a native perspective challenges the racial hierarchies coded into the original genre, but in such a way that the hierarchies themselves remain intact.

"a returning rather than a separation": Ceremony *as Liberation Narrative*

The second half of the novel traces Tayo's movement toward a different ethic, one that will allow him to return home without denying his hybrid identity or separating himself from any of the social groups that contribute to his multi-cultural milieu. This new cultural perspective, itself a product of the middle ground, allows Tayo to recognize that the interconnected threads of his life form a pattern rather than a tangle: "He cried the relief he felt at finally seeing the pattern, the way all the stories fit together—the old stories, the war stories, their stories—to become the story that was still being told.... He had only seen and heard the world as it always was: no boundaries, only transitions through all distances and time." (246). Tayo achieves this new understanding through a ceremony that revises his understanding of captivity, contact, and cultural mixture.

Tayo's family sends him to Betonie, a Navajo medicine man, in order to find the healing that the Laguna Scalp Ceremony did not provide. Betonie is himself a product of frontier mixture: his grandmother is a Mexican woman taken captive by Native Americans, who defines for herself a role in native culture as wife and professional partner to Descheeny, a medicine man famous for healing "victims tainted by Christianity or liquor" (150). Betonie's grandparents recognize that their world is changing as a result of inter-cultural contact, and they incorporate these changes into the ceremonies they perform: "But after the white people came, elements in this world began to shift; and it became necessary to create new ceremonies" (126). These changes frighten people who feel that the purity or authenticity of their culture has been compromised:

---

[8] See "Border Secrets: An Introduction," 1-39. For more on the way hybrid images transgress and threaten ideological structures, see Stallybrass and White's criticism of Bakhtin in their "Introduction," 1-26.

> The people nowadays have an idea about the ceremonies. They think the ceremonies must be performed exactly as they have always been done, maybe because one slip-up or mistake and the whole ceremony must be stopped and the sand painting destroyed. That much is true.... But long ago when the people were given these ceremonies, the changing began, if only in the aging of the yellow gourd rattle or the shrinking of the skin around the eagle's claw, if only in the different voices from generation to generation, singing the chants. You see, in many ways, the ceremonies have always been changing. (126)

Night Swan, the Mexican dancer, also speaks to Tayo about this fear.

> They are afraid, Tayo. They feel something happening, they can see something happening around them, and it scares them. Indian or Mexicans or whites—most people are afraid of change. They think that if their children have the same color skin, the same color eyes, that nothing is changing.... They are fools. They blame us, the ones who look different. That way they don't have think about what is happening inside themselves. (100)

According to Betonie's grandmother, these changes are a natural and necessary function of living cultures: "She taught me this above all else: that things that don't shift and grow are dead things" (126).

The desire to resist change, on the other hand, is represented as the product of witchery, which "works to scare people, to make them fear growth" (126). According to Betonie, this witchery is evil—a force that erodes love and sympathy, the feelings that bind people to one another, in order to produce destruction and death. The division of human beings into separate races—colonialism's self/Other binary—is part of this witchery. When Tayo tells Betonie that he saw Josiah among the massacred Japanese, Betonie responds by saying,

> "The Japanese," the medicine man went on, as though he were trying to remember something. "It isn't surprising you saw him with them. You saw who they were. Thirty thousand years ago they were not strangers. You saw what the evil had done: you saw the witchery ranging as wide as this world." (124)

Betonie's ceremonial story about the "contest in dark things" represents colonialist ideology—its belief in the separation of people and cultures, its advocacy of stasis and purity, its willingness to destroy the Other to maintain its (imaginary) separateness and hegemony—as unnatural, unhealthy, and evil.

Gaining a critical perspective on colonialist ideology allows Tayo to see that many of the problems he faces—the social problems that constitute the legacy of frontier—are the result of captivity. But in this revised understanding of the trope, captivity is defined not as forced and unnatural contact between peoples and cultures, but as forced separation from one's natural place within a middle ground. This form of captivity affects individuals, entire social groups, and even the natural world. Placing his experience in context with the Navajo Coyote Transformation rite (Bell), Tayo comes to understand his condition as one of captivity: "He recognized it then: the thick white skin that had enclosed him, silencing the sensations of living, the love as well as the grief, and he had been left with only the hum of the tissues that enclosed him" (229). In the Navajo story, Coyote throws his a coyote skin onto the hero, transforming him into a coyote; in Tayo's case, the "white skin" represents the context of Euro-American culture that forces him to repress his mixed identity in order to fit within the matrix of colonialist ideology. Similarly, the reservation system and the Japanese-American internment camps force minority groups to live within geographic and cultural boundaries artificially imposed by Euro-American culture in order to safeguard itself from the perceived threat associated with contact. Captivity-as-separation also affects the natural world, mapping colonialist ideology onto the landscape. Tse-pi'na, a mountain sacred to the Laguna people, has been taken captive by the white ranchers who logged the trees, killed off the animals, encircled the mountain with fencing, and renamed it "Mount Taylor." The fencing establishes boundaries that enforce the unnatural separation of this land from the Laguna people: "The people all knew what the fence was for: a thousand dollars a mile to keep the Indians and Mexicans out; a thousand dollars a mile to lock the mountain in steel wire, to make the land his" (188).

Betonie tells a number of stories that reflect this revised understanding of captivity, contact, and mixture. In the first, Betonie describes the experiences of his helper, Shush, who wandered away from his human family and was adopted by a family of bears. When the human family finds the child, he is acculturated and no longer recognizes himself as human. This story debunks the idea that contact must be unwilling and traumatic, and also the idea that mixture involves corruption or degradation: "It is very peaceful with the bears; the people say that's the reason human beings seldom return" (130). Shush's story helps Tayo to recognize his own situation. While the boy is happy enough to remain with the bears, his family wants him back. They ask Betonie to perform a ceremony that recalls the boy, step by step, to his natal culture: "It is a matter of transitions, you see; the changing, the becoming must be cared for closely" (130). The ceremony that Betonie performs—recalling Tayo to home, long life, and happiness—involves "transitions that had to made in order to become whole again, in order to become people our Mother would remember; transitions, like the boy walking in bear country, being called back softly" (170).

The "transitions" that free Tayo and his community from the evil of witchery/colonialism follow the Navajo Red Antway ceremony but also parallel another of Betonie's captivity narratives: the story of the storm clouds held captive on the mountain top. In one version of the story, the people become tainted by Ck'o'yo magic; as punishment, "Our mother/ Nau'ts'ity'i" takes the rain clouds away, resulting in drought and starvation for the people (48). Buzzard requires that Fly and Hummingbird perform a series of ceremonial tasks before he will purify the town of the evil. In the other version, the Ck'o'yo magician Kaup'a'ta gambles with the people, wins the storm clouds, and holds them captive for three years, again causing drought and starvation. Eventually, Spiderwoman teaches Sun how to defeat the Gambler and restore the clouds to their rightful place. In both stories, captivity associated with witchery—and therefore with colonialist separation—is undone through the performance of ritual actions that purify the community, restore the captives to their rightful place, and bring an end to drought and the suffering of the people. In Tayo's case, the transitions that will lead him back consist of ritual encounters with the spotted cattle, with a woman, and with the witches themselves..

Tayo's first ceremonial task involves freeing the spotted cattle from their captivity on the white rancher's property—symbolically located on the top of Tse-pi'na. The cattle themselves represent the strength that lies in multi-culturalism: Mexican cattle that are "at home" in the desert, able to forage for food and water and resist predators; Josiah believes that, when crossed with meaty European Herefords, they will provide food and income even during periods of drought. Tayo feels an ethical responsibility to make good on his promise to Josiah, but also to undo—where possible— the destruction wrought by colonialism. In cutting through the barbed wire around Floyd Lee's ranch, Tayo frees both the cattle and the sacred mountain from an illegal and/or unethical captivity, returning both to the more natural state of freedom.

During his mission to rescue the cattle, Tayo encounters Ts'eh, both woman and spirit, who helps Tayo locate himself in relationship to the environment.[9] She orients him to the landscape by introducing him to the star pattern and teaching him herbal lore. In their lovemaking Tayo uses her body to locate himself—"He was afraid of being lost, so he repeated trail marks to himself: this is my mouth, tasting the salt of her brown breasts; this is my voice calling out to her" (180)—after which, for the first time in the novel, he seems physically and emotionally at peace. Ts'eh offers Tayo love, and love offers Tayo relief from the grief and guilt that torture him:

---

[9] For more on the symbolic function of Ts'eh, see Allen (8), Mitchell (32-4), and Orr.

> The terror of dreaming he had done on this bed was gone, uprooted from his belly; and this woman had filled the hollow spaces with new dreams.... The dreams had been terror at loss, at something lost for ever; but nothing was lost; all was retained between the sky and the earth, and within himself. He had lost nothing. The snow covered mountain remained, without regard to titles of ownership or the white ranchers who thought they possessed it. They logged the trees, they killed the deer, bear, and mountain lions, they built their fences high; but the mountain was far greater than any or all of these things. The mountain outdistances their destruction, just as love had outdistanced death. (219-20)

In this passage, Tayo achieves the healing that he seeks throughout the novel. He now sees the destruction produced by colonialism and captivity, which he had understood as irretrievable loss, as insignificant in comparison to the power of love to overcome and undo it.

This moment of understanding represents Tayo's achievement of wellness, but not the end of his ceremony. Before he can complete his return, he has to face the witchery itself. This takes place in his confrontation with Emo at the uranium mine. There, Tayo's own story merges with that of his family, his region, his nation, and the world through the shared context of colonialism/witchery, as the entire world comes under the threat of nuclear destruction:

> There was no end to it: it knew no boundaries; and he had arrived at the point of convergence where the fate of all living things, and even the earth, had been laid. From the jungles of his dreaming he recognized why the Japanese voices had merges with Laguna voices, with Josiah's voice and Rocky's voice; the lines of cultures and worlds were drawn in flat dark lines on fine light sand, converging in the middle of witchery's final ceremonial sand painting. (246)

Tayo now recognizes the full implication of Betonie's multicultural vision, with its radical deconstruction of racial and ethnic difference: "From that time on, human beings were one clan again, united by the fate the destroyers had planned for all of them, for all living things" (246).

The challenge for Tayo after recognizing this pattern is to resist the almost instinctual urge to participate in the ongoing cycle of violence, anger, hatred, and revenge that sustains the witchery. Recognizing Emo as a destroyer and a witch—as Other—Tayo feels that violence against him would be justified and regenerative: "He felt certain his own sanity would be destroyed if he did not stop them and all the suffering and dying they caused—the people incinerated and exploded, and the little children asleep outside Gallup bars" (252). In this moment, Tayo comes very close to reverting to the logic of colonialism: to demonizing another human being, denying that person's humanity, and diminishing his own in the process. Earlier, Ts'eh had predicted this moment, telling Tayo that the fight against the witches is a fight for control of "the end of the story. They want to change it. They want it to end here, the way all their stories end, encircling slowly to choke the life away" (231-2). In killing Emo, Tayo would have lost touch with the healing he had so recently achieved, trading love for hatred, peace for violence, and reconciliation for revenge. By resisting the urge to kill, Tayo maintains the end of the story that he chooses for himself: a peaceful homecoming and a loving reunion with his family and his environment.

Ceremony does not end with Tayo's homecoming, but with a final act of story-telling through which he invites the Laguna elders, and by extension the entire community, to share in the healing he has experienced. Rather than filtering his experience through Euro-American or contemporary Laguna perspectives, both of which include the colonialist ethic of separation and purity, Tayo narrates his story through the multi-cultural ethic of Betonie's revisionist mythology. While the traditional captivity narrative emphasizes the difference between peoples and cultures, Tayo's story highlights their similarity and connectedness. Instead of supporting one group's violent and destructive domination of others, Tayo's story argues for the equality of cultures within a common humanity, for an ethic of mutual respect, and for the peaceful resolution of conflicts.

Silko's novel lacks the narrative dissonance that characterize the traditional captivity narrative—in *Ceremony*, story and discourse complement one another. By framing the novel with the word "sunrise," Silko reveals that the text functions as a Laguna ceremonial story. It is important not to read this narrative technique as excluding non-Laguna readers. Tayo returns to a Laguna community that bears the mark of contact with other cultures; even within the sacred space of the ceremonial hogan, Tayo sits on a metal folding chair appropriated from "ST. JOSEPH MISSION" (256). In describing Tayo's return to Laguna culture, she is pointing out a way for all Americans—and ultimately all human beings—to feel at home in what we increasingly recognize as a multi-cultural nation and world. Silko's novel asks its readers to accept the moral, ethical, and ideological implications of this vision. If, like Tayo, we accept the idea that cultural change is healthy and inevitable, and if we accept cross-cultural exchange as a healthy occurrence in a multi-cultural world, if we accept the humanity of all people and our inter-dependent relationship to the natural world, we can re-orient the frontier myth away from its ending in "regenerative" violence. By rejecting the destructive ideology that drove the colonial process, we can embrace the potential that always existed in frontier situations: the potential for respectful, peaceful, and mutually beneficial exchange across social borders. By signifying on the trope of captivity, *Ceremony* frees us to explore those possibilities in our present, rather than focusing on our failure to do so in the past.

Works Cited

Aldama, Arturo J. "Tayo's Journey Home: Crossblood Agency, Resistance, and Transformation in *Ceremony* by Leslie Marmon Silko." In *Cross-Addressing: Reistance Literature and Cultural Borders*. Ed. John C. Hawley. Albany: SUNY P, 1996.

Allen, Paula Gunn. "The Psychological Landscape of *Ceremony*." *American Indian Quarterly* 8 (1984): 81-93.

Bell, Robert C. "Circular Design in *Ceremony*." *American Indian Quarterly* 5.1 (1979): 47-61.

Calloway, Colin G. *New Worlds for All: Indians, Europeans, and the Remaking of Early America*. Baltimore and London: Johns Hopkins UP, 1997.

Castiglia, Christopher. *Bound and Determined: Captivity, Culture-Crossing, and White Womanhood from Mary Rowlandson to Patty Hurst*. Chicago and London: U of Chicago P, 1996.

Crosby, Jr., Alfred W. *The Columbian Exchange: Biological and Cultural Consequences of 1492*. Westport, CT: Greenwood, 1972.

Douglas, Mary. *Purity and Danger: An Analysis of the Concepts of Pollution and Taboo*. 1966. London and Boston: Routledge & Kegan Paul, 1986.

Drinnon, Richard. *Facing West: The Metaphysics of Indian Hating & Empire Building*. New York: Schocken Books, 1980.

Getz, John. "Healing the Soldier in White: *Ceremony* as War Novel." *War, Literature, & the Arts* 9.1 (1997): 123-40.

Harpham, Geoffrey Galt. *On the Grotesque: Strategies of Contradiction in Art and Literature*. Princeton: Princeton UP, 1982.

Harris, Joy Colleen. "Embodying the Texas Frontier: Notes Toward a Somatic Reading of Captivity Narratives. Unpublished M.A. thesis: U of Mississippi, 1996.

Mitchell, Carol. "*Cermony* as Ritual." *American Indian Quarterly* 5.1 (1979): 27-35.

Michaelson, Scott and David E. Johnson, ed. *Border Theory: the limits of cultural politics*. Minneapolis and London: U of Minnesota P, 1997.

Namius, June. *White Captives: Gender and Ethnicity on the American Frontier*. Chapel Hill and London: U of North Carolina P, 1993.

Orr, Lisa. "Theorizing the Earth: Feminist Approaches to Nature and Leslie Marmon Silko's *Ceremony*. *American Indian Culture & Research Journal* 18.2 (1994): 145-57.

Peacock, John. "Unwriting Empire by Writing Oral Tradition: Leslie Marmon Silko's *Ceremony*." In *Unwriting Empire*. Ed. Theo D'Haen. Amsterdam: Rodolphi, 1998: 295-308.

Pearce, Roy Harvey. *Savagism and Civilization: A Study of the Indian and the American Mind*. Berkeley: U of California P, 1988.

Ronnow, Gretchen. "Tayo, Death, and Desire: A Lacanian Reading of *Ceremony*." In *Narrative Chance: Postmodern Discourse on Native American Indian Literature*. Ed. Gerald Vizenor. Albuquerque: U of New Mexico P, 1989.

Rowlandson, Mary, Olaudah Equiano, and Others. *American Captivity Narratives*. Gordon M. Sayre, ed. Boston and New York: Houghton Mifflin, 2000.

Silko, Leslie Marmon. *Ceremony*. 1977. New York: Penguin, 1986.

Slotkin, Richard. *Regeneration through Violence: The Mythology of the American Frontier, 1600-1860*. Hanover, NH: Wesleyan UP, 1973.

—. *Gunfighter Nation: The Myth of the Frontier in Twentieth-Century America*. New York: Atheneum, 1992.

OStallybrass, Peter and Allon White. *The Politics and Poetics of Transgression*. Ithaca, NY: Cornell UP, 1986.

Swan, Edith. "Healing Via the Sunwise Cycle in Silko's *Ceremony*." *American Indian Quarterly* 12.4 (1988): 313-28.

Wald, Alan. "The Culture of 'Internal Colonialism': A Marxist Perspective." *MELUS* 8.3 (1981): 8-27.

White, Richard. *The Middle Ground: Indians, Empires, and Republics in the Great Lakes Region, 1650-1815*. Cambridge: Cambridge UP, 1991.

Since finishing her master's thesis on Somatic Readings of Captivity Narratives at the University of Mississippi in 1996, Joy Harris Philpott has been teaching English and history and working on curriculum development in high schools in Mississippi and Alabama. She is currently captivated four periods a day by her students at Hillcrest High School in Tuscaloosa, Alabama.

Peter Alan Froehlich is a Ph.D. candidate at the University of Mississippi. His dissertation, entitled "Frontier Grotesque in Southern Literature: Regional Use of a National Myth" traces the legacy of the frontier experience in southern literature and culture. He has published several essays on frontier myth in the work of William Faulkner.

Solemn Laughter:
Humor as Subversion and Resistance in the Literature of Simon Ortiz and Carter Revard

Jane Haladay
University of California, Davis

> As there has been so much said and written about the American Indians, with my tribe, the Klamath Indians, included, by the white people, which is guessed at and not facts, I deem it necessary to first tell you who I am, for which please do not criticize me as egotistical.
> Lucy Thompson *To The American Indian*

> Laughter—that is something very sacred, especially for us Indians. For people who are as poor as us, who have lost everything, who had to endure so much death and sadness, laughter is a precious gift.
> John (Fire) Lame Deer *Lame Deer Seeker of Visions*

Introduction

No single representation could adequately illustrate the variety of images which the Euramerican mind has been projecting for centuries onto the tan-skinned screen of the North American Indian. A kaleidoscope of qualities has been ascribed by white America to what it believes to be "Indians," these "Indians" merely a construct, in the words of Gerald Vizenor (Anishinabe) which are "the simulations of the 'absolute fake' in the ruins of representation, or the victims in literary annihilation" (1994:9). Yet while the profound biases, distortions, misunderstandings, assumptions, condescensions and outright hatred in colonial and post-colonial literary representations of Native American people are centuries old, it has not been until relatively recently—within the last one hundred years, as indicated by Lucy Thompson's words above written in 1916—that Native people have had opportunities to represent themselves to a significant degree in mainstream texts. Even this access has been controlled through the processes of translation and editorial preference. As recently as 1989, Arnold Krupat asserted that "there still remain those who assume that Indians have nothing to say worthy of critical scrutiny, that Indians are the academic responsibility of anthropologists or government bureaucrats, not of literary critics" (1989:9). Certainly, as Luther Standing Bear states in his autobiography *My People the Sioux*, "[t]he American Indian has been written about by hundreds of authors of white blood...[who] are not in a position to write accurately about the struggles and disappointments of the Indian." Standing Bear continues:

> White men who have tried to write stories about the Indian have either foisted on the public some blood-curdling, impossible 'thriller'; or, if they have been in sympathy with the Indian, have written from knowledge which was not accurate or reliable. No one is able to understand the Indian race like an Indian. (1975:v)

Of course, the truth of Standing Bear's words has not stopped Euramericans (some with the best, others with the worst intentions) from claiming to understand "the Indian race," or even to presume a superior understanding. And truth has not stopped the Euramerican mind from writing about Indian people as if it understood these objects of Otherness better than Native people have known themselves. Vine Deloria, Jr. (Standing Rock Sioux) wryly states that Native peoples' "foremost plight is our transparency. [Non-Indian] [p]eople can tell just by looking at us what we want, what should be done to help us, how we feel, and what a 'real' Indian is really like. Indian life, as it relates to the real world, is a continuous attempt not to disappoint people who know us" (1988:1). In constructing, disseminating and endlessly reproducing their "knowledge" about Indians since the earliest days of contact, Euramericans rapidly created specific categories of stereotypes to describe Native American people, all of which continue to exist in some form and to various degrees.

At the same time, Native people have illustrated a history of vigorous resistance to these stereotypes in their own performed and written literatures. Through their portrayals of Euramerican misperceptions, ignorance and savagery, Native writers have been able to turn the tables on false representations to challenge and refute them. I explore here the manner in which contemporary Native authors Simon Ortiz (Acoma) and Carter Revard (Osage) subvert the stereotype of the "Noble Savage" in two poems by accentuating both the racist fallacies in these representations and the fact of such images' continuing presence. (Many other examples exist in the writings of each author.) I specifically discuss how humor functions as a strategy of literary subversion in these poems, and suggest the authors' relationship to a larger, pan-tribal practice of Native American humor as social critique to counter Euramerican misconduct and colonial oppression.

At the heart of the controversy around misrepresenting Native people is the simple yet highly charged issue of just who is entitled to define a person's identity, who is in possession of this definition, and what constitutes "true" or "authentic" identity. In the case of North American indigenous peoples, the history of stereotyping began with earliest European contact, and has been perpetuated in all forms of mainstream media to serve the political and social needs of Euramerican society over time (among others, Robert F.

Berkhofer, Jr.'s *The White Man's Indian* [1978] and Francis Jennings' *The Invasion of America: Indians, Colonialism, and the Cant of Conquest* [1975] are two works which offer extended analysis on this complex topic). The very word "Indian," asserts Vizenor, along with "most other tribal names, are simulations in the literature of dominance.... The Indian was an occidental invention that became a bankable simulation" (1994:10-11). Often, this wild-west fantasy "Indian" of the dominant culture appears as the "vanished" Noble Savage or the psychotic Bloodthirsty Savage, each of which Ortiz and Revard confront in their work. While there is a great deal of overlap in the savage noble and murderous savage Euramerican representations of "Indians," we will focus here on the Noble Savage representation as rendered in Ortiz's poem "A New Story" (*Woven Stone* 1992:363-365) and in Revard's poem "Parading With The V.F.W." (*An Eagle Nation* 1993:13-14). These two complementary poems highlight the essentials of the Noble Savage stereotype, and vividly illustrate Revard's and Ortiz's creative ingenuity and humor in turning this stereotype upside-down.

Stalking the "Real" Indian: Savages Wild and Noble

Early Euramerican representations of the "Indian" as Natural Man drew from Euramerican perceptions of "the Indian's" exotic dress and/or partial nakedness, strange superstitions and ceremonies, and enigmatic relationship formations and lifeways. These perceptions were all extensively documented by the first "explorers" to the misnamed New World, who sent back to their homelands fantastic impressions in written letters, journals and reports. Robert F. Berkhofer, Jr. notes that "English and French explorers [after Columbus] found similar examples of the Golden Age still lived on earth among the Indians they met" (1978:73). As Berkhofer and others have discussed, these nomadic early Europeans were predisposed to render Indian peoples' complex social, linguistic, political and spiritual systems in terms with which they were already familiar, and to frame Native lifeways in languages of judgement with themselves as arbiters of moral correctness. "The primitivist tradition did not create the favorable version of the Indian," writes Berkhofer; "rather it shaped the vocabulary and the imagery the explorers and settlers used to describe their actual experience in the New World and the lifestyles they observed among its peoples" (1978:73).[1] This

---

[1] Primitivist ideology was firmly in place in the minds of educated Europeans by the time of the Renaissance. The philosophy conceived of a pristine, earthly paradise (past or present) in which humans lived simply and harmoniously in "nature," in contrast to the quagmire of political, social and material corruption in which many Europeans found themselves living at the time. For many, early encounters with indigenous peoples of the Americas "proved" the existence of primitivism's idealized Eden; Berkhofer's chapter "European Primitivism, the Noble Savage, and the American Indian" provides details on how specific period texts contributed to enforcing these ideas (1978:72-80).

early Euramerican image of the Indian evoked a pristine and earth-connected person (though crude and simple-minded) imbued with deep mystical and spiritual links to animals, plants, rocks, water and any other metonymical facet of Nature with a capital "N." This view defined the "noble" aspect of the Noble Savage, and these European representations of the "natural Indian," which took root as early as the fifteenth century, continue to flourish in generalized Euramerican conceptions of "Indianness." "From the very beginnings of European relations with indigenous Americans," Choctaw/ Cherokee writer Louis Owens observes, "the goal of the colonizer has been to inhabit and erase an ever-moving frontier while shifting 'Indian' to static and containable 'territory'—both within the trope of the noble and vanishing red man and within the more effective strategy that equated good Indians with dead ones" (1998:27). Through both colonial discourse and policy, then, this attitude necessarily relegated living Native people—those pesky, tenacious groups who refused to be erased—to becoming artifacts of the past, museum pieces in whom non-Indians might take a passing interest at an exposition or fair, but only to witness human curiosities that were justifiably headed for extinction because of their backward ways and inability to adapt to a superior civilization. Because of the success of early European text representations of fantasized "Indians," subsequent interactions between Europeans (and later, Euramericans) and *actual* Native people demanded that Native peoples' behavior conform to stereotypical colonial notions of "Indianness" rather than be comprehended on its own indigenous terms.

The reproduction of images both in graphics and text—what in more contemporary times we call "advertising"—has been crucial in fueling the marketability of static "Indian" representations. In postcards, souvenirs, clothing, literature, film and even food products, advertising exploits particular signifiers to create enticing images of "natural splendor" and "primitive" exoticism in association with Native peoples. In discussing the ways ads exhibit women's bodies with the material trappings of fantasized exotica, Mady Schutzman writes, "feathers, beads, twigs, shells, rope, exotic flowers, [and] undeveloped landscapes" are designed to infuse the human subject "with a raw incompleteness ready for processing into usable forms" by "the legendary colonizers" (1999:139). An identical phenomenon has long taken place in Euramerica's representations of the stereotypical "Indian." Despite this "raw incompleteness," however, Devon Mihesuah reminds us that non-Indians possess relentless and quite specific "expectations of what Indians should look like," and these expectations both seek and generate active reinforcement in the material world. "Indian men are to be tall and copper-colored, with braided hair, clothed in buckskin and moccasins," explains Mihesuah, "and adorned with headdresses, beadwork and/or turquoise," while "[w]omen are expected to look like models for the 'Leanin' Tree' greeting cards" (1996:9), complete with long black hair, brown skin that is not "too dark," anglicized features, and palpable sexuality via tight and/or scanty faux "traditional" dress. According to this thinking, "real Indians" cannot, for example wear suits, evening dresses or Birkenstocks; they cannot be imagined as articulate, well-traveled, highly educated professionals. In fact, these representational "Indians" can barely be conceived of as contemporary entities.

Yet Simon Ortiz and Carter Revard tease and invert the highly prized white creation of "Indian" as artifact, dress-up doll and passive consumer commodity. The stereotypical beads-and-buckskin props as part of the vanished Indian colonial repertoire are subverted by Ortiz in his ironically titled poem, "A New Story." Here, Ortiz playfully but pointedly emphasizes the persistent theme of Indian usefulness to the ongoing Euramerican agenda which promotes white romanticism toward anachronistic representations of American Indians, a theme "in which 'primitive peoples' [drop] out of history altogether in order to occupy a twilight zone between nature and culture" (Bennett 1994:143). The poem opens with a woman telephoning the speaker because she is "looking for an Indian," though we quickly realize that she is not looking for an actual human being at all. The woman asks Ortiz's speaker, "Are you an Indian?"

> "Yes," I said.
> "Oh good," she said.
> "I'll explain why I'm looking
> for an Indian."
> And she explained.
> "Every year, we put on a parade
> in town, a Frontier Day Parade.
> It's exciting and important,
> and we have a lot of participation."
> "Yes," I said.
> "Well," she said, "Our theme
> is Frontier,
> and we try to do it well.
> In the past, we used to make up
> paper mache Indians,
> but that was years ago."
> "Yes," I said.
> "And then more recently,
> we had some people
> who dressed up as Indians
> to make it more authentic,
> you understand, real people."
> "Yes," I said.
> "Well," she said,
> "that didn't seem right,

but we had a problem.
There was a lack of Indians."
"Yes," I said.
"This year, we wanted to do it right.
We have looked hard and high
for Indians but there didn't seem
to be any in this part of Colorado."
"Yes," I said.
"We want to make it real, you understand,
put a real Indian on a float,
not just a paper mache dummy
or an Anglo dressed as an Indian
but a real Indian with feathers and paint.
Maybe even a medicine man."
"Yes," I said.
"And then we learned the VA hospital
had an Indian here.
We were so happy,"
she said, happily.
"Yes," I said.
"there are several of us here."
"Oh good," she said.

Well, last Spring
I got another message
at the college where I worked.
I called the woman.
She was so happy
that I returned her call.
And then she explained
that Sir Francis Drake,
the English pirate
(she didn't say that, I did)
was going to land on the coast
of California in June, again.
And then she said
she was looking for Indians...
"No," I said. No. (1992:363-365)

The ironic humor in Ortiz's treatment of this poem's subject matter resides in both what is and is not said. Ortiz allows the enthusiastic white parade organizer to represent herself through the barrage of words she rains upon the Native vet, while the speaker's responses are primarily the monosyllabic and guarded affirmation "Yes." Ortiz's simple diction and short line lengths in the poem, combined with his repetition seven times of the speaker's words "'Yes,' I said," construct the sly illusion of a congenial conversation taking place between the parties, one in which the typically taciturn "Indian" may once again appear to be accommodating the more aggressive colonial agenda. The chatty parade organizer increasingly reveals her ignorance and stereotypical imaging of Native people, culminating in her desire for "a real Indian with feathers and paint." Her admission of the parade's having at one time used "paper mache Indians" calls to mind the extravagant tableaux of American world's fairs of the nineteenth century, which were characterized, in some cases, by their displays of exoticized "Indians." Frederick Hoxie writes of the 1876 Philadelphia exposition—"held in honor of the nation's centennial"—that "[f]ully half of the Government Building was given over to a display of Indian life" which included, according to local newspapers, "'all manner of curious things,'" one of which was "'a series of plains warriors made from papier-mâché'" (*New York Times*, March 29, 1976 and *Philadelphia Bulletin*, May 1876 in Hoxie 1989:86). Such lifeless constructions symbolized the nation's chronically conflicted but also changing attitudes toward Native people. Hoxie tells us that,

In the early twentieth century, shifts in popular perceptions reshaped the public image of the Indian and his place in American society...[Native Americans] came to symbolize the country's frontier past. In this new context, traditional lifeways were less disturbing, and the eradication of old habits ceased to be an overriding policy objective...Optimism and a desire for rapid incorporation were pushed aside by racism, nostalgia, and disinterest. (1989:112-113)

All three of these attitudes—racism, nostalgia, and disinterest—are demonstrated nearly a century later through the remarks of Ortiz's nice white lady parade organizer. She perpetuates the same representations of the "exotic primitive" Indian while believing she is portraying reality, evidenced by her use of the word "real" four times to describe the Indian type she seeks to make her parade "more authentic." Significantly, she never asks the speaker himself what he believes a "real Indian" might be, nor does she ask him his tribal identity; to her, all "Indians" are the same, are interchangeable, and any one would suffice for her purposes. Part of the ironic humor here, of course, is that now that the woman has actually *found* a real Indian, she can't shut up long enough to listen to him; again, the Indian is given no voice in the colonial metanarrative. At the same time, the parade organizer remains blithely oblivious to the irony in her observation that there seemed to be "a lack of Indians" available to fulfill her Anglo fantasy of authenticated Indianness. It does not occur to her that this type-casting is her own invention, nor that the intention of actual Frontier expansion by whites was to push Indians off their land and out of the picture. She is similarly blind to the fact that the site where she finally tracks down "an Indian" is in the Veteran's Hospital, a place where those wounded in battle—as so many Indians were in the "settling" of the Frontier, and have continued to be in subsequent wars fought on behalf of the United States—have ended up as a consequence of previous assaults on body, mind and spirit. She is simply happy to know that "there are several of [them]" to be found there.

Meanwhile, although the vet initially assents that there *are* "Indians" in the VA hospital, Ortiz complicates this ambiguous label by closing the poem with a suggestion that his speaker denies he is an "Indian" as defined by outsiders when he is approached at a later date for similar Euramerican exhibition. Rather than a denial of the speaker's Indian identity, this suggestion asserts *authentic* Indianness, not the lifeless papier-mâché representation sought by an unconscious colonial events coordinator. Ultimately, Ortiz subverts the racist stereotype which threatens to capture the poem's speaker by allowing the vet to have the last word in controlling his own participation in a second white attempt to represent "real Indians." When asked to participate in the recreation of Sir Francis Drake's "land[ing] on the coast of California" (and here Ortiz has his last bit of fun in the poem when his speaker characterizes Drake as "the English Pirate," then confesses parenthetically that the event organizer didn't say that, *he* did), the vet simply says "No," twice. His first "No" verbally refuses the event coordinator's attempted appropriation of his identity as "Indian," but it is the speaker's second No—it's own complete sentence, voiced without quotation marks— which indicates his ultimate rejection of colonial interference in manipulating indigenous identities. This final small but emphatic declaration resonates into the silence extending beyond Ortiz's last written word. *This* is the voice of the *real* Indian, and this open expression of dissent toward the Euramerican agenda for Native people as colorful relics initiates the "new story" referenced by Ortiz's title to the poem.

Carter Revard also engages "real Indian" stereotypes in a different type of parade poem, entitled "Parading with the V.F.W." These two poems present both poets' approaches in addressing the same central theme—the assertion of authentic Native identity in the face of destructive North American history—and also illustrate the similarities in each poet's sense of humorous play in communicating quite serious subject matter. In contrast to Ortiz's "A New Story," where the parade is in its earliest organizational stages when we enter the poem, "Parading with the V.F.W." opens *in medias res* with the assembly of a great number of Native people. Revard distinguishes these peoples' nations, and he names others who have figured prominently in U.S military conflicts.

>Apache, Omaha, Osage, Choctaw, Micmac, Cherokee, Oglala....
>Our place was ninety-fifth,
>and when we got there with our ribbon shirts

and drum and singers on the trailer,
women in shawls and traditional dresses,
we looked into the muzzle of
an Army howitzer in front of us.
"Hey, Cliff," I said, "haven't seen guns that big
since we were in Wounded Knee."
Cliff carried the new American flag
donated by another post; Cliff prays
in Omaha for us, being chairman
of our Pow-Wow Committee, and his prayers
keep us together, helped
by hard work from the rest of course.
"They'll move that 105 ahead," Cliff said.
They did, but then the cavalry arrived.
No kidding, there was this troop outfitted
with Civil War style uniforms and carbines
on horseback, metal clopping on
the asphalt street, and there
on jackets were the insignia:
the 7th Cavalry, George Custer's bunch.
"Cliff," Walt said, "they think you're Sitting Bull."
"Just watch out where you're stepping, Walt,"
Cliff said. "Those pooper-scoopers
will not be working when the parade begins."
"Us women walking behind the trailer
will have to step around it all
so much, they'll think we're dancing,"
was all that Sherry said.
      We followed
the yellow line, and here and there
some fake war-whoops came out to us
from sidewalk faces, but applause
moved with us when the singers started,
and we got our banner seen announcing
this year's Pow-Wow in June,
free to the public in Jefferson Barracks Park,
where the dragoons were quartered for the Indian Wars.
When we had passed the judging stand
and pulled off to the little park all
green and daffodilly under the misting rain,
we put the shawls and clothing in the car
and went back to the Indian Center, while
Cliff and George Coon went out and got
some chicken from the Colonel

> that tasted great, given the temporary
> absence of buffalo here in the
> Gateway to the West, St. Louis. (1993:13-14)

The manner in which Revard employs humor here has a direct relationship to some tribes' traditional uses in oral forms, a relationship also evident in Ortiz's humorous works. John Lowe writes that,

> ... even though we now know much more about Native oral traditions, many still assume that being a member of a 'tragic race' or 'vanishing Americans' precludes the existence of comic literature. But Indians, like Jews, blacks, and other oppressed peoples, have proved capable of taking what appears to be a tragic history, winnowing out and cherishing what contradicts it, and inverting the rest; thus the communal verbal tradition of joking lives, with a vengeance, providing a cornucopia of jokes and comic motifs for writers. (1996:196)

Throughout "Parading with the V.F.W.," Revard shows great incisiveness and glee in "cherishing what contradicts" the apparent "tragic history" of Native people and "inverting the rest" through communal joking. He begins his humorous counterattack on white hostility in the poem's eighth line, by joking that he hasn't "seen guns that big/ since [he was] in Wounded Knee." This bit of teasing follows immediately after the disconcerting discovery that Revard's group is placed ninety-fifth in the parade lineup, which forces them to look directly "into the muzzle of/ an Army howitzer in front of [them]."[2] Revard's humor relieves the tension and potential fear in this symbolic allusion to Euramerican military aggression against Indians, despite the ironic fact that all participants in this parade are supposedly united by their shared status as veterans who have fought for the United States. However, Revard's wit underscores the truth that Native people have long been forced to do battle both within and beyond U.S. terrain, and these conflicts are far from resolved. In our correspondence on this poem, Revard wrote,

> ... in "Parading With The Veterans Of *Foreign* Wars," I stress the "foreign" because every Indian person in the U.S. is a veteran of DOMESTIC wars waged by the US government against that person's nation, religion, language, and economic wellbeing. Our parading WITH the veterans is therefore ironically funny, because besides the

---

[2] In our correspondence, Revard explained that all the jokes and details in this poem are based on true events, a fact which substantially deepens the layers of irony in the poem.

fact that many of our men and some of the women are literally veterans of these Foreign Wars, there is this "Indian History" involved. (E-mail 3/6/00)

As the poem proceeds, no sooner do the marchers face down—through joking, prayers and "hard work"—the initial threat of the howitzer pointed straight at them than Revard announces that "the cavalry arrived./ No kidding." Revard's tongue-in-cheek phrase here defuses the anxiety inherent in the howitzer's focused aim and takes on a new layer of irony when we learn that the group is "the 7th Cavalry, George Custer's bunch" no less, "outfitted/ with Civil War style uniforms and carbines." Revard makes only three references to specific "wars" in this poem, and his choices are carefully interrelated. He first refers to Wounded Knee, in this case the second historical Wounded Knee event, the 1973 takeover on the Pine Ridge Sioux Reservation in South Dakota during which two hundred armed FBI agents, U.S. marshals and BIA police confronted a small but powerful group of not more than thirty Native men and women whose anger over a racist legal decision tapped their larger, longstanding outrage over the chronic injustices faced by contemporary Native people. The seventy-one day standoff between the U.S. government and Native American activists at Pine Ridge was the longest armed conflict in United States history after the Civil War more than one hundred years earlier, which is the second battle Revard names in his poem. The last named "war" in the poem, the "Indian Wars," in fact refers to the protracted, painful series of U.S.-Native conflicts lasting through the end of the nineteenth century as the United States sought to clarify once and for all their frantic wish that Native people become a "conquered race," and that despite powerful legal and moral contradictions, the Federal government's sovereignty would supersede that of Native nations. Some consider the first Wounded Knee event of 1890 to have marked "the end of the Indian Wars." But as Joseph M. Marshall, III (Sicangu Lakota) writes, "It could perhaps better be seen as the last well-known large-scale massacre in the long history of massacres of Indian people in North America" (1996:697). Through these three highly charged references to significant moments in North American colonial history and U.S.-Native relations that extend across centuries, Revard weaves a profound seriousness into the jocular festivities of parade day. As he reminds us in the quotation preceding this paragraph, the domestic wars forced upon Native peoples by U.S. colonial institutions are often daily, inevitable assaults.

Back at the parade, after the Native group sees the cavalry arrive, Walt joshes Cliff that "they think you're Sitting Bull," to which Cliff, the group's spiritual leader, retorts that Walt better watch his step (in more ways than one) if he wants to avoid contact with the cavalry's horse droppings. Sherry's final quip ends the men's exchange, and the poem's first stanza, with a barb against both the quantity of cavalry manure and the ignorance of non-Indian parade watchers who may mistake the women's fancy footwork for genuine "Indian" dancing. "Jokes like these," writes John Lowe, "enable a sometimes taciturn people to deal with infuriating and dangerous issues, especially relations with whites, which the Custer jokes also epitomize." Further, Lowe explains, such "verbal dueling also signals the speaker's confidence in his special joking relationship with a friend; the participants test and affirm their relationship through mock-insult" (1996:197-198), and so strengthen already close connections. Revard makes clear in the poem's second stanza that there is no avoiding the same old stereotypes entirely, and he reminds us of their consistent presence when "some fake war-whoops" greet the marchers "from sidewalk faces." We might read the blurry anonymity in this phrase, and the fact that Revard does not dwell on the sounds of the "sidewalk faces," as a sort of physical reduction of these ignoramuses to ground level. Within the same brief line, Revard has quickly moved on to highlight the majority of the spectators' positive reaction as "applause/ moved with us when the singers started,/ and we got our banner seen announcing/ this year's Pow-Wow in June,/ free to the public in Jefferson Barracks Park." Revard writes that,

> ... the poem's main point is the ironical jokes involved inviting all the people who would have no knowledge of Indians or Indian history (and "war whooped" from the sidewalks to express sympathy!) to come and dance with us in a place where the Dragoons were quartered during the Domestic Wars against Indian nations. Our dances therefore became a statement of our survival and a way of healing ourselves and offering friendship to those whose ancestors had warred on ours. (E-mail 3/6/00)

Symbols of that survival, healing and friendship close the poem, accompanied of course by more good humor. After moving past "the judging stand"—the omnipresent colonial gaze even in the context of an inclusive and high-spirited public celebration—Revard's group is rewarded by the beauty of spring and images of perpetual renewal in "the little park all/ green and daffodilly under the misting rain"; also, by a finger-licking-good meal. Revard has fun with the irony of his troops being fed by "some chicken from the Colonel," the poet's final reference to a member of the military, and in this case one whose rank has been radically reduced to that of purveyor of fast-food meals to the masses.[3] His humorous reference to the "absence

---

[3] Still, in his guise as the genteel and smiling symbol of longstanding Southern hospitality, Colonel Sanders in his crisp whites and trim beard resonates with the same brand of cultural nostalgia (in this case, America's belief in friendlier, simpler days filled with plenty of "down home" cooking and congenial family gatherings) that a number of spectators in Revard's poem continue to project on the parade's "Indians.

of buffalo" again illustrates Revard's ability to make us smile over what is in fact an extremely painful historical fact: the decimation and loss of this significant Plains peoples' food source, and the consequent changes in many Native peoples' lifeways, including many warrior societies. But Revard's joke accepts this bit of gastronomic acculturation, implying that when in Rome, eat pasta, and when in St. Louis, eat KFC; that is, at least until the bison return, which Revard assures us will happen with that single, clever adjective in the phrase *"temporary* absence." (We'll settle for chicken, he hints—*for now.*) The poem declares to The Powers That Be that Indian people are still here, both by opening with the list of living Native peoples visible in the V.F.W. parade, and by closing with a reference to the temporary absence of buffalo in the Gateway to the West. The ellipses ending the poem's first line extend the nations' numbers infinitely into the future to include all vital contemporary Indians and their children to come, and the poem's dominant iambic meter enhances the poem's feeling of forward movement: a drumbeat, heartbeat rhythm. There are no "vanished primitives" in Revard's parade, no papier mâché dummies on floats, no anachronisms nor savages. These are joke-telling, fast-food-eating, flag-waving, Omaha-Osage-English speaking *survivors*, bedecked in "ribbon shirts/...shawls and traditional dresses," singing, marching proudly, yet careful to avoid whatever literal or metaphysical obstacles might precede them in their journey.

Although both "A New Story" and "Parading with the V.F.W." address historical U.S.-Native military conflicts and European/Euramerican aggressions against Native people, we see significant differences in the way each poem focuses on "Indian" representations. Ortiz allows his Euramerican speaker the dominant voice in his poem, and in this manner the continuing existence of the Noble Savage in the Euramerican mind is revealed by the source itself. Ortiz delineates the Euramerican definition of "Indian" only to ultimately refute it through his speaker's simple, final denouncement: the false, externally imposed definition of who is Indian is denied. Revard's poem, while achieving a similar result, contrasts this technique by centering its dominant voice (or voices) from within Native culture. Throughout the poem, it is an internal definition of Indianness that is illustrated through the conversations and actions of the key players: those Apache, Omaha, Osage, Choctaw, Micmac, Cherokee, Oglala and other Native celebrants of the V.F.W. parade activities. Both parades in "A New Story" and "Parading with the V.F.W." express a version of "The journey theme [which] is pervasive in contemporary Native American poetry." Dakota poet Elizabeth Cook-Lynn believes that "[t]he oral traditions from which these expressions emerge indicate a self-absorption essential to our lives." Themes of personal journey and forward movement on behalf of one's larger cultural group "follow the traditions of native literatures which express as a foremost consideration the survival of the individual, thus the tribe, thus the species, a journey of continuing life and human expectancy" (1987:63). Ortiz's and Revard's parade poems, in their different but related expressions of survival and self-definition in accordance with cultural traditions, show strong parallels to each facet of Cook-Lynn's description of journey themes. At the conclusion of each poem, we are left with a sense that while the parade may be over, the journey is not. It will continue in new directions not following the dog-eared colonially drawn map of an established parade route, but will be determined by Native people themselves, in terrain that they will name.

Indian Representations for A New Millennium

Euramerican depictions of Native people as anachronistic earth-connected primitives doomed to perish are not problematic only because they are racist and inaccurate. This view of American Indians is additionally dangerous for the reasons Homi Bhabha outlines in describing the constrictions of the stereotype: "The stereotype is not a simplification because it is a false representation of a given reality. It is a simplification because it is an arrested, fixated form of representation that, in denying the play of difference (which the negation through the Other permits), constitutes a problem for the *representation* of the subject in psychic and social relations" (1994:75). In the "vanishing primitive" or Noble Savage depiction of Native Americans, thriving contemporary cultures become static dioramas contained behind glass in the Euramerican mental museum. Such images are comfortable and nonthreatening for those constructing them, and afford Native people little opportunity to break free and go about the business of living without further intrusion by the colonizers, because of the pressure to conform to the demands of omnipresent external and internalized colonial stereotypes. Yet as both "A New Story" and "Parading With the V.W.F." illustrate, writing itself can be an act of transformation which shatters the confines of Euramerican preconceptions, and liberates a breathing reality. Joseph Bruchac has discussed with Carter Revard the consistent theme of transformations in Revard's work. Of the poem "Dancing With Dinosaurs" (the title itself a delicious spoof on the late twentieth century film, *Dances With Wolves*, considered by a huge non-Native public to be a hallmark of "authentic" Indianness), Revard says, "what I'm talking about there is the way in which you transform yourself out of something which is an obsolete and extinct species, according to a lot of notions of Indians that non-Indians have, into something that stays alive" (1987:237). The themes of transformation and survival resonate not only in "Dancing With Dinosaurs," but within both authors' parading veterans poems, and throughout the body of Ortiz's and Revard's work generally.

"All of us, Native and non-Native, are ethnocentric at our deepest levels," claims Wendy Rose (Hopi/Miwok). "No amount of anthropological training or insight can abolish ethnocentricity (although we can become aware of it and learn to take it into consideration on a day to day basis)" (1984:18). It is not ethnocentricity in and of itself, Rose contends, that causes harm. What has remained a barrier to the cultivation of positive cultural ethnocentrism within any group in the United States is the Euramerican mainstream's assumption of a privileged stance over Native and other non-white cultures. Through the humor in their authentic portrayals of lived Native experiences, however, writers like Ortiz and Revard force the colonizers to recognize and consider more deeply the effects of delimiting Euramerican text stereotypes—Indian as "primitive" or "natural" or "savage," or any other dimensionless reduction—long promoted in colonial discourse as "fact." "Writing itself is not a neutral space," Nicholas Dirks reminds us. "In the last fifty years we have learned how much it matters from where we write, to whom we write, and more generally how writing is positioned in geopolitical, sociohistorical, and institutional terms" (1998:14). Ortiz emphasizes this point in asserting that,

> If the critic really looked at what Native America was and is today, he would have to undo the construct that America according to Western civilization and its rationalizations is. He would have to throw it all out. He would have to say this is all wrong; the Native American is indeed right. There is a real—not only a hesitation—denial of what the real America is; and the real America is the Native America of indigenous people and the indigenous principle they represent. That's the real America. The critics refuse to live with that. It's too fearful. They have to undo what they have learned. They have to admit that their perceptions have been wrong all along. (1990:115-116)

Through literature, contemporary Native authors Simon Ortiz and Carter Revard are actively engaged in the project of authentic cultural assertion that may one day finally puncture enduring Euramerican stereotypical representations of "Indians." Part of what motivates his writing, explains Ortiz, is his desire "[t]o express certain political and cultural Native American positions, to define and identify more closely the truth, to squash the stereotypes and replace them with the real thing" (1990:109-110). Revard meanwhile states that "One way to survive is to keep a sense of hope, of being able to find what works, what helps, the laughter and shared strength and awareness of good things and good ways" (Internet 1997). It is humor's inextricable alliance with cultural change—a critical element of community survival—that links Revard's and Ortiz's literary expressions to traditional Native patterns of oral storytelling events, and that makes these expressions imperative in an ongoing movement of Native literary resistance. For many Native people, humor's role in cultural survival has not only served to defend against outsiders but to outline proper behavior within tribal groups. Vine Deloria, Jr. has written, "When a people can laugh at themselves and laugh at others and hold all aspects of life together without letting anybody drive them to extremes, then it seems to me that that people can survive" (1988:167).

Revard and Ortiz are each part of the larger group of contemporary Native American writers whose work simultaneously deconstructs paralyzing and oppressive representations of their people, while actively constructing in print tribal and personal realities that, in continuing to be expressed, strengthen longstanding indigenous traditions of cultural affirmation. "To a great extent," Ortiz declares, "my writing has a natural political-cultural bent simply because I was nurtured intellectually and emotionally within an atmosphere of Indian resistance.... At times, in the past, it was outright armed struggle ... currently, it is often in the legal arena, and it is in the field of literature" (1987:193). As Ortiz suggests, more than one kind of weapon is required in the arsenal of resistance over time: sacred songs and subpoenas; prayers and police; writs and writing. Yet some elements remain constant throughout the struggle, and one is human beings' need to laugh. Without laughter, the enemy gains a stronger foothold, a fact Simon Ortiz and Carter Revard understand well. In much of their literature they offer readers an honest look at painful historical truths, while holding out eternal hope for the construction of new realities through the faith, recognition, and unity that humor brings. "In spite of the fact that there is to some extent the same repression [of Indian identity] today," Ortiz avows, "we persist and insist in living, believing, hoping, loving, speaking, and writing as Indians" (1987:194). The ugliness of centuries-old Euramerican "Indian" stereotyping is not funny, and may not be eradicated within our own lifetimes. Still, these poets offer a crucial perspective by insisting that ultimately, as Revard observes, "Comedy is worth more than tragedy anytime survival is at stake" (1998:90).

Works Cited

Bennett, Tony. "The Exhibitionary Complex." In *Culture/Power/History: A Reader in Contemporary Social Theory*. Eds. Nicholas B. Dirks, Geogg Eley, and Sherry B. Ortner. Princeton: Princeton University Press, 1994. 123-154.

Berkhofer, Robert F. Jr. *The White Man's Indian: Images of the American Indian from Columbus to the Present*. New York: Vintage Books, 1978.

Bhabha, Homi. "The Other Question, Stereotype, discrimination and the discourse of colonialism." In *The Location of Culture*. New York: Routledge, 1994, 67-84.

Cook-Lynn, Elizabeth. "You May Consider Speaking About Your Art..." In *I Tell You Now: Autobiographical Essays by Native American Writers*. Eds. Brian Swann and Arnold Krupat. Lincoln and London: University of Nebraska Press, 1987. 55-63.

Deloria, Vine Jr. *Custer Died For Your Sins*. Norman and London: University of Oklahoma Press, [1969] 1988.

Dirks, Nicholas B. *In Near Ruins: Cultural Theory at the End of the Century*. Ed. Nicholas B. Dirks. Minnesota: University of Minnesota Press, 1998.

Hoxie, Frederick. *A Final Promise: The Campaign to Assimilate the Indians, 1880-1920*. Cambridge: Cambridge University Press, (1984) 1989.

Krupat, Arnold. *The Voice in the Margin*. Berkeley, Los Angeles, Oxford: The University of California Press, 1989.

Lame Deer, John (Fire) and Richard Erdoes. *Lame Deer Seeker of Visions*. New York: Simon and Schuster, 1972.

Lowe, John. "Coyote's Jokebook." In *Handbook of Native American Literature*. Ed. Andrew Wiget. New York: Garland Publishing, Inc., (1994) 1996. 193-205.

Marshall, Joseph M. III. "Wounded Knee Takeover, 1973." In *Encyclopedia of North American Indians: Native American History, Culture, and Life from Paleo-Indians to the Present*. Ed. Frederick Hoxie. Boston and New York: Houghton Mifflin Company, 1996. 697-699.

Mihesuah, Devon A. *American Indians: Stereotypes and Realities*. Atlanta: Clarity Press, Inc., 1996.

Ortiz, Simon. "Simon Ortiz." In *Winged Words: American Indian Writers Speak*. Ed. Laura Coltelli. Lincoln and London: University of Nebraska Press, 1990. 103-119.

—. "The Story Never Ends: An Interview with Simon Ortiz." In *Survival This Way*. Ed. Joseph Bruchac. Tucson: The University of Arizona Press, 1987. 211-229.

—. *Woven Stone*. Tucson: The University of Arizona Press, 1992.

Owens, Louis. *Mixed Blood Messages, Literature, Film, Family, Place*. Norman: The University of Oklahoma Press, 1998.

Revard, Carter. *An Eagle Nation*. Tucson and London: The University of Arizona Press, 1993.

—. E-mail from the author, 6 March 2000.

—. "Introductory Words For A New Collection of Poems." The Internet Public Library Native American Authors Project. Website author Karen M. Strom <kstrom@hanksville.org>. Carter Revard and Karen Strom, 1997. Online <http://www-personal.si.umich.edu/~lmon/intro.html. 5 October 1999.

—. *Family Matters, Tribal Affairs*. Tucson: The University of Arizona Press, 1998.

—. "Something That Stays Alive: An Interview with Carter Revard." In *Survival This Way*. Ed. Joseph Bruchac. Tucson: The University of Arizona Press, 1987. 231-248.

Rose, Wendy. "Just What's All This Fuss About Whiteshaminism Anyway?" In *Coyote Was Here: Essays on Contemporary Native American Literary and Political Mobilization*. Ed. Bo Schöler. *The Dolphin* No. 9. Denmark: Seklos, c/o Department of English, University of Aarhus, 1984. 13-24.

Schutzman, Mady. *The real thing: performance, hysteria, & advertising*. Hanover and London: University Press of New England, 1999.

Standing Bear, Luther. *My People the Sioux*. Lincoln: University of Nebraska Press, 1975.

Thompson, Lucy. *To The American Indian*. Berkeley: Heyday Books, 1991.

Vizenor, Gerald. *Manifest Manners: Postindian Warriors of Survivance*. Hanover: Wesleyan University Press, 1994.

Jane Haladay is currently a Ph.D. student and associate instructor in Native American Studies at the University of California, Davis. The essay that appears here was taken from her M.A. thesis (University of Arizona, May 2000). Her current research focuses on Native North American writers' creations of and responses to literary representations of indigenous people.

Envisioning Anthropology: David MacDougall and the Next Culture

Mark Ingram
Goucher College, Baltimore, Maryland

Transcultural Cinema. David MacDougall. Edited and with an introduction by Lucien Taylor. Princeton, NJ: Princeton University Press, 1998. 318 pp. ISBN: 0-691-01235-0. Cloth: $59.50; Paper: $18.95. Halftones.

David MacDougall is an unusual anthropologist. Throughout his thirty-year career and twenty-two ethnographic films, he has maintained a stormy relationship with the concept of culture. Yet in light of anthropology's recent discord about the core concept of its discipline, MacDougall turns out to be more representative than he might at first appear. In MacDougall's newest book, *Transcultural Cinema*, readers can trace his evolution as a key figure in the development of visual anthropology.[1] These essays grow out of the confrontation between the two pursuits of MacDougall's life: cultural anthropology and documentary film. Two questions guide his writing: How can ethnographic film contribute to reconfiguring cultural anthropology? And how can an anthropological approach revitalize the increasingly conventional and formulaic genre of documentary film? He answers these questions in the capstone essay, contributing significantly to recent anthropological debates about the culture concept.

Anthropological culture wars

As an anthropologist teaching in a French department, I am often called on to explain the concerns, methods, and overall value of anthropology to my literary colleagues. This essay attempts to do the same for *Paradoxa* readers in discussing David MacDougall's *Transcultural Cinema*. MacDougall explores the creative potential of documentary film and the nature of film as a medium of representation, but his approach is best understood in the context of recent anthropological debates about culture.

What have recent anthropological "culture wars" been about, and why have many critics come to feel that the baby must finally be thrown out with the bathwater? Oddly, just as the term "culture" in the sense of "a distinct way of life" has become a ubiquitous reference in popular media, anthropologists seem to be rejecting it. As Robert Brightman notes in a study of the current status of the term, its diminishing legitimacy is evident in the

---

[1] For recent work in the growing field of visual anthropology, see Banks and Morphy 1997, and the *Visual Anthropology Review*.

substitution of the adjectival "cultural" for the nominal "culture" in many journal, book, and article titles. He adds that when the term is used, it frequently bears quotation marks indicating the author's ambivalence, self-consciousness, or censure (1995:510).

Brightman provides a summary of some of the more influential and often interrelated themes in recent critiques. Among these, the following four seem to me to be the most important. Critics claim that the concept of culture distorts our understanding of contemporary social diversity because it

1) Necessarily implies homogeneity and coherence, taking no account of intracultural variability, contestation, contradiction, and disorder,
2) is overly localist, ignoring movement and variation across geographic and political boundaries (representing what Johannes Fabian (1983) has referred to as the "culture garden" perspective in anthropology),
3) implies primordialism and ahistoricity versus human change, syncretism and invention, and most importantly,
4) emphasizes difference and hierarchy, causing anthropologists to ignore or neglect a humanistic concern for the many resemblances between "them" and "us" (see especially Lila Abu-Lughod's 1991 "Writing Against Culture").

For these reasons, a broad range of theorists have called for anthropologists to move beyond culture. Some have proposed that other concepts, such as Foucault's "discourse," or Bourdieu's "habitus," fill the void. As Brightman makes clear, recent critiques often rely on a selective and partial reading of previous formulations. Those that do not fit are frequently ignored or deemed unimportant, while those which best serve as a foil to contemporary claims are presented as emblematic of their era. The focus on new terminology has often obscured the ways the old "culture" expressed perspectives similar to those promoted by today's critics. As Brightman notes,

> In question is whether 'discourse' is better able than 'culture' to elucidate, for example, Malinowski's assertion in 1926 that 'human cultural reality is not a consistent logical scheme, but rather a seething mixture of conflicting principles.'(1926:121) (1995:533)

Still, in spite of Brightman's emphasis on continuities in anthropological debates, the recent attention to culture represents more than simply pouring old wine into new bottles. Recent critiques, whether or not they succeed in moving anthropologists "beyond culture," are efforts to adapt the anthropological enterprise to a new global context. Political, economic, and technological developments have dramatically changed the conditions for the practice of anthropology in the last thirty years. These include the changes in banking and international business often referred to as globalization, as well as the development and broader diffusion of visual and other information technologies. These technologies have expanded the discourse concerning culture by including those people whom anthropologists sometimes presumed to speak for in an earlier era.

Because of these changes, anthropologists have devoted greater attention to the politics of representation in filmic portrayals of culture. A good example is anthropologists' critical response to the film *The Gods Must Be Crazy* in the early 1980s.[2] Directed by Jamie Uys, this film was a huge international hit. It depicts the encounter between a group of "Bushmen" (!Kung San) and the modern world, including a white scientist and a band of bumbling black revolutionaries in South Africa. Reviewers called it "the year's wackiest movie, ... inspired looniness" (Newhouse Newspapers), "downright hilarious ... riotously funny" (Gannet Newspapers), "perfectly delightful" (WABC Radio), and "even funnier than it is eccentric" (*New York Times*)" (Volkman 1988:238).

Given its near-universal acclaim, it might appear that only stuffy, contrarian academics could find something to complain about. Part of what anthropologists criticized was, as might be expected, the inaccurate portrayal of the San in the film: the actors were shown in traditional dress rather than the modern clothes most San wore at the time, they hunted with bow and arrow rather than rifles, and the director added clicks to their speech so that their language would sound even more exotic to foreign ears. More troubling to anthropologists were the consequences of this portrayal for the San people. As shown in John Marshall's documentary film *N'ai. The Story of a Kung Woman* (which includes footage showing the making of *The Gods Must Be Crazy*), the San people in 1979 were in dire circumstances. Much of their land had been taken by the South African government and their reduced territory became an official homeland: "Bushmanland." This was administered by the South African government, and the San were incorporated within the apartheid system. Robbed of their self-sufficiency, the San had few sources of revenue. Prior to cattle-raising initiatives of the 1980s, one of the few available sources of employment was with the South African army. By a strange coincidence, Marshall and Uys arrived at the same time to film. The central figure in Marshall's film, *N'ai*, is also an actress in *The Gods Must Be Crazy*. Marshall's film depicts the terrible problems (tuberculosis, poor sanitation, depression, and constant fighting) facing the San due to the transition to a sedentary lifestyle on the crowded settlement.

For anthropologists, the central problem with *Gods* was not simply that it failed to capture the reality described in Marshall's film. It was that Jamie Uys promoted a vision of the San as so happy-go-lucky and different that

---

[2] The film provoked picket lines and a protest resolution at the 1984 Annual Meeting of the American Anthropological Association.

they seemed not to need the same considerations of social and economic justice as the rest of us. Uys' statements to the press encouraged this view, especially those regarding one of his actors, N!Xau. When he asked the San to participate in his film, he told reporters: "The Bushmen agreed ... because they are such nice guys that when you ask them for something, they say OK." Uys also told the reporter that paying wages was a mistake, because N!Xau had no use for money: "'I found out later that the money had blown away', Mr. Uys said" (Volkmann 1988:240).

The problem here is that such representations hide and even encourage the processes of exploitation faced by the San. As Toby Volkmann notes,

> *The Gods Must Be Crazy* perpetuates the myth that Bushmen are blissfully simple creatures, while its popularity persuades South Africa that the world wants to continue to see them that way. It is no surprise then that the film's immense international success is being used in Namibia to promote a plan to convert Eastern Bushmanland into a nature reserve where white tourists could admire wildlife, including bow-hunting Bushmen. This latest scheme may be even more devastating than alcoholism, tuberculosis, or militarization. Aside from museumizing and commoditizing the !Kung, it would bring an end to cattle raising, the one subsistence alternative on Bushmanland through which some !Kung have begun to reclaim a measure of economic independence and dignity. (Marshall and Ritchie, 1984) (Volkmann 246)

These issues contributed to a growing awareness among anthropologists of the implications of their work within a global politics of representation. It has become increasingly important for anthropologists to understand and address their works' political and economic consequences for their subjects. This has prompted more work devoted to initiatives of "indigenous media"[3] such as those of Australian Aboriginal groups. In Brazil, where miners have massacred Indians to drive them off wanted lands, anthropologists have called attention to indigenous resistance. The film *Kayapo: Out of the Forest* depicts Kayapo Indians fighting a government dam project at Altamira, and their savvy employment of the media and an international star (Sting) to publicize their struggle.

These developments prepared the ground for recent critiques of culture by directing attention to the need to emphasize similarities, as well as differences, across cultural lines. In films such as *The Gods Must Be Crazy*, natives are presented as blissfully simple and other-worldly creatures: the mirror opposite of civilized life with its stress, complications, and anxieties. In her critique of *The Gods*, Volkman concludes,

---

[3] "Indigenous media" refers to efforts to create locally based networks providing a voice to indigenous groups who had not previously had access to film and television media. For a discussion of anthropology and indigenous media, see Ginsburg 1991.

> Unlike E.T. or the brother from another planet, however, Xi and his
> fellow San are very much of this planet and this moment. The denial
> of this reality allows South Africa to continue to dispossess them of
> their autonomy, their history, and their land. (247)

It is precisely this fear that a description of cultural difference will assign indigenous groups to an exotic world apart from our own that has prompted some anthropologists to argue that we must move "beyond" culture. Similarly, documentary filmmakers such as Dennis O'Rourke have critically examined the assumptions underlying the Western quest for the exotic among indigenous peoples. O'Rourke's 1987 *Cannibal Tours* is about a group of European and American tourists in Papua New Guinea. His film portrays today's tourists as the direct heirs of a colonial legacy. Like Renato Rosaldo's discussion of "imperialist nostalgia" in popular films (1989), he underlines the ironies of Westerners seeking exotic thrills in areas where colonists formerly did all they could to eradicate the strange customs of the locals.

But O'Rourke is also careful to draw attention to his own exploitative picture-taking. In a scene from the film, a clearly uncomfortable Papua New Guinean man is surrounded by tourists who take pictures of him from the front, the back, and the side. O'Rourke says to the man, "It's a hard way to make a buck, isn't it?." But as O'Rourke himself points out in a filmed interview (*Taking Pictures*, 1996), the question is deeply ironic. Throughout the scene, O'Rourke himself is also filming the subject, and presumably also paying him. He too is a part of this "hard way to make a buck." O'Rourke's film draws out the ambivalent and troubling relationships embedded in the commerce of intercultural contact, whether in cultural tourism, "primitive" art (see Price 1989, Steiner 1995), or in the project of cultural anthropology itself. Perhaps for this reason, O'Rourke has always denied an "anthropological" aim for this film (see Lutkehaus 1989,[4] and for one anthropologist's review of the film, Bruner 1989).

David MacDougall, on the other hand, has maintained his investment in the anthropological enterprise throughout his career. His earliest essays argued for the legitimacy of film as a medium of ethnography as opposed to those who saw film simply as a research tool. His more recent work is informed by the contemporary debates about culture outlined above. He seeks to demonstrate how closer attention to "the particular expressive qualities of visual media" (272) can serve in reconfiguring anthropology and the

---

[4] "'I'm not an ethnologist, clearly,' he states. 'I'm happy they like my work. It's a compliment. But I'm not one and I don't want to be one. In fact, I'd hate to be one. We have to separate out film as an artistic statement, which is what I do; I'm an artist. I resent very much the implication that as soon as you make a film about an exotic culture suddenly you have to be called an ethnographic filmmaker.... In the end, I'm not against anthropology. I'm just somewhere else. I believe in doing good. I care and I have a moral purpose in doing what I do. A self-delusion, perhaps...'" (433).

concept of culture. But his concept of "transcultural cinema" extends beyond strictly disciplinary concerns by addressing the creative potential of all documentary film. This concept focuses on the unique possibilities for exploring intersubjectivity through film and other visual media. In this way, MacDougall both speaks to anthropological debates, and seeks to recast documentary film as a dynamic and creative genre. His newest work shows the evolution of his thought from his earliest essays and films up to today.

Beyond Observational Cinema?

Early on, MacDougall was known for being both the foremost practitioner of observational cinema, and its most serious critic. "Observational" cinema refers to an approach to documentary filmmaking which developed concurrently with "direct cinema" and "cinéma vérité" following the invention of portable synchronous sound in the early 1960s. The new technology made filmmakers less dependent on staged settings and allowed them to focus on more private aspects of their subjects' lives. Ethnographic films made in the observational style were intended to maintain a discreet distance from the subjects—as if the filmmaker were no more than a "fly on the wall," or as MacDougall himself puts it, "to film things that would have occurred if no one had been there" (129). This ideal is well expressed in MacDougall's description of his own technique when filming *To Live With Herds* (1972) among the Jie of Uganda:

> I used a camera brace that allowed me to keep the camera in the filming position for twelve or more hours, over a period of many weeks. I lived looking through the viewfinder. Because the camera ran noiselessly, my subjects soon gave up trying to decide when I was filming and when I was not. As far as they were concerned, I was always filming, an assumption that no doubt contributed to their confidence that their lives were being seen fully and fairly. (128-129)

Criticisms of the observational approach often note that this pretense to a "full" representation of the subjects' lives masks the many elements of filmmaking (camera angle, lighting, choice of subject, later editing) that shape the particular perspective of the film. Far from being an objective document of life as it would be without the anthropologist, every observational film presents its own partial perspective. Further, by minimizing interviews, observational films are criticized for denying a voice to the filmed subjects. In his 1972 article "Beyond Observational Cinema," MacDougall makes this point himself, criticizing fimmakers who refuse to accept the input of their subjects in the filmmaking process. Doing so, they

> ...inevitably reaffirm the colonial origins of anthropology. It was once the European who decided what was worth knowing about 'primitive' peoples and what they in turn should be taught. The

shadow of that attitude falls across the observational film, giving it a distinctively Western parochialism.... It is a form in which the observer and the observed exist in separate worlds, and it produces films which are monologues. (133)

But if MacDougall criticized the tendency of observational filmmakers to refuse the participation of their subjects in the filmmaking, he did not reject the observational style. On the contrary, unlike recent trends in documentary filmmaking which emphasize docudrama and first-person narratives, the MacDougalls have continued to refine an essentially observational approach to cinema. Lucien Taylor's description of this style (see also Myers 1988) is worth quoting at length:

> The laconic style of the MacDougalls' films shares neither the palpable provocation of cinéma vérité (which, in retrospect, appears as much a forebear of the expository interview as of the first-person film) nor the blue pencil of Direct Cinema, which typically confined its attention to intrinsically suspenseful situations and notable personalities (be they celebrities or eccentrics). But it is a style that is difficult in the end not to label 'observational' if only because its powers of observation are at once so unwavering and self-evidently partial. Again, this does not mean that it is not participatory, for if it is anything it is that; nor does it mean that it is not reflexive, for it is that, too. Indeed the contemporary predilection to reproach observational cinema for its 'plain style' and its naïve 'realism,' or to construe its gaze as distant or distantiating, as akin to that of a voyeur or a *surveillant*, has in many ways got the wrong end of the stick. For the truth is more nearly the opposite. Even as the MacDougalls highlight their own status as 'outsiders,' their films are remarkable for their affecting intimacy with their subjects. (pp. 7-8)

This "intimate" approach is central to MacDougall's efforts to renew documentary filmmaking by building on the best qualities of ethnography. For MacDougall, what is singular about ethnographic filmmaking is that it captures a unique moment of social and cultural exchange. Already in "Beyond Observational Cinema," he was impatient with treating the camera as a neutral instrument documenting external events. What is finally disappointing in the ideal of filming "as if the camera were not there," MacDougall states,

> ... is not that observation in itself is unimportant, but that as a governing approach it remains far less interesting than exploring the situation that actually exists. The camera is there, and it is held by a representative of one culture encountering another. Beside such an

extraordinary event, the search for isolation and invisibility seems a curiously irrelevant ambition. No ethnographic film is merely a record of another society; it is always a record of the meeting between a filmmaker and that society. (134)

For MacDougall, the recognition of the filmmaker's presence and impact on those he or she films is important not simply because of the political issues involving the representation of culture. It is also a question of acknowledging the broader web of social relationships which shape the creation of the film and the filmmaking encounter. The point is not so much to give a voice to filmed subjects, but to attend more closely to what they are already contributing to the process. It is also to recognize a broader range of perspectives within those contributions. In a 1992 epilogue to "Beyond Observational Cinema," he calls for a form of *intertextual* cinema:

> Through such an approach ethnographic film may be in a better position to address conflicting views of reality, in a world in which observers and observed are less clearly separated and in which reciprocal observation and exchange increasingly matter. (138)

In many ways, MacDougall has never really gotten "beyond" observational cinema. He remains committed to a style that explores intimacy and exchange in the ethnographic filmmaking encounter. This exploration is central to his concept of "transcultural cinema." MacDougall's ideas about "transcultural cinema" are an effort to revitalize the genre of documentary film. At the same time, they contribute to rethinking anthropological approaches to culture and cultural difference.

Transcultural Cinema

MacDougall's concluding essay begins with two definitions of "transcultural":

> Ethnographic films have been widely understood as transcultural, in the familiar sense of crossing cultural boundaries—indeed the very term implies an awareness and mediation of the unfamiliar—but they are also transcultural in another sense: that of defying such boundaries. They remind us that cultural difference is at best a fragile concept, often undone by perceptions that create sudden affinities between ourselves and others apparently so different from us. (245)

Here and in another of the new essays for this book, "Visual anthropology and ways of knowing" (Chapter 2), MacDougall makes a case for the advantages of visual representation over written ethnographies. Visual images, in contrast to written descriptions, are not limited by what can be expressed in a particular language. Films can convey a wealth of sensory detail and data which may otherwise be missed or insufficiently emphasized in a written account. MacDougall argues that films are better able to maintain the integrity of filmed subjects as individuals, rather than present them as representatives of a culture. Visual images ultimately undermine the totalizing qualities of writing through their presentation of excess, i.e., that which is not reducible to analysis and interpretation. For MacDougall, written ethnographies are governed by abstraction and generalization. Even when they include photographs, he notes, the caption usually points toward the subject's representativeness with respect to some aspect of cultural identity.

At times, MacDougall's promotion of ethnographic film as a kind of "visual communion" leads him to exaggerate its positive qualities and its differences from anthropological writing. Although Lucien Taylor notes that certainly no one today could claim that film is "unadulterated ontological revelation" (11), there are moments when MacDougall seems to suggest that the filmic image provides a direct pipeline to the truth about ethnographic encounters. "Images ... evoke the life experience of social actors, and also the experiences of fieldwork that always remain prior to anthropological description" (264). But these images are constantly reinterpreted and these interpretations are shaped in interaction with written accounts. In presenting images as the stuff of life in opposition to the abstractions of the written word, MacDougall downplays the inevitably partial picture of social life these images convey, and the way the reading of images, too, always involves a degree of abstraction and analysis.

In many ways, MacDougall's argument concerning the singular qualities of visual representation is best read as a description of the unrealized potential of documentary film. He has argued elsewhere that ethnographic filmmakers should approach filming as a way of creating circumstances in which new knowledge can manifest unexpectedly (see Taylor 1994). Although more documentary films are made today, they tend to be concerned primarily with subjects of topical interest. As Taylor notes, this has contributed to

> ... documentary, as a concept, being progressively evacuated of content, to its conflation with journalism, and to its infusion with the pieties that typically accompany either advocacy or reproof. Contrarily, MacDougall wishes to reclaim documentary as an arena of engagement with the world, one that actively confronts reality, and that in so doing is transformed into a mode of inquiry in its own right. (10)

Here MacDougall's concerns with documentary film as a mode of inquiry join his anthropological goal of reconceptualizing culture. In his view, previous conceptions of culture fail to fully account for the intersubjectivity of cultural knowledge, i.e., the ways individuals create social meaning publicly, in their interaction with others. Visual anthropology can provide a reorientation toward the visual, public world. In particular, ethnographic filmmaking can focus on exchange and interaction with filmed subjects rather than on subjects as exotic others. For MacDougall, the marginalization of ethnographic film in anthropology occurred parallel to a move in Twentieth-Century anthropology away from an understanding of people based on resemblance (evolutionist theories saw all people related with respect to a common trajectory), to one focusing on difference. This happened, he states, with the rise in linguistic study in mid-century:

> With language studies, anthropological conceptions of culture gradually shifted from the external to the internal, from visible artifacts and behavior to invisible knowledge and cognition. (255)

MacDougall sees this trend continued in the influential work of Clifford Geertz, to whom he attributes an overemphasis on the invisible dimensions of culture in his definition of it as "an historically transmitted pattern of meanings embodied in symbols, a system of inherited conceptions expressed in symbolic form by means of which men communicate, perpetuate, and develop their knowledge about and attitudes towards life" (1973:89).

Ultimately it is perhaps less the emphasis on the invisible dimensions of culture that MacDougall objects to than Geertz's argument that this system of signs is primary in shaping the public, visual world and in distinguishing one group of people (one "culture") from another. MacDougall's goal is not simply to redefine culture but to "rethink the contribution that culture makes to both lived experience and personal identity" as Lucien Taylor puts it (20). For MacDougall, the "transcultural" qualities of film, which make it difficult to translate one social system into the terms of another, offer an advantage over writing in that they direct attention to the individual rather than the social context. Noting that ethnographic films tend to situate "individuals as experiencing subjects" in specific social scenarios and narratives, MacDougall states that these narrative forms

> ... make possible a view of social actors responding creatively to a set of open-ended cultural possibilities, rather than being bound by a rigid framework of cultural constraints. ... Perhaps in the perspectives of visual anthropology, individuals will be seen more often to 'refract' such a culture than to typify it. 'Culture' as a category may shrink, taking a more modest place beside social, economic, historical, and psychological factors. (271)

The advantage of the camera is in recording the contingent and improvisatory qualities of these interpersonal performances. Films make it clear that individuals are writing the script as they go and doing so in a subtle process of sensory cues and probes, contextualizing their words and actions as they interact with others. For MacDougall, previous conceptions of culture were inadequate primarily because they portrayed individuals as slaves to discrete and invisible moral worlds. They failed to fully capture aspects of experience which the "transcultural" qualities of film help to bring forth and render visible.

MacDougall's conception of "transcultural cinema" thus extends beyond the concerns of documentary film and brings together his interests in filmmaking and cultural anthropology. He pursues the intersections between these interests and explores their potential for being mutually beneficial. The "next culture" for MacDougall is a considerably reduced one: he calls for a view of the world less focused on separate mental worlds and more centered on cross-cultural exchanges and affinities. At the same time, MacDougall also presents a medium for examining these exchanges by proposing that we rethink and recast documentary film so that it is no longer a static document but a "mode of inquiry." *Transcultural Cinema* offers new perspectives toward culture by centering on visual representation and its potential for exploring creativity across cultural lines.

Works Cited

Abu-Lughod, Lila. "Writing Against Culture." In *Recapturing Anthropology. Working in the Present*, ed by Richard Fox. Santa Fe, NM: School of American Research Press, 1991.137-162.
Banks, Marcus and Howard Morphy, eds. *Rethinking Visual Anthropology*. New Haven: Yale University Press, 1997.
Brightman, Robert. "Forget Culture: Replacement, Transcendence, Relexification." *Cultural Anthropology* 10 (4) (1995):509-46.
Bruner, Edward. "Of Cannibals, Tourists, and Ethnographers." *Cultural Anthropology* 4 (4) (1989):438-435.
Fabian, Johannes. *Time and the Other. How Anthropology Makes its Object*. New York: Columbia University Press, 1983.
Geertz, Clifford. *The Interpretation of Cultures*. New York: Basic Books, 1973.
Ginsburg, Faye. "Indigenous Media: Faustian Contract or Global Village." *Cultural Anthropology* 6 (1) (1991):113-130.
Lutkehaus, Nancy "Excuse Me, Everything is Not All Right: On Ethnography, Film, and Representation. An Interview with Filmmaker Dennis O'Rourke. *Cultural Anthropology* 4 (4) (1989): 422-437.
MacDougall, David. *Transcultural Cinema*. Princeton, NJ: Princeton University Press, 1998.
Malinowski, Bronislaw. *Crime and Custom in Savage Society*. New York: Harcourt Brace and Co., 1926.

Marshall, John and Claire Richie. "Where are the Ju/Wasi of Nyae Nyae?" Capetown: Center for African Studies, 1984.
Myers, Fred. "From Ethnography to Metaphor: Recent Films from David and Judith MacDougall." *Cultural Anthropology* 3 (2) (1988):205-20.
Price, Sally. *Primitive Art in Civilized Places*. Chicago: University of Chicago Press, 1989.
Rosaldo, Renato "Imperialist Nostalgia." *Representations. Special Issue: Memory and Counter-Memory*. Spring, No. 26, 1989.107-122.
Steiner, Christopher "The Art of the Trade: On the Creation of Value and Authenticity in the African Art Market." In *The Traffic in Culture. Refiguring Art and Anthropology*, ed. by G. Marcus, F. Myers. Berkeley: University of California Press, 1995. 151-165.
Taylor, Lucien, ed. *Visualizing Theory: Selected Essays from V.A.R. 1990-1994*. New York: Routledge, 1994.
—. "Introduction." In *Transcultural Cinema* by David MacDougall. Princeton, NJ: Princeton University Press, 1998.
Volkman, Toby. "Out of South Africa: *The Gods Must be Crazy*." In *Image Ethics : the Moral Rights of Subjects in Photographs, Film, and Television*, ed by Larry Gross, John Stuart Katz, and Jay Ruby. New York: Oxford University Press, 1988. 236-247.

Films Cited:

Cannibal Tours. 1987. Dennis O'Rourke. Dennis O'Rourke and Associates (Australia), 70 mins.
The Gods Must Be Crazy. 1980. Jamie Uys. Twentieth-Century Fox.
In and Out of Africa. 1992. Ilisa Barbash and Lucien Taylor. Research by Christopher Steiner. Berkeley, CA: University of California, Extension Center for Media and Independent Learning, 59 mins.
Kayapo, Out of the Forest. 1989. Michael Beckham. Disappearing World Series, 53 mins.
N!ai. The Story of a !Kung Woman. 1980. John K. Marshall and Adrienne Miesmer. Documentary Educational Resources/Public Broadcasting Associates, 58 mins.
Taking Pictures. 1996. Les McLaren and Annie Stivan. Vingan Pty Limited Productions, 56 mins.

Films of David MacDougall
(Film dates indicate year of production/year of release.)

1967. *J. Lee Thompson: Director.* Columbia Pictures. 15 minutes. (Director/Camera).
1968/89. *Imbalu: Ritual of Manhood of the Gisu of Uganda.* Richard Hawkins and Suzette Heald. 75 minutes. Commendation, RAI Film Festival, 1990. (Camera).
1968/70. *Nawi.* 20 minutes. (Director/Camera).
1968/72. *To Live With Herds.* 70 minutes. Grand Prix Venezia Genti, Venice Film Festival, 1972. (Director/Camera).
1968/74. *Under the Men's Tree.* 15 minutes. (Director/Camera).
1970. *Man Looks at the Moon.* Encyclopaedia Brittanica Films. 25 minutes. (Writer/Director).
1972/74. *Kenya Boran.* American Universities Field Staff. 66 minutes. (Co-Director/Camera).
1974/77. *The Wedding Camels.* 108 minutes. RAI Film Prize, 1980. (Co-Director/Camera).
1974/79, *Lorang's Way.* 70 minutes. First Prize, Cinéma du Réel, 1979 (Co-Director/Camera).
1975/77. *Good-bye Old Man.* Australian Institute of Aboriginal Studies. 70 minutes. (Director/Camera).
1977/78. *To Get That Country.* Australian Institute of Aboriginal Studies. 70 minutes. (Director/Camera).
1977/80. *Familiar Places.* Australian Institute of Aboriginal Studies. 53 minutes. (Director/Camera).
1978/80. *Takeover.* Australian Institute of Aboriginal Studies. 90 minutes. (Co-Director/Camera).
1974/81. *A Wife Among Wives.* 75 minutes. (Co-Director/Camera).
1978/82. *Three Horsemen.* Australian Institute of Aboriginal Studies. 54 minutes. Finalist, Greater Union Awards, Sydney Film Festival, 1983. (Co-Director/Camera).
1982/84. *Stockman's Strategy.* Australian Institute of Aboriginal Studies. 54 minutes. (Co-Director/Camera).
1982/84. *Collum Calling Canberra.* Australian Institute of Aboriginal Studies. 58 minutes. Finalist, Best Documentary, Australian Film Awards, 1985. (Co-Director/ Camera).
1982/86. *Sunny and the Dark Horse.* Australian Institute of Aboriginal Studies. 85 minutes. (Co-Director/Camera).
1982/86. *A Transfer of Power.* Australian Institute of Aboriginal Studies. 22 minutes. (Co-Director/Camera).
1986/87. *Link-Up Diary.* Australian Institute of Aboriginal Studies. 86 minutes. (Director/Writer/Camera).

1988/91. *Photo Wallahs.* Fieldwork Films/Australian Film Commission/ Australian Broadcasting Corporation. 60 minutes. Award for Excellence, 1994 SVA/AAA Film Festival; Commendation, 1992 RAI Film Festival; Honorary Mention, 1992 Golden Gate Awards, San Francisco Film Festival. (Co-Director/Camera).

1992/93. *Tempus de Baristas.* (Time of the Barmen). Istituto Superiore Regionale Etnografico/Fieldwork Films & BBC Televison. 100 minutes. 1995 Earthwatch Film Award; Golden Plaque, 1994 Chicago Film Festival; Commendation, 1994 RAI Film Festival; 1994 komedia Award (Freiburg). (Director/Camera).

Mark Ingram's cultural anthropology/French studies dissertation focused on the politics of culture in France and was based on fieldwork with a touring theater company. He has published in the *French Review*, *Anthropological Quarterly*, and *Quaderni*. With Florence Martin, he recently co-wrote an article on the documentary film *Mémoires d'immigrés* for the forthcoming *Moving Pictures/Moving Cultures: Cinemas of Exile and Migration*. He is currently writing an ethnography based on his fieldwork.

Hearths and Minds:
Violence and Domesticity in a Hopi Life

Jennifer Lei Jenkins
University of Arizona

The Hopi people of northern Arizona base their cultural identity in peace and balance. "Hopivötskwani," the Hopi way, is the middle path, that of mediation and compromise. As Helen Sekaquaptewa shows in her autobiography, however, such balance is forged in conflict. Sekaquaptewa's account of her early life in *Me and Mine* reveals an uneasy dialectic of violence and domesticity in Hopi culture. The very tenets of Hopi mythology emerge from periods of cultural crisis and change. Patterns of migration and rest, the interdependence of clans for village survival, and the awareness of white men as a presence in Hopi cultural destiny—all reflect a tension of communal and anti-communal impulses. In *Me and Mine*, Sekaquaptewa examines her tribal history at the turn of the last century, when Hopi lifeways were challenged by Anglo insurgence and settlement. As Sekaquaptewa tells it, the Oraibi Split fulfills a pattern of Hopi mythic history in which, in a culture under pressure, domestic ritual intensifies and becomes its opposite, violence.

The Hopi creation story and related mythology are stories of migration. The Four Worlds of the Hopi define stages of cultural existence through which the People passed on their journey to this, the Fourth World. In each case, migration was necessitated by bad behavior on the part of some of the people. As Edmund Nequatewa explains, profound domestic disorder provoked the first migration:

> About this time, when the men had been falsely forgiven, the women were going around and running wild after the unmarried boys, so that they might break the hearts of their husbands and so be revenged. Their families were neglected and their fires and cooking were left unattended. Among both men and women there was not a soul who could be happy in such sinful days, for there was murder, suicide, and every other wicked thing that made the days darker and darker. (2)

Adultery, immodesty, and spite dominate the people's actions against one another in this time of crisis. The chief, Yai-hiwa, was "broken hearted" (2) and consulted with his advisors. After four days of prayers and requests for aid, emergence into the next world came through the intervention of birds, obviously symbols of transcendence. This story establishes the fundamental importance of domestic order within Hopi society, and counsels recourse to nature in times of trouble.

As Mockingbird sang into being the names and languages of the Upper World, the people emerged through the *sipapu*.[1] Emergence into this Fourth World led to a period of wandering during which the various Hopi and *Bahana*, the white older brother, traveled East to meet the Sun. All Hopi groups fell away from *Bahana*, who raced ahead to touch his forehead to the Sun. Edmund Nequatewa and Harry C. James remind us that Hopi mythology, like that of many Native People, has always contained a white figure who brings prophecy or change or assistance to the People (Nequatewa, 23 n. 14; James, 9).[2] As the Hopi reached the mesas, the first group discovered a bear carcass, and took it as their clan totem. The Bear clan established a village at Oraibi, and subsequent clans had to bring an important ceremony in order to join the village (James, 18-19). This pattern was repeated at each village. Thus village administration and religious tasks were distributed amongst the clans from the start. Indeed, specific ceremonials remain the responsibility of specific clans. As not every village houses every clan, not every village can host every ceremonial, such as the Snake ceremony. Hopi mythology, then, conveys three broad issues: a pattern of migration and rest; an interdependence amongst clans for village survival; and a mythological recognition of white men. All three of these mythic tenets bear upon the events at Oraibi that lie at the core of the violence and domesticity in Helen Sekaquaptewa's *Me and Mine*.

---

[1] The *sipapu* is the gateway from the last world to this one, a hole said to be located near the headwaters of the Little Colorado; each kiva has a small hole in the floor, also called a *sipapu*, to commemorate the People's journey. "When Mockingbird's songs were finished, no more people were permitted to enter the Upper World through Sipapu—as the entrance-way was, and still is, called" (James, 8).

[2] Nequatewa's interlocutor, Mary-Russell Colton, offered the following explanation of this racial binary in 1936. It perhaps tells us more about Anglo wish-fulfillment than Hopi views of racial difference:

> The legend of the Bahana, white brother, or white savior of the Hopi is firmly established in all the villages. He came up with the people from the underworld and was accredited with great wisdom, and he set out on the journey to the rising sun—promising to return with many benefits for the people. Ever since, his coming has been anticipated. It is said that when he returns there will be no more fighting and trouble, and he will bring much knowledge and wisdom with him. The Spanish priests were allowed to establish their missions in the Hopi country because of this legend, for the people thought that at last the Bahana had come. *Since that time they have suffered many similar disappointments, but they are still expecting the arrival of the 'true Bahana'.*
>
> The origin of the word *Bahana* is unknown, though there are several theories. Today, this word is a term used to describe the coming of the Spaniards.
>
> The belief that a powerful white savior is expected is common to all the pueblos of New Mexico as well as those of Arizona. (Nequatewa, 108, emphasis added)

*****

Helen Sekaquaptewa had an extensive American education for a Hopi woman of her upbringing and generation. Born in 1898, she went to day school in New Oraibi (Kykotsmovi) and to Indian boarding schools in Keams Canyon and Phoenix. Yet not until she met Louise Udall in 1957 did Helen think to tell her story in print. Louise Udall was an extremely generous interlocutor for the times: her presence is virtually invisible in the text. Helen tells her story in her own words, and the organization of events is her own.[3] There are several notable as-told-to Hopi autobio-graphies from Helen's generation, most notably Don Talayesva's [b.1890] *Sun Chief* as told to anthropologist Leo W. Simmons, Edmund Nequatewa's [b. 1880] *Born a Chief* as told to anthropologist Alfred Whiting, and Polingaysi Qoyawayma's (Elizabeth Q. White) *No Turning Back* as told to Vada F. Carlson. *Me and Mine* is unique in its matter-of-fact discussion of Hopi life in the absence of an anthropologist's controlling hand.[4]

Me and Mine begins with a catalog of activities that defined Hopi existence: farming, harvesting, and grinding corn. The rules and morés of food cultivation dictated behavior, thereby inculcating Hopi children with communal values and responsibilities. From very early in her life, Helen observed the domestic arena as a locus of potential threat. The community plaza was a place of public observation and, often, public commentary on one's actions. Hopi cultural values were reinforced by the power of gossip and ridicule, and no infraction was too small for comment. Ruth Benedict noted this tendency in the neighboring Zuni culture, likening it to Apollonian orderliness in ancient Greek culture in her famous (or infamous) essay, "The Pueblos of New Mexico." Benedict contends that the Puebloan value of community over the individual is an Apollonian trait:

> The known map, the middle of the road, to any Apollonian is embodied in the common tradition of his people. To stay always within it is to commit oneself to precedent, to tradition. Therefore, those influences that are powerful against tradition are uncongenial and minimized in their institutions, and the greatest of these is individualism. It is disruptive, according to Apollonian philosophy in the Southwest, even when it refines upon and enlarges the tradition itself. (80)

Like their nearest neighbors, the Zuni, the Hopi encouraged conformity through social and religious ritual. Selfishness, arrogance, and individualism

---

[3] For an excellent discussion of the complex colonialist implications of as-told-to autobiographies, see Sands.

[4] For an extended discussion of the development and compilation of *Me and Mine* as an autobiography, see Bataille and Sands, 99-101.

were seen as threats to the community as a whole, and were punished on a scale ranging from mockery and humiliation to physical violence and even threats of decapitation, as was the case at the Oraibi Split.[5]

One story suggests that the very founding of Oraibi village was a result of such pressure to conform. Edmund Nequatewa recounts in his compilation of Hopi mythic history that the youngest brother of the chief [kikmongwi] at Shungopavi village on Second Mesa was violating royal privilege by skimming off others' crops without growing his own. The people grumbled but were afraid to rebuke Ma-chito, the brother of their leader. Only when the leader discovered this behavior did the community feel free to speak: "Then all the other men thought that was their chance to say something to him and they all called him down. That hurt him more than anything else, and he left all the corn right there and went home" (31). The youngest brother left the village to become a hermit in the rocks near Third Mesa. When discovered, he would not speak to emissaries, and even refused his wife's plea to come home. She eventually joined him in moving atop the mesa and building Oraibi village. As Nequatewa concludes, "From then on, in the other villages, whoever got mistreated or got mad at something went over there to live. When other clans drifted in, Ma-chito didn't have many questions to ask of them, but just brought them in, for he wanted to get ahead of his brother and have more people in a short time" (32). This near-parable about the founding of Oraibi reminds us that even in mythic Hopi prehistory, domestic life contains an element of fractiousness. Helen Sekaquaptewa amplifies this dimension of Oraibi's founding in her account:

> The Chief told his older son to go to the East where the sun rises, and live there with his people. This is the origin of the white man. The younger brother was to live in Oraibi. He was to send for his older brother in time of trouble. If the older brother should ever come and find the Oraibi people backsliding into their old ways, or departing from the traditions, he should cut off the head of the Oraibi Chief and this would end the trouble. (227)

---

[5] The dialectic of creation/destruction, order/chaos, life/death that Benedict characterizes as Apollonian/Dionysiac is readily apparent to European-descended observers of American indigenous cultures. From the Coronado expedition forward, Europeans and their followers have noted such dichotomies. Hopi culture, while grounded in the peaceful marriage of opposites, articulates opposition quite moderately. The terms in Hopi language which best approximate Benedict's reading of Apollonian and Dionysiac may be *yuku*, meaning "creation," and its negation, *yukuna*. *Yuki* carries the sense of making, as well as of orgasm and generative creation; *yukuna* means to finish, to finish off, or to destroy. This is opposition on the practical level. Alternatively, *qatsi*, or existence, is opposed to *hin qatsi*, chaos or pandemonium. Film buffs may know the term *koyaanisqatsi*, life out of balance, from the Philip Glass score; the corrective to that is *suyanisqatsi*, life in harmony. For more on Hopi language, see the invaluable and comprehensive Hopi dictionary, *Hopìikwa Lavàytutveni*.

Ma-chito's obstinacy in founding Oraibi village is pointedly contained and domesticated by the threat of sibling vengeance. Here communal domestic standards are established, and any "backsliding" to lower worlds or lower standards carries a capital penalty.[6]

*****

Of course, domesticity carries dual connotations in Native American studies. Juxtaposed with the morés and rituals of domestic life within the tribe are the American government's attempts to "domesticate" Native populations after the so-called "closing of the frontier" announced by Frederick Jackson Turner in 1893. Military-style Indian Schools and coerced participation in vaccinations, land-use reform, stock reduction, and Anglo education—all were geared toward "domesticating," that is, taming and subduing, the American Indian. Such attempts were rarely gentle, and often were fraught with violence. (The Wounded Knee massacre is an obvious example, and the increasing number of Indian School captivity narratives being published is testament to the violence with which American domesticity was imposed upon Native children.) The historic and geographic autonomy of the Hopi people posed a marked challenge to the U.S. government, one that was met with both overt and covert domestic plans.

Around the turn of the 20th century, much pressure was being put on Hopi parents to send their children to the day school off the mesa. Indeed, in 1890 the government established a quota for Hopi childhood education, with the U.S. Army as the enforcement agency (Rushforth and Upham, 126). Resistant parents were labeled "Hostiles" or traditionalists, and were deprived of the tools and government distributions of clothes and food staples that the "Friendlies," or progressives, enjoyed. Navajo policemen were hired to chase the children and take them, forcibly if necessary, to school. This prompted what Helen calls "a serious and rather desperate game of hide-and-seek" (8) with dire consequences: the entire domestic arena, from family home to village plaza, became both a hiding place and a place of exposure, an indeterminate space of both security and danger. In this climate, the security of Hopi traditionalism into which many retreated had the effect of endangering rather than conserving their houses, farms, and their very cultural posterity.

This duality dominates Helen's account of her early life in Oraibi, as the pressure of Anglo influence and schooling grew. Once "caught," the children of Hostiles were marched off the mesa to Oraibi Day School where they were stripped of Hopi garb, bathed, dressed in government-issue clothing, and given Anglo names; the bath and clothing were repeated every week,

[6] While Bahana, or the white man, holds the mythic role of cultural arbiter in this story, historically the Hopi have suffered at white hands and had by Helen's time cultivated a healthy distrust of white visitors from any direction.

and the Anglo names became indelible. Helen describes her mother, a dedicated Hostile, stripping her of "the clothes of the detested white man" and calling her by her Hopi name, Dewawisnima, every day when she got home from school (12). This daily vacillation between Hopi and Anglo garments, codes of hygiene, language, and names could only unsettle these children's sense of self and blur the line between familiar and strange. Under such pressure, Hostiles became ever more committed to tradition, while Friendlies sought increasingly rapid adaptation to Anglo ways. Thus, the outside threat to Hopi culture as a whole produced internal divisions and stern adherence by Hostiles and Friendlies to their respective choices of cultural standards.

Children of Hostiles and Friendlies alike reverted to traditional Hopi home life in their games: domestic rituals seemed to offer comfort in these fractious times. At the Oraibi Day School, daughters of Friendlies would play house with traditional Hopi chicken- and sheep-bone dolls during recess. Their play mimicked Hopi domesticity, as Helen describes:

> ... the little girl reenacted family life, speaking for the characters, cooking, feeding, training her children, and as the day ended putting them to bed. There would be a quiet time; then, a cock would crow, the chickens would begin to talk, and the mother would get the family started on another day. ... Bone women gossiped and discussed their families and neighbors. (16)

Schoolyard play reproduced the violence of Hopi life, as well. Helen, being from a Hostile family, was not invited to play house with the other little girls: "I liked to stand near enough to listen and watch, but when they discovered what I was doing they would drive me away" (16). This bullying extended to the afterschool walk home, where the Friendly children gathered and threw rocks at the Hostile children making their way up the trail to Oraibi. The power of didactic role-playing with dolls—what Benedict would call an Apollonian activity—is enforced by a conversely Dionysiac frenzy of bullying and rock-throwing.

Even within traditional, non-Anglo influenced Hopi culture, domesticating rituals often contained violent dimensions. Initiations, seasonal ceremonials, and religious training relied upon a blending of opposites. Helen explains the children's first religious initiation, into a Kachina[7] Society:

> Kachinvaki is the first ceremony in which Hopi children participate, being the initiatory step into society; it is also called "The Whipping." It is in the nature of a baptism—that is, to drive out "the

---

[7] Kachinas are animist spirits which oversee Hopi religious and material life. They exist as ideals, and are represented by humans in ceremonials and in carved figurines. Kachinvaki, then, is initiation into kachina society. Since the regularization of Hopi orthography, this word is spelled *katsina*.

bad." It occurs in the spring of each year in connection with the Bean Dance. (23)

The "whipping" is done by Whipper kachinas who are armed with yucca strips. Whipper kachinas are the enforcers: they accompany the Mother Kachina as her moral policemen, and they also accompany the Ogres, who are said to eat naughty children.[8] The Kachinvaki is a ceremony that members of the village all over the age of seven enjoy because they are "in" on the purpose and drama of it. This communal event binds generations and neighbors together in the education of children. It also impresses the young initiates with the importance of participation in community:

> When the day came for Kachinvaki, my mother dressed me in freshly washed clothes. First she wrapped an old belt around my waist, next to my skin. It went around two or three times and I wondered at the time why the two belts? ... As we left the house to go to the kiva [my godmother] gave me an ear of corn which I was to hold in my hand all during the ceremony. (24-5)

This ritualized robing and the corn as talisman mark the initiate: they set the child apart as one whose rite of passage must be observed by the community. The sense of being watched and singled out is—in a culture deeply committed to the group as social unit—almost as fearsome as the pending confrontation with the kachinas. The storyteller in the kiva tells the initiates a tale full of moral guidance; Helen recalls that she could not remember it afterwards because of her fear and anticipation. The storyteller slowly raises the pitch of excitement to create suspense amongst the children:

> The kachinas were watching at the edge of the village. At the proper time, the man on the kiva roof stood up, and this was the signal to the man on the housetop to also stand, and the kachinas knew that it was time to come on the run so as to appear and enter the kiva as the storyteller said, "They are coming closer. Now they are here." We heard the two whipper kachinas making a lot of noise as they stopped and clanked the turtle shells fastened to their legs. They ran around the kiva four times before coming down the ladder into the kiva. With the whipper kachinas came a mother kachina, carrying in her arms a big bundle of fresh yucca to serve as whips ....
> It goes fast, with much crying. When a whip gets limp a new one—four yucca branches—is taken. The whippers take turns with the lash, while the mother whipper urges them on....(26-28) [This is "why the two belts."]

---

[8] For an excellent introduction to katsina culture, see Secakuku.

Occurring as it does in the kiva, the nexus of clan and village activity, this ritual is clearly meant to reinforce clan and kinship relations and values. Its chaotic and violent elements function not to punish or expel children from the community, but to induct and contain them within the village, family, and clan. Once Hopi children have been through Kachinvaki, they are deemed members of the community: the violence of the ritual domesticates the children by both taming and enculturating them.

Although Helen confesses that after the initiation she was "upset and scared" (28), she laments the disillusionment that comes three days after the whipping. Following a house-to house gift-giving ritual by kachinas, an all-night dance is held, and initiated children are allowed to see kachinas with their masks off. This rite of passage takes children from being the beneficiaries of kachina ceremonies to sharing village responsibility for the various rituals which their clan societies sponsor. Helen ruefully comments:

> It was quite an ordeal for me. When I went back to my home I wished I didn't know that a kachina was a man with a costume and a mask, when all the time I had thought they were real magic. (29)

Clearly, this domestication into cultural and religious societies is a ritual of violence, even when implied and enacted rather than "real." The whipping is not meant solely to draw blood, nor is it meant to be strictly punitive. For a Hopi, the mere experience of being singled out for attention is a kind of violence: teasing, mocking, and gossip all exist within the community in order to enforce—with differing degrees of intensity—conformity to the group's values. Kachinvaki singles out children and confronts them with enforcer kachinas in order to demonstrate the consequences of deviance within a safe, controlled environment. The revelation of the man behind the mask shows that exposing the "real magic" is part of the domesticating process. This object lesson takes place in the contained, safe space of the kiva; back out in the village, the consequences can be much more severe.

The fracture of Oraibi Village, which occurred in the same year as Helen's initiation, is the extreme example of the violence latent in Hopi domestic ritual. The "Oraibi Split" was at heart a difference over the degree to which Euro-American culture and influence should extend into Hopi life. A key figure in this division was Lololma, who had been the head of the Bear clan at Oraibi and therefore purportedly a Hostile (James, 131). After being convinced by trader Thomas Keam to visit Washington D.C. in the 1880s he embraced government efforts to "modernize" his people by moving them down from Oraibi to the valley floor, closer to the government school (Rushforth and Upham, 124). After Lololma's death in 1900, the two factions each had a leader in Oraibi village and tensions escalated. Conflict arose over an outbreak of smallpox. Convinced that the Anglos meant violence to their homes, Hostiles at Oraibi closed the village to vaccinations and home fumigation by the U.S. Government. Oraibi had established itself as the core of traditionalist, Hostile belief, and Hostiles from other villages across the mesas moved to Oraibi (Whiteley, *Deliberate Acts*, 105). Such fracture and removal carried dire consequences: because specific ceremonies belong to specific clans, village religious life had been disrupted, in some cases permanently.

In July of 1906 the Hostiles in Oraibi were sponsoring the Home Dance, which sees the kachinas off to their homes in the San Francisco peaks until after the next harvest. This important final ceremony of the kachina season involves kachinas entering the plaza at intervals through the day, and resting outside the village in between. On this occasion, politics collided with religious observance, as Helen explains:

> As the kachinas came to a narrow passage, where two houses were only ten feet apart, they found their way blocked by strong men of the Friendlies who had stationed themselves strategically and stepped out[,] quickly forming a line shoulder to shoulder, barring the way and preventing the kachinas from going through.
>
> It was beneath the dignity of the kachinas to physically contest this challenge. They argued for about an hour, rehearsing the traditional respect due them, to no avail. In humiliation the kachinas turned back and retired from the plaza to the resting place and there disrobed. This was a deliberate insult on the part of the Friendlies, with all eyes upon them. The tension built up to a fever heat, until by the end of the summer there were threats of driving the Hostiles out of the village. (67)

The insult to and humiliation of the kachinas occurs through exposure: by denying their supernatural qualities and exposing them as mere men, the Friendlies breach not only the social code but the religious one as well. As Sekaquaptewa notes, "traditional respect" was due the kachinas. The "deliberate insults" by the Friendlies set "all eyes upon" the Hostile kachinas, drawing attention to them not just as mortals, but as humiliated mortal members of the clan out of favor in the village. This is violence against the domestic community as well as blasphemy.

Around this time people began recalling a prophecy about a division of Oraibi which said that one group would be driven out of the village and off the mesa. The determining factor would be a test of strength: one party would push the other over a line on the ground. Adding to the mix was a group of "immigrant" Hostiles who had been exiled from Shungopavi village on Second Mesa for refusing to get smallpox vaccinations. By the first week of July 1906 rumors of assassination plots, government involvement, and prophesied violence were rampant. It was in this context that the Home Dance disruption occurred. On September 6, 1906 Tewaquaptewa, leader of the

Friendlies, ordered the Shungopavis to leave the village; their refusal elicited threats of bodily removal, and then the Friendlies acted upon their threats. Helen Sekaquaptewa was a child of seven, and experienced this removal:

> There was a great commotion as the Friendlies carried out the Hostiles, pushing and pulling, the Hostiles resisting, struggling, kicking, and pulling the hair of their adversaries. The Hostiles were taken bodily, one by one to the northern outskirts of the village, and put down on the far side of a line which had been scratched in the sandstone, parallel to the village, some time before. (75)

Helen was among the women and children who were herded from the village by Tewaquaptewa's "Friendly" men, and recalls that, ironically, "they looked wild-eyed and exhibited real fanaticism, for this event was the result of deep traditions" (75). Eventually the conflict came down to a physical contest between Tewaquaptewa, the leader of the Friendlies, and Yukioma, the leader of the Hostiles. They faced each other across the Line and began pushing each other's shoulders. Yukioma, being older, taller, and thinner, was raised up by the Friendly crowd and passed over the Line. This determined the final expulsion of Hostiles from Oraibi. What Helen does not tell us is that the traditionalist Yukioma then went to the local whites and demanded the beheading of the progressive Tewaquaptewa as the prophesied and ordained penalty for abandoning Hopi traditions. The Indian Agent and the neighboring Mennonites refused to support this outcome, looking as Bahana had to the East—Washington—for mediation (Whiteley, *Bacavi*, 57-61). Within three days the Hostiles were forced to leave the vicinity of Oraibi and wander to the spring at Hotevilla, some eight miles away. Following the mythic pattern, they took specific ceremonies with them, religious rituals which were no longer performed in Oraibi. As other Hostiles sought to join the group at Hotevilla, they argued their cases in terms of the ceremonies and religious rites they could bring to the village. Eventually the villages of Hotevilla and Bacavi were established by these exiled Hostiles, and only in the 1960s did Oraibi recoup some of its lost clan ceremonies through marriages and adoptions. The price of enforcing domestic order on both sides was physical violence, and more importantly, perhaps, violence to the ceremonies and religious stability of both factions. For many years a condition prevailed of *koyaanisqatsi*, life out of balance, which in Hopi lore heralds the end of this world and a new migration.

The deeply-held feelings that led to the Oraibi split prevailed long after the founding of Hotevilla and its offshoot village Bacavi. When Helen returned home after thirteen years away at school at Keams Canyon and Phoenix Indian School, her Hostile family rebuked her for her education and Bahana clothing. After her mother's death from influenza, Helen's traditional right as the youngest daughter to her mother's house was usurped.

Despite being what Helen calls " a true Traditional all her life" (145), Helen's older sister Verlie defied custom and moved her own large family into the mother's house. Helen recalls that "[t]his placed me in an awkward position, a sort of outsider with no place nor part in the family" (151). By ousting her younger sister and defying the Hopi tradition of ultimageniture, Verlie did violence against the very way of life she despised her sister for leaving. In denying familial and property rights, Verlie attempted to make Helen a cultural orphan. This symbolic exile replicates, on a familial level, the Oraibi split and expulsion of members of the village. This time, however, the Hostile Verlie kept the house and the Anglicized Helen was left to wander.

What is remarkable about Helen Sekaquaptewa is the way in which she managed to honor both her education and her Hopi upbringing. Trained to be a "domestic" at the Phoenix Indian School, Helen brought Anglo ways back to Hotevilla after her marriage to Emory Sekaquaptewa. She canned food, used cloth diapers, sewed on a sewing machine, and took her babies to the Anglo doctor. She also made a home for her unmarried brothers, took in abandoned and orphaned children to raise along with her own, and followed Hopi custom in attending kiva ceremonials and upholding obligations to family and neighbors. In response to her domesticating efforts, she experienced local and symbolic violence: diapers and machine-sewn clothes disappeared off her clothesline, her neighbors blamed her for outbreaks of scabies amongst the animals and skin diseases amongst the villagers and "I was aware that my neighbors were talking about me, laughing at me, mimicking, and generally belittling me all the time. ... I could feel critical eyes following my every move" (187). Communal scrutiny, first experienced at Kachinvaki, remains in Hopi culture as a domesticating force, a form of acceptable violence within the village.

Me and Mine examines religious life, gender roles, and social morés as directly derived from this mythic context. Patterns of defensive domesticity and fractious violence seem endemic to the Hopi culture Helen Sekaquaptewa describes: the tales and tenets of Hopi prehistory contain this oppositional ethos, from the story of the founding of Oraibi through the prophecies of the Split. Again and again, in periods of cultural pressure, Hopi communal domestic practice intensifies and escalates to become its opposite as domesticity transforms into danger. In myth, oral tradition, and archival 20th century history, all degrees of cultural violence—from village gossip and scrutiny, fist-fights, exile, and threats of beheading—protected and enforced Hopi domestic values. Helen herself functions as a binary figure in her narrative: initially a conservative victim of the Friendlies' wrath at Oraibi, she later returned to Hotevilla as a force for change, only to incur Hostile condemnation for her progressive ways. Ever the iconoclast, Helen Sekaquaptewa resolves complex issues of clan history, cultural integrity, and prophecy by taking "a combination of what we thought was the good of both cultures" (186). In doing so, ironically, she embraces the Hopi sense of balance, effectively turning the dialectic of violence and domesticity into a synthesis, molding *koyaanisqatsi* into *suyanisqatsi*, life in harmony.

Works Cited

Bataille, Gretchen and Kathleen Mullen Sands. *American Indian Women Telling Their Lives*. Lincoln: University of Nebraska Press, 1984.
Benedict, Ruth. "The Pueblos of New Mexico." *Patterns of Culture*. Boston: Houghton Mifflin, 1959: 57-129.
Hopi Dictionary Project. *Hopi Dictionary/Hopìikwa Lavàytutveni*. Bureau of Applied Research in Anthropology. Tucson: University of Arizona Press, 1998.
James, Harry C. *Pages From Hopi History*. Tucson: University of Arizona Press, 1974; rpt.ed, 1994.
Nequatewa, Edmund. *Truth of a Hopi*. Flagstaff, Museum of Northern Arizona, 1936, 1967; Flagstaff: Northland Press, 1994.
—. *Born a Chief*. As told to Alfred Whiting. Tucson: University of Arizona Press, 1993.
Qoyawayma, Polingaysi (Elizabeth Q. White). *No Turning Back*. As told to Vada F. Carlson. Albuquerque: University of New Mexico Press, 1964.
Rushforth, Scott and Steadman Upham. *A Hopi Social History: Anthropological Perspectives on Sociocultural Persistence and Change*. Austin: University of Texas Press, 1992.
Sands, Kathleen Mullen. "Collaboration or Colonialism: Text and Process in Native American Women's Autobiographies." *MELUS* 22.4 (Winter 1997): 39-59.
Secakuku, Alph H. *Following the Sun and Moon: Hopi Kachina Tradition*. Flagstaff: Northland Press, 1996.
Sekaquaptewa, Helen. *Me and Mine: the Life Story of Helen Sekaquaptewa as told to Louise Udall*. Tucson: University of Arizona Press, 1969.
Talayesva, Don. *Sun Chief*. As told to Leo W. Simmons. New Haven: Yale University Press, 1942.
Whiteley, Peter. *Bacavi: Journey to Reed Springs*. Flagstaff: Northland Press, 1988.
—. *Deliberate Acts: Changing Hopi Culture through the Oraibi Split*. Tucson: University of Arizona Press, 1988.

Jennifer Lei Jenkins teaches interdisciplinary courses on cultures of the Americas, journey motifs in world literature, and will soon pilot a course on Orientalism in western art, literature and culture. She has written on gothic domesticity in Harriet Beecher Stowe and Henry James, on unholy pilgrimage in *Lolita*, and is currently working on a study of violence and domesticity in the literature of the Arizona-Sonora borderlands.

The Power of Kinship

Roger Dunsmore
University of Montana

Kinship, the fact of our relatedness to each other, has been the backbone of tribal existence not only in North America but throughout the world, and anthropologists have paid considerable attention to it. It gives rise to a very different kind of *self* than what is taken for granted in Euro-American culture where a form of truncated "individualism," the separate self in competition with others, has such overriding value. In contrast, the Native self became "co-extensive with the universe," to use Dorothy Lee's phrase. I want to show how this deep expression of kinship, or relatedness, was used to heal wounds within the tribe, how it is extended to other species, and what the implications of this might be. But first, a contemporary account so we will have a clear understanding of what is meant by Kinship, at least in one tribe.

Leslie Silko, the Laguna Pueblo writer, presents the force of this kinship or relatedness idea *within the tribe* through her character Auntie in the novel *Ceremony*. Auntie, with her strict Catholic morality, is one of the least attractive characters in the book, but her nephew, Tayo, understands the source of her fear and moralisms:

> An old sensitivity had descended in her, surviving thousands of years from the oldest times, when the people shared a single clan name ... from before they were born and long after they died, the people shared the same consciousness ... the ability to feel what the others were feeling in the belly and chest.... When Little Sister had started drinking wine and riding in cars with white men and Mexicans, the people could not define their feeling about her ... they were losing her, they were losing part of themselves.... For the people, it was that simple, and when they failed, the humiliation fell on all of them; what happened to the girl did not happen to her alone, it happened to all of them. (Silko, 1971, 70-71)

In this passage Silko makes abundantly clear that the meaning of Kinship goes far beyond what the so-called "dominant" culture means by the term. For the Lagunas, the sense of belonging to the people, of kinship, meant sharing "the same consciousness," it meant that what happened to one of them "did not happen to her alone, it happened to all of them." This is a clear expression of a self deeply connected to others who form what is called a tribe. The etymology of the word *tribe*, in fact, includes the Latin base word for *to become*, the future tense of *to be*. To be, fully, is to be a part of the people. That is *being* with a future to it. The individual is thus enhanced, not stifled, by a healthy collective. The intact social structure supplies an enabling framework. This is the paradox of individualism: when it is construed as set over against the social life of the people it becomes a destructive parody of itself. But when one's social roles are clear and valued, one is freed to fulfill them from the depths of the self.

Indian writer and anthropologist, Ella Deloria, considering her own people, the Dakota, devotes a whole section of her book, *Speaking of Indians,* to the role of kinship in Dakota life. "I can safely say," she says, "that the ultimate aim of Dakota life, stripped of accessories, was quite simple: One must obey kinship rules; one must be a good relative" (17). This deep obligation "to be a good relative" is embedded in the linguistic and religious structures of the Dakota. Deloria tells us, "The Dakota words 'to address a relative' and 'to pray'... are not really two; they are one (word). *Wacekiya* means both acts.... *Wacekiya* implies that in every meeting of two minds the kinship approach is imperative;... It is tantamount to smoking the ... pipe; in fact, to smoke ceremonially is to *wacekiya*" (20).

Deloria goes on to give an even more startling account of how kinship was used to heal the most serious wounds within the tribe, the murder of one Dakota by another.

> ... occasionally the power of kinship rose to its sublime height. The murder of a fellow Dakota was a crime punishable either through immediate reprisal by the kinsmen of the slain or a resort to the ancient ordeals....
>
> However, now and again, influenced by exceptionally wise leadership, the relatives of a murdered man might agree not to shoot the murderer or demand the ordeal for him, but instead to win his abiding loyalty through kinship. This they did by actually adopting him to be one of them in place of his victim.... I have a most impressive account of such an episode, which I transcribed in the Dakota language while old Simon Antelope, a well known, reliable Yankton, told it....
>
> The angry younger relatives debated the kind of punishment fitting the crime while their wise elder listened, seemingly in accord with them. But after a good while, he began to speak.
>
> 'My Brothers and Cousins, my Sons and Nephews, we have been caused to weep without shame.... No wonder we are enraged, for our pride and honor have been grossly violated. Why shouldn't we go out, then, and give the murderer what he deserves?'
>
> Then, after an ominous pause, he suddenly shifted into another gear:
>
> 'And yet, my kinsmen, there is a better way!'
>
> Slowly and clearly he explained that better way. They were men of standing, he reminded them, and therefore it was becoming

in them to act accordingly. He challenged them to reject the traditional and choose the better way. It was also the hard way, but the only certain way to put out the fire in all their hearts and in the murderer's.

'Each of you bring to me the thing you prize the most. These things shall be a token of our intention. We shall give them to the murderer who has hurt us, and he shall thereby become 'something to us' (an idiom for relative) in place of him who is gone. Was the dead your brother? Then this man shall be your brother. Or your uncle? Or your cousin? As for me, he was my nephew; and so this man shall be my nephew. And from now on, he shall be one of us, and our endless concern shall be to regard him as though he were truly our loved one come back to us.'

And they did just that. The slayer was brought to the council not knowing what his fate was to be. Steeling himself for the worst, he kept his eyes averted. He did not try to infer the decision by peering into the councilmen's faces....

But when the council's speaker offered him the peace pipe saying, 'Smoke now with these your new relatives, for they have chosen to take you to themselves in place of one who is not here,' his heart began to melt.

'It is their heart's wish that henceforth you shall be one of them; shall go out and come in without fear. Be confident that their love and compassion which were his are now yours forever!' And, during that speech, tears trickled down the murderer's face.

'He had been trapped by loving kinship,' my informant said, 'and you can be sure that he made an even better relative than many who are related by blood, because he had been bought at such a price.'

And what might easily have become burning rancor and hatred, perhaps leading to further violence, was purged ... from the hearts of all. (23-24)

This is the most compelling account I know of the power of kinship operating within a society to heal wounds inflicted by our human propensity for violence. One begins to understand why the Dakota had a single word for addressing a relative, for praying, and for smoking the pipe: *Wacekiya*.

II

The crucial thing to remember about the importance of kinship for Native peoples is that they did not confine their concept of it to the human sphere only, but recognized their participation in a wider kinship that extended to other species, to other forms of life. This recognition of a broader kinship, or relatedness, is *the* essential idea for grounding an environmental ethic, vision, practice.

In a dramatic statement about relationship to other species in which a pejorative term is transformed by verbal jujitsu we see this experience of connection in its starkest relief:

> The Indian believes that he is a cannibal—all of his life he must eat his brothers and his sisters and deer and corn which is the mother, and the fish, which is the brother.... All our lives we must eat off them and be a cannibal, but when we die, then we can give back all that we have taken, and our body goes to feed the worms that feed the birds. And it feeds the roots of the trees and the grass so that the deer can eat it and the birds can nest in the tree. And we can give back. But today we can't even do this, you know. They poison our bodies and we can't bury our people. We have to be put in boxes to wait for some life, you know, that's going to be.... we are all going to rise up, which is so ... different from the way we feel about our bodies and giving back. (Armstrong, # 245, p.160)

Implicit in this statement is an understanding that we are all related. The fact of being alive, of eating, involves us in deep debt to other species, which we must somehow pay back, at least in our death if not in our lives. Gratitude, then, becomes the most appropriate response to the other forms of life on which we depend. And though in this statement the other species mentioned are deer, corn, fish, grass, in works such as Silko's *Ceremony* even the fly, the green bottle fly in particular, has its place in the people's stories about how they have been able to survive in this world, and deserve respect, are not to be killed nonchalantly. Even the flies, for they can get through the cracks in the world to the four worlds below this one to carry messages to the All-Mother. *Mitakuye Oyasin,* [all my relations], the Lakota expression used variously, especially when emerging from the sweat lodge or to end a ceremony, expresses this overall sense of relatedness to all things.

I suspect that if there is such a thing as "original sin" lurking in the dark corners of the soul of Western man, it really isn't because sex is "dirty," or because we are simply too filled with desire and covetousness; if one looks from the expanded kinship perspective of Native peoples, it appears that the "original sin" beneath the surface of Euro-American theology might really have to do with the separation of ourselves from all other forms of life—which permits *us* to use *them* with little or no compunction about the use we make of them—their utility value overcomes their value as beings. So-called "progress," then, is dependent upon having turned on the other species, without acknowledging a debt or connection with them. It is this sheer ingratitude that has given rise to the many Native terms for Euro-Americans that translate as "grabbing creature" or "fat grabbers" or *suyapi,* from an old coyote story in Salish. This is not to condemn everything that Western society has created in the last 10,000 years, but it is to locate the enormity of the ecological work before us. What ecology entails is the reconsideration of all the other forms of life and our relationship to them in the interest of reestablishing balance, or harmony, morality and *proper behavior* in our way of living on this planet. The Native experience of kinship has this insight, this power within it. We feel this spirit in the wilderness. This is the depth of ecology we are obligated to accept.

Euro-America is haunted by, and has not recovered from, that moment in its early history as recounted in the *Book of Genesis*. According to the ancient beginning story, God said to Noah, on his emergence from the Ark...

> the fear of you and the dread of you shall rest on every animal of the earth, on every bird of the air, on everything that creeps on the ground, and on all the fish of the sea;   into your hand they are delivered. Every moving thing that lives shall be food for you and just as I gave you the green plants, I give you everything. (Genesis, 9, 2-4)

How chilling, and how different from the stories of connection recounted by Native Americans!

Leslie Silko's "Story From Bear Country," for instance, recounts how some individuals have been called out of their human selves all the way into animal form, in this case, into the world of bear.

> We can send bear priests
> loping after you
> their medicine bags
> bounding against their chests....
>
> They will try to bring you
> step by step
> back to the place you stopped
> and found only bear prints in the sand
> where your feet had been.
>
> .... When they tracked him the next day
> his tracks went into the canyon
> near the place which belonged
> to the bears. They went
> as far as they could
> to the place
> where no human
> could go beyond,
> and his little footprints
> were mixed in with bear tracks....

> There wasn't much time....
> He was already walking like his sisters
> he was already crawling on the ground.
> They couldn't just grab the child.
> They couldn't simply take him back
> because he would be in-between forever
> and probably he would die.
> They had to call him.
> Step by step the medicine man
> brought the child back.
>
> So, long time ago
> they got him back again
> but he wasn't quite the same
> after that
> not like the other children. (Silko, 1981, 204-09)

This "Story From Bear Country" takes place in a world where the lines of separation between humans and other species are not yet firm, where someone might be called over or out into another kind of existence. How that calling occurs is difficult to explain, she tells us, but irresistible. "You will never want to return/Their beauty will overcome your memory." Beauty has the power to call the "you" of this story both ways, to the world of the bears and back to human shape again. We have not under-stood the absoluteness of beauty in Native cultures, nor in ecology, as a primal power in all of nature. It is easy, for example, for Navajos to sell their jewelry or weavings because the power resides in the capacity to make them rather than in the objects themselves. Or consider the power of perfumes and the colors of flowers in attracting pollinators. How far this story of bear country is from "the fear of us and the dread of us." How far from "original sin." The call of the wild is the call of the beauty of the bears, and of that *place which belongs to them.*

In this Native story of kinship, the relationship between humans and bears is presented as close enough to be attractive, to be dangerous, to draw young humans into the bear world. Those who have been through the experience, and who have returned, are not the same again. Perhaps they become bear priests. But the story implies that humans need those who have been called out into the world of bears and others and never quite get all the way back again.

This story, like thousands more from Native peoples, speaks of transformation, of crossing over species boundaries, engendering connections among peoples who have not separated from other species. These stories also express another kind of human self, another, older way of being. They are stories of a greater kinship that Euro-America has chosen to forgot. They are the stories that are necessary now in order for us to re-member our selves among the earlier nations of the earth.

What are we to do with this information? It is beautiful and very moving, but most of us are not Lakota, we are not Laguna. We do not live the same lives as they did, and do. It makes us feel nostalgia for what has been lost. It makes us feel guilt at the role of Euro-American culture in the destruction of this older world. We wish for a different culture than the one we now live in.

But these old/new stories of relationship provide us with a vantage point from which to examine the values of Euro-American society. For instance, how important is kinship in American society today? Why have dogs and plants and stones been denied the sort of value that would enable us to respond to them as kin? What have we lost as a result of this denial? What kind of human being might be possible if we begin to act on the idea of the value of our relationships with all things? What sort of society or world might be possible if we embraced this indigenous perspective?

Further, how might people enact such behavior? What's astonishing about Simon Antelope's story is that it offers the possibility of a whole society acting in a way that shows what might be possible if such an outrageous precept as "love thine enemies" were taken seriously. Perhaps Jesus was speaking from older tribal knowledge?

When we read Silko's "Story From Bear Country" we are reminded of all the stories of children raised by wolves and wild dogs. It resonates with the old genesis story of the city of Rome, and its ancestral founders, Romulus and Remus, who were raised by a she-wolf. What is the meaning of that ancient connection to wolves as nurturing mothers in the foundation story of an empire not unlike our own?

We cannot become traditional Indians of North America, but their stories give us the opportunity to enlarge our views, our possibilities; they give us a greater set of alternatives. These stories ask us to ponder our own situation. They teach us that being human is a much richer experience than Euro-Americans imagine.

Further, let us compare Jesus's claim, "the Kingdom of Heaven is within you," with that of another teacher, a Lakota, *Miniconju* [Planters by the Water], John Fire/Lame Deer from his autobiography, *Lame Deer, Seeker of Visions*. His mother has just died and Lame Deer had gone up on a hill to pray, to ask for guidance and for help. He hears the voice of an eagle, "loud above the voices of many other birds ..."

> 'Let our voices guide you. We are your friends, the feathered people, the two-legged, the four-legged,... the creatures, little tiny ones, eight legs, twelve legs—all those who crawl on the earth. All the little creatures which fly, all those under water. The powers of each one of us we will share with you and you will have a ghost with you always—another self....'
>
> I was frightened. I didn't understand it then. It took me a lifetime to find out.

> And again I heard the voice amid the bird sounds,... 'You have love for all that has been placed on this earth, not like the love of a mother for her son, or of a son for his mother, but a bigger love which encompasses the whole earth. You are just a human being, afraid, weeping under that blanket, but there is a great space within you to be filled with that love. All of nature can fit in there.' ... [T]he voices repeated themselves over and over again, calling me, 'Brother, brother, brother.' So this is how it is with me. All of nature is in me, and a bit of myself is in all of nature." (Lame Deer, 126)

If we are not to be overwhelmed and shamed by the history of Indian/white contact, we need to find this Native version of the kingdom of heaven within us, to find that great space in us which can be filled with the love that is bigger than that between mother and son, which encompasses the whole earth, where "all of nature can fit." This experience opens for Lame Deer a "ghost self," as the eagle has told him, a self that will always be with him, a greater self than the egoic one. This experience of another self, which has within it to embrace and be embraced by all of nature, is ancient and widespread in the indigenous traditions of the world. It is one of the great gifts of our ancestral human heritage. Not to remember this will make us prey to a vast emptiness within that will be filled with lesser things—for nature abhors a vacuum.

How do we accomplish this? If it is true that there are spirit beings of birds and mountains and green bottle flies sharing this world with us, as all the traditional cultures of the world attest, and if it is true that we have within us a vast space that can be filled with a bigger love, that can contain all of nature, then it behooves us to learn to apprehend it, to be quiet, to listen to what comes from deep within and without. It behooves us to build again the skills that will allow us to perceive this beauty and then to generate it.

Perhaps we are not without aid in this undertaking. Consider this idea from Aboriginal Australia:

> Certain Australian (Aboriginals) assert that one cannot conquer foreign soil because in it there dwell strange ancestor-spirits who reincarnate themselves in the newborn. The foreign land assimilates its conquerors. (Jung, 49)

The primary task before us is to become native to North America, truly native to this place. To learn where we actually are and how to conduct ourselves appropriately here, to not impose habits of mind and being emanating from our foreign ancestry. The idea of the power of kinship, not only among ourselves but between ourselves and other life-forms, is central to this task. Not to become Indians, but to learn from their experience of this place. Basho, a 17th century Japanese poet puts it this way,

> Do not follow
> in the footsteps
> of the ancient ones.
> Seek what they sought.

Dorothy Lee, writing a generation ago in her book *Freedom and Culture*, describes the old Dakota values in terms that echo this kinship ideal:

> ... an individual had to, was responsible to, increase, intensify, spread, recognize this (experience of) relationship. To grow in manliness, in humanness, in holiness, meant to plunge deeper into the relatedness of all things. (p. 61-62)

This is a "humanism," worthy of the name, not the Greco-Renaissance "man is the measure of all things." If the Australian Aboriginals are right, and the ancestor spirits of this land—North, Turtle Island, America—will reincarnate themselves in us, then these old stories of kinship with murderers and bears (and corn and stones) will take us in, guide us in the proper conduct here in this place.

Finally, for those of us of European ancestry who take up these stories from Native America, it is necessary to study and preserve the history of the European invasion and domination of this continent over the past five hundred years. This history is so treacherous, so cruel and twisted that to refer to it as a holocaust or as a centuries-long genocide is to understate its destructive evil. We may be so affected by what has happened in Kosovo and Yugoslavia because we have been the Serbs here in North America for centuries. The historical record of the devastation of this continent, of its peoples and native species, by the invading Europeans is full, clear, and abominable. And it goes on. The combined Puritan forces nearly destroyed the Pequods within 17 years of landing at Plymouth Rock in 1637. The Puritans burned the Pequod's town to the ground and everyone left in it, giving those who were captured to the Pequod's enemies as slaves, and justifyied their activities by quoting scripture. Here are the words of John Mason, the leader of the Puritan forces:

> Great and doleful was the bloody sight to the view of young soldiers that never had been in war, to see so many souls lie gasping on the ground, so thick, in ... places, that you could hardly pass.... It may be demanded, Why should you be so furious? (as some have said). Shouldn't Christians have more mercy and com-passion? But I would refer you to David's war. When a people is grown to such a height of blood, and sin against God and man, ... there he hath no respect to persons, but harrows them, and saws them, and puts them to the sword, and the most terriblest death that may be. Sometimes the

Scripture declareth women and children must perish with their parents. Sometimes the case alters; but we will not dispute it now. We had sufficient light from the word of God for our proceedings. (Hauptman and Wherry, 73 and 76)[1]

It is worth noting that our revised versions of the Bible render this event much more palatable by saying that David "set the people to work with saws and iron axes and picks, and in the brick works," slave labor being more acceptable to us than genocide. The Puritans, however, worked from a harsher translation. Mason, the Puritan expeditionary leader, described their intent to "cut off remembrance of them (the Pequods) from the earth," and the General Assembly of Connecticut declared the very name "Pequod" extinct, until the name was resurrected in *A Son of the Forest by William Apess, a Pequod*, which appeared in the 1820s.

When the new American government could not pay its war veterans after the Revolutionary War they were given ceded Indian lands as payment, the government knowing full well that the soldiers would intimidate the Indians, because they were military men and armed fighters. The cases of bacteriological warfare against Indians are well-known. The use of whiskey to weaken whole tribes and affect their judgement during treaty-making was widespread.[2] The killing of Indian babies because "nits make lice" was not an uncommon practice. The accumulation of wealth from Indian lands was a means to achieve political power for Washington, Jefferson, Jackson, and a host of governors. Where did the land for the National Bison Range north of Missoula came from? 18,000 acres of land were taken in this century from the Flathead Reservation, and the paltry sums paid them were then used to administer the opening of the Reservation to white settlement in 1910.

The death, destruction and domination continues. Which is the most nuclear bombed nation in the world? The Western Shoshone, over, on and within whose land more than nine hundred nuclear devices have been detonated. Where are the toxic waste dumps in this country located? Why is the life expectancy of reservation Indian people little more than fifty years today? Why were the Navajos who worked the uranium mines for our first atomic bombs and reactors neither told of nor protected from the health hazards of nuclear radiation? Why do the radioactive tailings from those mines blow

[1] cf. II Samuel, ch. 12, 29-31: "And David gathered all the people together, and went to Rabah, and fought against it and took it.... And he brought forth the spoil of the city in great abundance. And he brought the people that were therein, and put them under saws and under harrows of iron, and under axes of iron, and made them pass through the brick-kiln; and thus did he unto all the cities of the children of Ammon."

[2] Indian whiskey was such a mixture of lime, gunpowder, strychnine, rattlesnake heads, axle grease, red ink, chewing tobacco and other lethal substances that traders could use to jack up the watered-down rot-gut, that many Indian people died from drinking it.

around on the Navajo Reservation to this day, and seep into their water, causing a much higher incidence of cancer than elsewhere(cf. Ward Churchill)?

If a hundred years from now the grandchild of an ethnic Albanian from Kosovo happens to visit her grandparents' old country and talks to some Serbs who live there, what would she feel if, even as they lived in her grandparents' house and farmed their fields, mined their minerals, lived off the fat of their land, they said to her: "That's all in the past. We didn't do anything to you. Why should we have hard feelings because of what was done a hundred years ago?" What are the consequences of ethnic cleansing in the United States? Here are the words of a Navajo high school student written in the late 1980s after we studied oral accounts of the Long Walk, wherein the Navajos, in the 1860s, were force-marched four hundred miles to a prison camp in New Mexico, during which pregnant women who couldn't keep up were taken to the end of the column and shot:

> I never knew so much hate
> could one person have
> as when I read about
>
> pregnant women getting killed
> because they could not walk anymore.
> I think the only really big thing that happened to me
> was that my emotions could not handle all the sorrow
> and it turned to anger.
>
> Only when it turned to anger
> did I relieve myself of this terrible burden.
> I killed a crow at one hundred yards
> with the wind blowing in gusts.
> It was an almost impossible shot.
> But one bullet was all I needed that day.
> I was surprised to see my bullet find its mark
> as the crow slid down into the ravine where it was standing.

Here we see pain carried inside the people for three or four generations, before it has a chance to be expressed. The memory of this long-standing pain is seared into the minds of these Najaho high school students today, as it had been seared into the minds of their parents and grandparents.

Today, as we take up these Indian materials, it is imperative that we understand how cultural imperialism continues. It means: Now that you have killed off the majority of us and taken most of our lands, you also want our cultures, our spirit, our dreams? Do you think you can take these things as easily as you took the land?

Given this historical situation, how should Euro-Americans treat Indian materials? We must begin by taking a long, hard look at the history itself, at the consequences of it. We must try to grow up in terms of our respect for the people, the land, the dreams and stories of Native America. Respect means patience, not covetousness. Respect means doing the work to know the history, to know the people, to actually share some of their pain and struggle. Respect means listening, but with clear discrimination. It involves learning something of our own ancestry: the Scots and Irish, for instance, were treated barbarously by the British, so it was no surprise to them how the Puritans treated the Indians. Respect means understanding that the history of the last five hundred years does have an effect on peoples' lives and thoughts and feelings, on their spirits. Respect means knowing you have to earn "a mind to obey nature." As Silko has Sunrise Woman say in *Ceremony*, "[I]t won't be easy." But it is time to begin. Ah ho!

Works Cited

Armstrong, V. I. *I Have Spoken*. Chicago: Swallow, 1971.
Churchill, Ward. *A Little Matter of Genocide*. San Francisco: City Lights, 1997.
Deloria, Ella. *Speaking of Indians*. University of South Dakota, Vermillion, 1983.
Hauptman, Laurence M., and Wherry, James D. *The Pequods in Southern New England, The Fall And Rise of an American Indian Nation*. Norman and London, University of Oklahoma Press, 1990.
Jung, Carl. "Mind and Earth." *Contributions to Analytic Psychology*. Trans. C.F. and H.G. Baynes. London: Routledge and Kegan Paul, 1928.
Lame Deer, J. F. *Lame Deer, Seeker of Visions*. New York: Simon and Schuster, 1972.
Lee, Dorothy. *Freedom and Culture*. New York: Prentice Hall, 1959.
Silko, L. M. *Ceremony*. New York: New American Library, 1977.
—. *Storyteller*. New York: Seaver Books, 1981.

Roger Dunsmore has taught American Indian Literature and Nature Poetry in environmental and wilderness studies programs at the University of Montana since 1969. During 1988-89 he trained teachers as the Humanities Scholar in Residence at Tuba City, Arizona on the Navajo Reservation. He has published two volumes of poetry, *On the Road to Sleeping Child Hotsprings* (1977) and *Bloodhouse* (1987), and three chapbooks. The title poem from his chapbook, *The Sharp-Shinned Hawk,* was nominated for a Pushcart Prize by the Koyukon writer Mary TallMountain. His collection of essays, *Earth's Mind, Essays in Native Literature,* was published by the University of New Mexico Press in 1997. During spring semester, 1991 and fall semester, 1997 he was the exchange fellow from the University of Montana to Shanghai International Studies University in the People's Republic of China.

As If an Indian Were Really an Indian: Uramericans, Euramericans, and Postcolonial Theory

Louis Owens
University of California at Davis

It is both awkward and very convenient that so much of what we loosely term postcolonial theory today is written by real "Indians"—critics with such names as Chakrabarty, Chakravorty, Gandhi, Bhabha, Mohanty and so on—so that, in writing or speaking about indigenous Native American literature, we can, if we desire, quote without even changing noun or modifier, as if an Indian were really an Indian. It is tempting, in light of this five-hundred-year-old absurdity, to coin a new identifier for the first inhabitants of this part of the world. On a continent colonized by Euramericans—my preferred term for Americans of European descent—and populated by heteroglot immigrants such as actual "Indians" from India, perhaps the best term for the original Americans would be Uramericans. Euramericans and Uramericans—the doubling and inescapable sound of mutual accusation has a ring to it ("You're American!"). And certainly it is true that for half a millennium Euramericans have been locked in a struggle for possession not merely of the American continent but of the Uramerican soul as well.

I am myself neither a real Indian like Gayatri Chakravorty Spivak or Satya Mohanty, nor a theorist, but merely a teacher who writes, a writer who teaches—and my reflections should be taken in that context. I also wish to borrow a caution from the seminal postcolonial writer Frantz Fanon who declares in *Black Skin, White Masks*, "Since I was born in the Antilles, my observations and my conclusions are valid only for the Antilles" (14). Following and narrowing Fanon's wise lead, I must say that in significant measure I am my own Antilles and therefore my observations and conclusions are valid for only myself.

Edward Said has written about "*strategic location*, which [he explains] is a way of describing the author's position in a text with regard to the ... material he writes about" (*Orientalism* 20). My own strategic location vis-à-vis what we have come to call Native American literature is a complicated and contingent one. Descended from Mississippi Choctaw and Oklahoma Cherokee peoples on both paternal and maternal sides—and thus Uramerican—I am also Euramerican, with Irish and Cajun French ancestors. Being thus only partly original or "Ur," my strategic location may be found in what I think of as a kind of frontier zone, which elsewhere I have referred to as "always unstable, multidirectional, hybridized, characterized by heteroglossia, and indeterminate" (*Mixedblood Messages* 26). In this sense, my work, like that of many other writers identified as Native American, might in fact accurately be described as what postcolonial theorists have called "migrant" or "diasporic" writing, for while I spent a large part of my earliest years in Choctaw country in Mississippi, I do not write from the heart of a reservation site or community and was not raised within a traditional culture. It would not be incorrect to say, in fact, that today in the U.S., urban centers and academic institutions have come to constitute a kind of diaspora for Native Americans who through many generations of displacement and orchestrated ethnocide are often far from their traditional homelands and cultural communities. Such a frontier / transcultural location is an inherently unstable position, and one from which it is difficult and undoubtedly erroneous to assume any kind of essential stance or strategy, despite many temptations to do so. In such space, authority is hard to come by.

A commonality of issues, shared by all of us who work in the field of Native American (Uramerican) literature, mark this unsettled zone of frontier, interstitial scholarship. Dipesh Chakrabarty has suggested that non-Western thought is consistently relegated to the status of what Foucault might term a "subjugated knowledge" or what others define as a "minor" or "deterritorialized" knowledge (Gandhi 43). Chakrabarty writes that while third-world historians "feel a need to refer to works in European history; historians of Europe do not feel any need to reciprocate.... We cannot even afford an equality or symmetry of ignorance at this level without taking the risk of appearing 'old fashioned' or 'out-dated'" (Chakrabarty 2). To Chakrabarty's lament, I would add that critics and teachers of Native American literature are in a similar position. We are very properly expected to have and exhibit a crucial knowledge of canonical European and Euramerican literature; if we fail to be familiar with Shakespeare, Chaucer, Proust, Flaubert, Dickinson, Faulkner, Eliot, Joyce, Pound, Yeats, Keats, Woolf, Tolstoy, Tennyson, and so forth—not to mention the latest poststructuralist theory—we are simply not taken seriously and probably will not have earned a university degree in the first place. That, it is presumed, is the foundational knowledge, the "grand narrative of legitimation" in our particular field. However, while I have a great fondness for and some knowledge of canonical Western literature, like Chakrabarty I have often noticed that the majority of my colleagues in various "English" departments around the U.S know very little if anything at all about Native American literature, written or oral; nor do they often exhibit any symptom of feeling it to be incumbent upon them to gain such knowledge. It may be pleasant to believe, as the guest editor of a recent issue of *Modern Fiction Studies* declared, that "Native American literature has become part of the mainstream" (Peterson 3), but, despite incremental change over the past couple of decades, it would only take a few minutes in the English Departments of most universities to be disabused of such wishful thinking, even in the Southwest, the heart of supposed "Indian Country," where in a recent department meeting at the University of New Mexico one of my former colleagues, a medievalist, airily dismissed Native American literature as a "fad." In fact, it would not take much time spent browsing through contemporary critical/theoretical texts—including especially those we call postcolonial—to discover an even more complete erasure of Native American voices. It seems that Chakrabarty's "symmetry of ignorance" applies even less to postcolonial theorists' awareness of Native American voices than it does to mainstream academia. Those of us attempting to find a theory appropriate to a discussion of Native American literature are expected to be familiar with the writings of Said, Bhabha, Trinh, et al, but there is no symmetry of expectation. While Native American literature is gradually finding a small niche within academia, one discovers an almost complete absence of Native American voices in works by major cultural theorists and respected writers. We find, for example, a surprising erasure of Native presence in Toni Morrison's *Playing in the Dark*, in which this Nobel-winning African American writer adopts the rhetoric of imperial discovery and cites Hemingway's "Tontos" as well as Melville's *Pequod* without ever noting an indigenous Native presence shadowing her figuration of blackness in America. Morrison can clearly summon up romantic Indians when she needs them for color, as in *Beloved*, but the Native fades into obscurity when serious theorizing is in order. The most extraordinary denigration of Native American voices is found, however, in Edward Said's *Culture and Imperialism*, where this celebrated father of postcolonial theory dismisses Native American writing in a single scathingly imperial phrase as "that sad panorama produced by genocide and cultural amnesia which is beginning to be known as 'native American literature'" (304).

We can add to this disturbing list Homi Bhabha's total silencing of indigenous Native Americans in his influential study, *The Location of Culture*. Bhabha gives the impression of being acutely aware of a wide panoply of minority voices in this book, referencing Hispanic and Black American writers, for instance, and extensively praising Morrison's *Beloved*, but nowhere, not even in a whispered aside, does he note the existence of a resistance literature arising from indigenous, colonized inhabitants of the Americas—the literature, that is, of Uramericans. How, one wonders, can this student of postcoloniality, difference, liminality, and what he terms "culture as a strategy of survival" (172), be utterly ignorant of or indifferent to such writers as N. Scott Momaday, James Welch, Leslie Silko, Louise Erdrich, Simon Ortiz, or, most incredibly, the Anishinaabe writer and theorist Gerald Vizenor? How, one wonders, can any serious student of the "indigenous or native narrative," the term Bhabha uses to define his subject, not read and deal with Vizenor's radically indigenous theory? Imagine what lengths Bhabha and other postcolonial theorists would have to go to in order to come to terms with Vizenor's "trickster hermeneutics"—which effectively subsumes poststructuralist and postmodern theory into a Native American paradigm and discursive system—or the work of poet Luci Tapahonso, who writes in both Navajo and English from a position deeply embedded in her Diné culture while moving freely within the academic diaspora, liberating and appropriating villanelles, sestinas, and sonnets to a Navajo voice and epistemology. It is difficult to take seriously any cultural/critical theorist who is ignorant of this rapidly growing body of work, or who, if he or she is aware of it clearly relegates it to a "minor," "subjugated, or "deterritorialized" knowledge worthy of only silence or erasure. Within this great silence, it comes as more of a surprise than it should to find Trinh Minh-ha, in *Woman, Native, Other*, paying careful attention to Laguna Pueblo writer Leslie Marmon Silko's storytelling and then at least noting such Native American writers as Momaday, Joy Harjo, Vizenor, and Linda Hogan in a chapter from her 1991 essay collection, *When the Moon Waxes Red*.

As we argue for the recognition of Native voices missing from such texts, and, concomitantly, a place on the literary and academic stage, we must be wary of what Rey Chow has called the language of victimization and "self-subalternisation" which, Chow points out,"has become the assured means to authority and power" (13) in the metropolis, a phenomenon Leela Gandhi refers to succinctly as the "professionalisation of the margin" (Gandhi128), and Gerald Vizenor calls "aesthetic victimry." And we need to examine carefully those Native American texts that do make it somehow from the margin to if not the center at least an orbital relationship with the homogenizing gravity of that center. Citing her own frustrating experience in a white-male dominated academic conference as an example, Gayatri Spivak warns that "The putative center welcomes selective inhabitants of the margin in order to better exclude the margin." Spivak—a "real" Indian in America—quotes Adrienne Rich, who says, "This is the meaning of female tokenism: that power withheld from the vast majority of women is offered to the few, so that it may appear that any truly qualified woman can gain access to leadership, recognition, and reward..." (Spivak107).

In mentioning postcolonial theory and Native American literature in the same breath, we should also keep carefully in mind the fact that America does not participate in what is sometimes termed the "colonial aftermath" or postcolonial condition. There is no need in the U.S. for what has been called the "therapeutic retrieval of the colonial past" in postcolonial societies (Gandhi 5). In *The Wretched of the Earth,* Fanon wrote, "Two centuries ago, a former European colony decided to catch up with Europe. It succeeded so well that the United States of America became a monster, in which the taints, the sickness, and the inhumanity of Europe have grown to appalling dimensions" (313). Regardless of whether we share Fanon's harsh critique of the imperial U.S., I think it is crucial for us to remember that the American Revolution was not truly a war to throw off the yoke of colonization as is popularly imagined, but rather a family squabble among the colonizers to determine who would be in charge of the colonization of North America, who would control the land and the lives of the indigenous inhabitants. America never became post-colonial. The indigenous inhabitants of North America can stand anywhere on the continent and look in every direction at a home usurped and colonized by strangers who, from the very beginning, laid claim not merely to the land and resources but to the very definition of the natives. While it may be true figuratively, as Fanon writes, that "it is the settler who has brought the native into existence and who perpetuates his existence" (*Wretched* 36), it is even more true, as Gerald Vizenor has argued, that the "Indian" is a colonial invention, a hyperreal construction. "The *indians*," Vizenor writes, "are the romantic absence of natives.... The *indian* is a simulation and loan word of dominance.... The *indian* is ... the other in a vast mirror ..." (*Fugitive Poses* 14, 35, 37).

In imagining the Indian, America imagines itself, and I know of no text that more brilliantly and efficiently illuminates America's self-imagining than Walt Whitman's poem "Facing West from California's Shores." Whitman speaks in his poem as and for America, and since it is a brief poem, it is worth quoting in its entirety:

> Facing west from California's shores,
> Inquiring, tireless, seeking what is yet unfound,
> I, a child, very old, over waves, towards the house of maternity, the land
>   of migrations, look afar,
> Look off the shores of my Western sea, the circle almost circled;
> For starting westward from Hindustan, from the vales of Kashmere,
> From Asia, from the north, from the God, the sage, and the hero,
> From the south, from the flowery peninsulas and the spice islands,
> Long having wander'd since, round the earth having wonder'd,
> Now I face home again, very pleas'd and joyous,
> (But where is what I started for so long ago?
> And why is it yet unfound?)

In her introduction to postcolonial theory, drawing upon Heidegger, Leela Gandhi writes that "the all-knowing and self-sufficient Cartesian subject violently negates material and historical alterity/Otherness in its narcissistic desire to always see the world in its own self-image" (39). In this extraordinary poem, Whitman articulates Euramerica's narcissistic desire to not merely negate indigenous Otherness and possess the American continent, but to go far beyond North America to what is implicitly "my" sea, "my" Hindustan, "my" Kashmere, "my" Asia, and so on. In her extraordinarily thorough "Translator's Preface" to Derrida's *Of Grammatology*, Spivak reminds us of Nietzsche's famous "will to power" and Nietzsche's explanation that "the so-called drive for knowledge can be traced back to a drive to appropriate and conquer" (*Of Grammatology* xxii). The imperial, "inquiring" American of Whitman's poetry calls to mind not only this Nietzschean will to power but also Spivak's point that "the desire to explain might be a symptom of the desire to have a self that can control knowledge and world that can be known" and that "the possibility of explanation carried the presupposition of an explainable (even if not fully) universe and an explaining (even if imperfectly) subject. These presuppositions assure our being. Explaining, we exclude the possibility of the heterogeneous." Spivak concludes that "every explanation must secure and assure a certain kind of being-in-the-world, which might as well be called our politics" (*In Other Worlds* 104-6).

The Euramerican "child" of Whitman's remarkable poem seeks to claim the originary moment, to claim possession of the womb of humanity in a great universalizing narcissism that subsumes everything in its tireless, inquiring quest after its own image, thereby excluding heterogeneity from the very womb, and it is pleased and joyous about the whole imperial endeavor. Leela Gandhi writes that "In order for Europe to emerge as the site of civilisational plenitude, the colonised world had to be emptied of meaning" (15). Whitman brilliantly comprehends this grand gesture in the Americas, and in his final question he even more brilliantly registers the ultimate, haunting emptiness the colonizing consciousness faces at last once it is forced to confront a world emptied of meaning outside of itself. Because there is no way back to that infinitely retreating moment of origin—and no explorer's route to a golden Uramerica—the green breast of this new world remains forever distant as it draws the Euramerican psyche onward. Whitman's question—"(But where is what I started for so long ago?/And why is it yet unfound?)"—resonates not merely through the heart of America's own metanarrative, leaving the Jay Gatsby's of America alone and painfully perplexed, but through the rest of the world marked by European narcissism and expansion. In Whitman's poem, America, having completed a stunningly deadly, self-determinedly innocent waltz across the bodies and cultures of Native inhabitants, seeks to claim not just the territory of the world but also the womb of humanity, seeding its own consciousness alone within that embryonic place of origin. This self-willed, brutal child looks to the "house of maternity" beyond "Hindustan," "Kashmere" and all of Asia to legitimize its claim to primacy and thus legitimacy as the inheritor of all. Conversely, the Euramerican seeks, profoundly, to be not merely Uramerican but simultaneously the only child and the father of all.

The large stride of Whitman's American moves across and through hundreds of indigenous cultures. These cultures are the Others who must be both subsumed and erased in a strange dance of repulsion and desire that has given rise to both one of the longest sustained histories of genocide and ethnocide in the world as well as a fascinating drama in which the colonizer attempts to empty out and reoccupy not merely the geographical terrain but the constructed space of the indigenous Other. And if we doubt the place of the imagined Indian in America's imperial self-construction, we can turn to Scribner's *Concise Dictionary of American History*, which explains that "The experiences of the Indian agencies with people of a race, color, and culture wholly unlike our own have been of great value to United States officials dealing with similar peoples throughout the world" (Andrews 463). Given the rather horrifying nature of United States officials' treatment of "Indians," the "similar peoples throughout the world" mentioned here would be well advised to read Scribner's dictionary and heed its warning.

Fanon has written that "Man is human only to the extent to which he tries to impose his existence on another man in order to be recognized by him." He adds, "In its immediacy, consciousness of self is simple being-for-itself. In order to win the certainty of oneself, the incorporation of the concept of recognition is essential" (*Black Skin*, 216, 217). European America holds a mirror and a mask up to the Native American. The tricky mirror is that Other presence that reflects the Euramerican consciousness back at itself, but the side of the mirror turned toward the Native is transparent, letting the Uramerican see not his or her own reflection but the face of the Euramerican beyond the mirror. For the dominant culture, the Euramerican controlling this surveillance, the reflection provides merely a self-recognition that results in a kind of being-for-itself and, ultimately, as Fanon suggests, an utter absence of certainty of self. The Native, in turn, finds no reflection directed back from the center, no recognition of "being" from that direction.

The mask is one realized over centuries through Euramerica's construction of the "Indian" Other. In order to be recognized, and to thus have a voice that is heard by those in control of power, the Native American must step into that mask and BE the Indian constructed by white America. Paradoxically, of course, like the mirror, the mask merely shows the Euramerican to himself, since the masked Indian arises out of the European consciousness, leaving the Uramerican behind the mask unseen, unrecognized for him/herself. In short, to be seen and heard at all by the center—to not share the fate of Ralph Ellison's Invisible Man—the Native must "act out" and pose as the absolute fake, the fabricated "Indian," like the dancing puppets in Ellison's novel.

If a fear of inauthenticity is the burden of postmodernity, as has been suggested by David Harvey in *The Condition of Postmodernity* among others, it is particularly the burden not only of the Euramerican seeking merely his self-reflection, but even more so that of the indigenous American in the face of this hyperreal "Indian." In *Midnight's Children*, Salmon Rushdie's character Saleem Sinai says, "above all things, I fear absurdity." Quoting Rushdie's character and reflecting on Sinai's predicament, Gandhi writes that "the colonial aftermath is also fraught by anxieties and fears of failure which attend the need to satisfy the burden of expectation" (5). America not only contains no "colonial aftermath," it also places no burden of expected achievement on the American Indian. On the contrary, for Native Americans the only burden of expectation is that he or she put on the constructed mask provided by the colonizer, and the mask is not merely a mirror but more crucially a static death mask, fashioned beforehand, to which the living person is expected to conform. He or she who steps behind the mask becomes the Vanishing American, a savage/noble, mystical, pitiable, romantic fabrication of the Euramerican psyche fated to play out the epic role defined by Mikhail Bakhtin: "The epic and tragic hero," Bakhtin writes, "is the hero who by his very nature must perish.... Outside his destiny the epic and tragic hero is nothing; he is, therefore, a function of the plot fate assigns him; he cannot become the hero of another destiny or another plot" (*Dialogic Imagination* 36). While the "Indian" holds a special and crucial place within the American narrative, the Native who looks beyond his or her immediate community and culture for recognition finds primarily irrelevance and absurdity.

Frantz Fanon declares that "The town belonging to the colonized people, or at least the native town, the Negro village ... the reservation, is a place of ill fame, peopled by men of evil repute. They are born there, it matters little where or how; they die there, it matters not where, not how.... The native town is a hungry town, starved of bread, of meat, of shoes, of coal, of light" (*Wretched* 39). Could this not be a description of Pine Ridge, South Dakota today, a hungry reservation town and the poorest county in America, home to the very Plains Indians so celebrated in America's fantastic construction of Indianness, the aestheticized subjects of such romantic and insidious films as *Dances With Wolves*? Fanon writes: "For a colonized people the most essential value, because the most concrete, is first and foremost the land: the land which will bring them bread and, above all, dignity" (*Wretched*, 44). Above all, Native Americans have been deprived of land, and of the dignity that derives from the profound and enduring relationship with homeland.

To understand this contemporary colonialism as it affects Native Americans, we need to recognize what Leela Gandhi, a "real Indian" writer and theorist, has called the "relationship of reciprocal antagonism and desire between coloniser and colonised." Gandhi suggests that "the battle lines *between* native and invader are replicated *within* native and invader" (4, 11-12). America's desire to control knowledge, to exclude the heterogeneous, and to assure a particular kind of being-in-the-world depends upon a total appropriation and internalization of this colonized space, and to achieve that end, America must make the heterogeneous Native somehow assimilable and concomitantly erasable. What better way to achieve that end than to invent the Indian as an Other that springs whole-formed from the Euramerican psyche? In *Black Skin, White Masks*, Fanon says simply that "what is often called the black soul is the white man's artifact" (14). It can be argued, and has been argued effectively by such Native American writers as Gerald Vizenor and Philip Deloria, that what is called the Indian is the white man's invention and artifact. In his book *Playing Indian*, Deloria documents exhaustively and persuasively America's obsession with first constructing the Indian as Other and then inhabiting that constructed Indianness as fully as possible. Deloria describes marvelous "Indianation" ceremonies in which white Americans induct one another into Indianness. In one such ceremony, a "spirit" voice intones, "The red men are my children. Long ago I saw in the future their destruction, and I was very sad." According to Deloria , the "spirit tells initiates that the only way to placate the mournful Indian shades is to preserve their memory and customs. The society's sachem then replies that the membership will accept the 'delightful task.' The ceremony concludes by offering the initiate complete redemption and a new life through mystic rebirth as an Indian child. 'Spirit,' prays the sachem, 'receive us as your children. Let us fill too the place of those who are gone'" (78).

Deloria comments: "Like all these boundary-crossing movements, however, Indianized quests for authenticity rested upon a contradictory foundation. In order to be authentic, Indians had to be located outside modern American societal boundaries. Because they were outside those boundaries, however, it became more difficult to get at them, to lay claim to the characteristics Indians had come to represent" (115). To extend Deloria's observation, I would also suggest that the artifactual "Indian," unlike the indigenous Native, could be easily gotten at because he or she was a pure product of America. Deloria also examines Natives who step into the Euramerican-constructed mask to play "cultural politics for social and political ends," actual indigenous Native Americans who "found themselves acting Indian, mimicking white mimickings of Indianness" (189). "If being a survivor of the pure, primitive old days meant authenticity, and if that in turn meant cultural power that might be translated to social ends, it made sense for a Seneca man to put on a Plains headdress, white America's marker of that archaic brand of authority" (189).

In the midst of such extraordinary torsions, where is the Native writer to locate her or himself, and how is that writer to find or have a voice in a world articulated through another language or knowledge system? Raja Rao described the challenge faced by the indigenous artist who writes in a colonizer's language by saying, "One has to convey in a language that is not one's own the spirit that is one's own" (Gandhi 150). Rao also said, "We cannot write like the English. We should not. We cannot write only as Indians" (Gandhi 151). Native Americans, with few exceptions, such as Navajo writers like Luci Tapahonso and Rex Lee Jim who write in both Navajo and English, do not have the option of writing and publishing in an indigenous language, and even more than those of whom Rao speaks, Native authors surely cannot "write only as Indians." After five hundred years of war, of colonial infantilization and linguistic erasure, cultural denigration, and more, how and where does the Native writer discover a voice that may be heard at the metropolitan center?

Homi Bhabha, borrowing from V. S. Naipaul's *The Mimic Men*, writes of "colonial mimicry," which, he declares, "conceals no presence or identity behind its mask" (*The Location of Culture* 86). Gandhi labels such mimicry the "sly weapon of anti-colonial civility, an ambivalent mixture of deference and disobedience" which "inaugurates the process of anti-colonial self-differentiation through the logic of inappropriate appropriation" (149-50). In glossing Bhabha's formulation, Gandhi argues that "the most radical anti-colonial writers are 'mimic men'" and that "the paradigmatic moment of anti-colonial counter-textuality is seen to begin with the first indecorous mixing of Western genres with local content" (*Postcolonial Theory* 150). Gandhi's description of such counter-textual mimicry would seem to apply well to such a work as Cherokee writer John Rollin Ridge's 1854 novel, *The Life and Adventures of Joaquín Murietta, the Celebrated California Bandit*, in which Ridge appropriates the genre of the western adventure/romance to tell a deeply encoded story of colonial oppression and brutality. Similarly, the Uramerican Okanagon writer Mourning Dove performed a brilliant and clearly subversive act of appropriation in her 1927 novel, *Cogewea, the Half-Blood: A Depiction of the Great Montana Cattle Range*, a novel that mimics the classic western romance with indigenous mixedbloods in the roles always reserved for European American cowboys. But neither Ridge nor Mourning Dove found acceptance in the centers that control textual production in America. Ridge, grandson of traditional Cherokee leader Major Ridge and founding editor of the *Sacramento Bee* newspaper in California, promptly vanished from the landscape of American literature to be rediscovered a century later in a kind of ethnographical salvage operation. Mourning Dove found it took not only collaboration with a white editor, but a dozen years and money earned from her labor in apple orchards and hops fields to get *Cogewea* published and then forgotten for half a century until its discovery by Native American scholars and feminist critics. Acceptance and recognition by the metropolitan center would not come for a Native American writer until 1969 when the Kiowa author N. Scott Momaday won a Pulitzer Prize for his first novel, *House Made of Dawn*. According to a member of the Pulitzer jury, an award to the author of this novel "might be considered as a recognition of the arrival on the American literary scene of a matured, sophisticated literary artist from the original Americans" (Schubnell 93).

I want to focus briefly upon Momaday's historic accomplishment. And in doing so, while keeping in mind that we are discussing a "colonial" rather than "postcolonial" text, it may be helpful here to borrow from the critic Timothy Brennan who argues that the "privileged postcolonial text is typically accessible and responsive to the aesthetic and political taste of liberal metropolitan readers. The principal pleasures of this cosmopolitan text accrue from its managed exoticism. It is both 'inside' and 'outside' the West...." Such texts provide a "familiar strangeness, a trauma by inches" (quoted in Gandhi 162). Bhabha declares that "The desire to emerge as 'authentic' through mimicry—through a process of writing and repetition—is the final irony of partial representation" (88). How does a colonial or postcolonial author—a collective whom I have earlier identified as "migrant" or diasporic in the postcolonial sense—achieve a text so accessible and responsive to metropolitan readers? Aijaz Ahmad suggests that "Among the migrants themselves, only the privileged can live a life of constant mobility and surplus pleasure, between Whitman and Warhol as it were. Most migrants tend to be poor and experience displacement not as cultural plenitude but as torment.... Postcoloniality is also, like most things, a matter of class" (Gandhi 164). It is not difficult to extrapolate from Ahmad's statement to the fact that most Native Americans live lives fashioned by generations of displacement with resulting impoverishment, suffering, and silence. While life for urban Uramericans can be difficult, the poorest and most desperate places in America are Native American reservations, populated by indigenous people who commonly live with as much as 85% unemployment, deplorable health care and even worse education, horrifying rates of alcohol and drug addiction, an epidemic of fetal alcohol syndrome, and the highest suicide rates and lowest life expectancy of any ethnic group in the nation—all the effects of profoundly institutionalized racism. It is apparently delightful to caricature Native Americans as sports mascots and in movies, but as long as the real people are hidden from sight on rural lands reserved for their containment, it isn't necessary for the dominant culture to even contemplate the Natives' quality of life. And before everyone protests, let me quote Jean-Paul Sartre, who wrote acutely in his preface to Fanon's *The Wretched of the Earth*, "Our worthiest souls contain racial prejudice" (21). How else could our worthiest souls live with Washington Redskins, Cleveland Indians, Atlanta Braves, Chief Wahoo, the Tomahawk Chop, and so on, all of which are merely the slightest indices of the far more profound currents that impoverish Native Americans in incalculable ways? Would we live so comfortably today with the New Jersey Jews, Newark Negroes, Cleveland Chicanos, Houston Honkies, Atlanta Asians, and so on? Entering the 21st century, would the city of Washington cheer a football team whose mascot scampered around at halftime in blackface or wearing a yarmulke and carrying a Menorah? Again, Bhabha adds an interesting note here when he writes that "the discriminatory identities constructed across traditional cultural norms and classifications, the Simian Black, the Lying Asiatic—all these are *metonymies* of presence. They are strategies of desire ..." (90).

America has in large part at least recognized the impropriety of such racial stereotypes as those Bhabha describes—the "Simian Black" and "lying" or "inscrutable" Asian—even if it has perhaps not relinquished them entirely. However, the same operative strategy of desire that for a very long time governed representation of other minority cultures clearly still controls Euramerican discourse representing the Native American Indian. Given the uncomfortable realities of most contemporary Native American lives, as we look around us in academia, I think it is perhaps time to recognize that what we are calling Native American literature is represented largely, if not exclusively, by the sorts of privileged texts Timothy Brennan describes and is created by those migrant or diasporic Natives who live lives of relatively privileged mobility and surplus pleasure. As a group, published Native American authors have an impressively high rate of education, most possessing not merely a university degree but at least some graduate work if not an advanced degree. We may go back to our families and communities periodically or regularly, we may, like N. Scott Momaday, even be initiated into a traditional society within our tribal culture, but we are inescapably both institutionally privileged by access to Euramerican education and distinctly migrant in the sense that we possess a mobility denied to our less privileged relations.

The question remains: what must the colonial, or postcolonial, writer—in this case specifically the indigenous Native American, mixedblood or fullblood—do to be allowed a voice like Shakespeare's cursing Caliban? Let us consider the Pulitzer Prize juror's words regarding Momaday's award for *House Made of Dawn*. What might such a statement as "the arrival on the American literary scene of a matured, sophisticated literary artist from the original Americans" possibly mean? I would suggest, as I have elsewhere, that these words indicate that an aboriginal writer has finally learned to write like the colonial center that determines legitimate discourse. Momaday so successfully mimicked the aesthetics of the center that he was allowed access. This—the evolution of the colonial subject to *something like* the level of the colonial master—fulfills the idealized, utopian colonial vision of reconstructing the colonial subject to reflect the colonizing gaze. To be heard at the center—to achieve both authenticity and recognition within the imperial gaze that controls dissemination of discourse—the Native must step into the mask and into Whitman's circle; and the more fully we enter that empowering circle, the more successful we may be. The most prosperous of such texts are both accessible to the aesthetic and political tastes of the metropolitan center and, perhaps more significantly, present to such readers a carefully managed exoticism that is entertaining but not discomfiting to the non-Native reader. Elsewhere I have called the most extreme versions of this publishing phenomenon "literary tourism." And, as I have also suggested in my book *Mixedblood Messages*, certainly N. Scott Momaday's Pulitzer Prize testifies to a Native American author's successful entry into that privileged circle. *House Made of Dawn*, with its very visible and pervasive indebtedness to classic modernist texts, is clearly "accessible and responsive to the aesthetic and political taste of liberal metropolitan readers." Just as clearly, Momaday's novel offers what Brennan calls a "managed exoticism." The Pueblo world of the protagonist, with its "familiar strangeness" and "trauma by inches," is never threatening or very discomfiting to its Euramerican readership, while it provides a convincing and colorful tour of Indian country, including titillating glimpses of Native ceremony and even witchcraft. Exoticism packaged in familiar and therefore accessible formulas, carefully managed so as to admit the metropolitan reader while never implying that the painful difficulties illuminated within the text are the responsibility of that reader, clearly *House Made of Dawn* is both "inside" and "outside" the West.

To say all of the above is not to deny the aesthetic or artistic achievement, or even the important political ramifications of Momaday's novel or many others that might be similarly described. *House Made of Dawn* is superbly subversive. Seen in this way, N. Scott Momaday becomes one of the "mimic men," to borrow V.S. Naipul's term, who realize a genuinely appropriationist and subversive end by packaging a text in sufficient imperial wrappings as to get it past the palace guards into the royal Pulitzer chambers. It is an impressive achievement, yet an achievement requiring extensive education of its author—all the way to a doctorate from Stanford University—within the knowledge system of the metropolitan center as well as careful crafting to conform to that center's expectations. A peripatetic citizen of the U.S. Native American diaspora, a modern "migrant" intellectual and artist, Momaday—like all the rest of us who find ourselves in somewhat similar if less celebrated circumstances—has not only entered the trajectory of Whitman's circular journey but has internalized that circle. Momaday's "strategic location" vis-à-vis the Pueblo world he wrote about in his first novel, like the strategic location of most Native American writers, is surpassingly complex, shifting, hybridized, interstitial and unstable.

Those of us working in the field of what we call Native American literature can and undoubtedly will chafe at the ignorance and erasure of Native American voices within the metropolitan center, and within what at times appears to be the loyal opposition to that center called postcolonial theory. And we can, and undoubtedly will continue to try to make our voices heard— to "give voice to the silent" as a recent academic conference termed the endeavor. However, such negotiations are never simple or free of cost. It seems that a necessary, if difficult, lesson for all of us may well be that in giving voice to the silent we unavoidably give voice to the forces that conspire to effect that silence. Finally, as we approach nearer to literate Euramerica, the circle within us may be almost circled, and like Whitman's America, we may be left asking, "But where is what I started for so long ago ...?"

Work Cited

Andrews, Wayne, ed. *Concise Dictionary of American History*. New York: Charles Scribner's Sons, 1962.

Bhabha, Homi K. *The Location of Culture*. London & New York: Routledge, 1994.

Bakhtin, Mikhail. *The Dialogic Imagination: Four Essays by M. M. Bakhtin*. Ed. Michael Holquist. Tr. Caryl Emerson and Michael Holquist. Austin: University of Texas Press, 1981.

Chakrabarty, Dipesh. "Postcoloniality and the Artifice of History: Who Speaks for 'Indian' Pasts?" *Representations*, vol. 37 (1992), pp. 1-26.
Chow, Rey. *Writing Diaspora: Tactics of Intervention in Contemporary Cultural Studies*. Bloomington: Indiana University Press, 1993.
Deloria, Philip. *Playing Indian*. New Haven: Yale University Press, 1998.
Fanon, Frantz. *Black skin, White Masks*. New York: Grove Press, 1967.
—. *The Wretched of the Earth*. New York: Grove Presss, 1963.
Gandhi, Leela. *Postcolonial Theory: A Critical Introduction*. New York: Columbia University Press, 1998.
Harvey, David. *The Condition of Postmodernity: An Enquiry into the Origins of Cultural Change*. Oxford: Basil Blackwell, 1989.
Owens, Louis. *Mixedblood Messages: Literature, Film, Family, Place*. Norman: University of Oklahoma Press, 1998.
Peterson, Nancy J. "Introduction: Native American Literature– From the Margins to the Mainstream." *Modern Fiction Studies* 45:1 (Spring 1999), pp 1-9.
Said, Edward W. *Orientalism*. New York: Vintage Books, 1979.
Said, Edward. *Culture and Imperialism*. New York: Knopf, 1993.
Schubnell, Matthias. *N. Scott Momaday: The Cultural and Literary Background*. Norman: University of Oklahoma Press, 1985.
Spivak, Gayatri Chakravorty. *In Other Worlds: Essays in Cultural Politics*. New York: Routledge, 1988.
Spivak, Gayatri Chakravorty. "Translator's Preface." Jacques Derrida, *Of Grammatology*. Tr. Gayatri Chakravorty Spivak. Baltimore: Johns Hopkins University Press, 1997.
Trinh, T. Minh-ha. *Woman, Native, Other*. Bloomington: Indiana University Press, 1989.
—. *When the Moon Waxes Red: Representation, Gender and Cultural Politics*. New York and London: Routledge,1991.
Vizenor, Gerald. *Manifest Manners: Postindian Warriors of Survivance*. Hanover & London: Westleyan University Press, 1994.

Currently Professor of English and Native American Studies at the University of California, Davis, Louis Owens is of Mississippi Choctaw, Oklahoma Cherokee and American Irish descent with a good dash of Louisiana Cajun French from Catahoula Parish. His publications include *Other Destinies: Understanding the American Indian Novel; Mixedblood Messages: Literature, Film, Family, Place; John Steinbeck's Re-Vision of America;* as well as five novels, with the most recent being *Dark River* (1999). Forthcoming works include *I Hear the Train: Inventions, Reflections, Refractions* (Oklahoma, fall 2001), a collection of stories and essays masquerading as non-fiction

A Multitude of Routes, Roads and Paths Transcultural Healing in A.A. Carr's *Eye Killers*

Jesse Peters
University of North Carolina at Pembroke

The removal, separation, and exclusion have never been right, no matter the reasons, reversions of scores, or, measure for measure, the wild taste of vengeance. Natives would be much wiser now to include others, to absolve the absence, embrace a common presence, and celebrate coincidence over exclusions. The reservation politics of sanguine modiation and blood count names is a curse of exclusion and dominance.
Gerald Vizenor (*Manifest Manners: Postindian Warriors of Survivance*)

In *Eye Killers*, novelist A.A. Carr constructs a world in which people, cultures, and belief systems necessarily collide and merge. By blending the popular Western myth of vampires with traditional Navajo and Laguna stories, Carr makes a bold statement about the fluidity and uncertainty of identity, not only for Native Americans, but for all of humanity. What makes this novel interesting and quite different from many Native American texts is that this zone of uncertainty brought about by transcultural contact is a positive space in which positive growth and change occur.

As Bakhtin has explained,

> For the writer of artistic prose ... the object reveals first of all precisely the socially heteroglot multiplicity of its names, definitions and value judgments. Instead of the virginal fullness and inexhaustibility of the object itself, the prose writer confronts a multitude of routes, roads and paths that have been laid down in the object by social consciousness. Along with the internal contradictions inside the object itself, the prose writer witnesses as well the unfolding of social heteroglossia surrounding the object, the Tower-of-Babel mixing of languages that goes on around any object; the dialectics of the object are interwoven with the social dialogue surrounding it. (278)

Carr is quite aware of the "multitude of routes, roads and paths" that surround both a text and the objects within that text. In fact, this inherent quality of dialogue, and indeed of existence, which Bakhtin has explained so well, the "heteroglot multiplicity" present in almost all situations of consciousness, is the driving force of this novel. Through the plot of the novel and the characters' actions, Carr explains how he believes heteroglossia affects identity.

Perhaps the best example of how heteroglossia shapes identity is found in the character of Michael Roanhorse; one of the first things a reader may notice about him is his religious complexity. His wife, Margaret, had been a strong Christian before her death. Even though Michael "wasn't as devout a Catholic as Margaret had been" (14), he still says a prayer for her soul, presumably to the Christian God. Also, each morning as he sits and drinks his coffee, he faces a "1958 July calendar with Jesus on the cross.... The picture on the calendar had been Margaret's favorite of all the portraits of Our Savior she owned, and she had often scolded his attempts to remove it" (14). Margaret's belief in Catholicism, along with Michael's ongoing respect for and understanding of that religion, speak to the complexities of faith found in many Native American cultures. According to James Treat,

> Native people who choose to identify themselves with Christian institutions, liturgical forms, teachings, or spiritual practices do so while bearing in mind the community circumstances, family precedents, and personal experiences that define their lives. Furthermore, many native Christians accomplish this identification without abandoning or rejecting native religious traditions.... To dismiss all native Christians as acculturated, anachronistic traces of religious colonialism, is to miss innum-erable demonstrations of their insightful historical and social analysis, their complex and sophisticated religions, creativity, and their powerful devotion to personal and communal survival. (10)

Indians who find spirituality in the Christian faith have neither betrayed their cultural heritage nor turned their back on it. In fact, it is the very merging of these beliefs, the immersion within a heteroglot religious identity, which allows them to survive.

In describing the religious faith of these characters, Carr makes it clear that there are no simple answers. Michael may not be much of a Catholic, but when he is first introduced in the novel, he has little faith of any kind. After Michael's brother died in Korea, he "had found the bar a suitable mourning place. A church to pray and think in, more silent and more intimately human than the wide desert flats or the valleys of juniper and pinon below Madrecita" (54). Eventually, his wife retrieves him from the bar, and "all of her family, in the Indian way, left him alone to find his lost heart. Soon, the changing seasons healed him" (54). Again, Carr illustrates the fact that the notion of faith and religion is a highly syncretic part of the lives of these characters, and Margaret, who is a devout Catholic, understands that her husband needs something other than a bar or a Christian church in order to heal.

After Margaret's death, what little Christian faith Michael had slowly fades, and he leaves the picture of Jesus above his table more out of love and respect for Margaret than for God. However, Carr explains that since the death of his Navajo grandmother, Michael has also abandoned the traditional Navajo ways he once respected and cherished:

> He had set all the Navajo curing chants aside after Nanibaa' had died from cancer. Nothing, now, could have gotten him to a sing even if not showing meant life or death for him. He had thought Nanibaa' the most powerful human being alive. Her presence was enough to drive away all of his childhood's most terrifying monsters. Seeing her pray every morning in her strong voice, singing in the east-facing doorway of her hogan, hair gray as iron, Michael had believed completely in her medicine and chants—in her Beauty Way. He had felt the power of them echoing in his soul. (62)

Even though he seemed to be completely invested in his grandmother's spiritualism, after she dies from cancer, Michael throws "his charred prayer sticks, eagle feathers, and bits of dried sage over the snowy edge of Canyon de Chelly" (62).

His rejection of traditional Navajo beliefs is a rare moment in Native American fiction. Carr constructs an Indian character who is not separated from his traditional, cultural faith because of ignorance, distance, or cultural poisoning through contact with the dominant society. Instead, Michael Roanhorse has chosen to give up the Navajo way because he failed to see its power, failed to see the importance of that faith to his own well-being and to the culture in general. And even though in some senses Michael is "healed" by the end of the novel, that process is a long and difficult one, full of physical, mental, and spiritual challenges. Carr never wants his characters or the choices they make to appear simple because, as his novel points out, it is in complexity, in syncretic notions of identity, that people survive.

In a discussion of metonymic and synecdochic representations within Native American narratives, particularly in autobiography, Gerald Vizenor writes,

> Metonymy ... is a trope, a figurative device that indicates a common reference by replacing one name with another; for instance, the pen is mightier than the sword. Synecdoche, on the other hand, is a word or name that substitutes the part for the whole, such as head count, hired guns, weasel words, and the simulations of indian cultures and traditions. (*Fugitive* 106)

When these terms are extended to construction of identity, one could say that to label a person Navajo, for example, would be to create that person metonymically through notions of what it may mean to be Navajo, rather than through his individual characteristics. On the other hand, to see a person or a character in a piece of literature as representative of a particular group or culture makes individual characteristics (synecdoche) paramount and may serve to homogenize that group or culture.

Either of these moves in Indian literature is dangerous, even though synecdochic representation may come closer to challenging preconceived notions of Indianness. In synecdoche, there may be a character who, since he is Navajo, informs the reader about what it is to be Navajo through his actions, thoughts, experiences, dialogue, etc. In metonymy, one would already know everything about the character once his status as Navajo is discovered. And, as Vizenor points out, "varionative[1] autobiographies would be synecdochic and move in the direction of integration, or the latent cast of native traditions, rather than metonymic simulations, or reductive associations, as causal reason and other connections" (*Fugitive* 107). The move from object to subject demands synecdoche because the act of speaking for oneself defies prescribed metonymic labels and stereotypes. However, that unique voice, that synecdochic moment that informs a reader's idea of a given native culture or of Indianness in general, may also have negative results because the reader could very well fail to see that a particular viewpoint is but one among many. Synecdoche runs the risk of becoming "an aesthetic renunciation of human sound and a native presence, an aversion to the creative maneuvers and ambiguities of visions and memories" (Vizenor *Fugitive* 108).

The postindian writer, who "must waver over the aesthetic ruins of indian simulations" (Vizenor *Fugitive* 15), has to find a new way to speak from within his or her experiences as "Indian" because "Natives, in either of these motives and associations [metonymy and synecdoche], are objects in the tropics of dominance" (Vizenor *Fugitive* 106). As Vizenor explains,

> Whatever the figurative directions, varionative autobiographies are dialogic circles, and the traces of presence are more originary, and generative, than structuralist representations. These literary devices and interpretations are neither the directions of narratives nor the thematic union of author intentions. (*Fugitive* 107).

In *Eye Killers*, Carr seems conscious of the "dialogic circle" that circumscribes any articulation of identity, and in his narrative he attempts to defy both metonymic and synecdochic tropes. His characters and plot defy stereotypes but also never make the argument for one simple way or solution.

Michael is a curious hero and one who denies simple interpretation, and Carr does not allow him to be either a metonymic or synecdochic representation of Indianness. At times in the novel, he seems very strong, and at others weak, both physically and spiritually. But his confused faith is, oddly enough, a source of both his strength and his weakness; he has been

---

[1] Vizenor defines varionative as "an uncertain curve of native antecedence; obscure notions of native sovenance and presence. The *varionative* traces of ancestors are scriptural, episodic, and ironic in narratives" (*Fugitive* 15).

prepared by traditional Navajo and Pueblo culture and religion as well as by Christianity to recognize the dangerous threat that vampires represent, but his wavering and incomplete spirituality make it difficult for him to combat the evil and save his granddaughter. However, it is precisely his lack of confidence which allows him and Diana to succeed in the end. Because he is not always powerful and sure of what action to take, he is forced to look for help, to learn new ways and new powers, ultimately realizing that one path is not always the only path and may, in fact, not even be the correct one.

Like Michael, Diana challenges stereotypes often found in Native American literature and, even more importantly, she represents the importance of acknowledging the heteroglot multiplicity of existence. Even though Diana has knowledge of the vampires and the experience of being in physical contact with Falke, she also has another characteristic which helps her in her struggles, both with herself and with the vampires. This characteristic is perhaps the most valuable tool of all; Diana is willing to change.

At one point in the novel, she realizes that she must "make a connection. Connect" (179), and as she learns more and more about Melissa, her family, and the vampires that have taken her, she gradually gets closer to making that connection. In order to connect, her preconceived notions of Indianness and whiteness must change. At first, because of her own self-doubt and her dependence on simple clichés to inform her about Michael's world, she is unable to see her important role in the unfolding battle against Falke. She thinks,

> I can't honestly believe I'm making a difference to Melissa's life by standing in this dusty old place while two old men sit in a forgotten kitchen guzzling coffee. I can't even understand what they're saying, much less plan any kind of strategy, break bread with them, make medicine, or whatever. (196)

But it is precisely this uncertainty, this conscious realization that beliefs (and people) are neither steadfast nor universal that gives Diana strength, and, like Michael, she becomes an example of the positive results associated with embracing a heteroglot environment and rejecting the synecdochic notions of identity she once held.

When she eventually decides to join the fight, it is with the realization that she doesn't know what to do, that she will need help. But what she does know is that to do nothing, to remain stagnant, will not allow her to make the connections that she needs to make in order to feel whole again. When asked to help fight, she says, "I'm not remotely Indian. Not even one-eighth" (244). But she soon realizes that it is not important who is Indian and who is not because the syncretic nature of this common evil, of this threat to humanity as a whole, negates qualifications based on blood quantum; identity is much more than a simple matter of blood. Diana learns that labels do not define people, they simply may help one to understand something about them.

As she spends more and more time with Michael, William, Doris, and Emily, Diana becomes more comfortable, and her sense of community, the connections to other people that she has been lacking, gradually return. When she first goes to William and Doris's with Michael, "she emerged from her car and locked the door, urging Michael to do the same" (156). Later, when she returns to their house to rest and eventually to prepare to fight, she gets out of her car "and shut the door without locking it" (241), an act symbolizing her growing security. As Diana gets to know the Native American people she spends time with as people rather than as simply Indians, and as she begins to recognize the fact that she is similarly accepted because of who she is, she becomes part of a caring and supportâve community. Eventually she is reborn, not only as a warrior who fights Falke, but also as a person who once again recognizes and experiences the value of human relationships, relationships that do not stop at cultural boundaries. Carr beautifully symbolizes this transformation as Diana looks at the sky: "The sky outside was featureless, what Diana imagined a baby chick might see before pecking itself out of its shell" (250).

Diana does not want to appropriate the culture she learns about out of a selfish need for spirituality or out of a need to define herself through others. Even though her confidence and self-reliance grow as she gets to know members of Navajo and Pueblo culture, the basis for that growth comes from responsible membership in a community, not from a romantic notion of Indianness. She decides to learn the Navajo stories and songs which will help her defeat the vampires, not to become Indian, but out of a desire to help Melissa and thus the community she is becomming part of. As Emily tells her, "You are with us now, Diana. That's a good thing, and requires your respect and strength" (286). In fact, Carr does not give his readers the feeling that Navajo or Laguna culture is better than the dominant Euramerican culture, or even that it is more powerful; the different cultures are merely both necessary parts of this particular story, parts that must work together if the enemy if healing is to occur. Though Diana may ultimately feel "as if she had come home" (272) as her link to Michael and his family grows, there is never the sense that she must, as a Euramerican, abandon the "destructive and inferior" ways of her past. She must simply understand, respect, and incorporate her past into the new ways she learns, a formula that Carr feels is the necessary one for any growth or healing to take place. Or as Paula Gunn Allen says, "In a word, there are so many discoveries to make, so many strange new lands to explore; questions rather than answers, information and insight rather than 'fact' and 'authority' become the goal and the source of human experience" (*Reservation* 11).

The complex, non-stereotypical characters of Michael and Diana, who work together as they face a common enemy, are representative of the dialogic circles inherent in a which is heteroglot in nature. Similarly, the enemies themselves, the vampires, teach them (and us) something about the dialogic nature of the world. These creatures exist outside human experience even though at one time they were human as well. Some, like Elizabeth and Melissa, exist in a liminal state between human and vampire, a state which demands that they negotiate between realities; they have some of the powers of the vampire, while still being able to access human feeling and emotion. Thus, they still have the ability to embrace heteroglossia and feel the power of change. But to exist completely as a vampire, as Falke does, is to exist in a timeless and unchanging state, both physically and psychologically.

In many ways, such an existence represents anyone who denies the movement and change inherent in a syncretic world. Existing without the uncertainty of change may appear to be an appealing alternative, one that hints at the comfort and power of certainty. However, to live this way, much like living as a vampire, demands that one must watch the world change from a stagnant and often isolated position. In order to survive, one who denies the evolving nature of existence, like a vampire, is forced to feed off of what he or she once was. Therefore, the pursuit and destruction of the literal and figurative state known as vampire becomes symbolic of reclaiming a positive concept of self through the acceptance of a reality that is syncretic, multiple, and fluid.

The liminality of existence explored in this novel, from Diana's and Michael's interactions with each other to the relationships between vampires and humans, are examples of what Louis Owens describes as the politics of frontier space: "Frontier, I would suggest, is the zone of trickster, a shimmering, always changing zone of multifaceted contact within which every utterance is challenged and interrogated, all referents put into question" (*Mixedblood* 26). This zone of "frontier" is not a damaging or destructive zone; it is a site of healthy and necessary contact in which discourse, and thus identity, is necessarily forged, evaluated and reevaluated. Just as trickster stories are "the stories of liberation and survivance without the dominance of closure" (Vizenor *Manifest* 14), so too is the frontier space that these stories inhabit a site of variation, accommodation, choice, action, and response.

It is important to note that it is not on the reservation, at his home, that Michael's return to faith occurs; he is in unfamiliar surroundings, faced by an unfamiliar enemy, in need of help from unfamiliar people. He does not have to turn his back on Euramerican culture in order to defeat the evil he faces; in fact, he realizes that he must incorporate new ways of seeing the world and find new sources of strength (attitudes symbolized by his friendship with Diana) in order to destroy Falke. Although he travels back and forth between Albuquerque and reservation land as he prepares to rescue Melissa, it is in the zone of the frontier that he is asked to reevaluate, and ultimately re-strengthen, both his spiritual power and his committment to fostering community over isolation.

Diana also discovers her power through contact with another culture. As discussed above, she slowly develops a connection to the community as she befriends Michael, Emily, Doris, and William. Herself in a strange world, faced with an unfamiliar enemy, and with growing concern for unfamiliar people, she is forced to consider what her role in this battle is going to be and whether or not she has the strength, or even the desire, to help. In the end, Diana decides to help because she learns what it means to take responsibility for others as well as for herself and that she can be strong in the face of opposition, lessons that become clear only in a frontier space of insecurity and uncertainty. As Doris tells her, "You are not Pueblo or Navajo, but you've told a story that Emily recognizes. And it's not only Melissa that needs healing. It is you too" (245). She goes on to explain that Diana's actions will have even greater ramifications: "It's time to heal the wounds that the government soldiers caused us, time to heal the hurt, the weeping, and distrust that still lives between our people. Emily has seen this in ceremony, Diana. You must accept it now" (245). Both Diana's personal healing and the possible intracultural healing she may facilitate would not have been possible without contact between cultures. Isolation would only serve to reinforce the manifest manners of dominance as well as the ignorance and misunderstanding that results from mentonymic and synecdochic representations.

Elizabeth, who constantly exists in the liminal, frontier state between human and vampire, also rejects isolation as she comes to understand herself and her existence through contact with Michael. Even though she has been loyal to Falke for centuries, she is acutely aware of the power Michael represents, a power that is associated with connection, growth, and change. She slowly understands that Michael's power stems from human interaction, human caring, human love, emotions that she, in her liminal state, is still able to feel but unable to take advantage of. Her relationship with Falke is not based on the same type of love she senses in Michael. When Falke tells her he loves her, she responds, "No, Falke. You never loved me" (72) because, as she finally realizes, Falke is incapable of love. He is a stealer of life, a thief of human joy and emotion, and for that, Elizabeth can never forgive him and eventually helps to destroy him. Elizabeth has been with him for centuries, and still she thirsts for human love. As Falke says, Elizabeth "chooses to remain human. Vulnerable" (72), but it is that vulnerability, that uncertainty that comes with emotion, which she clings to. As she realizes by the end of the novel, "Dreams and fantasy were fleeting. Memories were solid and gave strength. Like love. A power Hanna would never understand" (335). And it is that power, one that results from the shifting frontier space of love, that defeats Falke and saves Melissa.

Unlike Michael, Diana, and Elizabeth, Falke rejects the syncretic nature of frontier space and exists only in the comfortable territory of the past. When he enters a nightclub in the city, his lack of tolerance for change is evident:

> He adjusted his senses to the new atmosphere. Again, he listened. He recognized sounds originating from stringed instruments,

heavy drum beats. The people of this time had changed the delicate musical sounds into the squeals of slaughtered horses, the thunder of prideful angels. The music roaring from the walls and ceiling was not music; it was mere noise, lush and overblown as a spoiled carcass. (96-97)

Falke judges his environment from an ethnocentric and chronocentric point of view; he longs for the familiar drums of the past and can see little value in the changed present.

Though he believes that one should understand the ways of an enemy, a strategy not so very different from Michael and Diana's, Falke's understanding is not centered around the concept of healing or of constructive learning about the "new" world he finds himself in. As he arrogantly tells Hanna, "I will remain for a time in this city and study its modern way first. Know the ways of your enemy. His lifestyle and habits. His language. You will be better prepared to destroy him" (46). Falke's goal is the destruction of his enemies so that he, the embodiment of stagnant evil, can survive. It is because of his inability to adapt and change that he is defeated. A hundred years ago, he was destroyed by Native American people, and having learned nothing, again, in the present, he is overcome by a greater power, a power directly linked to a syncretic world of growth, love, and change.

Just as Carr suggests that liminality and the negotiation of frontier space are necessary aspects of the construction of identity as well as a source of strength, he also calls for a long overdue healing, not only for many of the characters in the book, but also for the world in general. And this healing must start with understanding, respect, and patience. Diana and Michael learn these strategies in order to heal themselves and aid in the destruction of Falke. But Carr also tells us that the people in the world, whether they be Euroamerican or Native American, have some things to learn as well.

Michael tells Diana a story that illustrates how important it is to listen to others and points out the fact that Indians often have something to learn from the dominant culture. He explains to her how three white doctors came to their village to help fight disease. At first, the people did not listen, but in time, they came to see the value in the advice of the doctors. He explains:

> Two of these doctors became my family. They cured me and my wife and they knew us. Not as bodies carrying plague, but as two stupid kids who hadn't learned to listen yet. We all of us in Madrecita finally listened, because of those two white people. And we gave those two doctors, a man and a woman, names in the Keresan language, my wife's language. It was decided by the old Pueblo men in their kiva, I think. I don't know where those doctors are now, but we still remember their names. (146)

A MULTITUDE OF ROUTES, ROADS AND PATHS 193

The Pueblo is able to survive literally and figuratively because they chose to listen, and that act of listening gave them the ability to negatiate the frontier space between cultures and to decide what information, if any, found within that space should be brought into their reality..

Morris teaches a similar lesson when he tells Diana,

> Our elderlies tell us that our children are the only real treasure we have now. Our land is being chopped into bits, scattered away. The uranium mine is poisoning our brains and bodies with sickness. I read and understand things. That is also the most important thing to us now. The ability to read. (202)

Morris understands the past, but he does not exist only there; he sees how the past has shaped the present, but he also looks to the future for positive change. And he knows that literacy, especially literacy in English, provides him with the power to listen, to learn, and eventually to fight for change. He continues,

> These young boys nowadays don't care nothing about reading nor writing correctly. Least, the ones I have seen. I've talked with our Indian physicists and doctors and teachers and my heart just busts with pride. But these other hotshots are just wanting to fistfight and complain. Their only concern is telling off the white man for stealing our land whilst standing by useless and watching it happen. (202)

He is primarily disappointed in the young people because they live in the past, much as Falke does, and want things to be like they were. The problem is that they are unwilling to navigate frontier space, unwilling to negotiate, unwilling to listen, unwilling to choose a different strategy to facilitate positive change.

The importance of listening, of healing within the transcultural space of the frontier, is best illustrated in an exchange between Diana and Emily. When Diana comes to stay with Doris and William, Emily tells her, "It is more than a vacation.... We are learning about each other. I will teach you some words in Keresan, if you want" (259). Diana, who is willing to learn, says, "Oh I don't know! Yes, I would like to learn Navajo, and Keres, maybe Tewa, too, if you have the time. For my own knowledge" (259). Emily says she is willing to teach if Diana has "the patience" (259). But it is not only Diana who wants to learn and has the patience to do so. When she asks Emily what she could give her in return, Emily says, "Maybe ... you could teach me to speak better English" (259). Learning the language of the other is the first step in understanding which, in turn, is the first step in healing.

At one point in Eye Killers, Michael tells Diana, "What we must do requires a lot of strength. And respect" (215), and in his words is the simple but powerful strategy that Carr sets forth for transcultural interaction. He is not concerned with teaching his readers about the atrocities of the past, nor is his present filled with Indians leading hopeless lives of alcoholism and poverty. His present is a highly hybridized reality which, rather than functioning as a tragic pollutant to Native American cultures, acts as a source of strength and healing. As Owens points out,

> Cultures can and indeed cannot do otherwise than come together and deal with one another, not only within the transcultural regions of frontiers or borders but also within the hybridized individual, Vizenor's "crossblood," who internalizes those frontier or border spaces. (*Mixedblood* 40)

All one has to do is understand and accept the syncretic nature of the world and negotiate that world with patience and respect.

For Carr, identity is never static, and *Eye Killers* is a revealing articulation of an important point made by Gunn Allen:

> And perhaps, as our traditions have always been about liminality, about voyages between this world and many other realms of being, perhaps crossing boundaries is the first and foremost basis of our tradition and the key to human freedom and its necessary governmental accomplice, democracy. Certainly, as both our literature and lives attest, that's how it seems to be. (*Reservation* 12)

Even though I would not agree that all Native American literature attests to liminality of tradition and the crossing of boundaries, I do believe that Carr's novel captures the spirit of this philosophy. Perhaps Owens, who includes Carr's work in what he calls a body of "hopeful, life-affirming literature" (*Mixedblood* 159), says it best: "It is a literature that, often invoking traditional stories, songs, and rituals with discretion, tells the stories of who we are today, not only yesterday, with humor and strength so that we may, as a people, continue to survive" (*Mixedblood* 159). That philosophy may not always be a popular one, but it certainly challenges the reader to learn an incredibly old, but often overlooked lesson.

Contact between cultures is something that Aaron Carr knows from personal experience; as a child, "he spent time at his grandfather's sheep camp west of Albuquerque. His grandmother and mother told him the myths and legends of his people" (Reed "Old West" D3). These stories, along with other cultural elements of being Navajo and Laguna, are important to Carr, but his life, and thus his art, are much more complex. He also has lived in Albuquerque most of his life; his writing has been influenced by many Western authors; and his film career, which itself influences his writing, has been influenced by filmmakers from all over the world. Does his love for German silent films or Thai food make him less "Indian?"

Some critics would say yes; they may talk about his lack of tradition or his inappropriate plot that gives a white character power. For example, Reva Gover believes that

> A.A. Carr is to be applauded for his efforts to "push the envelope" for Native American writers. However, by doing so does this lessen the importance of our people and their capabilities? In being responsible to our youth does he belittle our elders by making their efforts ineffectual and letting the "good whiteman" or in this case woman, save us? (84)

And she ends by cautioning readers to keep young, inexperienced, Native people away from Carr's work: "*Eye Killers* should be kept to the learned, those who know their culture and lifeways, and are secure in themselves as Indians. I definitely would not recommend this book to young adults still forming an idea of who they are" (84). In her opinion, this novel is not a "true" articulation of what it is to be Indian. Why not? Is it because the novel is "polluted" with instances of Euramerican culture? Is it because Indians aren't supposed to believe in vampires? Is it because Carr's Indian characters don't hate white people and resent the "tragedies" of the past? Whatever her reasons, Gover did not find the message she wanted to find in this novel. Perhaps it is because she is used to seeing, and more importantly, believing in the simulations of dominance, in metonymic concepts of Indianness, and in synecdochic characters that reflect that familiar clichÈd Indianness back to the audience.

Carr's best reply to these criticisms is *Eye Killers* itself, a novel that reflects an important reality for many contemporary Indian people, a novel that explains how tradition grows out of human experience, and that the syncretic nature of those experiences cannot be rejected or ignored. Some critics and reviewers have seen the merits of the work. Catherine Krusberg notices the fact that, even though the novel is certainly about vampires, there is a much deeper message behind the book. She says, "*Eye Killers* is a vampire tale much of the traditional European type but told in a very non-European way to fit its non-European setting, designed to reward the patient acceptance of following its threads in their juxtapositions of dream-vision and Western reality" (5). What she calls "dream-visions" is the Navajo/Pueblo reality and mythology which plays a major role in both the theme and narrative strategy of the novel. And another reviewer for *American Studies International* explains that

> ...the device of using a naive Anglo school teacher allows him [Carr] to inform the reader about Navajo history without becoming pedantic and his inspired choice of an abandoned movie theater as the home of one of the young women vampires permits wonderful flights of

imagination, joining American popular culture and Indian history. (Mergen 95)

The more readers are aware of the strategies that Carr uses in the novel and of the reality of the syncretic frontiers in which we all exist, the more well-crafted and artful they seem to find the book.

Steve Terrell adeptly points out that "A lesser writer would have taken a shortcut and made the protagonist a wise old medicine man, ready to throw down the hoodoo with the monster. But Carr makes Roanhorse far more interesting" (8). Michael is certainly an Indian man, but Carr challenges his readers by focusing on this character as a man rather than as an Indian. Being Navajo may be a large part of who Michael Roanhorse is, but it is not the only dimension that makes up his identity. Similarly, Diana's whiteness is not her defining quality, and her reactions to the Indian and vampire worlds that she encounters during the course of the novel are complicated and often unexpected. Her decision to help Michael defeat Falke is not based on romantic notions of Indian spirituality, and ultimately, her "initiation into the ways of Indian medicine is a metaphor for sharing knowledge between cultures" (Terrell 8), not a quest for personal gain or cultural appropriation.

The literal and figurative boundaries of "reservation life" ultimately do not exist for Carr. He takes his characters "off the reservation" not in an act of defiance, but merely in an act. And what they find there is not always and necessarily a hostile, angry world filled with unsympathetic, evil others. It is merely a different world, another experience which becomes a part of their own. Diana and Michael learn from each other during the course of the novel, and through their adventures, the reader learns something as well, something about the ways people and cultures can, and in fact do, exist together. As Chick Flynn says, "Steeped in myth and legend, the surprising final pages bring the story full-circle, and allow the healing process to begin, which is an element that has never before been introduced in vampire literature" (24). And for Carr, this healing process depends upon the fact that existence is not stagnant and must start with the simple, but often unheard idea that cultures that have been at odds with each other for centuries must begin that healing process together. This idea is far too rare in Native American literature.

More than merely a novel about destroying vampires, Eye Killers is also a statement about the ways in which identity is formed. As we see in the strategies that Diana and Michael implement as they confront evil, the willingness to acknowledge and accept change is a key element of understanding one's place in the world. Along with these changes comes the realization that the construction of identity, whether Navajo, Laguna, Indian, white, Irish, Euramerican, or any other label, takes place in a dialogically agitated environment. As Bakhtin explains, "The authentic environment of an utterance, the environment in which it lives and takes shape, is dialogized heteroglossia, anonymous and social as language, but simultaneously concrete, filled with specific content and accented as an individual utterance" (272). In order to understand an utterance, a label, or even a person's concept of identity, we must accept and negotiate the dialogic environment in which we find that utterance, label, or identity. Carr's novel suggests that the way to understand identity comes from embracing the syncretic nature of the world, not from denying that world. And to understand ourselves in dialogue with others is to heal.

Works Cited

Allen, Paula Gunn. *Off the Reservation: Reflections on Boundary-Busting, Border-Crossing, Loose Canons.* Boston: Beacon Press, 1998.

Bakhtin, M.M. *The Dialogic Imagination: Four Essays by M.M. Bakhtin.* Edited by Michael Holquist. Translated by Caryl Emerson and Michael Holquist. Austin: University of Texas Press, 1981.

Carr. A.A. *Eye Killers.* Norman: University of Oklahoma Press, 1995.

Flynn, Chick. "Eye Killers." Rev. of *Eye Killers* by A.A. Carr. *The Bloomsbury Review.* May/June 1995: 23-24.

Owens, Louis. *Mixedblood Messages: Literature, Film, Family, Place.* Norman: U of Oklahoma P, 1998.

Gover, Reva "Mariah" S. "*Eye Killers.*" Rev. of *Eye Killers* by A.A. Carr. *Red Ink* 5 (Fall 1996): 83-84.

Krusberg, Catherine B. "Vampires in Print." In *The Vampires Crypt.* Margaret L. Carter, Fall 1995: 5.

Mergen, Bernard. "Fiction—*The Lone Ranger and Tonto Fistfight in Heaven* by Sherman Alexie / *Eye Killers* by A.A. Carr / *The Death of Bernadette Lefthand* by Ron Querry / *Ghost Singer* by Anna Lee Walters." *American Studies International.* Oct. 1995: 94-96.

Reed, Ollie Jr. "Old West Writer Bryan Wins Spur for Elfego Bacabio." *Albuquerque Tribune.* 28 Mar. 1995: D3.

Terrell, Steve. *Eye Killers. New Mexico Magazine.* October 1995: 8.

Treat, James. *Native and Christian: Indigenous Voices on Religious Identity in the United States and Canada.* New York: Routledge, 1996.

Vizenor, Gerald. *Manifest Manners: Postindian Warriors of Survivance.* Hanover: Wesleyan U P, 1994.

—. *Fugitive Poses: Native American Indian Scenes of Absence and Presence.* Lincoln: University of Nebraska Press, 1998.

Darrell Jesse Peters is Assistant Professor of English and American Indian Studies. He has also published on the work of Louis Owens and Thomas King and is currently working on a book entitled *Only the Drum is Confident: Simulations and Syncretisms in Native American Fiction.* He also throws frisbees for his dog and fishes as much as possible.

Bodies of Memory and Forgetting: "Putting on Weight" in Leslie Marmon Silko's *Almanac of the Dead**

Beth Hege Piatote
University of Oregon

In Leslie Marmon Silko's novel, *Almanac of the Dead*, the body functions like a map for expressing many of the novel's central themes, among them the cannibalistic nature of capitalism, the force of sexual liaisons in shaping politics, the perversion of fertility and alienation from Mother Earth, and the consuming hunger for blood that drives a category of people known as The Destroyers. Among the most compelling themes is the question of survival or destruction in the face of colonial practices: the book's 30-plus characters are engaged in various ways in a war that, among other things, pits capitalism against Marxism, human boundaries against spiritual ones, and memory against amnesia. The narrative itself positions "story" against time by rejecting the familiar formula of a *Bildungsroman*, which generally ushers a single story line carefully through time. Instead, the 763-page *Almanac* uses an episodic structure and constantly shifting time and place orientation, thus functioning as a manual, handbook, or other type of reference book which offers the most graphic details on the processes of living and dying. These processes, both physically and metaphorically, are located in the body, and thus the body may serve as the locus of analysis, and as a map of two distinct trajectories of survival and destruction.

We may begin thinking about the *Almanac* at the beginning, although this is certainly not the only possible point of entry. Silko's novel opens not with prose but with a map, a key element of the work which has received little attention from scholars. The map is the first representation of borders in the book, and evokes both the capitalist and colonialist histories that the book so incisively critiques while also introducing the transcendence of borders through pan-Indian movements and alternative orientations to time. The map has some recognizable geographic features: it is shaped somewhat like the region of the southcentral United States and Mexico, and features a straight line border between what is assumed to be the U.S. (since it is not identified as such) and Mexico (which is clearly labeled). The Atlantic and Pacific Oceans appear on the map, as well as Haiti and Cuba. Different cities and sites (such as Tucson, Laguna Pueblo Reservation, Mexico City, Tuxtla Gutierrez, and "North to Alaska") where the novel's action takes place are identified, along with the names of most of the

---

* I am grateful to Shari M. Huhndorf for her comments on this paper, and for insights offered by her and other members of the Silko Reading Group at the University of Oregon: Jim Tarter, Jeff Ostler, and Scott Pratt.

characters. The map offers fragments of historic and prophetic story lines, and reveals the image of the giant stone snake, identified as the "ancient spirit messenger."

In addition, there are four textual notes, each of which contains a narrative thread that links the past, present and future. The note headed "The Indian Connection," for example, states that "Sixty million Native Americans died between 1500 and 1600. The defiance and resistance to things European continue unabated. The Indian Wars have never ended in the Americas. Native Americans acknowledge no borders; they seek nothing less than the return of all tribal lands." The reference to the ongoing (past and present time) Indian Wars locates the novel as a wartime epic, and the reference to the return of land reflects the importance of place and geography. But the notion of "acknowledg[ing] no borders" is not limited to physical topographies; when read with another note, the "*Almanac of the Dead* Five Hundred Year Map," it is clear that there are temporal implications as well. According to this note, "Through the decipherment of ancient tribal texts of the Americas the *Almanac of the Dead* foretells the future of all the Americas. The future is encoded in arcane symbols and old narratives." While the book is very specifically oriented to particular geographic places, the borders of those physical places are only part of the picture. The borders of time are also revealed on this "five hundred year map," and it is these borders, as well as colonial geographic ones, that Silko addresses in the novel (16-17).

The five-hundred year time frame explicitly places the text within the period of European colonization of the Americas. *Almanac of the Dead* is a powerful anti-colonial work, and the map is a key to decoding two distinct trajectories— one of continued destruction, and the other of survival, even rebellion—that the book suggests as potential responses to colonial processes. A third textual note, called "Prophesy," identifies an anti-colonial process at work in the book. It says: "When Europeans arrived, the Maya, Azteca, Inca cultures had already built great cities and vast networks of roads. Ancient prophecies foretold the arrival of Europeans in the Americas. The ancient prophecies also foretell the disappearance of all things European" (16-17). The key phrase, for the purpose of this analysis, is "the disappearance of all things European," because it speaks not of European people but of colonial processes. The distinction has to do with relationships. This "disappearance" is often portrayed in the book as a type of internal hunger—a consuming, self-destructive force located inside the body. "Things European" also refers to a spiritual vacuity, a fractured relationship between Europeans and their God and homeland, which is expressed through capitalism. This note implies that European colonialism is a consuming, destructive force that will ultimately turn upon itself, a theme that is played out in the self-destructive activities of some of the novel's major characters.

We may begin our analysis by reading the map because it is helpful for decoding the book: in the map, it is possible to see both the physical world and the temporal world at the same time. The body is the precise location in which these two worlds converge. Using the body as a map, we may focus on the effect of "putting on" weight, as seen in the experiences of the characters Menardo—whose ultimate destruction is brought on by his blind faith in his bulletproof vest—and Mosca, who suddenly puts on weight when a spirit moves into his body and communicates with him through his shoulder. I will show how Menardo's experience is a process of deadening an historic line (thereby participating in colonization), whereas Mosca's is a process of bringing historic and prophetic lines to life (thus resisting colonization and making revolution possible). Their actions are distinctly linked to time, memory and amnesia. The success of colonization relies upon a constantly imposed fracture of memory, place and culture in a way that paralyzes the colonial subject in the present moment. This is precisely the reason why Native Americans must "acknowledge no borders" if they are to survive. Menardo is clearly trapped in the present moment, and his paralysis has the effect of deadening both historic lines and future possibilities. In contrast, Mosca transcends the boundaries of present time and both resurrects the past and opens the possibility of alternative futures and sovereignties. I will tie the actions of these two characters and others to elements on the map by showing how they participate in the past and present Indian Wars, and how they contribute to a present and future "disappearance of all things European."

Mosca and Menardo—Identity

The bodies of Mosca and Menardo serve as maps because they reveal two distinct directions for navigating a colonized world. The two characters bear three important similarities. Both are Mestizos, although they are situated, in mirror fashion, on opposite sides of "the border": Menardo lives in Tuxtla Gutierrez and Mosca works with his uncle, Calabazas, in Tucson. Both have the ability to see into the spirit world, Menardo through his dreams and Mosca in his waking life. Both "put on" a protective layer upon their bodies in response to a sense that certain destabilizing forces are gathering around them. For Menardo, it is concern over the potential Indian uprisings in southern Mexico that may upset the political/social structure upon which his status depends; for Mosca, it is prophetic knowledge of a gathering force of spirits and hardships to come. How these two characters handle these three problems—identity, "seeing," and protecting the body—map the trajectories of destruction and survival in Silko's work.

In introducing the character of Menardo, Silko makes a striking narrative move by shifting from third-person to first-person voice. Menardo alone in the 763-page volume speaks in his own voice. In this passage, he describes "the old man," his grandfather, in terms that are both fierce and affectionate:

> Full of beer he used to get very serious, and when I was a young child, I felt frightened. It was then he bragged the ancestors had seen "it" all coming, and one time I interrupted to ask what "it" was, and he

waved his hands all around the shady spot where we were sitting and he
said, "The time called Death-Eye Dog." There was no one in the area
who could talk the way the old man did. (257)

In this passage, it is clear that Menardo's grandfather was attuned to a type of ancient knowledge that exists across barriers of time. His grandfather had the capacity to see, or perhaps to "recognize" time, and in this instance he identifies the period of colonialism as the era of the Death-Eye Dog. In this moment in which Menardo is both speaking in his own voice and revealing his grandfather's knowledge, he is locating within himself a link to the past which, in terms of the novel's main theme, is the only hope for moving into the future. He is actively contesting the fracture of memory by speaking with an historic consciousness, which challenges both colonization and the economic forces of capitalism that drive it.

As Menardo's brief narration (it is a mere three paragraphs) continues, he describes how his grandfather had shown an interest in European thought:

The ancestors had called Europeans "the orphan people" and had noted that as with orphans taken in by selfish or coldhearted clanspeople, few Europeans had remained whole. They failed to recognize the earth was their mother. Europeans were like their first parents, Adam and Eve, wandering aimlessly because the insane God who had sired them had abandoned them. (258)

This passage addresses the problem of alienation from "Mother Earth," a recurring theme in the novel. This section reveals the imposition of boundaries between humans and their "mother" as a distinct process of separation between the "parent" God and the European "children." In the absence of a relationship to "Mother Earth," it became possible for European notions such as capitalism and colonialism to arise, as these forces of exploitation depend upon the objectification of the other, be it environmental or human. Thus the spiritual fracture between Europeans and their God can be manifest in other forms, and it is precisely this process of alienation that Menardo undertakes when he effectively orphans himself from his lineage and attempts to re-create himself with a European identity.

As readers, we are able to watch this process from its inception. Immediately following the discussion of Europeans as orphan people, the narrative shifts back into third person, and Menardo is dis-located from his voice:

Menardo had loved the stories his grandfather told him about the old man who drank stinking beer and talked about and sometimes talked with the ancestors. Menardo had loved the stories right up until the sixth grade when one of the teaching Brothers had given them a long lecture about pagan people and pagan stories. (258)

It is in the moment that colonization sets in, here in the form of colonial narratives about native peoples, that Menardo loses his first-person voice. Subsequently, a set of decisions on Menardo's part reveal that he is moving toward a rejection of his own body, family, and (hi)stories in order to embrace "all things European." This is why Silko's narrative shift is so critical; by shifting from the intimacy of first-person to the more remote third-person voice, it is possible to experience Menardo's internal shift of subjectivity and, on another level, the separation of his voice from his body. This dis-location is a thoroughly colonial process.

At the same time that Menardo is finding his cultural/historical identity under attack, he is also being teased for two of his physical attributes: classmates make fun of his fat body and "flat nose," the latter taunt serving as slang for "Indian." Once his body explicitly and painfully signifies his "Indianness," and thus his inferiority, Menardo begins in earnest his quest to transcend his identity. By the end of this critical chapter, Menardo has constructed another narrative to explain his flat nose. He describes it not as a family trait (he is, after all, in the process of orphaning himself), rather taking the line from a famous boxer from Chiapas, Menardo says that his flat nose is the result of an injury inflicted by an opponent.

Menardo's path from adolescence is a desperate attempt to attain whiteness through imitation and association. He marries above himself, creating a union with the well-heeled Iliana, a descendant of one of the original European colonists of the area; and he establishes his own company called Universal Insurance. In selling his product to potential clients, Menardo's mind frame is revealed as classically colonial: "He was there, he told them, because the 'new world' could belong to them just as the old one had" (261). He socializes with the general, the governor, the judge and the police chief, all representatives of colonial power; and he has an affair with the young architect, Alegria, who traces her bloodlines to the conquistadors. His location near the border, which "leaked rabble-rousers and thieves like sewage pipe," (261) evokes not a single notion of solidarity with other Indians, but rather presents him with a unique business opportunity: Menardo's company becomes the first insurance group to guarantee protection against Indian-based political unrest. All of these acts contribute to the process of alienation that lead, ultimately, to Menardo's end when he puts on the white vest, a symbol of racial whiteness, a theme which we will investigate more thoroughly.

The figure of Mosca, in contrast to Menardo, reveals an entirely different construction of native identity, one which ignores rather than imposes borders, one which resists rather than participates in colonization. Again, the trajectories of fracture and healing are revealed through the body. Mosca's path to survival (and potential for healing) evokes a mandate of the map: the fight for the return of tribal lands. The *Almanac* calls for a convergence of spiritual powers from the North and the South to accompany the people as they rise up against 500 years of colonization. These spiritual powers do not recognize geographic, political, or temporal borders; and Mosca, whose body is an open conduit, is able to express these powers.

While Menardo aspires to whiteness, Mosca clearly rejects it for himself and abhors it in others. Mosca's relationship with his ancestors runs an opposite course from Menardo's: "Mosca had not always believed all the notions of the old tribal people, but he had seen for himself over the years that the old people had told the truth" (605). Whereas Menardo once loved the old people and their stories but came to reject them, Mosca's early skepticism was transformed over time into belief. Mosca keeps the stories of the people close to himself and his body is a conduit for messages from the spirit world. He believes that he has "a higher calling than ordinary men" (606) and is not afraid to die because of his understanding that the dead continue to participate in the struggles of the living.

Mosca's openness represents the role of boundary-crossing that is necessary for indigenous people to reclaim a relationship that has been fractured through colonization. The vessel of Mosca's body is one that changes shape over time in ways that reveal the importance of memory and prophesy in the struggle against colonization. For most of the novel, Mosca appears skinny and wiry and is so charged with electricity that he can't wear a wristwatch because it will malfunction. Electromagnetic fields also "acknowledge no borders" in their ability to cross vast boundaries and surfaces. Mosca's electromagnetism is compared to the type of communication that lizards and geese use to communicate across many miles, and also relates Mosca to the old Yupik woman in Alaska who has the power to make pilots' controls malfunction. This boundary-crossing relationship reveals a pan-Indian resistance to colonization and subverts politically imposed borders among indigenous peoples and others who are oppressed by capitalism. Mosca has the power to transcend or make meaningless any borders—political, geographic—between worlds, or beyond the body.

Seeing

In Silko's work, the ability to "see" has temporal as well as epistemological implications. Knowledge and recollection of the past are necessary preconditions for seeing into the future, and seeing into other realms (crossing the boundaries into the spirit world of the dead, for example) can illuminate the true nature of what is transpiring in this time and place. Silko employs a Mayan notion of time that is cyclical and repetitive, in which days and times recur, reflecting a cosmological difference from what is called "linear time," in which a series of days follow each other like soldiers, each distinct and singular and never repeating (Reineke 66). Silko writes on Mayan notions about time in a piece on the *Almanac* in her collection of essays, *Yellow Woman and a Beauty of the Spirit*:

> Since the days eventually returned, the Maya believed it was possible to know the future, if one understood the identities, or souls, of the days from their last appearance among humans. Certain people in touch with the spirits knew the days, weeks, months, and years intimately and could say exactly whether the days to come were peaceful, full of

plenty, or menacing and on the brink of disaster. The Maya people kept track of the days, and weeks, and months, and years in extensive almanacs. (136)

In *Almanac*, this concept of time becomes embodied: "The days, months, and years were living beings who roamed the starry universe until they came around again" (313). From this temporal frame, being able to "see" into the future does not come from the ability to imagine or conjure the "unknown," but rather from the *recognition* of that which is already known. The structure of Silko's novel, as an almanac itself, calls upon the reader to recognize time as it circulates through the work. One way to see time is to understand the human characters and their actions (or "reigns") as the embodiment of particular times. Thus the scenes in the book which are parallel can be conceptualized as the same "day." The same day may have occurred, for example, when the little grandparents are stolen from the Laguna people and when the movie crew films the giant stone snake, although in Gregorian time these events are separated by eighty years. The same "month" or longer period of time (reign) may be revealed whenever the plentiful cast of Destroyers (Beaufrey, Serlo, Trigg, Cortez, de Guzman, et. al.) clamor after blood, sex, and power. To say "the same day" is not to imply "the identical" day, but rather that the same forces were at work to create a particular "time." In Silko's work, it is incumbent upon both the characters and readers to "see" time. Moreover, the textual weight of *Almanac* functions against time, as its sheer volume ensures that most readers will have to experience the work over a period of time.

David L. Moore, in his essay on *Almanac*, addresses the responsibility of the reader to see by calling it a "ritual of witness," after the fashion of Tayo witnessing evil in Silko's earlier novel, *Ceremony*. Like the mythical Arrowboy, Tayo's gaze or "witness" of witchery has the power to confront evil. Moore's analysis is helpful in considering the relationship of the reader to the work's "textual brutality" (151). Indeed, Silko forces the reader to confront multiple violent and disturbing manifestations of bloodshed, brutality, cruelty, and perversion. In some passages, she indicts the reader's voyeurism and forces the reader instead to "see" by subtly shifting the perspective. For example, in the chapter "Video Surveillance," there is a progressive shift in perspective: Menardo thinks the police chief is imagining the governor and his young secretary from Chiapas together; then the judge thinks the police chief is remembering the "body search" he performed on the same girl; then the police chief is remembering watching the secret videotape of the governor with the girl; then suddenly the reader is "seeing" the governor rape the girl. This final move leaves the reader without a screen (the lens of the character) to hide behind, and thus the reader is forced to take on the role, to borrow Moore's terms, of either "voyeur" or "witness." Moore contrasts the two possibilities in this way:

Witnessing recognizes its own implication in the other, which it sees, while voyeurism, which is blind to the other, leaves the other in its own separation. Voyeurism commodifies and dehumanizes; witnessing recognizes and humanizes. Voyeurism crystallizes, witnessing circulates. (161)

An example of this blindness to the other can be found in Beaufrey: "the most bloody spectacles of torture did not upset him; because he could not be seriously touched by the contortions and screams of imperfectly drawn cartoon characters" (533). In contrast, the revolutionary leader Angelita la Escapia functions as a witness who continually calls forth the injustices of the past by reciting tribal (hi)stories, an act which in itself recognizes the connection to others that defies all boundaries. La Escapia ("the meathook") calls for revolution (a circulation of power) and is a leader in the current round of Indian Wars. Her recitation of history, her evocation of memory, places her on one side of the struggle, while Beaufrey's self-absorption and identification with the abstract notion of "sangre pura" Europeans places him on the other.

Menardo and Mosca, too, can be located on opposite sides of the revolutionary border by their ability (or inability) to "see." Menardo is desperately blind about a number of things: his wife's infidelities, the degree of loyalty he perceives from his servant Tacho, his status among the elite crowd he socializes with, and the death warnings that come to him in his dreams. Menardo's greatest blindness can be seen in his view of himself, his own identity—he fools himself into believing he has attained "whiteness" in the eyes of others. His self-absorption exists in inverse proportion to his self-awareness, a basic blindness that leads him into orchestrating his own mortal drama. When Menardo employs a security force to suppress indigenous uprisings, he is projecting his own suppression of indigeneity onto his people. Mosca, on the other hand, tends to be a more perceptive judge of character, such as when he criticizes Root's mother or Sarita and Liria for their love of whiteness. He accepts and understands the spirit messenger who moves into his body. He can identify witchery, and, perhaps most importantly, he can see differences. In a critical scene early in the book, Root and Mosca are the reluctant students of Calabazas, who marches them through the desert at night to teach them a lesson: "Those who can't learn to appreciate the world's differences won't make it. They'll die" (203). The ability to "see" is a basic tool of survival. In terms of the political struggle, then, Menardo's blindness puts him on the colonial side of the Indian Wars, while Mosca is clearly on the revolutionary side.

When Silko introduces Mosca she notes that his given name is Carlos and "Mosca" is a nickname given by Calabazas. Root calls Mosca by the English translation, "The Fly," and his visage fits the name: a wiry figure who wears large sunglasses that exaggerate his eyes. The name thus evokes the image of a creature who has a multi-faceted lens for sight, and Mosca has the gift that Silko identifies as one of the most important, which is the ability to "see." This ability is critical to survival because it is the way to understand relationships. While the processes of colonization and exploitive capitalism tend to obscure relations between people and place, "seeing" the relationships is often the first step toward revolution and/or a revolutionary act in itself. Some of the characters who can "see" include Tacho, who sees images of the present and future in the opal; the old Yupik woman, who can see into a crystal like a television set; Lecha, who sees the location of the dead; and Calabazas, who is able to see every nuance of the desert. As for Mosca, he "claimed he could remember everything, even being born. Though he had only been an infant, had sensed something was watching him from the ceiling. The first of thousands of things Mosca would 'see'"(603). Mosca also has the ability to detect witches in daylight. He can simply see them.

Menardo, too, has the ability to "see" through his dreams, although he suppresses it. For a while he confides the ominous content of his nightmares to his servant, Tacho, whose people are known to be able to interpret dreams. Tacho prompts, and Menardo readily invents, the most innocuous interpretations of the visions that are disturbing Menardo. Unable to deny completely the truth of his dreams, he awakens at night in a sweat and develops a stomach condition. The tool that eventually provides relief for Menardo is the gift of a bulletproof vest from Sonny Blue, which Menardo begins to wear to bed to keep his nightmares away. In this way, the vest, which is designed to protect Menardo from external forces, functions to protect him from internal ones instead.

Putting on Weight

In response to the political and social unrest moving northward from Chiapas, both Menardo and Mosca "put on weight" as a measure of protection. For Menardo, the weight is the white bulletproof vest. For Mosca, it is a layer of fat. It would seem that there is much less protection in the latter than the former, but in fact the fat prepares Mosca to survive, while the vest prepares Menardo to die. If we are to consider Mosca's and Menardo's bodies as temporal maps, these processes will reveal the future: Mosca expands with his weight, while Menardo's weight constricts him. Further, the notion of putting on weight contrasts with weightlessness, which is another representation of the "disappearance of all things European."

In Menardo's case, the vest is an unyielding and undynamic presence on his body. The vest is literally white, and thus it is the extension of his desire to clothe himself in "whiteness." Yet more significant than the protection that it offers from outside forces, it blunts his inner life forces. Considering that sexuality represents life force and fertility, the vest clearly functions to deaden Menardo in this respect. When he dances at the governor's house with Alegria, she twists away from him, complaining that the vest is crushing her. While his sexual relationship with his wife continues to disintegrate (she quits sleeping with him when he starts wearing the vest to bed), his affection for the vest is described in provocative terms: Alegria teases him of "fondling" his vest, and it is said that he touches the vest "tenderly" and "wanted to be alone" with it (324-5). The vest is elevated beyond other inanimate objects, but this comes only from Menardo's projections onto it and the faith Menardo places in it. Rather than performing its stated duty of protecting Menardo from outside forces, the vest serves to suppress his internal knowledge, robbing him of self-preserving instincts such as caution, prophesy, and wisdom. It deadens him from the inside out.

The image of dying from the inside out is one that appears several times in *Almanac*, and is linked to the "disappearance of all things European." This process is one that is reflected in a state of "weightlessness," as in the early sections about Lecha and Zeta's father, a geologist who "had been stricken with the sensation of a gaping emptiness between his throat and his heart" (121) and had dried up and died like a cactus in a drought. His corpse was marked by its weightlessness, and the process of his death "as if he had consumed himself" (123). Weightlessness, in this example and others, is the consuming spiritual vacuum that characterizes the Destroyers, the agents of colonization. A similar image is found in one of Silko's essays in *Yellow Woman*, in which she describes the process as follows: "You see that, after a thing is dead, it dries up. It might take weeks or years, but eventually, if you touch the thing, it crumbles under your fingers. It goes back to dust. The soul of the thing has long since departed" (25). In *Almanac*, she identifies through Tacho the prophesy that "whiteness" would consume itself: "The white man would someday disappear all by himself. The disappearance had already begun at a spiritual level.... All ideas and beliefs of the Europeans would gradually wither and drop away" (511).

To understand the nature of weightlessness, one must also consider the meaning of "weight." In Silko's work, "weight" is explicitly linked to story, history, prophesy, and time. It is thus linked to the forces necessary to bring about revolution. In the past and present Indian Wars, neither the living nor the dead have given up fighting. So it is critical for the revolutionary indigenous fighters to be open to the aid of those on the other side of the "border" of death. In the chapter, "The Weight of Ghosts," Calabazas tells a story about a man riding his mule, trying to pass through an area where many Yaqui people had been slaughtered by Mexican troops. But the ghosts in this area are restless and begin to pile onto the mule for a ride, which exhausts the mule. The man is told that it is not the mule's fault—it is the weight of ghosts, which weigh two or three times what they weighed in life. "The body carries the weight of the soul all the life, but with the body gone, there's nothing to hold the weight anymore" (191). Extrapolating from Calabazas' story, it is possible to see "weight" as the presence of disquieted spirits from the past who are attempting to move across landscapes of place and time. This "weight" is not separate from the story/history that created it. That is to say, while the spirits themselves have weight, the stories of the spirits also have weight. Here, too, the novel reveals the importance of this idea through form, in this case embedding the significance of "weight" in a story told by Calabazas.

When Mosca puts on weight, it signals the arrival and embodiment of history: "Mosca felt a burden, not his alone—ancient losses, perhaps to war and famine long ago" (607). The weight is also prophetic, manifest in the form of a creaky voice that settles into his shoulder. This mirrors the image of one of the heroic twin brothers to the south, who has a spirit macaw riding on his shoulder for guidance. Mosca is able to knit both history and prophesy together when he speaks of understanding the silent language of spirits: "Because talk was not necessary so long as you remembered everything you knew about your ancestors. Because ancestor spirits had the answers, but you have to be able to interpret messages sent in the language of spirits" (604).

Silko provides an interpreter of the "language of spirits" in a fat reader, a person who has the ability to "see" the future in the contours of the body. Mosca finds her through his friend Floyd, who is in prison for life. In the chapter where Mosca visits the fat reader, fat is described as a life-giving force, one related to sexual pleasure and physical survival, a contrast to the deadening language used to describe Menardo's white vest. Fat readers have the ability to communicate with fat, even to massage messages into the body to enhance and increase sexual pleasure, thus countering the sexual deadening that affects Menardo. The fat reader explains the relationship between pleasure and survival: "Thin ones tended not to be well attached to life. Without capacity for pleasure, thin ones preferred the sensation of denial or pain. Injury and illness could easily carry off a thin woman or man. Skinny ones burned up in fires and blew away in big winds" (604). This again raises the image of "weightlessness" as a consuming and destructive state.

The fat reader treats Mosca's body like a map, and like the *Almanac*'s map, it has both physical and temporal dimensions. She recognizes that Mosca has only recently put on weight, which links him to the future: "(f)at that had been with a person all of his life related to the past; fat that had appeared suddenly was related to events in the future" (608). She interprets Mosca's fat as a warning of hardships to come and instructs him to fatten up more. She also speaks of the danger of suppressing the knowledge of the body, particularly the knowledge of fat (or weight): "She was still amazed, she said, at today's people and their fear of body fat. The human body grew to the size necessary for its survival" (608).

Conclusion

What is most significant about Mosca and Menardo and their relationships to weight is the direction their weight takes them. Their bodies are maps of the past and the future. In the case of Menardo, he is born fat (with ancestral memory) but he rejects the weight of his past and takes on a different kind of weight—a faith in "all things European" as represented, ultimately, in the white bulletproof vest. In so doing, he positions himself on the European (colonial) side of the Indian Wars. Of course, he is also at war with himself. He does everything he can to deaden his senses against his indigenous identity—rejecting the old stories, his physical attributes, his own family, his prophetic dreams, his social situation (he sees himself as a peer among the political and military elite, when in fact he is a subject of their scorn). He creates borders around himself, and it destroys him. His trajectory shows how his path has diverged from being one with the People to being one of the Destroyers, capable of much evil had he not accidentally turned his destructiveness upon himself. In contrast, Mosca's trajectory is the path of survival. He is given hard lessons from Calabazas before he learns to "see" and to replace his skepticism with acceptance of the old stories. As he grows older, he takes on the weight of history; he opens his body to the knowledge of the spirit world. He positions himself on the indigenous side of the Indian Wars, and prepares for the coming hardships. He accepts that he may soon die as a result of this, yet he is not afraid to continue his efforts on the other side of this life. With both of these characters, given their comparable birth identities and places in life, they could have chosen either path (destruction or survival); the pairing of the two reveals two distinctly different outcomes for the resolution of the Indian Wars.

In an interview with Ellen Arnold, Silko acknowledged that the book is difficult to take in but a "strong remedy" for readers who do: "If you make it all the way through *Almanac*, it makes you strong" (7). The *Almanac* is a weighty book, full of stories, histories, spirits, and witness. In many ways, the book fulfills its own mandate of bearing witness, by forcing readers to see the ravages of colonization, relate the colonial past to the present, and draw relationships between violence and capitalism. Its evocation of violent histories works against the tide of amnesia. At the same time, it implicates native peoples in colonial processes while drawing distinctions between Europeans and "all things European." The emphasis on processes and relationships of power, both external and internal, is at the core of the work, and shows that any series of choices (related to blindness or seeing; and the imposition or transcendence of borders) can lead to destruction or survival. To quote Silko's words to Arnold, "[W]hat matters is how you feel and how you see things, and not how you are on the outside. ... That's why in *Almanac* the only hope for the retaking of the Americas is that it's done by people of like hearts and like minds" (26).

Works Cited

Arnold, Ellen. "Listening to the Spirits: An Interview with Leslie Marmon Silko." *SAIL* 10.3 (1998): 1-33.
Moore, David L. "Silko's Blood Sacrifice: The Circulating Witness in *Almanac of the Dead*." In *Leslie Marmon Silko: A Collection of Critical Essays*. Ed. Louis K. Barnett and James L. Thorson. Albuquerque: University of New Mexico Press, 1999. 149-183.
Silko, Leslie Marmon. *Almanac of the Dead: A Novel*. New York: Simon and Schuster, 1991.
—. *Yellow Woman and a Beauty of the Spirit: Essays on Native American Life Today*. New York: Simon and Schuster, 1996.
Reineke, Yvonne. "Overturning the (New World) Order: Of Space, Time, Writing, and Prophesy in Leslie Marmon Silko's Almanac of the Dead." *SAIL* 10.3 (1998): 65-83.

Beth Hege Piatote is a graduate student in Comparative Literature at the University of Oregon where she also teaches in the School of Journalism and Communication. Her research interests include comparative ethnic literatures and Native American representation. Currently she is working on essays dealing with representation of Plateau peoples in Oregon museums.

Imagining a New Indian: Listening to the Rhetoric of Survivance in Charles Eastman's *From the Deep Woods to Civilization*

Malea Powell
University of Nebraska at Lincoln

This is a story

The story I tell here is an invitation to a new imagining of Charles Eastman's *From the Deep Woods to Civilization* (hereafter *Deep Woods*, 1916). In his now-classic essay, "The Man Made of Words," N. Scott Momaday offers this advice: "We are what we imagine. Our very existence consists in our imagination of ourselves. Our best destiny is to imagine, at least, completely, who and what, and *that* we are" (103). Gerald Vizenor takes Momaday's advice seriously and theorizes that "the shimmers of the imagination are reason"; they are "the liberation of the last trickster stories," the traces of "tribal survivance" (*Manifest Manners: Postindian Warriors of Survivance* 14-15; hereafter *MM*). What both Momaday and Vizenor are arguing for is an imaginative liberation of indigenous peoples from the stories that have been told about us, those mythic American stories that insist on nobility or ignobility, savagism or civilization. My tellings in this essay depend not so much on the fact that the discourses of American imperialism exist/ed as they do on listening to the *use* to which Eastman put those discourses, the ways in which he represents and imagines new possibilities for Native survivance. Eastman is a subject here, a participant in his own textual making and re-making as well as in his refigurings of Indian-ness. In order to hear his figurations, I'll begin with an abbreviated recounting of the context of Eastman's life and then move to my central argument—that in imagining Native people's survivance in relation to Euroamerican cultural dominance, Eastman creates a new *Indian-ness*, a new way to be Indian in the "white man's" world.

Telling a Life

Charles Alexander Eastman was, by most accounts, "the most prominent American Indian of the early twentieth century" (Hauptman 389). Born in 1858 on the Santee Sioux (Dakota) reservation in Minnesota, Eastman was, at least genealogically, no stranger to the import of Euroamerican culture in

Indian country.[1] He was the great-grandson of Cloud Man (Mahpiya Wichasta), one of the "earliest converts to the civilization programs among the Santees" (Wilson 11), and was the grandson of the noted Euroamerican artist Captain Seth Eastman and Stands Sacred (Cloud Man's daughter) and the son of their daughter, Mary Nancy Eastman, and Many Lightnings (Jacob Eastman). In the aftermath of the Great Sioux Uprising of 1862, Eastman (then Ohiyesa) fled with his paternal grandmother Uncheedah to Canada until his father reappeared and persuaded him to go to school.[2] Ohiyesa became Charles and began attending the Santee Normal School in 1875. Eastman spent the next fifteen years of his life gaining and mastering the "modern ideal of Christian culture" (*Deep Woods* xvii), working his way through Beloit College, Knox College, Kimball Union Academy, Dartmouth College and Boston University Medical School.

In November of 1890, at the age of 32, he arrived at the Pine Ridge Agency, South Dakota, to accept his appointed post as Physician. By January (1891) he was caring for those Lakota who had survived the massacre at Wounded Knee. Eastman clashed with the Indian agent there and was eventually harassed into resigning his post.[3] He moved to St. Paul and by 1893 his essays were being published in magazines like *Nicholas* and *Harpers*, and he had delivered a speech, "Sioux Mythology," at the World Colombian

---

[1] Most accounts of Eastman's life, including his own in *Indian Boyhood* and *From the Deep Woods to Civilization,* mark his isolation from white culture during the first eleven years of his life despite his maternal family's clear relationship to whites.

[2] The Uprising took place in June of 1862 when the Santee, near starvation due to the exploitive practices of corrupt Indian agents, were denied the rations and annuities that had been guaranteed them by treaty. Many Native people fled to Canada to escape retribution from the U.S. government while others were forced onto reservations in what is now Nebraska and the Dakotas. 303 Santees were sentenced to hanging, 38 were actually hanged by order of President Abraham Lincoln. It was the largest public hanging in the history of the United States. Those who escaped death did so by converting to Christianity—this group included Jacob Eastman, who spent three years in the federal penitentiary in Davenport, Iowa before he converted and was released to reclaim his family.

[3] Eastman's gripe at Pine Ridge was with the Indian agent there, Captain George LeRoy Brown, a Civil War veteran. The controversy was concerned with a government payment of $100,000 to "non-hostiles" at Pine Ridge for losses to their property and livestock during the Wounded Knee massacre. A Special Agent James Cooper was put in charge of disbursement of the funds. Lakotas began complaining to Eastman immediately that they weren't receiving their rightful shares of the money. A series of conflicts ensued, ending with a public battle of words in the Eastern press which had Elaine Goodale Eastman condemning Herbert Welsh, who had sided against Eastman. Brown publicly stated that he was "convinced either that his [Eastman's] knowledge of the English language is utterly at fault, or that he willfully mis-states facts." Eastman was consistently represented as deceitful, disrespectful of white authority, and prone to incite Indians against whites. He was suspended from his duties at Pine Ridge and moved his family to St. Paul.

Exposition. Through his writing, Eastman gained the reputation as an educated Indian. From St. Paul Eastman's path is complicated—he worked for a while as an International Secretary for the YMCA, then went to Washington, D.C. to advocate for the restoration of Santee treaty rights (abolished after the 1862 uprisings), then in 1899 accepted a temporary job as an agent for Captain R.H. Pratt at the Carlisle Indian School.

In 1902 Eastman's first book, *Indian Boyhood*, was published. Shortly afterwards, Hamlin Garland, who was in charge of a massive "re-naming" program to obtain "standard" last names for Indian people as a way to protect their property rights, appointed Eastman as his Renaming Clerk, a position he held until 1909.[4] In 1910, Eastman obtained a grant from the University of Pennsylvania museum to study and collect Indian folktales and artifacts. While studying the Ojibway (Anishinaabe), his writings became more nature-centered, more philosophical—a "renewed" Eastman wrote *The Soul of the Indian* in late 1910. In 1916, the other half of his autobiography, *Deep Woods* was published. In 1923 (following a slew of financial problems and dissolution of his marriage), Eastman was appointed to the office of U.S. Indian Inspector by the Coolidge administration. As a part of his duties, Eastman was ordered to investigate several rumors surrounding the existence of Sacajewea (Louis and Clark's "Indian guide").[5] Fired from that position, he moved to Chicago in 1925 (to be near the Newberry Library collections) and began working on a new manuscript. In January of 1939 Eastman suffered a severe heart attack. He died January 11, 1939 and was buried in Detroit's Evergreen Cemetery.

Throughout his career of service as a doctor and inspector for the Indian Bureau, as a spokesman for the Boy Scouts, and as a founder and officer of the Society of American Indians, he "tested the hard-won standard" of Euroamerican "civilization" (*Deep Woods* xvii). His writings (several articles

---

[4] This re-naming project was originally conceived of by Indian Commissioner Thomas Morgan (1890) in response to passage of the Dawes Act(1886): "the inheritance of property will be governed by the laws of respective States, and it will cause needless confusion and, doubtless, considerable ultimate loss to the Indians if no attempt is made to have the different members of a family known by the same name on the records"(qtd in Prucha 673-674). Ignored until 1902, the re-naming project was put into practice at the urging of Hamlin Garland. Though Eastman was the most successful renaming agent, revising the names of about 25,000 Siouxan families, "Garland's plans for other tribes did not work as well" and officials in Washington, D.C. lost interest. For more information, see Francis Paul Prucha's *The Great Father*.

[5] During the late nineteenth- and early twentieth-century there was considerable debate surrounding Sacajawea, who served as a guide for the Lewis and Clark expedition. Many claimed that she hadn't really existed at all since her identity was difficult to pinpoint. In the BIA's 1924 study, she was identified as a woman named Porivo, a Shoshoni who had been adopted and raised in a Hidatsa village in North Dakota and later married to a French fur trader (Toussaint Charbonneau).

and eleven books) have generally been characterized as commentary on the dissonance he observed between "Indian" and "White" cultural values. In those writings, Eastman seems determined to build an "uneasy alliance" through "consolidat[tion of] Christian and Sioux values" (Wong 142). Even if we see Eastman only as the reformers of his time did—as a "sample of what can be done for these [Indian] people by education" (Morgan, qtd in Wilson 72)—he would still stand as "a seminal figure in the development of contemporary native American intellectualism and literature" (Churchill 152). What I want to suggest here is that we see him as something more than that exemplary civilized Indian, that we see him, instead, as an early Native intellectual who learned to *use* the schools and tools of Euroamerican culture in order to speak out on behalf of Native peoples, to correct misconceptions about the "savagery" of tribal life, and to refigure the possibilities of Indian-ness for future generations.

Listening

My listenings to Eastman focus on *From the Deep Woods to Civilization*, the text in which Eastman represents his encounters with Euroamerican cultural values through its system of education. My claim here is that Eastman *uses* both late-nineteenth and early-twentieth century beliefs about Indians, and that he both capitulates to and destabilizes the ideological basis of those beliefs in order to imagine a new kind of Indian-ness. Methodologically, this means hearing his *use* of figures of popular identification—the Indian, the Civilized Man—not as the simple reproduction of dominant discourse but as the means whereby he becomes *a subject who can be heard* inside the arena of dominant discourse. In his text, Eastman simultaneously creates himself as "the Indian" and "the Civilized Man" in ways that are clearly tactical and rhetorical. He imagines and represents himself as a crossblood subject, "authentic" as both an Indian and a citizen. I use the word "crossblood" here in Vizenor's sense of the word, the "double others" who are "the discoveries of the ecstatic separations of one another from the simulations of the other in the representations of an 'authentic' tribal culture" (*MM* 45). Crossbloods are "a postmodern tribal bloodline" (*Crossbloods* vii-viii) who participate in what W.E.B. DuBois called "double consciousness"—"always looking at one's self through the eyes of others" (*Souls* 45).[6] This "doubly" participatory pole constructs a different kind of

---

[6] There are definite philosophical connections between W.E.B. DuBois's *The Souls of Black Folk* (1903) and Eastman's *The Soul of the Indian* (1911), a link that Eastman's final chapter of *Deep Woods* tropes in its title "The Soul of the White Man." DuBois and Eastman both spoke during a session of The First Universal Races Congress in London, England (1911). I believe that Eastman saw his own work, and that of the Society of American Indians, as similar to that of DuBois in establishing a cadre of "race intellectuals" within American culture.

subject, one who is an active participant in the cultural economy of both the "deep woods" and "civilization."

The concept of tactical authenticity is grounded in my understanding of Michel de Certeau's articulation of *use* practices in relation to systems of culture in *The Practice of Everyday Life* (1984). According to de Certeau, *use* is both a productive practice—it makes something—and an act of consumption—it turns an already made product into something else. De Certeau delineates two kinds of *use* through which humans interact with systems of culture—strategies and tactics. Strategies are "circumscribed as proper" (xix), they postulate "a place that can be delimited as its own and serve as the base from which relations with an exteriority composed of targets or threats can be managed" (36). Strategies are, then, actions that are delimited by the propriety of the system, connected to the power of the system, and sustained by it. Tactics, contrarily, are not proper; in other words, they don't recognize the propriety of the system as binding and have no sense of "a borderline distinguishing the other as a visible totality" (xix). Tactics are "calculated action[s] determined by the absence of a proper locus" (37), a production of knowledge determined by its absence, not its presence, in discourses of power which are "bound by [their] very visibility" (37). The place of the tactic, then, is "the space of the other" (37).[7] Those who engage in *use* as a tactic, then, are able to consume and not be consumed, "to remain other within the system" that has seemingly assimilated them, to maintain "their difference in the very space that the occupier [is] organizing" (32). This pose, this insinuation without delimitation, is clearly related to Vizenor's crossblood as well as to the trickster, a figure who is a space of liberation, a "communal sign," a "concordance of narrative voices" (*Narrative Chance: Postmodern Discourse on Native American Indian Literatures* 12; hereafter *NC*). Trickster inhabits the "wild space over and between sounds, words, sentences and narratives" and remakes them into something else (*NC* 196). By enumerating instances of tactical authenticity and by listening to his careful critiques of Euroamerican cultural institutions like capitalism and Christianity, we can begin to hear the rhetorical refigurings in *Deep Woods* which argue for a kind of reconciliation and balance that, instead of marking the inevitable end of "the Indian," ultimately produces a crossblood subject, a new *Indian-ness*.

In *Deep Woods* Eastman's representational tactics perform a number of functions: they authenticate Eastman as "Indian" and as "civilized Indian"; they educate the turn-of-the-century Euroamerican audience about "Indians" with representations that the culture can imagine as "real"; they educate that

---

[7] De Certeau's example of tactical *use* is that made by *los indios* (the indigenous inhabitants of Central and South America) of the products of Spanish colonization: "the Indians often used the laws, practices, and representations that were imposed on them by force or by fascination to ends other than those of their conquerors; they made something else out of them; they subverted them from within" (32).

same audience about the negative aspects of "civilized" society when viewed through the eyes of a so-called savage. Rhetorically, Eastman becomes a "real" Indian immediately. As *Deep Woods* opens, readers are directed to his previous work, *Indian Boyhood*, both in the foreword and in the first paragraph of the first chapter where he explicitly refers to the event that closed *Indian Boyhood*—the arrival of his father and his "long journey" into Euroamerica (*Deep Woods* 1). This connection seems important since Eastman tells the story of his own Indian-ness in *Indian Boyhood*, a book that begins by asking: "what boy would not be an Indian for a while when he thinks of the freest life in the world?" (3). That boyhood story is briefly re-told in *Deep Woods*: "From childhood I was consciously trained to be a man," "to adapt myself perfectly to natural things," to "have faith and patience" and "self-control and be able to maintain silence," "to do with as little as possible and start with nothing most of the time, because *a true Indian* always shares whatever he may possess" (1-2 emphasis mine). This re-telling is important since this time, in *Deep Woods*, the story of his Indian-ness will be told alongside and in relation to the story of his acculturation to white society. Eastman clearly sets out to view this process of acculturation, and of the Euroamerican society whose values he encounters, through his understanding of Indian-ness.

Eastman displays this mixed way of seeing and understanding, whether he is describing Indian or White cultural practices. In describing his traditional Indian upbringing, Eastman tells us that his "tribal foes" are mere rivals like those of a college athlete, that he had "no thought of destroying" them (2). He emphasizes his qualifications as a man: "Thus I was trained thoroughly for an all-round out-door life and for all natural emergencies. I was a good rider and a good shot with the bow and arrow" (5). To an audience still deeply attached to the romance of the frontier, this rugged preparedness would have marked him clearly as masculine, both in terms of their imaginings of what Indian people value as well as in terms of their own Euroamerican gender values. At 15, Charles Eastman was poised on the edge of "a man's life" when his father, the recently converted Jacob Eastman, appeared and painted for him "a totally new vision of the white man, as a religious man and kindly" (7).

Through the weight of "filial duty and affection," Eastman agrees to take the "perilous journey" that his father required of him. Eastman attended school in Flandreau, at first "an object of curiosity" who cut his hair and adopted the clothing of the other schoolchildren (21). He did so in an effort to accept his father's challenge to become a different kind of warrior, one who sees the English language and books as "the bows and arrows of the white man" (16), who finds that learning the English alphabet is like his "bird's track and fish-fin studies" (23). Eastman puts the most powerful equivalences between Indian-ness and white-ness into his father's voice: "'The way of knowledge,' he continued, 'is like our old way of hunting"

(29); "'Remember, my boy, it is the same as if I sent you on your first warpath. I shall expect you to conquer'" (32). These early equivalences especially reinforce Eastman's representation of himself as a "real" Indian, for even as he undergoes the "civilizing" process, he does so to remain Indian, to carry out the duty of a warrior, to obey his father "to the end" (50).

Even so, it seems as if "a mingling of admiration and indignation" creeps into Eastman's texts when he offers his father's seemingly wonder-filled descriptions of Euroamerican culture (8):

> But here is a race which has learned to weigh and measure everything, time and labor and the results of labor, and has learned to accumulate and preserve both wealth and the records of experience for future generations. You yourselves know and use some of the wonderful inventions of the white man, such as guns and gunpowder, knives and hatchets, garments of every description, and there are thousands of other things both beautiful and useful. (8)

Remember, Eastman has just told us how wonderful and whole his childhood was, a childhood lived in harmony with nature, characterized by contact with the physical world and by a reverent sense of spirituality (2). What Eastman then offers his readers, in the words of his father, is a culture utterly different than that of the Santee—a material culture whose inventions are weapons of "the white man's warfare for spoliation and conquest" (2). It is just a few pages until Eastman's descriptions of the "strange appearance of [the] schoolchildren" at Flandreau who are dressed in yet another example of the "wonderful inventions" of Euroamerican culture (8,21). And it is this very material culture that Eastman himself will critique throughout *Deep Woods*: "evidently there were some disadvantages connected with this mighty civilization, for we Indians seldom found it necessary to guard our possessions" (62). Given even these small pieces of textual evidence, it becomes difficult to not read Eastman's "admiration" as ironic and pointed.

Many of Eastman's early observations in *Deep Woods* can be read doubly as commentary about the ways in which early twentieth-century Euroamericans conceived of Indians and as a warning to those dominant cultural readers as well. For example, on encountering the schoolchildren at Flandreau, Eastman writes: "I realized for the first time that I was an object of curiosity, and it was not a pleasant feeling. On the other hand, I was considerably interested in the strange appearance of these school-children" (21). While it's certainly possible to read this as straight explication, when read doubly the two sentences express more than a young boy's discomfort in strange surroundings. At the same time as Eastman acknowledges that Indians are the objects of a Euroamerican gaze, he also establishes himself as having the ability to look back. Given the position of the observation—in the first quarter of the text—it rhetorically establishes Eastman as both subject and object in his own text. Although many Euroamericans will read *Deep Woods* in order to satisfy their curiosity about Indians, there will always be an Eastman looking back at the "strange appearance" of his dominant culture audience.

Because Eastman poses as the "Indian informant" in his text it is necessary that his audience find him to be "civilized" as well in order to believe his positive representation of Indian people and culture. Again, the use of equivalences between Indian and Euroamerican culture works to construct him as knowledgeable about the workings of civilization. One can read his long narrative of education as one way to convince Euroamerican readers that he is, in fact, civilized since he is successful in the terms set down by the dominant culture. Eastman also shores up his status as "civilized" by linking himself to important and influential white people. One of the first instances of this occurs while Eastman is at Yankton:

> Next to my own father, this man [Dr. Alfred Riggs] did more than perhaps any other to make it possible for me to grasp the principles of true civilization.... Associated with him was another man who influenced me powerfully toward Christian living. This was the Rev. Dr. John P. Williamson, the pioneer Presbyterian missionary. (48)

Both Riggs and Williamson were missionaries, the sons of well-known early Presbyterian missionaries Stephen R. Riggs and Dr. Thomas S. Williamson.[8] In fact, it was with the help of Dr. John Williamson that the group of Indians which included Jacob Eastman had been able to establish the settlement at Flandreau in 1869. Dr. Alfred Riggs was the superintendent of the Santee Normal Training School, the school that Eastman was attending in 1871, also where Eastman's brother, John, worked as a teacher. What Eastman does in this passage is to offer his tutelage under the supervision of two of the most successful Indian assimilationists of the time as proof of his inculcation in Christian values. He learned "civilization" from the best of them.

Further, Eastman figures Riggs as a surrogate father in the above passage, a significant representation given that Jacob Eastman died in 1876, just as Charles was preparing to enter Beloit College, a move made possible through the recommendation and support of Riggs. Eastman links descriptions of

---

[8] Stephen Riggs and Thomas Williamson were Presbyterian missionaries sent by the American Board of Commissioners for Foreign Missions to minister among the Santee. Williamson established one of the most successful missions among the Santee at Lac qui Parle. Riggs became an authority on Siouxan languages (he wrote and published The Grammar and Dictionary of the Dakota, 1852). Their sons, John Williamson and Alfred Riggs continued their work among the Santees. Alfred Riggs's Santee Normal Training School was the first educational institution that taught in both English and Indian language (in this case, Sioux). Riggs was much criticized for this bilingual approach to civilizing.

both events in two contiguous paragraphs at the end of the third chapter of *Deep Woods*. The first paragraph describes how Eastman felt when offered the chance to attend Beloit: "This was a great opportunity, and I grasped it eagerly, though I had not yet lost my old timidity about venturing alone among the white people" (50). The very next sentence, the first in the following paragraph, tells of his father's death. Eastman writes: This was a severe shock to me, but I felt even more strongly that I must carry out his wishes" (50). Eastman's text links the efforts of Riggs to offer him a larger, though still intimidating, participation in the world of Euroamerica through education with the dying wishes of his father for him to "set [his] feet in the new trail" (50). Eastman follows the trail marked out for him by his father and Riggs and, as a result, is able to construct an almost five-page resume of his own philanthropic deeds in the final chapter of *Deep Woods* (182-193). Eastman writes that he "was invited to represent the North American Indian at the First Universal Races Congress in London, England, in 1911" (189) and refers to his "work for the Boy Scouts" (193). He combines this with a litany of the important people that he had met and/or corresponded with: "a very pleasant occasion of my meeting men and women distinguished in literature was the banquet given to Mark Twain on his seventieth birthday" (190); "had the honor of acquaintance with many famous and interesting people" followed by a page-long list of public figures and clergymen whose "large circle not so well known to the public, but whose society has been to me equally stimulating and delightful" (192). This affiliation tactic helps to mark Eastman's class status as well. Despite the fact that he suffered from financial troubles for most of his life, Eastman had status as a public figure and was aware of himself as living "more or less in the public eye" (192).[9]

[9] Interestingly enough, Eastman's financial troubles were nearly as famous as his writings. In fact, they were a topic of discussion—as an anonymous reference, of course—in Francis E. Leupp's *The Indian and His Problem*, published shortly after Leupp left his position as Commissioner of Indian Affairs. Eastman's large family (Charles and Elaine had six children) was difficult to support on the pay he received during his various engagements with the Indian Bureau, and he was never as financially independent as he seemed to want to be, though his situation seemed to get better after his publication of six books (1911-1918) and their subsequent foreign editions, his lecture tours and the opening of the summer camps in 1915. That Eastman's financial affairs were a topic of public speculation is, I think, important in terms of how Eastman's claim to "civility" was being worked through and disputed in the dominant culture. His financial problems rarely appear in Eastman's own texts, only in texts written about him. Since the money Eastman received (mostly from Alfred Riggs and Frank Wood) was used directly to support his own wife and children it seems possible that mention of them would hurt Eastman's representation of himself as a "civilized Indian," a successful citizen who happened to be Santee, given the dominant cultural notions concerning masculinity and its responsibilities and the popular notion that "Indians" were too lazy to support their families. Also little mentioned in Eastman's writings are the frequent assaults on his morality, his truthfulness and his tendency to foment conflict with Indian agents. For example,

This status gains him credibility in the eyes of his early twentieth-century Euroamerican audience who can be assured that he is "like them" in some respects because he circulates easily amongst people who are not only "like them" but who are role models for them.

Textual and symbolic affiliations are an important part of Eastman's process of authorizing himself, not just as a "civilized Indian," but also as a highly regarded member of the elite of white society. The *use* of linkage and affiliation with this elite society, combined with the display of his knowledge about Indians, are central components of Eastman's tactical authentication. Interestingly enough, it is this representation of affiliation with the Euroamerican elite that often lessens his credibility as anything but a "representative of sell[ing]-out and assimilation by [contemporary] radical indigenists" (Churchill 152). This label of "sell-out" is confusing, I think, especially in light of Eastman's persistent critiques of the very characteristics of Euroamerican culture that were argued to be primary components in "saving" the Indian. For example, in *Deep Woods*, Eastman *uses* the space of authority he created through affiliation and display of "Indian" expertise to launch direct and indirect critiques at capitalism and Christianity.

Eastman's direct critiques are most potent when they are aimed at the Euroamerican obsession with material wealth and at the institution of Christianity. In the final chapter of *Deep Woods*, "The Soul of the White Man," Eastman speculates on the problems with "civilization." He writes: "when I reduce civilization to its lowest terms, it becomes a system of life based upon trade" (194). He links what he sees as the Euroamerican focus on making money to an American desire for supremacy in the very next sentence: "The dollar is the measure of value, and might still spells right; otherwise, why war?" (194). It is wise to keep in mind that *Deep Woods* was published in 1916, in the midst of World War I and during a time of intense neo-imperial rivalry. Put next to Eastman's earlier commentaries about tribal rivalries, that Indians had "no thought of destroying a nation, taking away their country or reducing the people to servitude" (2), this simple observation becomes a powerful critique of early twentieth century American imperialism.

Eastman's diagnosis of Christianity as it is practiced by most Euroamericans is even more biting. He calls it "a machine-made religion ... supported by money, and more money ... too many of the workers were after quantity rather than quality of religious experience" (141). His linking of white

---

Eastman is said to have left his position as physician at Crow Creek (1900-1903) because of "immoral conduct" with the superintendent of the school there, Miss Augusta Hultman. Miss Hultman was dismissed from the school after having engaged in "unladylike" behavior with Eastman. Eastman was allowed to remain but the agent there, Harry Chamberlain, later claimed that Eastman was stirring up discontent among the Indians at Crow Creek. Seen as a threat because he spoke Dakota and other Siouxan dialects, Eastman was soon offered another position. For more information, see Wilson.

religious practices to the desire for money, and that desire to the conditions of war is quite provocative. In all of Eastman's commentary about Christianity and capitalism there is a single argument running underneath—that the Indian way was better. Though he regularly admits the necessity of Native people learning about white cultural values, it is his own synthesized version of bicultural education that appears again and again. So although he is sharply critical of Euroamericans' inability to practice the tenets of Christianity— "how is it that our [Indian] simple lives were so imbued with the spirit of worship, while much church-going among whites [Christians] led often to such very small results" (141)—he doesn't lay the blame for that inability on the religion itself. He writes that "it appears that they [whites] are anxious to pass on their religion to all races of men, but keep very little of it themselves," and then tempers that critique with the observation that "the white man's religion is not responsible for his mistakes" (193-195). The blame is on the desire for material wealth, a desire that Eastman locates in Euroamerican civilization itself when he writes: "we also know that many brilliant civilizations have collapsed in physical and moral decadence" (195).

Eastman's critiques are not all as explicit as the ones above. For example, he juxtaposes a penetrating description of Beloit College—"The college grounds covered the site of an ancient village of mound-builders"—with a historical bookmark—"it must be remembered that this was September, 1876, less than three months after Custer's gallant command was annihilated by the hostile Sioux"—and a reminder of his Indian-ness—"I was especially troubled when I learned that my two uncles whom we left in Canada had taken part in this famous fight"—next to a surprising image of white civilization — "when I went into town, I was followed on the streets by gangs of little white savages" (52-53). This two-page series of juxtaposed observations has a powerful effect. Eastman represents here the significance of where he is (on ancient Indian lands), how he got there (by leaving so-called savagery behind him), and what he finds there (white savages). In doing so, he simultaneously inhabits more than one "authentic" position and, in doing so, critiques the cultural beliefs that create those authenticities. He links himself to "real" Indians through his uncles, and participates in being "civilized" in his representation of Custer as "gallant" and in his being "troubled" at finding his relatives involved in the Little Big Horn incident. At the same time, though, his close relationship to the Natives who fought against Custer is implied alongside his observation of "white savages." In "subvert[ing] the language usually limited to describing Native Americans and appl[ying] it to Euro-Americans" (Wong 149), he surfaces the complexity of the stories being told and re-told about Indians, implicitly critiquing the intertwined nature of beliefs about savagism and civilization, whether Indian or white.

Even more so, Eastman's descriptions of Dartmouth offer a stunning critique of Euroamerican imperialism, most effective in the "gentleness of polemic" he displays (Churchill 152). Of Dartmouth he writes: "thinking of the time when red men lived here in plenty and freedom, it seemed as if I had been destined to come view their graves and bones" (65). While some may read this as further proof of Eastman's belief in discourses of Manifest Destiny and the Vanishing Indian, I hear this as establishing a connection to a past and a people that those "red men" couldn't have imagined, a connection similar to the one that contemporary scholars can establish with Eastman. His musings about Dartmouth and Indians certainly sound like resistance: "No, I said to myself, I have come to continue that which in their last struggle they proposed to take up" (65). Eastman's text here is clear—the indigenous peoples of New England have been killed off, but he will continue their struggle, he will become "a sort of prodigal son of old Dartmouth ... the New England Indians, for whom it was founded, had departed well-nigh a century earlier, and now a warlike Sioux, like a wild fox, had found his way into this splendid seat of learning" (68).

For Vizenor, this deliberately ironic pose is what identifies Eastman as a "postindian warrior," that he encounters his enemies "with the same courage in literature" as his ancestors "once evinced on horses" (*MM* 4). For me it seems significant that most scholars avoid focusing on these descriptive passages, passages that clearly reveal Eastman not only as not helpless in the face of civilization, but also as purposefully using its tools in order to continue an indigenous struggle against Euroamerican imperialism. It's a trickster move that Eastman makes when he drops these "innocent" comments on his journey from the "deep woods" to "civilization." For Vizenor, and for myself, these comments mark the trail of the postindian warrior who has "learned to use metaphors as the simulations of survivance" (51). In using the metaphors of dominant discourse, Eastman marks himself as a subject within it, not just as a victim subject to it. In doing so I hear him imagine a new Indian-ness, one that is not "a fictional copy of the past" (*IB* vi).

This re-imagining begins in *Deep Woods* with Eastman's representation of his father's views about civilization, that "there was no alternative for the Indian" (16), and quickly becomes his own, "it was the new era for the Indian" (33). While Eastman does not flinch from describing the injustices perpetrated against Indian peoples by whites, neither does he paint his acquisition of the tools of civilization as a mark of the "inevitable" disappearance of indigenous peoples. In fact, he sees it as a way to maintain the existence of Indians, although not the same "Indian" being reproduced by Euroamerican desire:

> I wished that our [Sioux] young men might at once take up the white man's way, and prepare themselves to hold office and wield influence in their native states. Although this hope has not been fully realized, I have the satisfaction of knowing that not a few Indians now hold positions of trust and exercise some political power. (65-66)

Later on in *Deep Woods*, Eastman offers further commentary on "the Indian" by complicating early twentieth-century notions of race/ethnicity. His point about the theatricality of race/ethnicity is made with a story about his "Armenian friend" who "conceived the scheme of dressing me in native costume and sending me out to sell his goods. When I wore a jacket and fez ... I did very well. For business purposes I was a Turk" (70). This is a performance that is replicated in the frontispieces to *Deep Woods* and one of Eastman's earlier texts, *The Soul of the Indian*, which offers a picture of a bare-shouldered Charles Eastman in a full Plains-style warbonnet staring into the distance. Titled "The Vision," the likeness works to authenticate the stories and explanations of "Indian" religion it accompanies, and to mark the teller of those stories as a "real" Indian. Contrarily, the frontispiece picture in *Deep Woods* is of Eastman in a starched white-collared shirt and suit, a likeness that works similarly to authenticate him as civilized.

I hear these habitations as tactical. Through these images and the textual parallels to them throughout his writings, and within the text of his life, Eastman navigates the simple binary contradictions assumed to exist between savagism and civilization.[10] He understands Indian people *as living cultural entities*, not as destined-to-disappear victims of national sympathy and nostalgia. Shortly after the "Armenian" scene in *Deep Woods* is an explicit display of that understanding. Eastman is walking around Northfield with Mr. Moody who points out a roadside stone—"this stone is a reminder of the cruelty of your countrymen two centuries ago. Here they murdered an innocent Christian" (74). Eastman's reply is openly direct and challenging: "it might have been better if they had killed them all. Then you would not have had to work so hard to save the souls of their descendants" (74). What I hear in this passage is two-fold: Eastman following the logic of extermination to its final conclusion—they should have killed them all—but also replying to centuries of intervention from the "Friends of the Indian"—how to kill the Indian and save the man. Underneath his words is a challenge to the myth of the inevitability of the disappearance of "the Indian." As Eastman points out here, the so-called disappearance of Native peoples has hardly been either inevitable or easy; it has been the desired end

---

[10] My work on Eastman (as well as other American Indian intellectuals) relies heavily on the analysis of Euroamerican ideology provided by Roy Harvey Pearce's *Savagism and Civilization: A Study of the Indian and the American Mind* (1953, 1987). Pearce begins his text by saying "this is a book about a belief," a belief that "forced Americans to consider and reconsider what it was to be civilized and what it took to build civilization" (xvii). Pearce claims that this belief in "the savage" arose from a certitude about American progress over all obstacles, and was the product of an understanding of the Indian as "one radically different from their proper selves" (4). Early American colonists "worked out a theory of the savage which depended on an idea of a new order [Euroamerican civilization] in which the Indian could have no part" (4).

of hundreds of years of deliberate action, an end made difficult by the refusal of even the most "civilized" Indian such as himself to forget.

In his essay "Socioacupuncture: Mythic Reversals and the Striptease in Four Scenes," Vizenor tells the story of Tune Browne, a "mixed-blood tribal trickster" who "never wore beads or feathers or a wristwatch; he never paid much attention to time or to his image until he became an independent candidate for alderman" (185). In the face of public evaluation, Browne remakes himself into an "Indian" and poses "in braids and feathers" to authenticate himself. Even so, he loses the election. Afterwards, he attends "the first international conference on socioacupuncture and tribal identities" and, standing by a photographic representation of himself, Tune Browne strips (186). His striptease is accompanied by references to anthropologic emulsions: Edward Curtis's photo, "In a Piegan Lodge," the alarm clock removed, the authentic tribal image invented and captured by the photographer; and, Alfred Kroeber's Ishi, "the last survivor of the Yahi tribe in California," held captive in the anthropology museum at the University of California at Berkeley (187-188). Browne performs the "sovereign striptease" of the trickster and even the ideas of "the Indian" vanish along with the investors and colonialists who had believed them. Vizenor claims that tribal cultures have been "colonized in a reversal of the striptease" (189). The dominant discourses about "the Indian" that Eastman *uses*, then, are the patches, the clothing that hides Tune Browne's nakedness. Yet it is this nakedness that Eastman remakes in his refusal to cease to be Indian even as he takes on and displays his mastery of the accouterments of civilization.

Eastman's final comments in *Deep Woods* are often cited as proof of his "struggle" with civilization, part of a depiction of the civilized Indian as an inherent contradiction, torn between worlds. What I hear in them, instead, is Eastman's final representation of himself in *Deep Woods* as a practitioner of survivance.

> I am Indian; and while I have learned much from civilization, for which I am grateful, I have never lost my Indian sense of right and justice. I am for development and progress along social and spiritual lines, rather than those of commerce, nationalism, or material efficiency. Nevertheless, so long as I live, I am an American. (195).

For Eastman's new Indian, being Indian and American is not a contradiction. It is not easy, and there are no rules for negotiating the confluence of the discourses from which this new Indian-ness, this crossblood, arises. But Eastman's text serves as an example, a new imagining, a way to move "from the earlier inventions of the tribes" and to "surmount the scriptures of manifest manners with new stories" (*MM* 5). *Deep Woods* does offer contemporary Native scholars some ways to begin our own re-imagining. Eastman is (seemingly) a willing participant in multiple Euroamerican cultural discourses; he is aware both of how those discourses work and of how they imagine Indians; and, he looks back into the eyes of his Euroamerican readers and shows us what their world looks like from his point of view. Eastman goes beyond double consciousness, complicated enough in itself, and doubles that consciousness again.

Eastman makes it patently clear throughout *From the Deep Woods to Civilization* how utterly short that journey from the "deep woods" to "civilization" really is. And in using this title, he refigures the founding trope of Euroamerican civilization whose settlers "tamed the wilderness" and created agrarian order in its place. In reminding us of the manifest-ness of the destiny of Native peoples on this continent, Eastman *uses* the common Euroamerican justification for hundreds of years of colonization and genocide and forces contemporary Native scholars to ask: "Could there have been a wiser resistance literature or simulation of survivance at this time? What did it mean to be the first generation to hear the stories of the past, bear the horrors of the moment, and write the future?" (Vizenor *MM* 51). Eastman himself claims that his only objective in writing *Deep Woods* was "to present the American Indian in his true character" (187), a truth that had little to do with Euroamerican imaginings of the noble savage. In presenting his "true Indian," Eastman creates a rhetoric of survivance, a *use* that requires persistence, intelligence and humor as it imagines a new Native subjectivity, a new Indian-ness, a word warrior, and a new beginning for us all.

Works Cited

Churchill, Ward. Rev of Ohiyesa: Charles Eastman, Santee Sioux, by Raymond Wilson. *Western American Literature* 19.2 (1984): 152-154.

De Certeau, Michel. *The Practice of Everyday Life*. Trans. Steven Rendall. Berkeley: U of CA P, 1984.

DuBois, W.E.B. *The Souls of Black Folk. 1903*. NY: Dover, 1994.

Eastman, Charles Alexander. *Indian Boyhood*. Alexandria, VA: Time-Life, 1993. Rpt. 1902 ed., McClure, Phillips, New York publ.

Eastman, Charles Alexander. *From the Deep Woods to Civilization*. Boston: Little, Brown, and Co., 1916.

—. *The Soul of the Indian*. Lincoln, NE: U of NE P, 1980. Rpt. 1911 ed., Houghton Mifflin, Boston publ.

Eastman, Elaine Goodale. "Foreword." *From the Deep Woods to Civilization*. By Charles Eastman. Alexandria, VA: Time-Life, 1993. Rpt. 1902 ed., Mclure, Phillips, New York publ. xvii- xviii.

Hauptman, Laurence M. Rev. of Ohiyesa: Charles Eastman, Santee Sioux, by Raymond Wilson. *Pacific Historical Review* 53.3, 1984: 389.

Leupp, Francis E. *The Indian and His Problem*. New York: Charles Scribner's Sons, 1910.

Momaday, N. Scott. "The Man Made of Words." *Literature of the American Indians: Views and Interpretations.* Ed. Abraham Chapman. NY: Meridian, 1975. 96-110.

Niess, Judith. *Native American History: A Chronology of a Culture's Vast Achievements and Their Links to World Events.* NY: Ballantine Books, 1996.

Pearce, Roy Harvey. *Savagism and Civilization: A Study of the Indian and the American Mind.* Rev. ed. of *The Savages of America.* 1953. Berkeley: U of CA P, 1988.

Prucha, Francis Paul. *The Great Father.* Lincoln: U of NE P, 1995.

Vizenor, Gerald. *Crossbloods: Bone Courts, Bingo, and Other Reports.* Minneapolis: U of MN P, 1976.

—. *Manifest Manners: Postindian Warriors of Survivance.* Hanover: Wesleyan UP, 1994.

—, ed. *Narrative Chance: Postmodern Discourse on Native American Indian Literatures.* Norman: U of OK P, 1989.

—. "Socioacupuncture: Mythic Reversals and the Striptease in Four Scenes." *The American Indian and the Problem of History.* Ed. Calvin Martin. NY: Oxford UP, 1987. 180-191.

Wilson, Raymond. *Ohiyesa, Charles Eastman, Santee Sioux.* Urbana: U of IL P, 1983.

Wong, Hertha Dawn. *Sending My Heart Back Across the Years: Tradition and Innovation in Native American Autobiography.* NY: Oxford UP, 1992.

Malea Powell is an assistant professor of English at the University of Nebraska where she teaches undergraduate and graduate courses in American Indian Literatures, the History of Rhetoric and Critical Theory. She has published essays in several scholarly volumes, such as *Race, Rhetoric & Composition* (Gilyard), and *Native American Literary Strategies for the Next Millennium* (Griffin and Hafen), and in journals such as *JAC: a journal of composition theory*. She is currently working on a book project entitled *Extending the Hand of Empire: American Indians and the Indian Reform Movement, 1880-1920* and is the new general editor of *Studies in American Indian Literatures.*

"Sacred Thresholds"
Transformation and Liminality in the Novels of Linda Hogan

Linda Palen Ruzich
California State University, Sacramento

Linda Hogan's overriding value of caretaking the earth and all its inhabitants is exemplified in her efforts at the Birds of Prey Rehabilitation Foundation. There she cleans cages, feeds and grooms animals which have been damaged by their contact with humans, and observes the paradox that people are both the wounders of these animals and their healers. She spends much time raking the compound and reflects that...

> The word *rake* means to gather or heap up, to smooth the broken ground. That's what this work is, all of it, the smoothing over of broken ground, the healing of the severed trust we humans hold with earth. We gather it back together again with great care, take the broken pieces and fragments and return them to the sky. It is work at the borderland between species, at the boundary between injury and healing. (*Dwellings* 153)

The birds and other animals at the foundation are there primarily because of contact with the contemporary world: most have been hit by vehicles or shot by hunters. So the existence of the organization is a recognition both of the value of the creatures it is designed to help and the negative impact which the modern world has on them. It is a place which straddles the world of man and the world of beast, a place to repair a little of the damage done at the collision of those two worlds. In this liminal area belonging exclusively to neither human nor animal, healing of both species occurs.

This sense of the perimeters of life pervades the novels of Linda Hogan. It is in the interstices of places and events where conflict occurs and damage is done; it is also the site of healing, growth and change. At the boundaries Hogan's characters are faced with injury and difficult choices; it is there that for some, transformation takes place. Renewal occurs when the earth is valued, when people spend time to listen to the terrestrial call of God, best heard in those marginal places on the edge of human activity. In *Dwellings* Hogan writes,

> In the traditional belief systems of native people, the terrestrial call is the voice of God, or of gods, the creative power that lives on earth, inside earth, in turtle, stone, and tree. Knowledge comes from, and is

shaped by, observations and knowledge of the natural world and natural cycles. In fact, the word *God* in the dictionary definition means to call, to invoke. Like creation, it is an act of language, as if the creator and the creation are one, the primal pull of land is what summons. (85)

As the land is increasingly deforested, covered with asphalt, mined, drilled, and dammed, it becomes increasingly difficult for indigenous people to find untampered earth on which to live, grow and worship. Hogan's characters renew their internal balance as they are able to renew their relationship with the land. Because the land and the people are one, it is only at the fringes where "civilization" has not yet reached that these people are able to find a center in the tribal rituals and society that allows them to achieve reintegration after the splintering effects of their experience with the dominant culture.

That belief is seen in *Mean Spirit*, Hogan's fictionalized account of the historical events which took place when oil was discovered in the Osage country of Oklahoma in the 1920s. The byproducts of greed of the white community—extending to the federal government level—are well documented even by the FBI. The new-found wealth of the financially unsophisticated Indians left them vulnerable to murder and fraudulent schemes; the black treasure underground left the landscape vulnerable to devastating exploitation as well. The Hill Indians, as they came to be called, began to leave the town of Watona, "the gathering place," some sixty years prior to the story's events in order to escape the influx of whites. They had been warned by old Lila Blanket, the river prophet, that the Blue River predicted the loss of their lands and way of life to the coming of the whites. By the 1860s, the town was already considered a "limbo between worlds" (6) by the peaceful native people. The town represents the point of impact between the native and European cultures, a place which becomes increasingly typified by materialistic greed and calloused indifference to human life and the environment as the white-run oil companies take over, and the Indians who own(ed) the land are forced into retreat. Watona is where the Hill Indians go to collect their monthly checks for their mineral rights, where they spend their money very differently from those with European values, and where they are systematically defrauded of their earnings, their land, their freedom, even their lives.

The devastation wrought by the white encroachment is profound: Grace and Sara Blanket, John Thomas, Walker, Benoit and others are murdered; the people's earnings, lands, and livelihoods are stolen; the earth is savaged by the oil industry; the sacred eagles are slaughtered for souvenirs. Nevertheless, there are whites who, when confronted with the atrocities committed by their compatriots, cross the border of their own culture to embrace the values and lifestyles of the spiritual native people, among them Rev. Joe Billy's wife Martha, the Catholic priest Father Dunne, and John

Hale's former girlfriend, China. Dr. Black, who performs insurance exams for the evil John Hale, notices that a number of the recently-insured die mysteriously and writes to the Bureau of Investigations of his suspicions, thus redeeming himself of his unknowing part in the duplicitous scheme. He is described as having "the defeated look of an honest man in a world gone wrong" (154). It is the doctor's letter which sets in motion the investigation which ultimately leads to the arrest and conviction of John Hale, the worst of the offenders in the story, and also brings Stace Red Hawk, a Lakota Sioux who works for the Bureau, into Watona and into inner conflict with his own life and career choices. Watona provides opportunity for unscrupulous machinations against the earth and the people and creatures which occupy it; paradoxically, it also provides occasion for those few who choose to live life in balance and harmony and simplicity.

The destruction of the land is not less heinous than the destruction of lives in this book. In this novel, as is common in Native American belief, earth is portrayed as a feminine entity, and like a woman, earth is vulnerable to rape. "Earth is a woman 'complaining through an open mouth, moaning sometimes and sometimes roaring with rage' (Hogan 145) as sweating laborers drive [oil] pipe into her, inch by inch" (Brice 132). Those perpetrators are men who "... are disconnected from woman as mother, lover, or earth" (Brice 133). The earth itself (herself) protests the actions of the boorish newcomers to the region. Spontaneous fires and explosions occur after the ground is savaged by the oil drilling; a vehement wind and rain storm unexpectedly sweep across the country when Grace Blanket is murdered. The very elements of the universe are anguished, it seems, by the injustice all around.

Renewal and transformation occur when the earth is valued, when people spend time to listen to the terrestrial call of God, best heard in those marginal places on the edge of human activity. Belle Graycloud retreats to her womb-like potato cellar to pray ceremonially for days, then emerges (from Mother Earth) strengthened, able to help her family and community cope with their multiple losses and lead the fight to save the sacred bats. Her cellar is a cave-like place; both are cool, mysterious, and damp, a halfway point between under and above ground. Sorrow Cave at the edge of town is home to the bats, which are holy to the Osage people but feared by the white community and therefore endangered. The bats themselves are liminal creatures; they fly, though they are not birds, and they are mammals, though they are air-born creatures. They are active at twilight, which is neither light nor dark. By her withdrawal in quest of healing and guidance, Belle herself evokes an image of the bats: she likewise retreats to a womb-like subterranean interior —mysterious, vulnerable, and holy. After her time apart she is enabled to guide Nola Blanket through the loss of her mother Grace and the indignities of Indian school and to comfort her own daughter Lettie through the loss of her lover Benoit, murdered by thugs of the aptly-named Sheriff Gold. She is strengthened enough to endure the painful search through Tar Town for her grandson Ben, who is sinking in the quagmire of alcoholism, materialism and despair. At the pain she sees around her there she notes that "Human skin became something else, a wall, a membrane between the worlds of creation and destruction" (275). It is a fragile membrane indeed.

Like the tribal people who revere them, the bats are in grave danger of extermination by the town's dominant white power culture. Belle stands at the mouth of the cave and risks her life for the creatures by refusing to leave when Sheriff Gold comes to shoot the bats. In the face of her obstinate courage the sheriff and his men temporarily retreat, giving the Osages time to create a hole in the wall of the cave through which the bats escape to an opening on the opposite side of the hill. Thus the sacred bats and the people who hold them holy mutually guide and protect each other, each inhabiting a dangerous place on the margin of the conflicted world and each led by the other to a place of relative safety.

Stace Red Hawk, like Belle Graycloud, seeks refuge in solitude to reflect on the events around him and his response to them. Sent by the Bureau of Investigation to Watona to probe increasing reports of crime on the Osage reservation, he becomes increasingly convinced that the native people are being routinely victimized both by the explicit actions of the local white settlers and by the implicit policies of the federal government. Resisting the agency's pressure to complete a quick report, Red Hawk retreats to the town's surrounding hills. There he considers the bewildering assortment of facts he has uncovered and attempts to deal with the increasing dissatisfaction he experiences; he works as a tribal man in the employ of a government he believes is covertly involved in the destruction of the Osage people and their land. His seclusion is interrupted by his encounters with Michael Horse, and their growing friendship and trust becomes pivotal in his decision to leave the agency and return to a tribal life with the Hill people.

In this novel, meaningful life is possible only when living in harmony with land, water, the animal kingdom, other people. Fear and greed, a "mean spirit," disrupt the natural balance and bring grief to self and others. Those who engage in sacred devotion, who retreat to the margin between the material and spiritual worlds, experience transformation and redemption. The Grayclouds, accompanied by Red Hawk, are last seen in their simple wagon fleeing their flaming house and the murderous Tate to join the Hill people at the edge of the reservation. They have lost family members, their land and livelihood, and all their belongings, but "... the Grayclouds' sense of oneness with the earth is undiminished by their dislocation from place" (Brice 128). It is at that borderland where they will begin life again, transformed survivors all.

In her second novel, *Solar Storms*, Hogan focuses on the healing which takes place as boundaries are blurred or erased. The novel is set along "Poison Road," so named because of the poison that had been set out there by settlers to eliminate the remaining wolves and foxes which threatened their cattle and pigs, European imports otherwise incapable of surviving the cold polar climate. The actions of the settlers leave the land pillaged and unable to sustain the people who live there. Forests have been denuded, logjams have made the river too shallow for the fish to survive, beaver and fox populations have disappeared through trapping. The starving people have been reduced to eating the cyanide-laced deer which the hunters have used to bait their traps. The taint of that poisoning is handed down from one generation to the next, both literally and symbolically. The land and its native people are truly in need of healing from the profound injury and contamination introduced by the white incursion.

Lyrically, Hogan merges three primary elements in this novel—water and earth and mother. She tells the story of the milkstone, a rock which flowed with healing, milky water, that had been dynamited by a bishop because he was convinced that any cure which did not come from God was the devil's work (66). The novel's narrator, Angel, is greatly in need of such soothing, refreshing waters, just as she is in need of nurturing, caring, mothering. Her childhood has been just as surely "dynamited" as the milkstone of the story. She literally has been cut off from mother's milk as well as from her place in family and culture and location. She returns to a place where aged wisdom and youthful questioning, ancient customs and contemporary technology, native ecology and Euro-American land dominance collide, and those conflicts are internalized within her as much as they are manifest in the external world.

The first person with whom Angel has contact is her aging greatgrandmother, Dora-Rouge, who exists on the border between this world and the next, often conversing with her long-departed husband, Luther. The scarred adolescent arrives at the home of her long-lost relations too emotionally battered by abuse at the hands of her mother and by insensitivity in a succession of foster homes to bond with anyone. At the outset Angel finds a place in her newly-discovered family: she tenderly cares for DoraRouge, feeding and carrying the frail woman. The trust she gradually develops in this far-away place with this great grandmother who has one foot in this life and the other in the hereafter is the first step in Angel's long voyage toward emotional restoration and womanhood.

The wounded teen soon learns the story of the much-beleaguered last glacier bear that her grandmother Agnes had come to love and ultimately chose to kill as an act of mercy (an event which presages the ambiguous and compelling action of *Power*, Hogan's third novel). Throughout the story, Agnes (and later, Agnes' daughter-in-law, Bush) wears the coat, now threadbare, made from the bear's hide. Agnes tells her granddaughter, "When I wear this coat, Angel, I see the old forests, the northern lights, the nights that belong to something large that we don't know" (54). The coat contains the presence of the bear as it was meant to live, wild and free in ancient forests. When wrapped in its warmth, its wearer is nurtured in a womb-like environment. The paradox is that the living bear, caged by its captor, had to be killed in order for its spirit to live. The coat, then, becomes a metaphor for the history of the Beautiful People; the past, though gone, guides, informs, comforts, and identifies them as those who live(d) in harmony with the land and its cycles of life.

When we first meet the narrator, Angel, she is a teenager looking for an escape from the series of foster homes in which she has lived her life. As a youngster she suffered abuse at the hands of her ice-hearted mother, Hannah, who treated her daughter in the same horrific manner which she herself endured. Angel's face and psyche are disfigured from events of which she has no memory and which are therefore all the more powerful. The scars on her face are evidence of injuries from which she has healed physically but from which she continues to suffer psychologically. Having received a letter and a few well-worn dollars from Dora-Rouge, Angel arrives nervous and uncertain at Fur Island, which exists at the boundary of time, just as she is looking forward and backward simultaneously, teetering precariously between youth and adulthood.

Angel has returned to her newly-discovered family "like rain falling into a lake" (26). At this place, called the Navel of the World, where frogs mysteriously emerge from the mud after years of drought to begin their life, Angel, too, gradually begins her own emergence from the drought of her early years. As Angel later recalls the vines which wound their tentacles inside Bush's house, she describes "Those hungry, reaching vines that wanted to turn everything back to its origins—walls, doors, a ladder-back chair, even a woman's life. They wanted to cover it all and reclaim the island for themselves" (73). In this place at the border of time and space she begins to reclaim her own life and recover her lost identity and her joy.

Throughout the book we see a landscape which exists at the "boundary between land and water" (67). "It was the north country, the place where water was broken apart by land, land split open by water so that the maps showed places both bound and, if you knew the way in, boundless. The elders said it was where land and water had joined together in an ancient pact, now broken" (21). As winter sets in, the lines between land and water become blurred; snow and ice cover the land, and the water of the lake freezes, becoming an extension of the shore. Even the division between earth and sky is erased: "A cold firmament, beautiful and frightening, solid and alive. I could hear it, the tribe of water speaking" (118). "Time vanished when we were frozen inside," Angel says. She and Bush go outside and in "... a moment of silence ... we heard the sound of the northern lights ... and I heard the shimmering of ice crystals, charged by solar storms" (119). The storms represent the whirlwinds of conflict between warring societies, white and Indian, as well as the internal conflicts of the troubled teen. The storms are literal events as well, reminding us that the forces of the universe are eternal and omnipotent and will overwhelm mankind's puny (and often destructive) attempts at control over them.

The water images in this northern place are ambiguous, at times life-giving, at others, life-taking, and in this dual capacity provide a metaphor for a harsh reality. The reader, like Angel, gradually comes to know Hannah, who came to Agnes, Bush and Dora-Rouge out of the storm, literally washed up on shore by whirlwind-whipped waves. Her heart is ice, water in one of its lethal forms. As Angel reflects on her own cold birth, she says, "... I belonged to that winter ... I arrived in the place where traders had passed with sleds of dead, frozen animals ... I was born in a house of snow" (108).

At the center of the lake surrounding Fur Island is Hungry Mouth, a treacherous circle of water that never freezes, a death-trap for unwary people and animals. It swallows tipsy trappers, inexperienced young deer, and Frenchie's daughter. Significantly, Angel comes to know the source of the scars on her face: her mother had savagely bitten her, thereby demonstrating another kind of "hungry mouth," which had eaten away Angel's love, identity, and appearance.

Eventually, Angel and her "three mothers" journey toward the far north country of their ancestors where they encounter the Se Nay River, which has become a raging torrent after engineers had diverted the water of the Big Arm River into its channel. It is at this site that Agnes makes her crucial pact with the river, eventually forfeiting her own life for the safe passage of the intrepid little band, a covenant kept this time by both parties—Agnes and the river.

But water also is a source of life. Frogs emerge from the primordial mud after the drought is over; fish and turtles thrive in the lake and rivers. Bush is a person more at home in and with the water than on land. She earns cash by assembling turtle skeletons and almost becomes one with the water as she paddles in her canoe. Part of Angel's healing occurs as she learns to swim. "Think turtle," instructs Bush, and with that admonition Angel, like her mentor, becomes part of the natural world, the essential shift toward redemption for all of Hogan's transformed characters.

It is the journey and the contacts she makes in that far country which complete Angel's recovery begun months earlier. By the time the little group has reached "the territory's outermost edges," the teen has encountered danger and deprivation of an intensity few will ever experience. Her back and muscles ache from the relentless privations of traveling by canoe and sleeping on the banks of rivers. She has swum under lake surfaces to see the pictographs inscribed by the ancient ones on cliff walls now submerged, gone for all succeeding generations because of the dam construction further north. She has tenderly carried the tiny Dora-Rouge over land passages and learned that vital, health-giving plants have been lost forever because of the destruction of the land. She returns from a quest for redroot, a medicine the failing Agnes needs to survive, to see what appears to be a "small raft of blue flowers" (208). It is, of course, Agnes, buried under a mound of the fragrant blossoms, floating between sky and water, transformed by death, the completion of the bargain she had made with the river god. As she protests in disbelief and grief, Angel is wrapped by Bush in the bear coat Agnes will never wear again. She wakes during the night to a vision of Agnes and the bear, walking together through the sky, both of whom are beautiful and renewed.

Angel hears the story of the old woman Eho, the keeper of animals, who bargains with water to be with the whale she loves; the parallels between Eho and Agnes, who bargained with the river to join the bear she treasured, clearly make this story a re-living of that ancient tale. The myth embedded within the novel serves several purposes. Certainly it connects the contemporary plot with the ageless beliefs and culture of this tribal people, who have been so stripped of dignity, land, community, even life itself.

In so doing, it validates the vision, the meaning which the Beautiful People make of their existence, though so little of their former life remains. It provides a sense of continuity to a people whose future is threatened, and it is one thread in the fabric of Angel's growing sense of belonging to her clan and to her family. And as Jennifer Brice points out, "Any incarnation of the force that created, and continues to create, the world crosses boundaries of time, place, belief, and culture to convey the greatest truths, which must necessarily be spiritual" (139).

Additionally, the embedded myth serves two other literary purposes, functions discussed by Louis Gates in *Signifying Monkey*. Gates posits that the use of embedded myth decodes the action of the novel and provides indeterminacy. The Eho story valorizes and makes sense of Agnes' death; her vow has made possible their safe passage through unnavigable water and has allowed her to join the spirit of the bear she has loved since childhood. At the same time, it deconstructs our notion of fixed completion. The myth is timeless, without discrete beginning or ending; so, too, by association is the present human enactment. This tale is but one of many instances of Eho's poignant visits to earth. The story, like creation, is never completed but is a recursive cycle constantly being re-told, renewed, re-born, re-visioned.

Though from another time and another culture, Martin Buber provides eloquent commentary on the process at play in Hogan's use of myth. In his introduction to *The Legend of the Baal-Shem*, Buber describes the steps by which he came to gather and set down the teaching of the zaddiks, those Hasidic rabbis whose ecstasy comes from entering the mythos of the universe. Buber relates his experience this way:

> I have received it and have told it anew ... I have told it anew as one who was born later. I bear in me the blood and the spirit of those who created it, and out of my blood and spirit it has become new. I stand in the chain of narrators, a link between links; I tell once again the old stories, and if they sound new, it is because the new already lay dormant in them when they were told for the first time. (10)

Hogan, too, tells the stories which are at once old and new. The story of Agnes is now a link in the chain that is Eho, and that is the chain which in turn links to the rest of the world. The myth embedded here, then, reflects circularity, the connection of all things in a continuing cycle of life. "Its end is already contained in its beginning, and a new beginning in its end" (Buber 13). Because the contemporary story is so intricately related to the fable, the present working out of the myth is then elevated; it, too, becomes mythic, sanctified by inclusion. And Angel, too, becomes sanctified as she becomes part of that mythic circularity, connecting to her people's culture and history.

It is at their journey's destination that Angel meets her mother for the first time since her early childhood, and comes to know why the priest referred to Hannah as a "miracle in reverse" (100). Hannah wears clothes in layers as protection against being hurt again or known; underneath is a body covered in scars. She is the "sum total of ledger books and laws" (100), representing the rape of the land, the people, and the culture at the hands of the white intruders. As Angel shares her mother's last moments, she comes to grips with the torment which created Hannah's icy heart, her cold, dangerous spirit. Even as Hannah breathes her last, Angel hears the cries of a baby, a sister she rescues. Angel's transformation is complete as she provides her sister the love and protection she herself never received from Hannah. Like Bush's turtle skeletons, Angel has reassembled her life; she is restored to dignity, identity, self-respect, love. "She," as Miss Nett eloquently says, "is a girl who turned into a human" (295). Her heart is no longer frozen but warmed by relationship with family, community, earth, and the spirits which inhabit all.

"This is the place where clouds are born and I am floating" (1). Thus begins *Power*, Hogan's third novel, which, like its predecessors, takes place in the intermediacies, beginning as it does suspended between earth and sky. Again the narrator is an adolescent, somewhere between youth and adulthood, who lives in an outlying place between land and water, in this case a Florida swamp. Like Angel, Omishto is initially unschooled in the ways of her people and has no recognized place within her tribal community. We first see Omishto as she sleeps in a boat because she is uneasy living at home, where her step-father's glances are intrusive and lewd. She is dismayed with her mother's and sister's easy embrace of the white world and feels like an outcast at school. She is drawn to Ama, like herself a Taiga, but she is initially uncertain what to make of the woman who will become her mentor.

Ama lives in an old shack which literally sits on the "wrong" side of Fossil Road, midway between the white community and the Kila village of the Taiga people, and she represents a life that locates itself outside of established norms. Embracing fully neither the white world nor the old ways of the Panther Clan to which she belongs, Ama makes her own way through the swampy land which nourishes the plant and animal life she loves. Believing the Euro-American way to be destructive and the Taiga way to be outdated, she creates a place for herself on the margins of both cultures. Omishto comes to this place on the perimeters as an uncertain child and leaves as a powerful woman.

"Mystery is a form of power," Hogan tells us in her epigraph. Omishto learns from Ama to embrace the mystery of nature, of life itself, and that is what ultimately gives the young woman a place of power. Ama lives in reverential awe of the beings that inhabit her world, as do her relatives in the Kila village. Unlike them, she wears tennis shoes, works for the white community on occasion for needed cash, and speaks English, peripherally incorporating two diverse cultures. Ama is an ambiguous figure, mysterious like the panther whose spirit she represents and worships. Omishto describes her mentor as a woman who "... lives in a natural way at the outside edges of our lives, and she 'keeps up relations,' as she says, with nature and the spirit world" (16-17). "... seeing is inside her," Omishto says of Ama. That vision comes at enormous cost and with incalculable reward. Ama is viewed with disdain by the white world and dismay by the Taiga people, and because Omishto associates herself increasingly with Ama, she herself becomes increasingly marginalized.

The opening event of the novel is a hurricane of horrific proportions. As the storm approaches, Omishto reflects, "The wind is a living force. We Taiga call the wind Oni. It enters us all at birth and stays with us all through life. It connects us to every other creature" (28). She also comes to know that Oni is tobacco and breath and God (41), song and prayer (177). It is power, for it tells a story as words are carried through air (178). It is the word spoken by Sisa, the panther, when there was just air and water, the word which called all things into being (182). And in the "rush of weather," Omishto hears "the wind (say) its own name, 'Oni'" (41).

The storm turns the world upside down. In this place the boundaries between dry land and water, earth and sky have been blurred by the storm; the edges between the old world and new have also been challenged. Old Methuselah, the foreign tree on tribal land, is downed, demonstrating nature's ultimate supremacy over Euro-American attempts to impose human order on the environment. Planted by white settlers, the tree represents the Caucasian presence on native land, and during the storm, Omishto's dress, symbolic of her adaptation to a westernized culture, is ripped from her and hangs from the tree's downed branches. Her life, like the region around her, is forever changed. For not only is great devastation created by the hurricane, the fury unleashed by Ama's hunting of the panther, sacred to the Taiga and protected by law as endangered by the white society, tears apart the tentative peace of the social order in the area, and places Omishto into the forefront of the controversy.

After the hurricane has passed, the two women are exhausted. Before they can recover, however, Ama inexplicably begins tracking the panther, taking the confused Omishto with her. Deeper and deeper into the dark forest they go, and deeper and deeper into mystery. Ama has spent her life protecting the panther from school boys who would shoot it for sport. It is holy to her, as to the other Taiga people. She has an immutable bond with all living creatures, but her strange behavior in this case is beyond explanation to Omishto, who is driven by forces she cannot explain to participate in an event which is reprehensible to her. Why kill an animal so central to the traditional people when, like them, so few still exist? To make matters worse, Ama does not take the body of the animal to the tribal elders for the proper ceremony which would ensure the return of the sacred creature's spirit. Ama has committed two taboos within her own culture and violated the white culture's law by killing a member of an endangered species. By so doing, she has guaranteed censure against herself and the young woman who accompanies her and who looks to her for guidance.

After Ama is arrested, Omishto sees all around her the storm-damaged land and realizes that all of life has been blown off track by the wind. "Two worlds exist," she thinks. "Maybe it's always been this way, but I enter them both like I am two people. Above and below. Land and water. Now and then" (97). She thinks of Ama and knows that like this twilight place, the woman she admires is neither here nor there, right nor wrong. Divisions have blurred. "We are surrounded by matter, but time disappears from us," thinks Omishto. "Or maybe, as Ama says, there are other worlds beside us all the time and every now and then we cross over and enter one, and every so often, too, one passes over and enters ours" (55).

As she reflects, Omishto recalls the myth of Panther Woman, who sings the sun up each morning, who keeps the world in balance, who keeps the world alive. A storm blows one day with such force that it blows a hole between the worlds. Following a panther into that other world, she finds a dying world, rivers aflame, animals sick, land choked with foreign vines. Sadly, the only way for her to return to her own world is to sacrifice the panther. Sacrifice means "to send away"; the animal will go to the spirit world where its essence can then return to the people who love it and begin the needed repair to the earth and its inhabitants (111). The woman, now transformed into a cat-like creature, goes to live in a place between worlds, opened by a storm. Ama surely is the modern appearance of this ancient legend. She has shot the starving, sickly animal partly to put it out of its misery. More importantly, she has sent it to the world of the spirits in order for it to return, renewed to the people who worship it and able to encourage the people as they face an uncertain future. Had Ama given the panther to the Taiga elders as required, their dismay at its puny, flea-bitten state surely would have left them dispirited, demoralized, unable to face the "sharp wounds of survival" (141).

Nevertheless, both Omishto and Ama must face both the legal and social consequences of their deed, no matter how they explain it to themselves. Ultimately acquitted for lack of evidence in federal court, they are brought before the tribal council at the Kila village, where they face a harsher judgment. For the Taiga, killing a panther is not simply illegal; it is a sacrilege.

As Omishto tells her narrative of the events of that awesome night, she is torn inside. She has promised Ama that she will explain in full what happened that night with one exception: she will not reveal the condition of the panther. That fact she has sworn not to divulge under any circumstances. As the tribal review progresses, Omishto realizes that Ama is in danger of receiving a death sentence by the Taiga people. She longs to explain that the reason Ama did not present the cat to the elders was that its sickly condition would demoralize the whole community. She knows that the tribe would forgive Ama if it knew she killed the cat out of kindness, and the young woman desperately wants to defend her mentor. Nevertheless, she does as Ama has insisted and simply relates the events as she experienced them. Ama is banished: she may not appear on tribal land nor speak to any member of the community for four years, a sentence so harsh that she may not survive. Omishto is heartbroken. She realizes, though, that Ama is the sacrifice for this people. The elders believe that "She is the between thing, like a wall that was built and stands between what is now and what could have been" (186). By turning Ama away, the tribal council believes that wall is torn down and their world will be restored.

The land and the social fabric have been rent by the storm; nevertheless, out of the chaos new life emerges. "This was how the world was created, ... out of wind and lashing rain. 'We were blown together by a storm in the first place.' It was all created out of storms. The mud was blown in with the trees and the seeds of growing things already planted in it" (44-45). Like the ancient tree Methuselah, Omishto's roots in the white culture have been torn asunder. Ama has sown in Omishto the seeds of respect for the earth and the Beautiful People of her origins, seeds which will be germinated in the soil enriched by her mentor's role modeling and by her acceptance into the Taiga tribe. In a final ceremony of healing, Omishto awakes to find her arms and legs raked by the claws of the magnificent cat, which is the hovering spirit of this trickster Ama/Panther Woman. This ceremonial raking calls to mind the "smoothing of broken ground" to which Hogan refers in *Dwellings*. The young woman leaves Ama's crumbling house so that it can complete its return to the elements of which it was made, and she returns to the Kila village to join her ancestral community. The tremendous storm has cleansed the land surrounding the reservation of its Euro-American presence; already the resurrection fern is uncurling its verdant fronds. It has also severed Omishto's ties to the western culture, and she has re-established her claim to a place among her people. In a small but significant sense, a new world has been created out of this powerful storm.

Again, Hogan's use of the Panther Woman myth within the story brings this current tale into that continuing, recursive chain of narration which places it in the body of legend. The convergence of myth and plot in this novel, as in *Solar Storms*, serves to deconstruct Euro-centric notions of linear time and bounded space. In discussing Leslie Marmon Silko's *Almanac of the*

Dead, Janet St. Clair notes that, "... time and space—those cornerstones of modern Western thought—become the eviscerated signifiers of a radically limited vision" (St. Clair 87). So, too, Hogan's vision serves to enlarge those notions and incorporate them into a holistic unity. The myth explicates the connection between the woman/panther/storm, and elevates Omishto and Ama into the enduring corpus of legends which are integral to the Taiga culture. Because Omishto inherits the mantle of Ama, the young woman becomes the next link in the chain of tradition for her people. No longer a confused adolescent, the powerful, newly-adult Omishto joins Ama and the Panther Women before her as the present telling of the ancient story.

In her novels as in her work at the Rehabilitation Foundation, Linda Hogan has raked, gathered up, smoothed the broken ground in the lives of those who have been wounded by the world. It truly is "work at the borderland" (*Dwellings* 153), and in that liminal space her characters undergo both testing and healing ceremonies which renew them to wholeness and simultaneously place them within the mythic traditions of their respective people.

Works Cited

Brice, Jennifer. "Earth as Mother, Earth as Other in Novels by Silko and Hogan." *CRITIQUE: Studies in Contemporary Fiction*. 39.2 (Winter 1998): 127-139.

Buber, Martin. *The Legend of the Baal-Shem*. Trans. Maurice Friedman. Princeton: Harper and Row, 1955. 7-32.

Gates, Henry Louis, Jr. *The Signifying Monkey: A Theory of African-American Literary Criticism*. New York: Oxford Press, 1988.

Hogan, Linda. *Dwellings: A Spiritual History of the Living World*. New York: Simon and Schuster, 1995.

—. *Mean Spirit*. New York: Ballantine Books, 1990.

Hogan, Linda. *Power*. New York: W. W. Norton & Co., 1998.

—. *Solar Storms*. New York: Simon and Schuster, 1995.

St. Clair, Janet. "Uneasy Ethnocentrism: Recent Works of Allen, Silko, and Hogan." *SAIL* 6.1 (Spring 1994): 83-98.

Works Consulted

Ackerberg, Peggy Maddux. "Breaking Boundaries: Writing Past Gender, Genre, and Genocide in Linda Hogan." *SAIL* 6.3 (Fall 1994): 7-14.

Allen, Paula Gunn. *Grandmothers of the Light: A Medicine Woman's Sourcebook*. Boston: Beacon Press, 1991. xiii-32, 107-110, 165-170, 205-233.

Allen, Paula Gunn. *The Sacred Hoop: Recovering the Feminine in American Indian Traditions*. Boston: Beacon Press, 1992. ix-29, 54-75, 102-117, 165-183.

"An Interview with Linda Hogan." *The Missouri Review* 1997: 110-134.

Balassi, William, John F. Crawford, and Annie O. Eysturoy, ed. *This Is About Vision*. Albuquerque: U. of New Mexico Press, 1990. Patricia Smith Clark. "Linda Hogan." 141-155.

Barfoot, C. C., ed. *Beyond Pug's Tour: National and Ethnic Stereotyping in Theory and Literary Practice*. Atlanta: Rodopi, 1997. A. Robert Lee. "'I Am Your Worst Nightmare: I am an Indian with a Pen': Native Identity and the novels of Thomas King, Linda Hogan, Louis Owens and Betty Louise Bell." 445-467. Juan E. Tazon. "The Evolution of a Stereotype: The Indian in English Renaissance Promotional Literature." 125-132.

Baria, Amy Greewood. "Linda Hogan's Two Worlds." *SAIL* 10.4 (Winter 1998): 67-73.

Bell, Betty Louise. "Introduction: Linda Hogan's Lessons in Making Do." *SAIL* 6.3 (Fall 1994): 3-5.

Blair, Elizabeth. "The Politics of Place in Linda Hogan's *Mean Spirit*." *SAIL* 6.3 (Fall, 1994): 15-21.

Bloom, Harold, ed. *Native American Women Writers*. Philadelphia: Chelsea House Publishers, 1998. 38-49, 50-60.

Bruchac, Joseph. "Survival Comes This Way: Contemporary Native American Poetry." *A Gift of Tongues: Critical Challenges in Contemporary American Poetry*. Ed. Marie Harris and Kathleen Aguero. Athens: U. of Georgia Press, 1987. 196-205.

—. *Survival This Way: Interviews with American Indian Poets*. Tucson: U. of Arizona Press, 1987. "To Take Care of Life: An Interview with Linda Hogan." 119-133.

Carew-Miller, Anna. "Caretaking and the Work of the Text in Linda Hogan's *Mean Spirit*." *SAIL* 6.3 (Fall 1994): 37-47.

Casteel, Alix. "Dark Wealth in Linda Hogan's *Mean Spirit*." *SAIL* 6.3 (Fall 1994): 49-68.

Coltelli, Laura. Winged Words: *American Indian Writers Speak*. Lincoln: U. of Nebraska Press, 1990. 55-68, 71-86.

Steinberg, Marc H. "Linda Hogan's *Mean Spirit*: The Wealth, Value, and Worth of the Osage Tribe." *Notes on Contemporary Literature* 25.2 (1995): 7-8.

Linda Palen Ruzich teaches English at California State University, Sacramento, and at American River College, Carmichael, CA. Her interest in Native American culture led her to participate in work projects among the Ch'ol in Chiapas, Mexico, and in study trips to Albuquerque and Santa Fe, NM. She authored the guide for college instruction of American Indian literature, *Storytelling as Ceremony and Survival: Teaching Native American Literature*.

Travelling the Hyperreality of Indian Simulations: Gerald Vizenor's *Darkness in Saint Louis Bearheart*

Elvira Pulitano
University of New Mexico

> The simulations of Manifest manners are treacherous and elusive in histories; how ironic that the most secure simulations are unreal sensations, and become the real without a referent to an actual tribal remembrance.... Manifest manners are the absence of the real in the ruins of tribal representations.
>
> Gerald Vizenor, *Manifest Manners*

> There is, then, an America of furious hyperreality, which is not that of Pop art, of Mickey Mouse, or of Hollywood movies. There is another more secret America ... and it creates somehow a network of references and influences that finally spread also to the products of high culture and the entertainment industry. It has to be discovered.
>
> Umberto Eco, *Travels in Hyperreality*

Umberto Eco's *Travels in Hyperreality* (1986) begins with a witty description of a realer-than-real image of two beautiful naked girls, an image that turns out to be a holograph. According to the author, "Holography could prosper only in America, a country obsessed with realism, where, if a reconstruction is to be credible, it must be absolutely iconic, a perfect likeness, a 'real' copy of the reality being represented" (4). Eco illustrates his thesis by taking us on a journey through America's "fortresses of solitude," especially through the monuments and museums of Southern California that testify to what he calls the "crèche-ification of the bourgeois universe"— Hearst Castle, the Madonna Inn, the Getty Museum, Forest Lawn Cemetery, the Palace of Living Arts at Buena Park. The American desire to create substitutes for reality that are more "real" than the original produces, as Eco shows, a kind of Absolute Fake, the "fac-simile" that is really "fac-different" (11).

Contemporary Anishinaabe novelist, poet, and essayist Gerald Vizenor has adopted Eco's concept of hyperreality to show how the Euramerican cultural invention of "Indianness" reduces tribal people to specimens preserved in amber, artifacts enclosed in animated museums without a living, "actual" self-definition. In *Manifest Manners* (1994), Vizenor claims that Indians become "simulations of the 'absolute fakes' in the ruins of representation, or the victims in literary annihilation" (9). Similarly, in the most recent *Fugitive Poses* (1998), he argues that the "*indian* is poselocked in portraiture, intaglio, photogravure, captivity narratives, and other interimage simulation [sic] of dominance" (146). As defined by cultural studies theorist Jean Baudrillard, the term *simulation* implies "the generation by models of a real without origin or reality: a hyperreal" (*Simulations* 2). In a passionate attack against ethnology, Baudrillard condemns Western civilization for driving the Indian back into the "glass coffin of the virgin forest," making him the simulation model for all conceivable Indians before ethnology. "For ethnology to live, its object must die," he claims in *Simulations*, a statement that best conveys the notion of the Indian frozen in time, "cryogenized," "sterilised," protected to death and in death. More important, Baudrillard observes, is the fact that American society itself bears the marks of the science of simulacra with its desire to completely catalogue, analyze, and then artificially revive, as though real, a mere hallucination of truth (*Simulations* 13-20). In strategies that both parallel and draw from Eco and Baudrillard, Vizenor creatively and imaginatively theorizes the "postindian" condition in an attempt to overcome "the simulations of dominance" (*Manifest Manners* 4).[1]

At the heart of Vizenor's writing lies the intent to discard the institutional and academic stereotypes "invented" for Native Americans by Euramerican culture, to liberate his characters and readers and win for all the freedom of realistic growth and continual becoming. In work after work, Vizenor's pen is raised against what he calls "terminal creeds," or beliefs that impose a false meaning on phenomena, that silence questions, and force agreement. Unable to change and adapt to new situations, and unable to account for the complexity and particularity of actual conditions, terminal creeds lead their bearers to isolation and, ultimately, to annihilation. Vizenor conceives of these beliefs as especially destructive for Native American people since they tend to confine and imprison Native Americans in the static, unchanging domain of words as they were once confined in the reservations. In one of his earlier works, *The Everlasting Sky*, he writes:

> The dominant society has created a homogenized history of tribal people for a television culture. Being an Indian is a heavy burden to the *oshki anishinabe* because white people know more about the *indian* they invented than anyone. The experts and cultural hobbyists never miss a chance to authenticate the scraps of romantic history dropped by white travelers through the *indian country* centuries ago. White people are forever projecting their dreams of a perfect life through the invention of the *indian*—and then they expect an *oshki anishinabe* to not only

[1] According to Colin Samson, Vizenor, in *Manifest Manners*, "combines the word 'post' and 'Indian' to avoid capitalizing 'Indian,' an occidental invention that has no referent in tribal languages and culture (*Loosening the Seams* 292). Similarly, Robert A. Lee notes that "Vizenor ... has positioned himself as postindian, an ongoing pursuer of all simulations that essentialize or ossify tribal people (Introduction to *Shadow Distance* xi).

fulfill an invention but to authenticate third-hand information about the tribal past. (15-16)

In accordance with postmodernist and poststructuralist theories, Vizenor attempts to subvert the power of language by breaking the language down in the sense of re-imagining it. He conceives of this agenda as a "breaking out of boxes" (Bruchac 290). On a metaphorical level, Vizenor claims, these boxes are designed and built by the dominating discourse and become a vehicle through which the dominant literature or social science discourse determines its authority. Vizenor wants to transgress the limitations set and imposed by "the culture of dominance" on Native American literatures through a recreation of the real that bears "simulations of survivance" (*Manifest Manners* 5). In this deconstructive act, he employs trickster discourse as "agonistic imagination" and aggressive "liberation" ("Trickster Discourse" 196). Trickster discourse becomes the countervailing force through which Vizenor attempts to overturn again and again the very process of writing.

My intent in this essay is to show how Vizenor's trickster discourse reconstructs and *re-imagines* the "real," causing the liberation of the signifier "Indian" from the absolute fake of hyperrreality. Specifically, I will refer to his first novel *Darkness in Saint Louis Bearheart*, a narrative that, in Alan Velie's words, is "first and foremost a trickster novel"("The Trickster Novel"131) in structure and content, with the trickster figure as the omnipresent, pervading element. Using Eco's collection of essays on the American "more to come" consumer culture, I will explore how Vizenor's "travels" through the ruins of America's high-tech culture ("the ruins of Western civilization") ultimately represent a direct attack against our modern life and civilization; they become a harsh critique of our culture of "affluence" that continuously and obsessively demands "more and more" and that adopts a philosophy of immortality as duplication in order to dominate the relationship with the self and the past.

Since its first appearance in print in 1978,[2] *Bearheart* has been criticized for its shocking, often graphic and extended depiction of physical violence. In the afterword to the 1990 reprint of the novel, Louis Owens mentions the risks of teaching such a book, as he discovered several years ago, learning that three students in one of his American Indian fiction courses, had reported him to a dean:

> My sin was including *Bearheart* in my syllabus. The three students, all mixedblood women raised in Southern California, had known how to respond to the familiar tragedies of Indians—mixedblood or full—played out in novels by other Native American

---

[2] The novel was reprinted in 1990 with the title of *Bearheart: The Heirship Chronicles*.

writers. But *Bearheart* with its wild humor upset them. Not only was there sexual violence in the novel, but even transsexual Indians. Indians in the novel were capable of cowardice, as well as courage, of greed and lust, as well as generosity and stoicism. And, according to the students weaned on film versions of Hollywood Indians, Native American people could never be like that. (247-48)

Even an established scholar of Native American literature, Kenneth Lincoln, has characterized *Bearheart* as "carnage, cocksucking, and throwaway dirty talk," and after discussing the novel, he asks, "So, why all this funny talk, fellatio, criptic comedy, and mindless violence?" (*Indi'n Humor* 156, 158).

In *Writing in the Oral Tradition*, Kimberly Blaeser notices how, over the years, Vizenor has offered several answers to Lincoln's question by producing texts that attempt "to break down what he sees as civilized illusions with uncivilized language, to state what good taste dictates should not be stated, partly to force a recognition of our most basic energies"(184-185). Indeed, Vizenor attempts throughout *Bearheart* to force readers—both Indians and non-Indians—to reconsider their own "terminal beliefs," those inflexible ground rules that determine the way we look at the world, whose values, and very identities result in empty bundles of words, bereft of meaning.

Just as the characters in *Bearheart* suffer because of their vanities and their attachment to words, we as readers are also challenged to reconsider our values and idiosyncrasies. Throughout the narrative, *Bearheart*, with its ruthless depiction of sex and violence and with its consistently crude language,[3] continuously thwarts our expectations, violates our notions of morality, and overrules again and again our desire for resolution and closure. Much of *Bearheart* is indeed disturbing, but Vizenor's fiction is no more astonishing than everyday reality and has to be conceived within a well-defined plan. In a personal interview with Blaeser, the author talks about his intent in the novel:

> I am not approaching any bourgeois reader with comfort. I have an objective.... I would, with this book, choose to confront the bourgeois expectations of the American audience.... I think literature ought to engage, upset, confront, disrupt, liberate people from their reading habits which reflect their worldview and compulsive behavior, inhibitions, religion, whatever, as the great life, as civilization. They ought to be tested, disrupted, and confronted. (*Writing in the Oral Tradition* 186)

---

[3] For a discussion of the physical violence in the novel, see Jon Hauss' article "Real Stories: Memory, Violence, and Enjoyment in Gerald Vizenor's *Bearheart*."

By unmasking all rules, revealing their true nature as fragile social constructs, Vizenor aims at provoking the reader's response, forcing us to reconsider the way we look at the world. As early as *Bearheart*, in 1978, before the works of Eco and Baudrillard were available in English, Vizenor was already moving toward a critical position that, anticipating these major European theorists, argues for the reader's active role in becoming co-participant and co-creator of meaning, and discovering the possibility of "survivance" beyond the text.

As one of the most prominent figures in contemporary reader-response theory, semiotics, and cultural critique, Eco provides valuable tools with which to approach Vizenor's writing. Eco's theories on the work as an "open text," in which interpretation is significantly limited by the semiological nature of the text itself, as well as his notion of the active role of the reader in this "ambiguous" process of decoding narratives,[4] define concepts that Vizenor has constantly used in his work in attempts to explore manifestations of the tension between oral and written. Moreover, Eco's views on *comic* or *carnevalesque* as transgression, a notion that has its manifestations in medieval times but that dates back to an ancient heritage (the classics), fits neatly with Vizenor's idea of the trickster and the liberating possibilities of trickster discourse.

In an essay entitled "Frames of Comic Freedom," Eco, following Bakhtin, states:

> Carnival is the natural theater in which animals and animal-like beings take over the power and become the masters. In carnival even kings act like the populace. Comic behavior, formerly an object of a judgment of superiority on our part, becomes, in this case, our own rule. The upside-down world has become the norm. Carnival is revolution (or revolution is carnival): kings are decapitated (that is, lowered, made inferior) and the crowd is crowned. (3)

Later, in the same essay, Eco indicates how humor determines the basic structures of a text:

> Semiotically speaking, if comic (in a text) takes place at the level of *fabula* or of narrative structures, humor works in the interstices between narrative and discursive structures: the attempt of the hero to comply with the frame or to violate it is developed by the *fabula*, while the intervention of the author, who renders explicit the presupposed rule, belongs to the discursive activity and represents a metasemiotic series of statements about the cultural background of the *fabula*. (8)

---

[4] See *The Role of the Reader* (1979) and *The Limits of Interpretation* (1991); see also *The Open Work* (1989) and *Interpretation and Overinterpretation* (1992).

Eco's love of paradox, as well as his quirky, sometimes outrageous sense of humor become particularly significant in *Travels in Hyperreality*, which aims at exposing the ideology of a culture in which "the completely real" is identified with "the completely fake." Consider, for example, the intentionally transparent language—accompanied by a cool, dispassionate voice—of the passage in which Eco provides evidence to support America's desire for hyperreality:

> And so we set out on a journey, holding to the Ariadnethread, an open-sesame that will allow us to identify the object of this pilgrimage no matter what form it may assume. We can identify it through two typical slogans that pervade American advertising. The first, widely used by Coca-Cola but also frequent as a hyperbolic formula in everyday speech, is "the real thing"; the second, found in print and heard on TV, is "more" in the sense of "extra." (7-8)

Or, in another example, where he presents his intentions to the reader:

> This is the reason for this journey into hyperreality, in search of instances where the American imagination demands the real thing and, to attain it, must fabricate the absolute fake; where the boundaries between game and illusion are blurred, the art museum is contaminated by the freak show, and falsehood is enjoyed in a situation of "fullness," of *horror vacui*. (8)

Humor as a tool of liberation and a means to achieve balance, humor that, in Bakhtin's terms, assumes political significance, is the matrix out of which Vizenor's writing originates. As noted by Louis Owens, "the trickster discourse of Vizenor's fiction resembles Bakhtin's definition of Menippean Satire," (*Other Destinies* 226), Vizenor's goal being always that of testing and exposing ideas and idealogues. Owens quotes Bakhtin:

> The familiarizing role of laughter is here considerably more powerful, sharper and coarser. The liberty to crudely degrade, to turn inside out the lofty aspects of the world and world views, might sometimes seem shocking. But to this exclusively and comic familiarity must be added an intense spirit of inquiry and utopian fantasy. In Menippean satire the unfettered and fantastic plots and situations all serve one goal—to put to test and to expose ideas and idealogues.... Menippean satire is dialogic, full of parodies and travesties, multi-styled and does not fear elements of bilingualism. (*Other Destinies* 226)

A sharp, and crudely shocking sense of humor characterizes the narrative in *Bearheart* with no other reason than keeping people alert to their own survival and power to heal. The novel begins with a "Letter to the Reader," a section that functions as a prologue and establishes the trickster quality of the narrative. In this section, we first encounter the author of this tale-within-the-tale, old *Bearheart*, the mixedblood shaman comfortably settled in the BIA offices. He has written the book we will read and assumes the role of trickster in the attempt to defy hypocrisy and "terminal creeds." Responding to an AIM female radical who asks him about the content of the book, he says that the book is about "sex and violence," in the form *of "travels through terminal creeds and social deeds escaping from evil into the fourth world where bears speak the secret language of saints*" (xii-xiv, italics mine). From the outset, then, Vizenor involves us in a dialogue between text and text, author and author, revealing the complex and multiple nature of authorship, a characteristic of both oral tales and poststructuralist/postmodern texts.

A futuristic fantasy, *Bearheart* depicts the cross-country journey of a group of "pilgrims" from the Cedar Circus on the White Earth Indian reservation toward Pueblo Bonito in Chaco Canyon, New Mexico, a place of passage into the fourth world. Proude Cedarfair—mixedblood Anishinaabe shaman and the fourth in a genealogy of Proude Cedarfairs—and his wife Rosina are forced to leave the Cedar Circus when the national economy collapses owing to the depletion of fossil fuels. Corrupt tribal officials lust after the timber and do not hesitate to kill all the representatives of the Cedar Nation who attempt to stop them. Accompanying Proude and his wife on this journey through the disintegrating America's high-tech culture is a bizarre collection of displaced persons, mostly mixedblood Indians, who represent various figures from Native American mythology as well as human values and virtues.[5] Indeed, this postmodern, post-apocalyptic phantasmagoria embeds, from the very beginning, emergence and creation myths from American Indian oral tradition, as well as the pervasive yet elusive presence of the trickster whose ultimate goal is that of liberating and activating the reader's imaginative powers.

In his analysis of the trickster motif in the novel, Velie claims that to Vizenor, "trickster is first and foremost a sign in the semiotic sense, a sign in a language game, a comic holotrope" ("The Trickster Novel" 131). This means that Vizenor's idea of the trickster is primarily conceived in a linguistic context; trickster thus becomes a way to attack the dominant bourgeois postcolonial world view. In the tradition of Rabelais—a tradition that Bakhtin describes

---

[5] According to A. La Vonne Brown Ruoff, echoes of the Ojibwe myth "Manabozho and the Gambler" appear in the episode of the novel in which Cedarfair and the other pilgrims gamble for life with Sir Cecil Staples. In addition, Vizenor's emphasis on bear transformation is a motif based on the role of the bear as a renewer of life in the Ojibwe oral tradition. See "Gerald Vizenor: Compassionate Trickster," 67-73.

as "fantastic realism" and that Vizenor calls "mythic verism"[6]—*Bearheart* employs laughter in the form of trickster discourse. As Vizenor points out,

> The trickster and comic liberator craves chance in agonistic imagination to lessen the power of social science and bourgeois humanism ... the comic liberator is a healer in language games, chance, and postmodern imagination; the trickster, as a semiotic sign, "denies presence and completion," that romantic "vital essence" in tribal representations, and the instrumental language of social science. ("Trickster Discourse" 192)

While recognizing the trickster signature of the novel and the overall subversive nature of trickster's discourse (a subversion of the Western mode of classification), Velie, however, misinterprets the nature of trickster identity when he claims that Proude Cedarfair and Benito Saint Plumero, or Bigfoot, represent two opposite sides of trickster ("The Trickster Novel" 134-135). As a culture hero who leads the pilgrims through the ravages of a futuristic world, Proude, Velie posits, represents the positive side of the trickster. Like the Manabozho in traditional Anishinaabe tales, he has the ability to change shapes, and at the end of the novel, we see him transforming into a bear before escaping into the mythic fourth world. On the other hand, Benito Saint Plumero, mixedblood clown, endowed with an enormous penis named President Jackson, embodies the "priapic character of the trickster, having sex anywhere, anytime, with anything" ("The Trickster Novel" 134).

To an audience familiar with Vizenor's theories on trickster nature, this reading appears quite problematic grounded as it is within a Western, binary mode of thinking with its tendency to split and categorize realms or types of beings. In response to academic theories about trickster, Vizenor presents his own view on "the comic holotrope." Not wholly human, animal, or god, but simultaneously none and all of these beings, the "polyedric" trickster, according to Vizenor, blurs these classic distinctions and mediates between contradictory forces in an attempt to balance the world with "unusual manners and ecstatic strategies." In addition, Vizenor argues that the "the trickster is comic in the sense that ... he represents a spiritual balance in a comic drama rather than the romantic eliminations of human contradictions and evil" (*The People Named the Chippewa* 3-4). Vizenor's formulation of the trickster creed as expressed by Third Cedarfair in *Bearheart* is "Outwit but never kill evil.... The tricksters and warrior clowns have stopped more evil violence with their wit than have lovers with their lust and fools with their power and

---

[6] Vizenor's definition of "mythic verism" expresses a concordance between naturalism and verisimilitude. In "Trickster Discourse," he claims: "verisimilitude is the appearance of realities; mythic verism is discourse, a critical concordance of narrative voices, and a narrative realism that is more than mimesis or a measure of what is believed in the world" (190).

rage" (15). Vizenor follows this same creed in his "trickster writing." His weapon is harsh satire and humor. He plays the clown while launching his attacks indirectly against romantic entrapments and terminal creeds.

According to Louis Owens, most of the pilgrims in this "Chaucerian pilgrimage, to varying degrees, do suffer from the illness of terminal creeds" (*Other Destinies* 232). Bishop Omax Parasimo, wearer of "metamasks" which allow him a series of metamorphoses, is "obsessed with the romantic and spiritual power of tribal people," an idea originating in the Euramerican version of Indianness. Matchi Mawka, another pilgrim, assumes the role of professional victim when he sings what Owens defines as a "lament of lost racial purity" whose refrain is "Our women were poisoned part white." Finally Belladonna Darwin-Winter-Catcher is the most obvious victim of terminal creeds, as she foolishly attempts to define what "Indian" means and remains trapped within her own preconceptions (*Other Destinies* 232).

Indeed, Vizenor's main attempt throughout *Bearheart* is to force readers to reconsider their own "terminal beliefs," which are essentially static, destructive systems of beliefs. By subverting all rules, and transgressing the limitations set by the dominant social constructs, he encourages readers to relinquish their moral stances and to re-valuate/reimagine things on their own merit. In this revolutionary/deconstructive intent, Vizenor is not so far from the author of *The Name of the Rose* who travels the length and breadth of America in search of places that probe the boundaries of realism, copies that promise more than the original: wax museums, halls of fame, theme parks, zoos. "Is this the taste of America?," Eco asks, wondering from "what depth of popular sensibility" this taste is forced on the public "to the point of exacerbation" (*Travels* 7). Eco's travels become an attempt to answer these interrogatives, an effort to understand America's furious demand for hyperreality with its tendency to create the "natural as constructed as artful" in the name of the "Absolute Fake."

Eco's questions regarding the culture of hyperreality provide intriguing insights into an analysis of Vizenor's notion of the invented Indian, a notion that runs through the core of *Bearheart*. "What but the Indian constructed as artifact could we expect from the culture of the *Absolute Fake*?" Vizenor seems to posit, adding that as an artifact, the Indian poses perfectly for a "cultural striptease" in the bankable simulations of contemporary America. In the introductory essay to his anthology, *Native American Literature*, Vizenor writes: "The American Indian has come to mean *Indianness*, the conditions that indicate the once-despised tribes and, at the same time, the extreme notions of an exotic outsider; these conditions are advocated as *real* cultures in the world. The simulations of the outsider as the other subserve racial and cultural dominance" (1).

The pilgrims' travels through the ruins of America's high-tech culture in *Bearheart*, their supernatural, wild, and bizarre adventures, trace Vizenor's journey into the hyperreal America in search of places that probe the boundary between the simulation of the invented Indian and the humorous "survivance" of the postindian. By continuously blurring the line between real and hyperreal, the novel, with its apparently amorphous and hard-to-define form, and its unusual, non-linear plot, fulfills the intentions of trickster tales, subverting the static and confining definitions of (Western) literature, and working toward liberating and activating the reader's imaginative powers.

Despite the imagined futuristic world of the novel, real towns mark the stops of the pilgrims as they travel Westward along the route that takes them across Minnesota, Iowa, Oklahoma, and New Mexico, traveling on foot through a country that has run out of oil. After leaving the Scapehouse, the pilgrims, still driving a convertible, pick up Zebulon Matchi Makwa, "a talking writer and drunken urban shaman," and then continue towards Belladonna's house. The narrative voice describes the consequences of oil shortage, while significantly addressing the novel's ecological concerns:

> Since the end of gasoline, weeds were growing over the asphalt roads. Tough flowers crept over the unused shoulders of the road and sprouted from cracks and potholes. Bigfoot avoided the late summer flowers and green weeds down the center of the road. In time trees would take root and turn the cement and asphalt to dust again. (51)

The fact that the country has run out of fuel becomes extremely significant in the context of what Eco defines as America's "paradise of consumer culture." "For a Californian, leaving his car means leaving his own humanity, consigning himself to another power, abandoning his own will," Eco hyperbolically writes as he approaches Disneyland, the quintessence of "consumer ideology," a place where the essential condition to enter is "to abandon the car in an endless parking lot and reach the boundary of the dream city in special little trains" (*Travels in Hyperreality* 48). On the same issue, Baudrillard observes:

> What draws the crowds [towards Disneyland] is undoubtedly much more the social microcosm, the miniaturised and *religious* revelling in real America, in its delights and drawbacks. You park outside, queue up inside, and are totally abandoned at the exit. In this imaginary world the only phantasmagoria is the inherent warmth and affection of the crowd, and in that sufficiently excessive number of gadgets used there to specifically maintain the multitudinous affect. The contrast with the absolute solitude of the parking lot–a veritable concentration camp—is total. (*Simulations* 23-24)

As imaginative as the infantile world of Disneyland might appear, a mere play of illusions and phantasms, both critics suggest that this "well designed carnival" significantly traces the objective profile of America, a country where technology can give us more reality than nature (and humans) can. In the views of Eco and Baudrillard, Disneyland is a perfect model of all the entangled orders of simulacra, a space of the regeneration of the imaginary.

Interestingly enough, when technology implodes, the postapocalyptic world of *Bearheart* reveals a phantasmagoria that revels in a hyperreal America. In a world strictly determined by high technological standards, where gasoline has become a matter of life or death, the scenario portrayed by Vizenor indeed prefigures a tragic outcome, while becoming a clear parody of our capitalistic/consumer culture. No longer able to drive, Americans lose their self-definition as a people always on the road. No longer able to work or feed themselves, they are deprived of one of the most important goals in a capitalist society: the ability to produce. In a final, desperate struggle for survival, the pilgrims in *Bearheart* attempt to satisfy their most basic needs and raw urges, revealing in the process very disturbing qualities. Numerous scenes of explosive violence and cannibalism, vividly portrayed from the beginning of the novel, clearly show human beings grappling with the basics of life and death, good and evil, forcing us to see the characters in the light of altered circumstances. In Vizenor's view, their behaviors challenge static definitions of the stereotyped/hyperreal "Indian," the "invented" victim of the "simulations of dominance."

A chapter entitled "Kitchibiwabik Osidaman" portrays the adventures of Benito Saint Plumero with a bronze statue. A clear parody of the victims of "terminal creeds" who cannot live without dreams and visions—what Vizenor labels "the traditional bullshit" anthropologists are constantly obsessed with—this chapter also fits neatly Eco's idea of the Absolute fake as characterizing the taste of America: "Well, bronze she is, but not in real life. In the real life of my dreams and visions she is a soothsayer, a pioneer representing the sources of rivers and thunders and the snow and sunshine. She is the curve and color of the earth and the breath of our lives" (*Bearheart* 83). This "lifeless" other in whom Benito's desire seems to find a safe repository is taken away from him by a man whom Benito thinks is crazy. After killing the man, Benito rescues the statue from the river where it had been drowned. Since then, the statue has been traveling with him, giving him "a vision without loneliness."

Visiting several wax museums between San Francisco and Los Angeles, as well as several "enchanted castles" winding down the curves of the Pacific Coast, Eco is remarkably impressed by "the masterpiece of the reconstructed mania" and of *giving more* and better, particularly evident when the "industry of absolute iconism" deals with the problem of art. As he walks though "authentic" reproductions of Leonardo's *Last Supper*, Michelangaelo's *David* and *Pietà* and the various art pieces that fill the castle of William Randolph Hearst in a variety of styles ranging from the Renaissance to the eighteenth century, to the modern period, he notes:

The striking aspect of the whole is not the quantity of antique pieces plundered from half of Europe, or the nonchalance with which the artificial tissue seamlessly connects fake and genuine, but rather the sense of fullness, the obsessive determination not to leave a single space that doesn't suggest something, and hence the masterpiece of bricolage, haunted by *horror vacui*, that is here achieved. (23)

Horror vacui, Vizenor would claim, becomes crucial within the context of the "academic monologue" of anthropologists who invented the Indian according to their own principles and methodologies; they needed a visible past, a visible continuum, and a myth of origin to impose methodological inventions of cultures and to maintain those inventions so as to maintain their own power. In an interview with Laura Coltelli, Vizenor points out:

> Everything in anthropology is an invention and an extension of the cultural colonialism of Western expansion.... Anthropologists believe they are right and what they have methodologically constructed is true because of the socioscientific method. They got a bundle of bad methodologies which have distorted the human spirit since anthropologists have been eagerly pursuing the invention of culture—and they invented culture. Culture doesn't exist. They invented it. (*Winged Words* 161)

The principles and methodologies used by anthropologists also operate within the context of the reconstructive mania of hyperreal America. A country so furiously obsessed with the past and so consciously aware of the lack (or rather lack of recognition) of history, hyperreal America must continually reexperience/reconstruct a credible and objective past in order to control the definition she has constructed about the past. In addition, Eco notices, this ideology to reproduce the Past, the quintessential symbol of America's entrepreneurial colonization, effectively reflects the apocalyptic philosophy of the Last Beach according to which Europe is declining into barbarism and something has to be done to preserve its treasures (*Travels* 36). J. Paul Getty's oil empire, with its perfect copies of Greek statues and Roman temples, with its polycrhome marbles, colonnades and Pompeian-wall paintings, is a perfect example of this philosophy. In Eco's terms, "it develops its thirst for preservation of art from an imperialistic efficiency, but at the same time it is the bad conscience of this imperialistic efficiency, just as cultural anthropology is the bad conscience of the white man who thus pays his debt to the destroyed primitive culture" (*Travels* 39).

According to Vizenor, as a consequence of the power dynamics involved, anthropologists silenced tribal cultures, separating them from the spontaneity of being alive and unpredictable, and from the spontaneity of play. The wild game of imagination embodied in trickster's comic worldview cannot occur within anthropologists' socioscientific theories and tragic discourse. Vizenor contrasts academic invention, viewed as lifeless and false, with tribal imagination, conceived as vital and true. In *The People Named the Chippewa*, he writes:

> Traditional people imagine their social patterns and places on the earth, whereas anthropologists and historians invent tribal cultures and end mythic time. The differences between tribal imagination and social scientific invention are determined in world views.... To imagine the world is to be in the world; to invent the world with academic predicaments is to separate human experiences from the world, a secular transcendence and a denial of chance and mortalities. (27)

Trickster signature and trickster dialectic, for Vizenor, are the keys to imagining and recreating the world. The chapters dealing with the Evil Gambler in *Bearheart*—narratively and philosophically set at the center of the novel—provide a means to theorize about the infinite possibilities of trickster discourse, a discourse that embodies contradictions, indeterminacy, and freedom, the ultimate salvation from "terminal creeds," and cultural narcissism. Sir Cecil Staples, "the monarch of unleaded gasoline," is Vizenor's parody of the solipsistic American sociopath, as well as a corrupted trickster, what the trickster could become through greed and lack of tribal values. Louis Owens compares him to a "malignant Moby-Dick of the Heartland," the product of a general failure of responsibility to the community (*Other Destinies* 236). On the other hand, Nora Barry notices a resemblance to Joseph Conrad's corrupt culture hero Kurtz who, in *Heart of Darkness*, appears as an "animated image of death carved out of ivory," adding that, like Kurtz, Sir Cecil hoards not ivory but gasoline ("Chance and Ritual" 16-17). Abducted from a dysfunctional suburban couple, Sir Cecil was raised in a trailer careening across the continent, doused with pesticides, and deprived of any tribal or communal identity. Representing a radical break from the natural world, he is quite at home in a culture of petroleum, industrial waste, insecticides, and death. As he explains, "Killing is too easy, thousands of people do it everyday to others and themselves. Nothing new, no surprises. That plastic film known as social control hanging over the savage urge to kill was dissolved when the government failed and the economic world collapsed "(126). In the novel's imagined world of violence and chance, Sir Cecil has dedicated himself to balancing the world with "evil." As his sign announces:

> The monarch of Unleaded gasoline
> Living or dying for gasoline,
> gamble for five gallons
> New traps and old tortures

follow the rows of abandoned cars to the altar trailers
open for evil business. (*Bearheart* 103)

Despite his trickster qualities, Sir Cecil does not trick to liberate or to balance good and evil through humor. The false center of his terminal creed is the belief that Good and Evil, Life and Death balance the world, and that nothing is lost or gained when such forces stand in contrast, since everything is chance. He states: "evil will still be the winner because nothing changes when good and evil are tied in a strange balance" (131). Consequently, his role in the novel is to serve as a test for Proude Cedarfair who has to save the pilgrims by gambling with him. Unlike Sir Cecil, Proude rejects the notion of hegemonic binaries that informs the Evil Gambler's terminal creed:

We are not equals...we are not bound in common experiences.... We do not share a common vision. Your values and language come from evil. Your power is adverse to living. Your culture is death.... Death is not the opposite of living, but you are the opposite of living. Your evil is malignant. The energies to live are never malignant. (132)

The evil character that Sir Cecil reveals originates from the same spiritual weakness to which, to some degree, each of the pilgrims will succumb. When confronted by the Evil Gambler, the pilgrims offer piles of words for personal strength; ironically, however, as Maureen Keady convincingly argues, that list of words appears to be "a condensed version of their own personal stories" and will determine the pilgrims' tragic fate. Lilith Mae—the white woman who had sexual intercourse with two boxer dogs while teaching on an Indian reservation—lists "boxer," "coxer," "springer," while Bigfoot, with his "President Jackson" lists a series of American presidents ("Walking Backwards" 63). By contrast, Proude lists the names of the pilgrims, demonstrating his will to risk everything in order to conquer evil, since names hold power, life, creation. In *Manifest Manners*, Vizenor points out how "Native American identities are created in stories, and names are essential to a distinctive personal nature"(56). Elaborating on Vizenor's statement, Elizabeth Blair, in an article focusing on the "postmodern language games" of the novel, notes how Vizenor's names and masks evoke the inevitable fluidity of identity as it is recreated in stories. In stories, author, narrator, characters, listeners, and readers have the ability to shapeshift through the liberating possibilities of language, avoiding the "trap of freezing the word on the page" ("Text as Trickster" 88).

Proude's credo that "we become the terminal creeds we speak" accounts for the suicide of Lilith Mae, after she loses her game with the Evil Gambler. A firm believer in terminal creeds, Lilith lacks the spiritual strength necessary to face the game, since, as Vizenor claims, "she did not know the rituals of spiritual balance and power" (116). Interestingly, the chapters that follow the Evil Gambler section portray the demise and disintegration of the group. One by one, the pilgrims fall victim to their own vanities and terminal creeds. Despite Proude's bravery in outwitting the Evil Gambler, he cannot change the pilgrims' wills, nor save them from themselves. As Keady points out, the novel enacts a sort of "survival of the fittest" theory and the fittest, in *Bearheart*, are those who adapt and change ("Walking Backwards" 65).

Discussing the dangers of contagious hyperreality in our time, Baudrillard claims that "it is now impossible to isolate the process of the real, or to prove the real," since "hyperreal events, no longer having any particular contents or aim, are indefinitely refracted by each other" (*Simulations* 41-42). This significantly affects power and the way it operates in society. Power today is threatened by simulation; "it risks the real, it risks crisis, it gambles on re-manufacturing artificial, economic, political stakes" (44). Describing the characteristic hysteria of our time, Baudrillard labels it as

> ...the hysteria of production and reproduction of the real. The other production, that of goods and commodities, that of *la belle époque* of political economy, no longer makes any sense of its own, and has not for some time. What society seeks through production, and overproduction, is the restoration of the real which escapes it. That is why *contemporary "material"* production is itself hyperreal. (44)

While acknowledging the fact that every society has, to a certain extent, perpetrated a discourse of production and reproduction of the real,[7] Baudrillard claims that today's material production is scaled-down to mere refraction, a hallucinatory resemblance of the real caused by the law of supply and demand; it becomes a commodity dependent on mass production and consumption and, as a commodity, it is no longer subject to violence and death. If this is the scene surrounding our non-referential world—a rather gruesome scene—is there any possibility of conveying the "real meaning," restoring the value of words and, more importantly, the values that words express? In the infinite play of simulations and representations, is there any possibility of using creativity and freedom to find a centered sense of self? Vizenor's final chapters in *Bearheart* seem to provide an answer to these interrogatives.

The "Bioavaricious Regional Word Hospital" is a brilliant example of Vizenor's complex and sophisticated ideas concerning the nature of language. In such a "hospital," scientists attempt to find the causes for a national breakdown in communication; by using a "dianoetic chromatic encoder," they attempt to "code and reassemble the unit values of meaning in a spoken sentence" (167). According to Owens, the "Bioavaricious Word Hospital"

---

[7] Eco himself mentions how the Roman patrician "yearned for impossible parthenons" and that, having helped to bring down Greece, he guaranteed its survival "in the form of copies" (*Travels* 20).

suggests a metaphor for the Euramerican colonial endeavor with its "indisputably bioavaricious impulse" to impose authoritative discourse on indigenous people, the privileged discourse of Euramerica, where language is inextricably "fused with authority" (*Other Destinies* 237). At the Bioavaricious Regional Word Hospital, any attempt at reformulation and recreation of the world by means of language is repudiated. Words are confined by static definitions, and meaning is nailed down into a single presence. An analysis of the structure of the sentences in this chapter—characterized by an abundance of passive forms—better clarifies Vizenor's assumptions:

> The last stop on the word hospital tour *was* at a glass enclosed room *surrounded* with electronic instrument panels. Doctor Wilde Coxwain and Justice Pardone Cozener *were volunteered* to enter the room for a demonstration of the conversation stimulators. With regenerated bioelectrical energies and electromagnetic field, conversations *were stimulated* and *modulated* for predetermined values. Certain words and ideas *were valued* and *reinforced* with biolelectric stimulation. (168; italics mine)

Even the attempt of those who would dissect the language and discard its meaning seems equally lifeless and coercive:

> "What does word hospital mean?" asked Inawa Biwide.
> The tall woman in uniform gestured to one and two for permission to respond to the question.... What does word hospital mean? Well, a word is a word is a spoken or printed combination of sounds with meanings determined in the usage of time and social taste. The word hospital means" ... "We get your meaning," said Matchi Makwa interrupting the tall woman. (166)

Vizenor's notion of continual questioning without a single, ultimate answer is here fully manifested. In "Trickster Discourse," he refers to the theories of Jacques Lacan who warns us "not to cling to the illusion that the signifier answers to the function of representing the signified, or better, that the signifier has to answer for its existence in the name of any signification whatever" (Lacan quoted in Vizenor, "Trickster Discourse" 189). The liberation of the signifier enacted by Lacan gives Vizenor the opportunity to develop his notion of "comic holotrope in trickster narrative." He claims that "comic holotropes comprise signifiers, the signified, and signs" ("Trickster Discourse" 190), suggesting a kind of discourse in which meaning is not pinned down to a single definition. Vizenor's beliefs that words should open up, rather than close down possibilities, make him celebrate Bakhtin's notion of *dialogism* as opposed to the isolated utterances of tragic monologues in the literature of dominance.

Within this context, trickster discourse becomes a challenge to the reader. In a comic tribal world view in which the audience actively takes part in the traditional storytelling process, the trickster assumes a crucial role in this act of "pushing up the audience's consciousness," making them reformulate and reimagine themselves. Similarly challenging and aggressive is Vizenor's writing in his attempt to break the boundaries of print and bring life to the static conditions of written ideas. In a personal interview with Blaeser, Vizenor states:

> We can be prisoners, and we are, in our bodies. But we can liberate our minds. Tribal people were brilliant in understanding that a figure, a familiar figure in an imaginative story, could keep their minds free.... I'm going for trickster consciousness because it's an ideal healing, because it disrupts the opposites and that creates the possibility for discourse that's communal and comic. (*Writing in the Oral Tradition* 162)

When applied to the notion of Indian simulations and the whole idea of the Indian as the "absolute fake," Vizenor's concept of the "comic holotrope" in trickster consciousness becomes the most powerful weapon to *re-invent the invention*. Whereas material cultures are possessed and continue to be invented in museums, Vizenor effectively exposes/removes/relocates, and rewrites the sign "Indian," fulfilling the role of "word-maker" in the contemporary "word-wars."

In one of the final chapters of *Bearheart*, entitled "Terminal Creeds at Orion," Vizenor enacts the final "word-game" on Indian simulations. In this town framed by "a great wall of red earthen bricks," a further metaphor for entrapment and confinement, Belladonna-Darwin-Winter-Catcher is asked to talk about "tribal values." As the most obvious victim of terminal creeds, she recites her creed about Mother Earth along with a series of worn-out clichés and romantic stereotypes on Indian identity:[8]

> We are tribal and that means that we are children of dreams and visions.... Our bodies are connected to mother earth and our minds are part of the clouds.... Our voices are the living breath of the wilderness.... I am different than a white man because of my values and my blood is different.... We are different because we are raised with different values.... Tribal people seldom touch each other ... we do not invade the personal bodies of others and we do not stare at people when we are talking.... Indians have more magic in their lives than white people.... (194)

---

[8] Belladonna's fate as a terminal believer has received a substantial amount of critical attention. See, among the others, Velie (1982), Owens, and Blaeser.

During her "tribal sermon," a hunter interrupts Belladonna with a series of questions that trap her in logical inconsistencies. Finally, when he asks the question in which is embedded the entire meaning of the novel, "*What does Indian mean*?," Belladonna's blindness in recognizing her role as a victim of terminal beliefs is fully manifested. She states: "Are you so hostile that you cannot figure out what and who Indians are? An Indian is a member of a recognized tribe and a person who has Indian blood" (195). In a flat, impassive tone, the hunter replies: "Indians are an invention.... You tell me that the invention is different than the rest of the world when it was the rest of the world that invented the Indian.... Are you speaking as an invention"? (195). In speaking as an invention, Belladonna poses as the hyperreal, the absolute fake of Indian simulations. In Baudrillard's terms, she becomes the frozen, cryogenized savage who "proclaim[s] at last the universal truth of ethnology" (*Simulations* 16).

Vizenor's harsh satire is relentless. Sentence after sentence, question after question, the hunter "destroys" Belladonna and her deadly views of the "static Indian." As the hunter explains: "Surviving in the present means giving up on the burdens of the past and the cultures of tribal narcissism.... No other culture has based social and political consciousness on terminal creeds.... Survival is not narcissism.... (198). In *Manifest Manners*, Vizenor calls for the "trickster hermeneutics of liberation" to deny the "obscure maneuvers of manifest manners" (66). Again and again, he upholds the same basic concepts to survival: balance, humor, imaginative liberation, continuance, and stories. If stories and humor become the energy that heals, the emblematic image, of the "spider building his web on the wind," in *Bearheart*, becomes the key metaphor to survival, suggesting a continuing deconstructing and reconstructing of the real, the ultimate weapon against the dangers of simulations.

Indeed, by the end of the novel, few of the pilgrims have survived to make the ascent, the metamorphosis into the fourth world. Belladonna is killed by poisoned cookies, a clear metaphor for her own self-pride and superiority; Little Big Mouse, in her attempt to identify the cripples as romantic figures, is torn to pieces by some of the victims of this modern technological world, humans horribly disfigured by chemical manufacturers; Bishop Paramasimo burns to death, after being struck by the lightning of "Master Stranger." Even though Judge Pardone Cozener and Doctor Wilde Cozwaine escape violent deaths, and succeed in finding a secure place at the Bioavaricious Word Hospital, their decision to stay there clearly suggests defeat since at the "Word Hospital" language is dissected and discarded into lifeless, static definitions.

As the pilgrims move westward, they stop at "The Palace of the Governors" in Santa Fe, New Mexico, defined by the narrator as an "adobe ghost town." Here, the pilgrims are made prisoners by the "new governors" who order an inquisition into "witchcraft and shamanism." Both Rosina and Proude are questioned since "no witches and shamans are permitted in [the new] nation." The fate of Sun Bear Sun, at the end of the chapter, is the direct consequence of his terminal beliefs in words. Being "locked in the past without visions" (234), Sun Bear Sun remains a prisoner of words, or a "honest fool answering unanswerable questions" (234). In his effort to explain himself to the soldiers, he falls victim to their games while revealing his misplaced faith. While the other pilgrims escape, "climbing through the smoke hole over the palace," Sun Bear Sun is left to his own destiny.

A further symbol of the danger of clinging to terminal beliefs, those "ruins of Western civilization" that trap Indians and non-Indians alike into constricted, lifeless roles, "The Palace of the Governors" also alludes to Euramerica's attempt to recreate the past by making the Indian an "ideal museum specimen."[9] In this context, a city like Santa Fe with its annual Indian Market and many other tourist attractions, including false adobe constructions, becomes emblematic of what Eco defines as "authentic ghost towns" of a century and more ago, Western cities that pretend to be "the real thing," but that once again offer us only simulations of the real—hyperreal. Even though the Palace of the Governors in Santa Fe is a "real" adobe construction dating from Spanish colonial times, the irony lies in the fact that the "real" artifact is now a simulation of colonization, a further symbol of Euramerica's revisionist attempt to erase and replace the historical past.

When the pilgrims arrive at Chaco Canyon, we finally see Proude and Iniwa Biwide follow the vision of the giant bear in the morning of the winter solstice and ascend to a new existence in the fourth world. Rosina, who has betrayed Proude with Bigfoot, is left behind, gazing at the bear tracks in the snow, the last sign of her husband in this world. Proude's note suggests his faith in her, and, despite her spiritual weakness, we assume that she will join her husband in the fourth world.[10] As critics have pointed out, the end of the novel suggests the importance of spiritual strength and continual self-imagining to preserve cultural integrity and transcend "the ruins of the culture of dominance."[11]

---

[9] Vizenor uses this expression to represent the tragic case of Ishi, the last representative of a Northern California tribe who was kept for five years in the U.C. Berkeley museum where he furnished amusement and study to the anthropologists of the University of California. See his essay "Ishi Obscura," in *Manifest Manners*, 126-137.

[10] According to Owens, the character of Rosina, at the end of the novel, bears resemblance to Changing Woman, the most revered of the Navajo Holy People, symbol of harmony and balance in the natural world. See *Other Destinies*, 239-240.

[11] See Owens, *Other Destinies*, 240; Velie, "Gerald Vizenor's Indian Gothic ," 84-85; Keady, "Walking Backwards into the Fourth World: Survival of the Fittest in *Bearheart*," 64-65.

At the end of his journey through hyperreal America, Eco attempts to come to terms with some of the dramatic questions to which he has been exposed in the culture of the Absolute Fake. Visiting various marine cities and artificial jungles along the coasts of California and Florida, he notices how the theme of hyperrealistic reproduction involves not only Art and History, but also Nature. Even though he finds these places enjoyable and all the more positive, adding that they should actually exist in what he calls "the Italian civilization of bird killers," he is clearly disturbed by their symbolic threat. Comparing the Marinelands to the wax museums, Eco argues that the Marinelands are definitely more troubling than other amusement places since here nature, almost regained, is instead "erased by artifice precisely so that it can be presented as uncontaminated nature" (*Travels* 52). Whereas in the art museums, all is sign but aspires to seem reality, in the Marinelands, all is reality but aspires to appear sign. He writes: "Thus in the entertainment industry, when there is a sign it seems there isn't one, and when there isn't one we believe there is. The condition of pleasure is that something be faked" (*Travels* 52). "Universal taming" becomes, for Eco, the final essence of this "apologue on the goodness of nature," a contrived and well-designed plan that discourages any kind of intellectual revolt and fosters instead the passive attitude of submitting oneself to the falsification industry.

As a scholar concerned with problems of language, communication, and semiotics in general, Eco shows how we are surrounded by "messages," products of political and economic power, and pushes us to analyze and criticize them. Like Vizenor, Eco believes in the liberating power of language and in the infinite possibilities and ambiguities of the word. To the visitor who, in Disneyland, enters his "cathedrals of iconic reassurance" and who "will remain uncertain whether his final destination is hell or heaven, consuming thus new promises," Eco provides thought-provoking tools that, in the long run, might help him to destabilize the iconic reassurance of hyperreal America. If literature—as Roland Barthes argues—has the power to liberate our minds with its dishonest and healthy trick, then we need to be considerably alert as we travel with Eco through the Fortresses of Hyperreal America. Similarly, as we travel with Vizenor through the ruins of Indian simulations, we must continually remember the wild realm of play within language that, trickster-fashion, intends to trick and shock us into self-recognition and knowledge.

As much as *Bearheart* is a narrative about the world's end, it is also about the beginning of a new world, a narrative of "survivance." Survivors actively engage themselves in the ongoing process of thinking and creating their own lives. Those who survive are those who continually evolve. If stasis and terminal beliefs characterize the victims, vitality and adaptability characterize the survivors. Survival, for Vizenor, becomes a consistent, delicate balancing, achieved primarily through the vehicles of story and humor. He claims that "we can tell stories to ourselves and prevail." As

Blaeser points out, the most powerful stories, according to Vizenor, "are trickster stories of liberation and comic survivance," stories that teach us how to balance the forces of good and evil (*Writing in the Oral Tradition* 64). Vizenor himself forcefully makes the point in *Fugitive Poses,* claiming that stories are "liberative," autonomous creations and "traces of natural reason" (1).

If the American imagination obsessively demands "the real thing" and, to attain it, must fabricate "the absolute fake," if the Indian becomes the ultimate simulation of America, an invention to contravene America's *horror vacui* of the past, a narrative such as *Bearheart,* devoted to the deinventing and at the same time reinventing of the Indian, brilliantly conveys Vizenor's notion that "some upsetting is necessary." To contravene the absence of the real in all the fabricated versions of Indianness, Vizenor suggests that we must move on from, or leave behind this academic invention. *Bearheart* celebrates the postindian mixedblood, the "word warrior," whose humor, tricksterism, and "agonistic imagination," delivers an ironic answer to the supremely farcical and all the more dangerous simulations of manifest manners.

Works Cited

Barry, Nora. "Chance and Ritual: The Gambler in the Texts of Gerald Vizenor." *SAIL* 5.3 (1993): 13-21.
Baudrillard, Jean. *Simulations.* New York: Semiotext(e), 1983.
Blaeser, Kimberley. *Gerald Vizenor: Writing in the Oral Tradition.* Norman and London: U of Oklahoma P, 1996.
Blair, Elizabeth. "Text as Trickster: Postmodern Language Games in Gerald Vizenor's *Bearheart*." *MELUS* 20. 4 (1995): 75-90.
Bowers, Neal and Charles L. P. Silet. "An Interview with Gerald Vizenor." *MELUS* 8.1 (Spring 1981): 45-47.
Bruchac, Joseph. "Follow the Trickroutes: An Interview with Gerald Vizenor." *Survival This Way: Interviews with American Indian Poets.* Tucson: U of Arizona P, 1987. 287-310.
Coltelli, Laura. *Winged Words: American Indian Writers Speak.* Lincoln and London: U of Nebraska P, 1990. 155-182.
Eco, Umberto. "The Frames of Comic 'Freedom'." *Carnival.* Ed. Thomas A. Sebeok. New York: Mouton Publishers, 1984. 1-9.
—. *Interpretation and Overinterpretation.* Cambridge: Cambridge UP, 1992.
—.*The Limits of Interpretation.* Bloomington: Indiana UP, 1990.
—. *The Name of the Rose.* New York: Warner Books, 1984.
—. *The Open Work.* Cambridge, MA: Harvard UP, 1989.
—. *The Role of the Reader.* Bloomington: Indiana UP, *1979.*
—. *Travels in Hyperreality.* Trans. William Weaver. San Diego: Harcourt Brace Jovanovich, 1986.

Hauss, Jon. "Real Stories: Memory, Violence, and Enjoyment in Gerald Vizenor's *Bearheart*. *Literature and Psychology* 41. 4 (1995): 1-16.

Keady, Maureen. "Walking Backwards into the Fourth World: Survival of the Fittest in *Bearheart*. *American Indian Quarterly* 9.1 (1985): 61-65.

Lee, Robert A. (ed.). *Loosening the Seams: Interpretations of Gerald Vizenor*. Bowling Greeen, OH: Bowling Green State University Popular Press, 2000.

Lincoln, Kenneth. *Indi'n Humor: Bicultural Play in Native America*. New York: Oxford UP, 1993.

Owens Louis. *Other Destinies: Understanding the American Indian Novel*. Norman and London: U of Oklahoma P, 1992.

Ruoff, A. LaVonne Brown. "Gerald Vizenor: Compassionate Trickster." *American Indian Quarterly* 9.1 (1985): 67-73.

Velie, Alan. *Four American Indian Literary Masters: N. Scott Momaday, James Welch, Leslie Marmon Silko, and Gerald Vizenor*. Norman: U of Oklahoma P, 1982.

—. "Gerald Vizenor's Indian Gothic." *MELUS* 17.1 (1991-92): 75-85.

—. "The Trickster Novel." *Narrative Chance:Postmodern Discourse on American Indian Literatures*. Ed. Gerald Vizenor. Albuquerque: U of New Mexico P, 1989. 121-139.

Vizenor, Gerald. *Bearheart: The Heirship Chronicles*. Minneapolis: U of Minnesota P, 1990. Reprint of *Darkness in Saint Louis Bearheart*. Saint Paul: Truck Press, 1978.

—. *The Everlasting Sky: New Voices from the People Named the Chippewa*. New York: Crowell-Collier Press, 1972.

—. *Fugitive Poses: Native American Indian Scenes of Absence and Presence*. The Abraham Lincoln Series. Lincoln: U of Nebraska Press, 1998.

—. *Manifest Manners: Postindian Warriors of Survivance*. Hanover and London: UP of New England, 1994. Reprint: *Manifest Manners: Narratives on Postindian Survivance*. Lincoln: U of Nebraska P, 1999.

—. *Native American Literature: A Brief Introduction and Anthology*. Ed. Gerald Vizenor. New Yok: Harper Collins, 1995.

—. *The People Named the Chippewa: Narrative Histories*. Minneapolis: U of Minnesota P, 1984.

—. *Shadow Distance: A Gerald Vizenor Reader*. Hanover, N.H.: Welsleyan UP/UP of New England, 1994.

Elvira Pulitano is currently completing her Ph.D. in English at the University of New Mexico. A Fulbright scholar from Italy, her research interests include Native American Literature, Critical Theory, and Nineteenth-century American Literature. She has previously contributed to *SAIL* with articles on contemporary Native American drama.

Towards a Tribal-Centered Reading of Native Literature: Using Indigenous Rhetoric(s) Instead of Literary Analysis

Kimberly Roppolo
Baylor University

> When outsiders can read between every stitch of beadwork, every wrap of quillwork and every brushstroke, then our stories will be told.   —Del Iron Cloud on his philosophy of art

In an essay entitled "Native Literature: Seeking a Critical Center," Anishinabe critic Kimberly Blaeser has suggested that when scholars have attempted dialogic, or Bakhtinian, readings of Native American Literature, they have fallen short because the "native half to that vision has been conspicuously absent" (56-57). She argues that we need

> ... a way to approach Native Literature from an indigenous cultural context, a way to frame and enact a tribal-centered criticism [a way to] seek ... a critical voice which moves from the culturally-centered text outward toward the frontier of 'border' studies, rather than an external critical voice which seeks to penetrate, appropriate, colonize, or conquer the cultural center, and thereby, change the stories or remake the literary meaning. (53)

To rephrase that, we have been reading *against* Western notions, or at least explicating against them, instead of *from* Native ones; we have been forcing Native ideas onto a western ontological framework.

However, no one has fully articulated a more Native way of reading literary texts or, to strike at the heart of the matter, a corresponding way in which the readings offered by such a practice could be explained in writing. For one thing, Native American cultures are very diverse, and articulating a theory of reading/explicating that could apply across those cultures would be extraordinarily difficult. On the one hand, tribal cultures are autonomous entities—each maintaining distinct heritages and histories. The differences in these cultures cause us to be positioned differently as readers. A Chirachua friend has, for instance, a very different reading of N. Scott Momaday's *House Made of Dawn* than I have as a reader of Cherokee/Choctaw/Creek heritage.

On the other hand, however, there is a strong Pan-Indian culture in the Americas today as well. It is a culture that has grown out of the ashes of colonization: new fire, new life. It is a culture of reservation boundaries—sometimes shared with those who were our traditional enemies. It is a culture of shared, syncretic spiritual experiences, particularly in relation to the Native American Church. It is a culture of relocation programs. It is a culture of the American Indian Movement. It is a culture of pow wows, and frybread. It is a culture of children who have gone off to universities and found family in Native student associations. As William S. Penn writes in *As We Are Now: Mixblood Essays on Race and Identity*:

> Only a few can remake themselves as full-blood essentialists. The rest have grown up influenced by a mixture of Native traditions as a result of their participation in urban Indian centers such as those in Los Angeles or Chicago where Hopi children learned Apache ways, or Nez Perce children learned Osage dances. (2)

And this common culture, Pan-Indian and Intertribal, is a culture of literature, of writing, of storytelling, of songs. English, despite the ironies pointed out by Ashcroft, Griffeths, and Tiffen in *The Empire Writes Back* (5), is its lingua franca. Even as we wish to celebrate and preserve our individual languages, we must also celebrate our shared language of English. It is our language of survival because it is the language of the Peoples now in terms of our common experiences and interests. Seeing our relation to one another does not erase individual tribal difference, it strengthens it.

A brief review of the history of criticism of Native American literature shows that some attempt to find a shared, more tribal-centered way of approaching these texts is needed. Across the board, whether critics are of Native or non-Native descent, what Blaeser protests against is present. Traditional literary criticism posits both the artist and the product as objects to be analyzed, rather than recognizing the artist as an agent negotiating meaning with an audience, placing the critic in the role of archeologist or anthropologist, a role that, in the opinion of many Native people, has led to cultural imperialism and exploitation. This "anthropologism" happens when well-meaning critics explain cultural aspects of Native texts, attempting to catalogue discrete chunks, and, in the process, fostering misrepresentation of the whole in the same way as museum exhibits of artifacts, thus leading to the same sense of transferred ownership: the artifacts now belong to the exhibitors, to the viewers, and the cultural "knowledge" now is the "intellectual property" of the critic. Mainstream criticism is simply not appropriate for every "American" literature that makes up our multifaceted canon. Paula Gunn Allen says,

> The beginning issue ... is not one of whether we can adequately discuss all the literature written in the United States since the beginning of the century (or the beginning of the nation), because,

given our existing critical tools and the epistemology that gave rise
to those tools, we cannot.... What we must devise, then, are critical
strategies that do not descend only from Anglo-European criticism,
for example, the Western Masculinist Aristocratic Tradition, for that
tradition of necessity speaks only to and from itself .... (147)

Though Allen asserts that we need to find a shared way to address American
literature as a whole, which indeed we do need to do, my purpose here is to
assert that we need to first find a way to talk about our own stories
appropriately. Blaeser, referring to a lesson taught by the character Uncle
Luther in Louis Owens' *The Sharpest Sight*, puts it this way:

> We must first 'know the stories of our people' and then 'make
> our own story too.' And then ... we must 'be aware of the way they
> change the stories we already know' for only with that awareness
> can we protect the integrity of the Native American story. One way
> to safeguard that story is by asserting a critical voice that comes
> from within the tribal story itself. (61)

While I do not want to claim a privileged epistemology, one where
mainstream criticism is *never* productive, *never* an appropriate enterprise, I
do believe that articulating a tribal-centered criticism is a much-needed and
Foucauldian assertion of power. As Paula Gunn Allen observes, "Even our
few solid backers in academe perceive us as extensions of the great white
way.... Our capacities as creative, self-directing, self-comprehending human
beings are lost in the shuffle of ideology and taxonomy" (164). Native
American academics are continually subjected to the mindset noted by
Eduardo Galeano: "Throughout America, north and south ... the dominant
culture acknowledges Indians as objects of study, but denies them as subjects
of history" (qtd. in Stone ix). To assert ourselves as subjects, we must claim
our own ways of making meaning, and we must give back to our Peoples in
our roles as American Indian intellectuals. It is, as Elizabeth Cook-Lynn
points out, an issue of sovereignty:

> Indian Nations are dispossessed of sovereignty in much of the
> intellectual discourse in literary studies, and there as elsewhere their
> natural and legal autonomy is described as simply another American
> cultural or ethnic minority. Scholarship shapes the political,
> intellectual, and historical nation-to-nation past as an Americanism
> that can be compared to any other minority past. (127)

We must, along with Ray Young Bear's character Edgar Bearchild, declare:
"For too long we have been misrepresented and culturally maligned by an
ungrateful country of Euro-American citizens who have all but burned their

own bridges to the past. I will not tolerate such transgressions of my being and character" (*Black Eagle Child* 140).

But finding a tribal-centered critical voice is not merely a political assertion on the part of American Indian academics. Though a great deal of the cultural literacy necessary to understand Native American texts has come from critics writing in the mainstream, though the scholarship has been done with honorable intentions, the appropriation, the cutting away, the splaying—the byproducts of mainstream modes of criticism—is offensive to many Native people.[1]

David Payne's description of his experiences with Native literature is a good example.

> Like most scholars old enough to worry about their cholesterol, I was taught to believe that good criticism spoke with the anonymous voice of a master rationalist, a sort of also-ran scientist, who dissected literary works like dead cats fresh out of the formaldehyde. I have since not only learned more ways to skin a cat, but to develop enough respect for cats to leave them fuzzy and contrary. I like them living in disdain of me (like stories) far more than splayed out on a lab table (like texts). And no matter how sharp a critic may hone in on a work/writer/movement, I now believe he's always telling me a personal story, not a universal narrative aimed at decoding a text (85).

Payne sees evidence of an evolution in approach in the latest works by Louis Owens and by Paula Gunn Allen—both mixed-bloods— works which contextualize the critic rather than positing the work as an object separate from him or her (85-89).[2] And in a few other critical works, Native and mixed-blood scholars have assumed similar stances, with the critic acting in the role of what Margaret Szasz calls a "culture broker," someone who can interpret between cultures.[3] Notably, this is seen in Allen's and Owens' earlier works, *The Sacred Hoop: Recovering the Feminine in American Indian Traditions* and *Other Destinies: Understanding the American Indian Novel*;

---

[1] As Geary Hobson says,
> The assumption seems to be that one's "interest" in an Indian culture makes it okay for the invader to collect "data" from the Indian people when, in effect, this taking of the essentials of cultural lifeways, even if in the name of Truth or Scholarship or whatever, is as imperialistic as those simpler forms of theft of homeland by treaty. (101)

[2] The works I am referring to are Owens' *Mixed-Blood Messages: Literature, Film, Family, Place* and Allen's *Off the Reservation: Reflections on Boundary-Busting, Border-Crossing: Loose Canons*.

[3] Elaine Jahner recognized that critical analyses of Native literature was an exercise in cross-cultural communication as early as 1977.

in the essays in Jeanette Armstrong's critical anthology *Looking at the Words of Our People: First Nations Analysis of Literature*; in P. Jane Hafen's "Pan-Indianism and Tribal Sovereignties in *House Made of Dawn* and *The Names*"; and in Greg Sarris' *Keeping Slug Woman Alive: A Holistic Approach to American Texts.* One recent review is also worth noting in this regard: Betty Booth Donahue's "Observations of another Trotline Runner: A Critical Discussion of D.L. Birchfield's *Oklahoma Basic Intelligence Test.*"

Nevertheless, a telling comment by Donahue shows that even this repositioning of the critic is not enough. Donahue feels compelled to apologize because literary criticism violates Native ideals:

> It goes without saying that writing a piece of literary criticism that interprets a work violates the principles of Choctaw epistemology, since [in this worldview] the hearer/reader must do his or her own independent thinking. Because literary critics, Indian and non-Indian alike, are enmeshed in a publish or perish *Catch 22*, this Cherokee critic will write and hope that Choctaw readers will overlook the inappropriate activity. (68)

Mainstream literary criticism arises from both a philosophy and a rhetoric that is antithetical to those of traditional Native cultures. To accomplish what Blaeser has suggested, to create a tribal-centered literary criticism, we have to subvert the accepted modes of criticism structurally as well as hermeneutically. We need the rhetoric of the argument to be more "indigenous" if we want the end result of that argument to be more indigenous, because a good rhetoric and its epistemology are inextricably tied. At least they are if we interpret "rhetoric" the way it is defined in composition theory: i.e., a "rhetoric" is an organized system of language whose primary function is to convey an idea, an argument.

Though I do not mean to speak for everybody, I *suspect* that for many Native readers and writers, the accepted mode of academic discourse inhibits our readings of texts, because the kinds of arguments put forth in standard literary criticism differ vastly from how we are taught to communicate, and the kinds of readings explicated in academia are certainly antithetical to the way in which we are taught to view the world. The diverse tribal cultures in North America remain heavily and richly oral, despite the changes brought on by colonization—the very changes which have created the cultural context in which Native literature written in English has evolved, the changes that necessitate the kind of explication mainstream literary criticism requires. In fact, our existence hinges, both on a spiritual level from one perspective and on a cultural level from another, on the fact that we remain "storied Peoples." "Listening" is a very important influence on our reading. And a traditional oral rhetoric is still very much apparent in our written literary works.

Between Indian and white world(view)s, to paraphrase the title of one of Szasz's books, there is a cross-cultural rhetorical obstacle. As Luther Standing Bear wrote nearly seventy years ago in *Land of the Spotted Eagle*: "Oratory receives little ... understanding on the part of the white public, owing to the fact that oratorical complications include those of Indian orators." Articulating a Native rhetoric has been complicated by those very differences, structural, philosophical, and semantic. Consider the words of Clifford Crane Bear, Northern Blackfoot director of the Glenbow Museum in Calgary: "Theories are somebody's guess. Through our oral history, we were told never to use theories. We were told to use what we were taught.... The first thing my grandfather taught me was that the Earth is our Mother. Respect her." Though this comment was made in reference to museum studies, I would suggest examining the semantic difference can offer resolution to our problem in literary studies. Crane Bear's comment reveals both an epistemology and an ontology, one I would suggest that is common to many tribal peoples in North America. Moreover, this epistemology and ontology offer a theory of reading and understanding tied to a theory of communicating. American Indian Peoples have a theory of metaphysics, with all of its corresponding parts—but it is not traditionally articulated in conventional academic is discourse. Vine Deloria says that "tribal peoples are as systematic and philosophical as Western scientists in their efforts to understand the world around them. They simply use other kinds of data and have goals other than determining the mechanical functioning of things" (41). Native articulation of philosophy—of who we are and how we see the world, of what our position in it is in relation to the rest of Creation— has been accomplished by indirect discourse. We are taught by story, and we explain by story, not by exposition.

In contrast, mainstream academic discourse depends on linear argument—an argument that proceeds through a series of points, each of which is a small chunk of information, connected by the sort of logic for which verbal thinking is most conducive. This contrast can be shown using the metaphor made commonly known by Leslie Marmon Silko's widely taught and studied novel *Ceremony*. The spiderweb illustrates a Native ontology and epistemology, and not just because of its role in the stories of Southwest tribes. The spiderweb, the work of the Creator-Grandmother, is what is real, both seen and unseen. All of this creation is one story, the story which we as human beings inhabit. We can affect this story through our words, thoughts, and actions. And, like a web, if one strand is broken, the whole is affected. If someone wants to communicate something about this reality to someone else, there are an infinite number of connections between the speaker and the listener—and the story is all of the rest of the web. The speaker, knowing this, must pick a strand to follow. The listener must meet him or her at the point of connection. This is quite different from the rhetorical triangle of composition and communication theory, in which the noetic field is depicted with the speaker (subject) at one corner of the triangle, the audience (object) at a another, the particular aspect of reality being discussed at the third, and the text in the middle.

In linear discourse[4] narrow theses are easier to work out. In fact, for those who think broadly or holistically, who see reality as an interwoven series of relationships in which everything is ultimately connected, thought is difficult to convey by this means. Thinking in smaller, verbal chunks changes the way the brain schematizes information, the way it stores and retrieves it. Verbal thinking allows, and, in fact, encourages, a thinker to move from point A to the related point B, and so forth, on to Z because the brain schematizes bits of information in relation to the ones it has already schematized. Very broadly speaking, the line of connection is known as "logic." But since it addresses only one kind of thinking, this definition does not encompass every kind of "logical" thought, though it may be that other forms of logical thought seem "illogical" to those accustomed only to mainstream discourse. As Leslie Marmon Silko said in her presentation "Language and Literature from a Pueblo Indian Perspective":

> For those of you accustomed to a structure that moves from point A to point B to point C, this presentation may be somewhat difficult to follow because the structure of Pueblo expression resembles something like a spider's web—with many little threads radiating form a center, criss-crossing each other. As with the web, the structure will emerge as it is made and you must simply listen and trust, as the Pueblo people do, that meaning will be made. (48-49)

---

[4] During a reading by Robert Bly at the 2000 Beall Poetry Festival at Baylor University, Waco, TX, March 27-30, 2000, he and Carolyn Kizer both publicly bemoaned the use of linear thinking and suggested it was inferior to Eastern thought. Whereas Bly has offended many Native Americans in the past with his indiscriminate borrowing of Native motifs (the "Iron John" controversy) and whereas Native American cultures have often been hastily compared to Eastern cultures, I believe examining Bly's comment here can be profitable.

I would assert that Eastern thought, like Native American thought, is more holistic and syncretic, rather than linear and analytic. And there is now a scientific basis for this assertion, at least in terms of the differences between Eastern thinking and mainstream Western thought. University of Michigan social psychologist Richard Nisbett and his colleagues have recently completed several studies comparing European Americans to East Asians. At the last American Psychological Association annual conference in Washington, Nisbitt said: "We used to think that everybody uses categories in the same way, that logic plays the same kind of role for everyone in the understanding of everyday life, that memory, perception, rule application and so on are the same," Nisbett said. "But we're now arguing that cognitive processes themselves are just far more malleable than mainstream psychology assumed." *Psychological Review* has scheduled the publication of his research results.

With mainstream academic arguments, associational leaps are forbidden. It is not permissible to jump from point A to point Q, for instance, the way a holistic thinker forced to explain an idea linearly tends to do. The thinker sees the connection, sees the whole picture. The problem is that the reader or listener, trying to duplicate the thinking of the speaker or writer, as we as humans do when we use our receptive language capacity, can't see the connection. It's not that the holistic thinker is illogical, he or she simply uses a different sort of logic.

In most, if not all, Native cultures—there's always the possibility when dealing with many individual cultures as similar entities that unnoticed exceptions will exist—argument doesn't proceed the way it does in academic discourse, at least traditionally. Argument is done by analogy, by association, by means of indirect discourse because while we value community, the rights of the individual to make his or her own decisions are also valued. The idea is that the only way to really learn something is to learn it for yourself. Donahue says:

> In an interview, the Reverend Mr. Randy Jacob, a Choctaw scholar from Broken Bow, Oklahoma, explains that the well-composed American Indian text is designed to confuse the hearer or reader. In the oral tradition, good story tellers do not tell all of the story. The hearer/reader must supply the missing parts of a narrative and comprehend the point of the work by means of his or her own intellectual efforts. For this reason, many oral works do not move along a chronological plot line in which first one event happens and then another. Works in the oral tradition seldom demonstrate cause and effect. Events transpire, and the hearer/reader must infer possible cause and effect, significance, and chronology if such categories are necessary for comprehending the meaning of a narrative. Since a narrative assumes different meanings as the interpretive abilities of the hearer/reader change with age and experience, narrative, like the hearer/reader, stays in a constant state of interpretive motion. All of this is not to say that there is no truth to a story; it is to say, however, that truth or meaning must be perceived by a Choctaw in his own time and in his own way. (68)

What Luther Standing Bear referred to as "oratory" serves, in rhetorical terms, as argument in Native cultures. This can be seen in examples from everyday conversations. Barbara Duncan recalls the time she told her Cherokee friend, Hawk Littlejohn, about some relationship difficulties she was experiencing. Rather than saying she was "co-dependent," Littlejohn told her this story:

You know, once there was an old man crossing over Soco Gap ... going East from Cherokee towards Maggie Valley. And it was the fall of the year, and it was cold. And just as he got over the top of the gap, and was starting down, he looked down and saw a rattlesnake laying there beside the trail. And it was frozen, about frozen to death. And because he was ani-yunwiya, one of the real people, he had compassion on his relative. And he reached down and picked up that rattlesnake and put it inside his shirt to warm it up. Well, he was coming down the mountain, and he felt the snake move a little bit. And he came down a little further, and the snake moved a little bit more. Come on down the mountain, and the air was getting warmer, and the snake was moving around. Come on down a little more, and the snake was moving around, and it bit him. And he reached inside his shirt and pulled the snake out and said, "Why'd you bite me? I picked you up and saved your life, and now you've bitten me and I might die!" And the snake said, "You knew I was a rattlesnake when you picked me up."

I sat there for a minute taking this in. "You knew I was a rattlesnake when you picked me up," Hawk repeated.

"Uh huh," I said, "and this means?"

"If you know somebody's a rattlesnake," he said, "you don't have to pick them up." (16)

Straightforwardly saying that a person was bad for Duncan would have been rude, not only because speaking badly of people is typically considered so, but also because Duncan's foolishness would have been pointed out. Furthermore, despite the emphasis on the group among tribal peoples, Native Americans highly regard an individual's autonomy in making personal decisions. Littlejohn, while he obviously cares enough for his friend that he would like to see her out of a destructive relationship, avoids directly telling her what to do. Had Duncan been accustomed to indirect discourse, the story alone would have sufficed. Even when she indicates with her question that she does not see how the story relates to the earlier portion of their conversation, Littlejohn finds other ways to imply this rather than fully explicating his "reading" of her situation. In short, he uses "synthesis" rather than "analysis" to help his friend. It is not surprising that this is the mode Duane Big Eagle points out is the one more common for problem-solving for Native peoples.[5]

I think the search for a tribal-centered criticism might start with an assertion by Blaeser, in which she builds upon the argument of Dennis Tedlock:

---

[5] In "Notes for Teachers on Native American Cultures," written for publication in his *Generations: Our People Say*, compiled by the California State Department of Education.

> Traditional native literature has always entailed both performance and commentary, with, in ... Tedlock's language, "the conveyer" functioning as the "interpreter" as well. We get, says Tedlock, "the criticism at the same time and from the same person...". In a similar fashion, contemporary texts contain the critical contexts needed for their own interpretation and, because of the intertexutuality of Native American literature, the critical commentary and contexts necessary for the interpretation of works by other Native writers. (59-60)

In other words, the traditional stories told in *Ceremony* alongside the contemporary narrative act as *indigenous critical argument*; they are interpretations of the story of Tayo and Ts'eh in a tribal context and in a tribal rhetoric. This certainly can be born out by examining the literature, oral to written, in which argument is made, *interpretation* is made, again and again by the same method. However, in accordance with Blaeser's suggestion above and in line with a Pan-Indian epistemology, a "reading" made in this fashion is not closed, that it is not the only reading that can be made by synthesizing the text with other tribal knowledge(s) and by using *forms* which arise out of both the oral and written bodies of Native literature. I would suggest that a Native person, offering an interpretative comment, if he or she is in-line with the culture from which he or she originates, would not purport that his or her reading is the *correct* reading or the *only* reading. Unlike mainstream Western philosophies, Native belief-systems are open-epistemologies, leaving room for change and growth, believing that Truth, with a capital T, can be expressed by infinite means. In Cherokee culture, for instance, the colors which symbolize the directions also symbolize a number of other things. Moreover, all of these colors change when a person is practicing "medicine," or using them for spiritual purposes. Just as these open-epistemologies allow for spiritual syncretism—because they place the focus on the signified rather than the signifier—they also allow for open-ended interpretation, many different ways of expressing the "meaning" of the text. So while a Native text may, and indeed, usually does, contain within itself critical commentary, the number of readings for that text is infinitely larger.

While the difference between linear and holistic thinking is only one of many differences between Western and Native American discourse that may have application in literary theory,[6] it is my hope that this article will offer

---

[6] This article evolves from a much larger project on Native rhetoric and literary theory in which I am currently engaged. In this, I also suggest that tribal-centered rhetoric should display an awareness of the spiritual power of words, utilize repetition and recursivity, defy genre boundaries, employ meaning-filled gaps (which manifest themselves in the oral tradition as pauses, and value paradox, as it is valued in Native thought. A tribal-centered rhetoric should strive toward communally-made meaning, with an experiential-based auctoritas and an accruing context of meaning. Borrowing

possibilities for tribal-centered readings coming from within both the culture and the literature, that is, based on those within the texts themselves. Articles such as Lee Hester's "Pishukchi: One Choctaw's Examination of the Differences in English and Choctaw Language Use" and Patricia Penn Hilden's "Ritchie Valens is Dead: *E Pluribus Unum*," though written for other disciplines, offer good models of a more tribal-centered discourse in academic writing. Moreover, Dean Rader (non-native) has proven with his presentation at the American Literature Association's Symposium on Native Literary Strategies for the New Millenium (Puerta Vallarta, Mexico, November 29-December 3, 2000), that a Native rhetoric can indeed be used for literary criticism—and that one does not necessarily need to have Native ancestry to do so, just a willingness to respect and value Native cultures, rather than trying to dissect the artistic productions of these cultures and make them one's individual intellectual property.

Works Cited

Allen, Paula Gunn. *Off the Reservation: Reflections on Boundary-Busting, Border-Crossing: Loose Canons*. Boston: Beacon, 1998.

—. *The Sacred Hoop: Recovering the Feminine in American Indian Traditions*. Boston: Beacon, 1992.

Armstrong, Jeannette. *Looking at the Words of Our People: First Nations Analysis of Literature*. Penticton, BC: Theytus, 1993.

Ashcroft, Bill, Gareth Griffiths, and Helen Tiffin. *The Empire Writes Back: Theory and Practice in Post-Colonial Literatures*. New York: Routledge, 1989.

Big Eagle, Duane. "Notes for Teachers on Native American Cultures." E-mail to the author, 26 August 1999.

Blaeser, Kimberly. "Native Literature: Seeking a Critical Center." Armstrong 51-62.

Cook-Lynn, Elizabeth. "American Indian Intellectualism and the New Indian Story." *Natives and Academics: Researching and Writing about American Indians*. Ed. Devon A. Mihesuah. Lincoln: U of Nebraska P, 1998. 111-138.

Crane Bear, Clifford. "Reclaiming Artifacts Through Oral History." Native American Symposium. Southeastern Oklahoma State University. Durant, OK. 15 Nov. 1997.

Deloria, Vine. *Spirit and Reason*. Golden, CO: Fulcrum, 1999.

---

from Craig Womack's *Red on Red* , I also suggest that a tribal-centered rhetoric should have a mimetic function and utilize Native humor—an important argumentative tool in a Native context—as well as being, for Native critics, an act of love for our Peoples.

Donahue, Betty Booth. "Observations of another Trotline Runner: A Critical Discussion of D.L. Birchfield's *Oklahoma Basic Intelligence Test.*" *SAIL* 11.3 (1999): 66-79.

Duncan, Barbara, ed. *Living Stories of the Cherokee*. Chapel Hill: U of North Carolina P, 1998.

Hafen, P. Jane. "Pan-Indianism and Tribal Sovereignties in *House Made of Dawn* and *The Names.*" *WAL* 34.1 (1999): 6-23.

Hester, Thurman Lee, Jr. "Pishukchi: One Choctaw's Examination of the Differences in English and Choctaw Language Use." *Ayaangwaamizin: The International Journal of Indigenous Philosophy*1.1 (1997): 81-90.

Hilden, Patricia Penn. "Ritchie Valens is Dead: *E Pluribus Unum.*" Berkeley: U of California P, 1997, 219-52.

Owens, Louis. *Other Destinies: Understanding the American Indian Novel*. Norman: U of Oklahoma P, 1992.

Payne, David. Rev. of *Mixed-Blood Messages: Literature, Film, Family, Place*, by Louis Owens, and *Off the Reservation: Reflections on Boundary-Busting, Border-Crossing, and Loose Canons*, by Paula Gunn Allen. *SAIL* 11.2 (1999): 84-89.

Penn, William S. *As We Are Now: Mixblood Essays on Race and Identity*. Berkeley: U of California P, 1997.

Rader, Dean. "Native Screenings." Native American Literary Strategies for the Next Millennium. Paper delivered at the conference of the American Literature Association. Puerta Vallarta, Mexico. 2 December 2000.

Sarris, Greg. *Keeping Slug Woman Alive: A Holistic Approach to American Texts*. Berkeley: U of California P, 1993.

Silko, Leslie Marmon. "Language and Literature from a Pueblo Indian Perspective." *Yellow Woman and a Beauty of the Spirit*. New York: Touchstone, 1997.

Stone, Albert E. "Foreword." *Black Eagle Child*, by Ray A. Young Bear. New York: QPB, 1997. ix-xv.

Szasz, Margaret Connell. "Samson Occom: Mohegan as Spiritual Intermediary." *Between Indian and White Worlds: The Cultural Broker*. Ed. Margaret Connell Szasz. Norman: U of Oklahoma P, 1994. 61-78.

Womack, Craig S. *Red on Red: Native American Literary Separatism*. Minneapolis: U of Minnesota P, 1999.

Young Bear, Ray A. *Black Eagle Child*. New York: QPB, 1997.

Kimberly Musia Roppolo is a doctoral student at Baylor University, specializing in Native American Literature. She has published reviews in *News from Indian Country* and *Studies in American Indian Literatures*, and poetry in the University of Arizona Press anthology *Children of the Dragonfly*. She is the 2000 recipient of the Wordcraft Circle of Native Writer's and Storytellers Award for Academic Research Paper of the Year.

Wisdom of the Elders:
Geary Hobson, P. Jane Hafen, Jeane Breinig, Clifford E. Trafzer, Carol Miller, Louis Owens and Vine Deloria

Kimberly Roppolo
Baylor University

I am tempted to start this introduction with the Tsalagi story of Turtle and Beaver, but that would be too obvious.

Instead, just let me say that this all started over a cup of coffee and more than a few cigarettes. Like all good Wordcrafters visiting Albuquerque, NM, I found myself sitting in Dr. Lee Francis' favorite coffee shop, surrounded by swirls of smoke and imbibing caffeine in quantities previously unthinkable. I was, at Dr. Francis' behest, getting to know David Willingham, who was working on putting together this special Native American issue of *Paradoxa*. If you've read my article just previous to this compilation, you will understand much of the conversation in which we were engaged—like any other young academic, I was doing what my elders, both Native and non, had stressed that I must: trying to get published. In this particular instance, we were discussing the paper I had just presented at the Southwest and Texas Regional Popular Culture Association Meeting and talking about issues in the study of American Indian literatures and the somewhat paradoxical situation I was finding myself in trying to assert what Robert Warrior and Elizabeth Cook-Lynn's work suggested: some academic sovereignty, at least in relation to my dissertation. In it, I propose that a more tribal-centered rhetoric for academic discourse is an appropriate assertion of this sovereignty. In fact, I voiced my concerns that so many of our so few college graduates seem to be going home forgetting how to communicate with their elders, that they have internalized the discourse of the dominant culture via the academy so well that they have almost entirely lost their cultural grounding, that the academy was doing an excellent job, in short, of promoting colonization, of causing death by assimilation. During this conversation, I suggested that validating a more tribal-centered discourse for writing about Native Studies issues—and other academic material as well—could perhaps allow American Indian students the opportunity to value our own ways of thinking and communicating, rather than seeing those ways as inferior to those of the mainstream and therefore as something that should be abandoned in the struggle to advance themselves educationally. Whereas I acknowledge the fact that academe is a Western construct, I do not believe that utilizing more traditional—and I use Craig Womack's definition here of "traditional"—methods of discourse construction takes us out of dialogue with our non-Native colleagues. It simply shifts the loci of the dialogic and includes the American Indian half of the dialogue.

David apparently thought about this conversation for a while.

A year later, more or less, David asked me to send out a letter he had composed to senior American Indian scholars, requesting that they address some of the issues that arose in our prior conversation and others that David and Kate Shanley, who was the guest editor for this issue, had identified in putting it together. Let me quote from the letter here:

> [Kim] has suggested that aspiring young Native American scholars have difficulty positioning themselves within the "academy." How can they take part in the dominant culture discourse surrounding Native American cultural productions and still preserve their allegiance to their Native American community? How can they be part of both worlds without damaging or compromising their position in either? How can they analyze and present their findings to the larger scholarly community without betraying their Native birthright, without abandoning their language, without forsaking their cultural expectations and violating communal confidentiality? Is "inventing" a Native American theoretical discourse the only morally and philosophically acceptable alternative?

While this explanation of my concerns was somewhat more dramatically stated than the terms in which I had conceived them—in fact, I felt a little like a neo-noble savage, an academic Cherokee princess engaged in a musical adaptation of a Lynn Riggs play, let's say—I thought the issues at the heart of the questions were something about which all young American Indian academics could use advice from our elders. This was a rare opportunity to seek guidance from our *anteposados*, as my Cohuillatec friends would term them—those who had gone before and, lest I offend anyone, those who are definitely *still going*.

The responses varied.

Geary Hobson gives concrete advice on the daily reality of being an American Indian academic. He suggests that no matter how much lip service there may be in the academy toward making a space for American Indian voices, that in truth, the American Indian voice is generally unwelcome and, in fact, unrecognizable as an Indian voice. This is complicated by the fact that despite their best intentions, our non-Native friends may often erase our voices by attempting to speak for us. Hobson does, however, feel that there is much work for young American Indians in academe and encourages us to keep struggling to carve out the space for our voices.

P. Jane Hafen offers that the issues concerning young American Indian academics apply to all Indians off the rez. She suggests survival tactics of forming and engaging Pan-tribal communities, while maintaining specific tribal identity. She notes that Native models of "friendship and mentoring" can help us help each other to lessen racial antagonism and further knowledge of Native cultures and history in the mainstream academic community.

Jeane Breinig notes that her education and her academic position have allowed her to work for and with her tribe in ways not possible otherwise. Her current work on the oral history of the Haida, for instance, is made feasible only within the context of it being part of the way she makes a living—otherwise, she couldn't afford financially or time-wise to do this for her people, work that she feels committed and compelled to do.

Clifford Trafzer shares that he often uses an American Indian rhetorical style in delivering his presentations because the reactions from tribal elders who may be present is more important to him than the reactions of academics who might discount traditional rhetorical styles as being "culturally inappropriate" for the academy. Trafzer also suggest that visits and oral interviews with elders are some of the most important and authoritative sources we can use to inform our work. He goes on to share just a few examples of how elders have worked with him in his scholarship.

Carol Miller gives an insightful history she labels "Academe as Indian Country"—a history that some of us currently finishing Ph.D.s are too young to remember. She admits that the academy can be an unfriendly place for American Indians and that conflicts between culture and career can arise. But she stresses that, yes, we can succeed in both worlds, that indeed there is much important work still to be done. She suggests, like Hafen, that American Indian models of community can make achievement in this somewhat alien environment possible and that by forging these ties, American Indian scholars can thrive and do work that will ultimately benefit our peoples and academe as a whole.

Louis Owens and Vine Deloria, Jr. had considerably different takes on the questions posed to them. Owens questions whether or not an American Indian discourse can exist, given the bi-cultural nature of the enterprise in which we are engaged. He reinforces the belief that the dialogic approach, employed by him and others, notably Gerald Vizenor and Kimberly Blaeser, is still, in his opinion, the best option we have for what we do.

Finally, Deloria—I am here barely resisting calling him "the Venerable Vine," as some of us do out of the utmost respect, but in the teasing fashion common with "All Our Relations"—seems quite unconvinced that any of us have any motives that are not entirely self-serving. Dr. Deloria has certainly earned the right to voice his opinion, grumpy or not, not only by virtue of his age and the traditional respect accorded to elders, but also because of the incredible work he has done in the academy and with respect to activism. In short, Deloria thinks we need to be wanting more from these careers than to be, as he put it to me, "the house pets of universities." He thinks we need to worry about our Peoples first. I agree. But Deloria's body of work alone shows that there is an achievable middle ground, that we can work for our

Peoples from within the academy *without* being sellouts, without being "apples."

I do think that the suggestions of all of these elders need to be taken into account. We need to work first for our Peoples. We need to find and forge and nurture community wherever these careers may take us. We need to claim our place and make a space for our voices within the academy for the good of our peoples and for the academy as a whole. And we need to keep continually in mind that we are only one of many generations, that what we do is grounded in the dreams of our ancestors and will give birth to the worlds our children will inhabit.

Indian Academics Must Speak for Themselves

Geary Hobson
University of Oklahoma

First, Indian people in university systems must face up to the fact that, when Indian people have employment in universities, such as the University of Oklahoma (where I am), or small schools such as Mesa Community College or Phoenix College (in Arizona), that no matter how many Indian students there may be on campus, how many Indian faculty, how many Indian custodians, cooks, bottle washers, etc., and even Indian administrators, there is very little accommodating room for Indian worldviews by the people who run the show. Despite how presidents and deans and chairs will deny this statement in the most vociferous tones, still Indian views are clearly not welcomed. Indeed, even when officials are faced with views they have little or no resources or knowledge to recognize them as such. This does not mean that the Indian academic should not make it known that he or she retains different worldviews. Quite the contrary. We must at all turns speak out for the accommodation of Indian worldviews.

Given that Indian faculty on college campuses will most likely constitute a tiny minority, we will often need as much support from friendly non-Native faculty as we can get. Here, however, is a dilemma. Most often our friends will outnumber us, as is to be expected. But Indian academics must stop allowing our friends to speak for us. This happens all too frequently. Despite the most sincere wishes of our non-Indian friends that Indian voices be heard, this will generally not deter them from speaking for us, or standing-in for us in the often important deliberations affecting Indian people. Whenever this happens, you no longer, of course, have an Indian viewpoint. I don't care how many books a particular White colleague in history or literature may have published about Indians, their own personal worldviews will most likely not be Indian worldviews. All too often, Indian people put up with this sort of eegch [shit], probably because, ultimately, we are too nice to say anything about these kinds of things. Recall how Black scholars in the 60s and 70s did not tolerate their White friends speaking for them. Indian people need to do this, too. I mean no disrespect to all our White colleagues by saying these things, but, the bottom line for me is, damnit to the White Man's Hell, let Indian people speak for Indian people.

This is my opinion. These are my words. Quite likely, I have by now offended everyone in the house by saying them. I'm sorry if I have. However, I decided a few years ago, as I came into elderhood (or dufferdom, as the less kind would have it), that I wasn't going to be just another "nice" old guy sitting in the corner collecting dust. I still have a bark–and a bite. There is still an incredible amount of very important work to be done in academia, and I have great hopes that many of the younger Indian scholars now making their marks will eventually go on to accomplish much that the Elizabeth Cook-Lynns and Vine Delorias were addressing a few years back. This is our real and best hope.

More than Intellectual Exploration

P. Jane Hafen
University of Nevada, Las Vegas

The questions Kim Roppolo poses go beyond the institutional structures of the academy and can be asked of any indigenous persons not living on their homelands. For the approximately two-thirds of off-reservation Indians, the challenge of maintaining connections to home communities extends beyond the intellectual confines of academia. To survive in an alien environment, we must never forget our homes and families, where we are from and who we are. We may seek refuge in pan-Indian associations and urban communities, but we must always remember our own Peoples. That sometimes means sacrificing prestigious positions at powerful schools in order to stay close to our roots, as Alfonso Ortiz did when he left Princeton to return to New Mexico.

Ortiz and many others also have set examples of friendship and mentoring. Tenured and established Indian scholars can help create a community devoted to indigenous issues by supporting each other in our work. Elizabeth Cook-Lynn has done this through her editorship at *Wicazo Sa Review*. We can encourage and mentor younger scholars through reviews and conversation. We can and must encourage standards of excellence. Respect for tribal distinctions allows for differences in approach. While institutional organizations, such as the MLA, may be venues of opportunity, they also have traditional and colonial relationships with native Peoples and literatures. As we establish a cadre of Indian scholars we can develop our own networks and organizations that will protect and respect tribal nations, our histories, our cultures and our literatures.

We must also recognize that many non-Indians will, of necessity, teach and research American Indian topics. Our responsibility is to train these scholars, as well, to be sensitive and responsible to tribal concerns.

Working in academia offers a unique opportunity for Native scholars to utilize institutions to educate others and to overcome racism, or in the words of Joy Harjo and Gloria Bird, to reinvent the enemy's language. We must be doubly prepared: to answer the demands of the academy in its own language and to assert our own imperatives. In the classroom we can influence willing students, Indian and non-Indian, to see the complexities of tribal nations, the vitality of Indian languages and communities, the power of languages. We can correct misconceptions and engender understanding and respect. We can offer students the strength of their own stories.

Finally, as American Indian scholars, we must remember that which compels our work. What we do is never mere intellectual exercise, but it impacts real peoples, real tribal heritages. The implications are those of survival.

To Native Scholars, Just Starting Out

Jeane Breinig
University of Alaska, Anchorage

First of all, I think if I had to do it over again, I would. For me, the degree and positions allow me to do the kind of work I'd probably not have been able to do if I hadn't gone on to get the PH.D and began an academic career. I'm not sure where I would be or what I'd be doing, but I doubt that I would be able to afford to work on the research that I now do as part of my job. Currently, I'm working on an elders' interview, oral history project with my own group (Haida). Because of my education, I'm in a unique position to help with this in ways people outside of my community could not. Prior to getting an academic job, I wanted to do this (and had done some of it already), but realistically finding the time and energy to do the work while holding down a non-related full time job was difficult. Strangely enough, academia does allow us an odd kind of (constrained?) freedom to create a space for our own intellectual work as only we can define it. But we have to claim that space.

On the other hand, if the non-Native academic world decides my intellectual accomplishments are "unworthy" of their approval, and I'm sent packing—well, okay. I did a lot of other kinds of work before I took this job. Only now I'm a better writer and (I hope) a better thinker. Maybe this sounds kind of corny, but I guess what it boils down to for me is the recognition that I'm only going to be on this earth for a "little bit" of time and maybe if I'm lucky I can do a "little bit" of good.

Sharing with Native Communities and Elders

Clifford E. Trafzer
University of California at Riverside

Several years ago I gave a talk at the University of Minnesota, and during the talk, I kept using traditional narratives to illustrate my subject. When I finished my lecture, one Native American graduate student asked me how I got away with using oral traditions among non-native academics because "they" did not think or work in this manner of storytelling. I remember saying that I was presenting in a manner most appropriate for me and that I did not care what the "scholars" thought about the presentation and methodology. However, I told this person that I did care what tribal elders thought about the presentation, having often presented in the same manner using the same stories among many diverse elders.

The views of tribal elders about my work, the presentations, and published materials mattered most. When writing historical works, I always share my manuscripts with some elders, tribal libraries, and tribal councils about whom I am writing. Of course I cannot reach everyone, but it is important to share your work with the community or communities, families, and individuals.

I was a keynote speaker one year at the Oregon Indian Education Meeting at Warm Springs, and after finishing my talk, an elder called down the hall asking if I was the fellow who had published a book on the Palouse Indians. When I said I had written such a book, she asked why I had not visited her on the Umatilla Reservation to talk since the man on the cover of the book was her great-grandfather and I had written about her family. I told her that I had been on the Umatilla Reservation to visit a family who had been referred to me by the Jim family on the Yakama Reservation. When I arrived to introduce myself, the elder I met did not want to talk about those days because they were so sad. I missed a wonderful opportunity by not meeting the person who had called out to me at the meeting, but we had a nice visit and I was much the richer because of the discussion. I have used that oral interview since, even though it was not included in the book, and I have remembered the visit as if it had been yesterday.

Oral interviews and visits with elders enrich our work more than anything. When I conduct oral interviews, I share the transcript and tapes with the person and families about whom I have worked, and I listen to their criticisms.

The tribal council on the San Manuel Reservation invited me to work with them on a book on Serrano Indians—the ancestors of the people at San Manuel. I have researched with their cultural committe, and attended ceremonies, funerals and sings. Soon I will share a completed manuscript on the history of Chemehuevi Indians with the tribal councils of the Twenty-Nine Palms Band and the Chemehuevi Valley people because I am writing about *their* people. I do this to stay close to the tribal scholars who know best whether or not I have represented them correctly—both through historical documents but also through their oral histories. If I enter an area that is too sensitive to discuss in a published work, I withdraw it from the narrative. This has rarely happened, even when discussing the most personal and sacred issues. I share my work, thoughts, and ideas with elders because but I have the utmost respect for the people.

The sharing of work, documents, photographs, stories, etc. is most helpful to me, and the elders help me keep things in perspective. Listening, sharing, and learning from tribal elders is most important for all of us working as academics, being true to Indian people and to our presentations in the written and spoken word. We may not always get it right, but we must make our best effort to continue to learn and grow from older men and women who learned their lessons during their own lives and carry with them the treasured knowledge of the people.

In a recent telephone conversation, Eleaonore Sioui, Turtle Clan Mother of Wyandot-Huron people, was very patient with me as she tried to explain the importance of her healing methods. In my mind, knowledge of medicinal plants was the foundation of her work, but she corrected me more than once, explaining that words were her most powerful medicines, and plants followed. I am writing a biography of Eleaonore and want to get this right, so I have thought about her words a great deal since our last conversation. Our words have meaning and we must choose them carefully. We are guided in our works and words by such elders as Eleaonore Sioui who have had lifetimes of experience and education. They carry with them the knowledge of their mothers, fathers, grandmothers, grandfathers, aunts, uncles, and generations of elders. They have much to share with us.

Academe as Indian Country

Carol Miller
University of Minnesota

American Indian literature, at least in its print-language shapes, is a quite young body of work, and American Indian Studies as an inter-discipline in higher education is even younger. We have now had about thirty years to gather empirical answers to the questions attached to the roles American Indian scholars play within the sometimes inhospitable institutional environments of the academy. These questions are most often framed around contending cultural allegiances: is it even possible for Native teachers and scholars to carve out successful academic careers while maintaining accountability to the constituencies of their tribal communities and nations? One of Leslie Silko's characters in *Ceremony* points the way to an answer: "... It isn't easy. It never has been easy." But ultimately that answer is a resounding—and crucially significant—yes. My conclusion is based on my own interdisciplinary readings of Native literature and scholarship in the context of ten years of experience in the earliest-founded Department of American Indian Studies in the country, whose fortunes, over three decades now, have much to teach us.

Native scholars—and, especially, our students at every point in the educational pipeline—must claim their right to their vital place in American colleges and universities. They should do so knowing that their insider representations of Native communities and sensibilities are directly linked to the cultural authority that will secure those communities for the generations coming after us. It's time to move beyond the defensiveness that fixated generations of us upon the problematics of identity politics, that kept us, and our students, in the margins of academic pursuit. Our right to be here is no longer equivocal, no longer a matter of mere "survivance." Our objective should be to model for our students not an adversarial and minimal survival in an alien environment but an expectation of achievement and influence in a setting that may be adapted to our own self-determined ends.

This tenacious place at the institutional table we set for ourselves was not, of course, always available—not for us, and not for many others as well. We do not forget that the ideal of the ironically identified "founders," was, after all, a homogeneous white, male, Protestant America, an agrarian, timeless space created by the theft of indigenous homeland. It was an ideal intended to contain and infantilize "others"—women, African Americans, and American Indians who, unlike Black Americans, were perceived as at least potentially assimilable. And, of course, the baggage we all bring to any discussion of academe as Indian country is another memory—an ongoing suspicion of education which was from the first a tool of assimilation.

But participation in education, especially higher education, as a right of citizenship would not come easily for any within those marginalized groups. World War II—the framing of the conflict between freedom and Fascism—may have sparked a new impetus for a pluralist society and a less hypocritical democracy, but the post-World War II boom in educational opportunity, made possible by public policies like the GI bill largely by-passed American Indians like my father, whose seventh grade education precluded him not only from the opportunity but even from the dream of a subsidized college education. It would take another twenty years and the energized Civil Rights Movement of the 60s to bring Indian faculty and Indian programs into universities. But even then, and perhaps never more so than at this moment, our tenuous position would be jeopardized by every one-step-up-two-steps-back wafting of the political wind.

So where are we now? What have we as Native scholars learned to this point about being accountable to our own cultures and communities? From hard experience, we've learned that successful recruitment and retention depend most of all upon refusing to accept the blame for, or being complicit in, strategies that are certain to fail. We know, for one thing, that we must be effective over the long term in sustaining access through the academic pipeline and increasing our critical mass of new cadres of Indian students and graduate-trained young faculty to teach them. We've learned that token recruitments and short-term commitments to peripatetic academic entrepreneurs have not paid off. Revolving doors do not build programs, but they do eventually provide the excuse for institutions to say "I told you so"—and retreat from whatever commitments have been won.

We know too that we need to protect our young faculty by insisting on that critical mass necessary for support and empathy. In this regard, we need, for example, to work for multiple hires, for long-term planning and commitment by key administrators. Crucially, we need to stand between our young colleagues and the burn-out that results from exponential service assignments that junior faculty should never be expected to assume.

We need too to pay attention to the "fit" between the faculty and institution. Tribal colleges and research institutions have related but not identical missions, student populations, and professional expectations. Effective recruitment and retention focus on attracting and supporting faculty who want to be where they're hired and are supported well enough so they're able to stay there. That might mean support that emphasizes research and teaching for some; it might mean support that emphasizes teaching and community outreach for others. It certainly means acknowledgement of the particular and culturally grounded responsibilities that American Indian faculty assume—responsibilities which many of their non-Native colleagues do not share.

Only when efforts to recruit and retain Indian faculty result in some version of genuine cultural community within the institution will that destructive revolving door close long enough for programs to build a credible record of success and productivity. This is important not just for the short-term goal of increasing our numbers. What we know is that "Indian country," wherever it exists, depends upon relational being and reciprocity.

Only when that community is allowed to form in whatever configurations are possible in particular institutional settings will we become less dependent upon the uncertain climate created by the disinterest, or even the largesse, of transient administrators and flash-in-the-pan resources. Such configurations may be centered around American Indian Studies Departments or Programs, such as the one here at Minnesota, or they may be dispersed more widely in cross-campus disciplinary departments. But somehow there must be possibilities of cultural community located within the institution if we are to be able to resist the old pressures of assimilation and instead have a chance at influencing and transforming the spaces and demands of "academe."

And just what might we influence and transform? Among other things, we might reshape pervasive CEO styles of leadership by modeling consensus alternatives drawn from our own cultural histories. We might revise careerist obligations that are seen among many of our administrators and colleagues to represent much higher priorities than family and kinship responsibilities. And we might introduce ideas of meaningful functionality in our research that have less to do with counting pages of publications and more to do with what Scott Momaday identified years ago in *House Made of Dawn* as another kind of tenure that may be associated with the ways of knowing of those who have lived here for twenty-five thousand years and more.

If these aspirations are naïve, perhaps all of us—younger and older scholars and teachers—may be guided by a more universal standard of accountability. Perhaps we now should think of ourselves as having the same obligations that our colleague Elizabeth Cook-Lynn has asserted Indian people have the right to ask of their writers: "Where were you when we defended ourselves and sought clarification as sovereigns in the modern world?" (*Why I Can't Read Wallace Stegner and Other Essays: A Tribal Voice*. Madison: University of Wisconsin Press, 1996.)

Part and Whole: Dangerous Bifurcations

Louis Owens
University of California at Davis

In response to your question, I have to say how can Native writers and teachers not participate in the wider critical dialogue? If we are interested in Native American literature, for example, we read and study John Milton Oskison, who graduated from Stanford University; John Joseph Mathews, who graduated from the University of Oklahoma and studied at Oxford; D'Arcy McNickle, who graduated from the University of Montana and studied at Oxford; N. Scott Momaday, Ph.D. from Stanford; Gerald Vizenor, M.A.; Leslie Silko, M.A.; James Welch, M.A.; Thomas King, Ph.D.; Louise Erdrich, M.A.; Carter Revard, Osage medievalist and graduate of Oxford; Betty Louise Bell, Ph.D.; Kimberly Blaeser, Ph.D.; Paula Gunn Allen, Ph.D.; and so on and so on.

Native American writers have the highest percentage of graduate degrees of any grouping of American writers; the published Native writer without a university degree is the exception here.

We can extrapolate from these writers to all Native Americans. Where does "traditional culture" end and something else begin? Who will make such decisions? Can we actually imagine that cultures are not formed in dialogue, that transculturation is not the condition of culture formation? That the syncretic cultural migration and distillation of the Kiowa that N. Scott Momaday describes so beautifully in *The Way to Rainy Mountain* is not every culture's experience? How can we peel away the complexity of cultural and intellectual realities that form and inform us to find an essential something that may be endangered by dialogue, both internal and external? The question at hand is clearly earnest and important, but I believe it points us toward an impossible and dangerous bifurcation of identity and voice, with the key word being "part." How can we not take "part" in the comprehensive critical dialogue when the "part" we take is inseparable from the whole that we are?

No More Free Rides

Vine Deloria
University of Colorado

It is very sad being asked how young scholars can benefit from the mainstream while appearing to be authentic Indians. I fear we have raised a generation of sell-outs who have no commitment to the Indian Community. Indian scholars should be representing the values and beliefs of the Indian people to the larger society. Of course they will be in jeopardy—that's what happens when you take a leadership role—which most people seem unwilling to do.

If my generation had adopted this attitude, the currrent generation would have nothing today. We went out and fought for more scholarships and opportunities even though we never had these benefits ourselves. But this generation is doing nothing for the people that come. They keep themselves in a little intellectual ghetto and throw around big words like "sovereignty" and think they are doing something. Not likely. If Clyde Warrior were alive today he would puke at what is happening.

In the last several years Indians have been attacked by the academic community—Kennewick Man, Pueblo cannibalism, and Krech's anti-Indian environmentalism. We've heard nothing from the younger generation of Indian scholars. If people want a place in the world of tomorrow they have to get out there and take it. No more free rides.

Review of *The Insistence of the Indian: Race and Nationalism in 19th Century American Culture*

Martha A. Bartter
Truman State University

The Insistence of the Indian: Race and Nationalism in Nineteenth-Century American Culture. Susan Scheckel. Princeton UP, 1998. 197 pp., notes, index, bibliography.

Americans have felt guilt and shame over the treatment of both Indians and Blacks from the very first contact on this continent. Surprisingly often these feelings have led to a peculiar confusion of the two groups, so that conquest of the Indian seemed to equate to conquest of the guilt of holding other humans in slavery. As the nation faced the recurring crises leading to the Civil War, it also waged wars of conquest against the Plains Indians and shamefully removed the Five Civilized Tribes from their eastern lands—where they had begun to imitate white culture too successfully—to already occupied Indian Territory in the West. Moreover, the very founding of the nation depended upon occupying land originally held by Indian peoples. Finding some way to incorporate these apparently incompatible visions of a "free, democratic nation" required both revisionist history and a kind of unofficial propaganda campaign to define the "national character" acceptably. In *The Insistence of the Indian*, Susan Scheckel looks at the ways in which these feelings and this confusion shows up in art and literature of the early nineteenth century.

Scheckel is working over well-plowed ground here, as she admits in her opening chapter; in fact, her care in asserting the precise area she covers in this work gives the impression of having faced a dissertation committee. Still, given the limitations she has imposed, this work does develop some very useful topics. She reminds the reader of the alteration in relative power that had taken place by the early 18th century, from the time that the Indians held vast territories and made powerful alliances with European powers, to the time that Henry Clay could note that "We are powerful and they are not" (4). Yet this shift in power had come at a very high moral cost. Andrew Jackson, who had depended on his Indian allies in the War of 1812 could now declare that "Our conduct toward these people is deeply interesting to our national character" (5). As Scheckel points out, the term "interesting" reflects the contemporary belief that enlightened self-interest forms the basis of all civilization, while at the same time distancing "these people"—the very Indians who had supported him, and who counted on his support—

from national responsibility. Looking at the novels of James Fenimore Cooper, dramas featuring Pocahontas, captivity tales as problematized by the story of Mary Jemison, the contrast between the lived experience of Black Hawk and his novelized *Life*, and finally at the bas relief and sculpture in the capital building in Washington, Scheckel explores the shifting paradigm of Indian-white relationships and the ways that art reinforced white preferences.

The handling of these topics is intensely interesting, and at the same time vaguely troubling. For example, Cooper's highly influential novels certainly affected the assumptions of many 18th century readers, especially those lacking immediate contact with living Indians. Yet Scheckel discusses only one novel in depth, *The Pioneers*. This novel certainly embodies the points she wishes to discuss, and metaphorically lays the Indian to an honorable rest in the grave of Chingachgook while making of Natty Bumppo a "national hero for providing the means to confront and defer the national guilt that cannot be resolved" (40). It also, as Scheckel notes, raises and fails to resolve the kinds of issues that later permitted the forced removal of the Cherokee nation from Georgia. But *The Pioneers* is only one novel among the many that Cooper penned, and perhaps not the most popular one of the day. One could wish that Scheckel had at least glanced at whatever changed in Cooper's depiction of the Indian from one work to the next, and also what impact this made on his reading audience.

Scheckel does do this kind of diachronic assessment in her next chapter, where she discusses the stage productions based on the tale of John Smith and Pocahontas. Comparing the main themes of two popular plays—one focused on race and gender, and one focused on national anxiety over the use and abuse of power—she shows how, over time, the play came to stand for an "idealized production (and reproduction) of the American nation" (42). She begins by explaining why the Pocahontas theme seemed essential to the early 19th century stage: many still saw the theater "as potentially disruptive of the social order and class distinctions," but a "national drama," one which told of the origins of the nation, could hardly be seen as dangerous (43). Since the Virginia colonies held, for many, a kind of reverential place in history, this story (which could be rewritten more or less at will, due to the scantiness of documentation) made an ideal dramatic subject. By dramatizing the character of Pocahontas as "both child of the New World, embodying its innocence and its fruitfulness, and mother of the 'infant colony,' displaying all the feminine virtues associated with the nineteenth century American definitions of the true woman," these dramas simultaneously celebrated the birth of a nation and—as Pocahontas left her people for marriage with a white settler—rejected any Indian claim to the land. (51).

In her next chapter, Scheckel discusses one of the most popular late 18th and early 19th century literary genres, the captivity narrative, but with a significant difference. Much of the titillation of this kind of narrative comes in recounting the sexual danger the captive woman faces, making it a respectable version of soft porn. Scheckel does not dwell on this, but points out that symbolically, the captive woman is equated with the nation, and her safe return to her family reincorporates the society. The work Scheckel examines here, however, is *A Narrative of the Life of Mrs. Mary Jemison*, the "white woman of the Genesee," who signally failed to reincorporate herself either to Indian or white society. Jemison married several times, each time to an Indian man; her children chose to see themselves as Indian, and Jemison herself chose to live in a "frontier" between the white and Indian worlds. Only when the Seneca were forced onto a reservation and Jemison's home was surrounded by white settlers did she "abandon the middle ground... where she had built her home and spent most of her life, to find yet another home among her 'kindred and friends' on the reservation" (97). (I should think a comparison of Jemison's narrative on these issues with that of John Tanner would make a fascinating study in contrasts.) Scheckel neatly points out the ways in which the white editor attempts to make Jemison's narrative fit the captivity mold, and the ways in which it stubbornly refuses to do so.

Throughout the work, Scheckel points out the relevance of the literature to the removal of the Cherokee, a saga continuing throughout the period covered by the literature she discusses. Her penultimate chapter deals with the *Life* of Black Hawk, a Sauk chief whose attempt to prove invalid the treaty that deprived his people of their land led to the abortive "Black Hawk war." In the process, she discusses the alteration of attitude about land treaties. These changed from formal negotiations with Indian nations as sovereign equals to spectacles in which the Indians played a (possibly unintentional) role as actors without real power. Thus, even though the Supreme Court, by majority decision, upheld the rights of the Cherokee to keep their land, it questioned the propriety of permitting one sovereign nation to exist within another. Less noted, perhaps, is the way in which the states of Georgia and South Carolina held the federal government hostage by their threats to secede if they did not acquire the Cherokee holdings. During this uneasy period, President Jackson decided to send Black Hawk and his party—until then prisoners following the "war"—on a tour of eastern cities. Jackson's "ostensible purpose was to exhibit to the Indians the power and prosperity of the American nation in order to convince them that any future resistance would be pointless" (107). Scheckel points out the irrelevance of this ploy, given the ease with which the Indians had been defeated. Nor did the public need to see captive Indians to prove their impotence; this also had been thoroughly achieved (at least east of the Mississippi) by 1830. Instead, Scheckel claims, the tour addressed the moral issue of proper treatment of a "vanishing race." Once back with his people, Black Hawk himself initiated the process of recording his autobiography. Scheckel notes that "Black Hawk simultaneously remains warrior, prisoner, and chief, still fighting a battle for justice that will never be concluded, a conflict in which the Indian no longer fights for a place in the land of his fathers but rather for his place in the history of (white) America" (114).

Scheckel concludes her study with a assessment of the sculpture of whites and Indians displayed in Washington. If the scene showed peaceful negotiations, it was disesteemed; if white man and Indian struggled, even though no victor was shown, the victory was automatically granted to the white man. On the cover of Scheckel's book one sees a buckskin-clad frontiersman holding a struggling Indian warrior with apparent ease; the Indian carries a tomahawk, while the much larger frontiersman, who wears something that looks rather like a Roman helmet without the plume on his head, has no weapon. Horatio Greenough's full group is displayed in this chapter, as it was placed "to the right of the staircase on the east facade of the U. S. Capitol" prior to 1920 (144). Behind and to the left of the two men one can see a seated woman holding a child, huddling away from the conflict, while on their right a dog calmly wags its tail. No contest here; the apparently confident white man stands much taller than the Indian, who looks up with the same startled expression he might show if a tree fell on him. Oddly, Scheckel does not discuss this disparity of size, nor explain the mysterious sweep of fabric from the Indian's captured arm, nor note the casual drape of the Indian's breechclout (strongly reminiscent of the decent covering allowed Christ on the cross). She concludes her work with a discussion of Leutze's panoramic "Westward Ho!" Unfortunately, the reproduction in the text is not sufficiently large (nor, in black and white, sufficiently clear) to help the reader discover the points Scheckel makes about the painting. But her summation of the artwork—and the other works she has discussed—seems well documented: "even when Indians were marginalized, as in Leutze's patriotic art, they continued, through their very exclusion, to frame the meaning of the nation" (151).

Martha A. Bartter teaches American Literature and American Indian Literature at Truman State University, Kirksville MO. She is the author of *The Way to Ground Zero: The Atomic Bomb in American Science Fiction* (Greenwood, 1988), and is currently editing a volume of Utopian essays.

Review of *Leslie Marmon Silko: A Collection of Critical Essays*

Susan Bernardin
University of Minnesota, Morris

Leslie Marmon Silko: A Collection of Critical Essays. Eds. Louise K. Barnett, James L. Thorson. Preface by Robert F. Gish. Albuquerque: University of New Mexico Press, 1999. ISBN 0-8263-2033-3. 319 pages.

In a 1998 *SAIL* (*Studies in American Indian Literatures*) review of a work by Choctaw writer D.L. Birchfield (coincidentally published within a special issue on Silko's *Almanac of the Dead*), Robert J. Conley addresses Birchfield's elusive narrative form:

> So just what kind of a book is *The Oklahoma Basic Intelligence Test*? To what category does it belong? The only one I can think of is that category of Native literature which most troubles non-native readers, editors, and literary critics, that peculiarly Native category of Momaday, Silko, and Vizenor. It's a category in which the writer creates his own genre with each book he writes. (95)

As Conley suggests, a hallmark of much Native literarture is its shape-shifting forms, signatures of a field in motion (and formation), forms whose effects include disrupting and destabilizing certain expectations—readerly, critical, and marketplace—of the relation of text and context, form and meaning, writer and reader. Conley's invocation of this "Native literary phenomenon" also serves as an apt introduction to Leslie Marmon Silko's texts, a body of work whose unpredictable movements may belie its rootedness in a sustained, Pueblo-based view of land, identity, story, and community. One of the astonishing aspects of the Silko literary phenomenon has been her canonization and wide reception outside the relatively small universe of Native literary studies, particularly given the radical epistemological and political challenges posed by her works. Not only is she one of the few contemporary Native writers to have achieved both national recognition and national publishing opportunities (along with Scott Momaday, Louise Erdrich, and more recently, Sherman Alexie), but her work has generated a veritable mini-industry of articles, book chapters, conference panels, and monographs. It is also a testament to the richness and diverse appeal of her texts that the first published collection of essays on Silko's work, purposely (and wisely) steers mostly clear of the by-now exhaustively analyzed *Ceremony*, while embracing a wide range of critical and theoretical approaches to her other, lesser known major works: *Storyteller* and *Almanac of the Dead* (Silko's most recent novel, *Gardens in the Dunes* (1999), appeared too late to be addressed by this collection). *Leslie Marmon Silko: A Collection of Critical Essays* remedies what co-editor Louise K. Barnett calls the "long overdue" need for sustained critical attention to Silko's work by offering up thirteen essays and a concluding bibliographic essay and extensive reference section. In her introduction, Barnett suggests that ethnic and gender divisions within U.S. literary studies have hampered such critical attention, and therefore argues that Silko "should be confined to no special classification or restricted field. Although she speaks passionately for her Pueblo culture, she also speaks from the borderland where cultures and languages meet and from a modernist literary praxis" (1). This statement, along with the information that this book's genesis was a panel proposal for reading *Almanac of the Dead* as modern *Divine Comedy*, suggests that the volume will try to emulate Silko's own radical crossings of generic, cultural, geopolitical, and linguistic borders. At their best, these essays do so, showing how Silko's texts model a politics and praxis of cultural transformation. At their worst, some of these essays pursue routes of theoretical inquiry that seem to bypass Indian Country altogether.

Although the introduction does not explicitly identify unifying threads in the collection, I found that many of the essays can be linked by their articulations of how Silko enacts her worldview in the construction of her texts, and how that worldview gets elaborated, complicated, even globalized, in her later work. Organizationally, the volume honors Silko's sense of "interior and exterior landscapes" by framing the collection with Robert Nelson's "A Laguna Woman," a brief but richly detailed map of the cultural and geographical space that has shaped Silko as a mixedblood writer, leaving its imprints all over her fiction. Raised in a familial and cultural "contact zone," Silko, Nelson suggests, has followed the same arc of departure and return as some of her characters, even as she currently lives at a distance from the Keresan landbase. Daniel White's "Antidote to Desecration" similarly roots Silko's nonfiction pieces (collected in her 1996 volume *Yellow Woman and the Beauty of the Spirit: Essays on Native American Life Today*) in a Pueblo philosophy characterized by "a complex web of relationships that must be kept in balance" (136).

Another cluster of essays attends to how her mixed-genre masterpiece *Storyteller* (1981) likewise weaves, through its structural, thematic, and narrative forms, the web of identity, language, land, and story comprising Pueblo philosophy. Helen Jaskoski's "To Tell a Good Story," provides nuanced close readings of the eight short stories within *Storyteller*, which she argues "share a common thematic concern: the nature of language and its function in maintaining identity, especially in a world of conflicting cultures, values, religions, and idioms" (87). Just as Jaskoski foregrounds these stories as "metafictions on the nature of story" (87), Linda Krumholz finds that *Storyteller* "epitomizes a metacritical text; every piece can be read for the story it tells and for its story about storytelling and the role of stories" (64). Krumholz's fine essay, "Native Designs: Silko's *Storyteller* and the Reader's Initiation," additionally tackles the ways in which Silko thwarts critical appropriation of her work by shifting "the reader's discursive ground" through a text that "redefines power" away from dominant cultural "connotations ... of dominance, objectification, and manipulation, and rewrites it as a term conveying spiritual knowledge, profound interrelationships, and respect and responsibility for all things" (82). Attentive to non-Indian readerly response and responsibility, Krumholz locates *Storyteller*'s power in compelling its readers "to learn a Laguna Pueblo reading practice" (82). In a related vein, Elizabeth McHenry's "Spinning a Fiction of Culture" attends to the ways in which *Storyteller*'s narrative innovations—its textual and thematic refusals of conventional expectations of genre, authorship, and meaning-making—decenter readers unfamiliar with Pueblo orality. Importantly, McHenry also notes that Silko's subversion of genre forms "should not be mistakenly associated with 'experimental' literature" (102), but rather with the demands of forging a narrative "true" to the complexity of Laguna storytelling. By enacting such a "politics and poetics of innovation" (116), Silko's *Storyteller*, McHenry writes, emerges as a "written text that alters its reader's perceptions of the project of writing culture" (116).

The final six essays turn from Silko's generic border transgressions seen in *Storyteller* and *Ceremony* to the profoundly challenging, profoundly disturbing border transgressions displayed in her 1991 "novel" *Almanac of the Dead*. Indeed, this volume will probably prove most helpful to those readers left unglued by *Almanac of the Dead*, what Craig Womack calls "one of the most important books of this century" (252). In aggregate, the *Almanac* essays illustrate Silko's (playful?) claim to an interviewer that "if you make it all the way through [*Almanac*], it makes you strong" (7). The very best of these ambitious, richly provocative essays is David L. Moore's "Silko's Blood Sacrifice: The Circulating Witness in *Almanac of the Dead*." In this intricately detailed, critical complement to the narrative design of *Almanac*, Moore's essay situates the text as "prequel" to Silko's previous works by looking at "two refrains in *Almanac* that echo and amplify *Ceremony* and *Storyteller*: the witness of death, through the trope of the Tayo/Arrowboy myth, and the narrative of circulation of life and death, through the trope of blood itself" (150). Not only does Moore help the hapless reader make sense of an overwhelming text (Daria Donnelly's essay tells us that there are "763 pages, 72 important characters, 12 locations, 500 years of history" (246)), but he fluidly and persuasively places *Almanac*, a text often read as sharply incongruent with her earlier works, within a network of mutually constitutive meanings. Moore is also one of the few contributors to ground his analysis within a network of American Indian theory and criticism by weaving in perspectives of Harjo, Vizenor, Owens, Momaday, and Deloria, among others.

Moore's essay is notable as well for its engagement with *Almanac*'s transformative effects on readers, as it compels them "to sacrifice their egos, their epistemologies, and their ideologies on the rebuilt altar of history in *Almanac*" (151). Echoing previous essays on *Storyteller*'s relationship with its readers, Moore explores how *Almanac*'s elaboration of the "power of cultural regeneration" (152) resides in the vital act of witnessing, both for the characters inside the narrative, and ultimately, outside, as the text "gradually interpellates the reader of *Almanac* as witness" (162). Like the haunting question, "what did you learn today?," posed in D'Arcy McNickle's *Wind From the Enemy Sky*, an earlier novel of cross-cultural violence and violent border crossings, Moore's essay implicates the listener/reader as a pivotal participant in making meaning out of the horrors of *Almanac of the Dead*.

Two other contributors also undertake the problems of reader response and responsibility magnified by *Almanac*, which, according to Donnelly, has been "judged harshly; [because] the scope of the book seemed unmanageable, the subject matter grim, the tone incendiary." (245). While Moore and Donnelly address the relentless horrors of genocide, sexual violence, torture, and murder permeating the text, Janet St. Clair turns her attention to one of the thorniest interpretive challenges posed by *Almanac*: the stereotypes it seems to reinforce through its host of monstrous gay male characters. St. Clair works to negotiate what she considers to be Silko's hyperbolic use of homosexuality as "metaphor of the insane solipsism and androcentric avarice that characterize the dominant culture" (207), with her vexation that the "metaphor works precisely because it taps into the very stereotypes that have led to the continuing oppression and denigration of gay males in America" (216). Deferral of satisfactory narrative resolution also accompanies Donnelly's reading in "Old and New Notebooks: *Almanac of the Dead* as Revolutionary Entertainment," of the novel's efforts to create "a revolutionary consciousness": "This comical and wending assemblage is set side by side a narrative so brutal that the reader yearns for an apocalyptic resolution" (253). Similarly, by viewing *Almanac* as modern-day Commedia, Janet M. Powers, in "Mapping the Prophetic Landscape in *Almanac of the Dead*," notes that "Silko's intensely disturbing novel is intended to shock her readers into full awareness of environmental and moral degradation" (261).

By circling out from the Southwest and United States to international cross-cultural settings for her last two novels (*Gardens in the Dunes* is set partly in Europe), Silko is putting into narrative practice her belief that "those who would make the boundary lines and try to separate them [people in Europe and indigenous peoples in the Americas], those are the manipulators ... to get rid of this idea of nationality, borderlines, and drawing lines in terms of time" (9). The critical implications of Silko's move toward transnational contexts make her work more available, but also more vulnerable, to a variety of theoretical approaches. In "Material Meeting Points of Self and Other," Ami M. Regier offers a sharp, highly engaging consideration of how "objects" in *Almanac* serve "as highly charged sites of cross-cultural politics" (187). And yet her concept of fetish discourse is partly anchored to Frank Hamilton Cushing's problematic formulations of his work with the Zuni, without any counterbalancing indigenous sources. (On a side note, she also refers to T seh in *Ceremony* as "a very earth-motherish woman," 197). Meanwhile, Caren Irr's essay, "The Timeliness of *Almanac of the Dead* or a Postmodern Rewriting of Radical Fiction," claims Silko as a "postmodern radical novelist" (225), without addressing Silko's own critique of postmodernism in her well-known essay on Louise Erdrich's *Beet Queen*, or other scholarship on Silko and postmodernism (Krupat; Castillo).

Awash in Derrida, Lukács, Heidegger, and Benjamin, the essay also links Silko's *Almanac* with U.S. protest fiction of the 1930s, with nary a mention of similar Native literary traditions of "protest." Yet another essay, "Silko's Reappropriation of Secrecy," by Paul Beckman Taylor, reveals its author's distance from the field by repeatedly using dated or otherwise problematic language such as "sacred lore," while reinforcing generalizations about, and binaries between, "the Indian" and "the Anglo" that he ostensibly dismantles with his study. Given that a number of these contributors' first fields is not in American Indian literary studies, it is perhaps unsurprising, but ultimately indefensible, that some of these analyses are so strangely decoupled from relevant Native literary theory or criticism. In a review essay, Patricia Penn Hilden asks in relation to several books on representations of Native peoples: "Do these works move the center from the West to the worlds of the Rest?. . .have [they] crossed into the borderlands?" (527). Inhabiting the "world of the Rest," Silko's fiction demands that her readers cross the borderlands and visit her there.

Works Cited

Arnold, Ellen. "Listening to the Spirits: An Interview with Leslie Marmon Silko." *SAIL (Studies in American Indian Literatures)* 10:3 (Fall 1998): 1-33.
Conley, Robert J. "The Oklahoma Basic Intelligence Test: New and Collected Elementary, Epistolary, Autobiographical and Oratorical Choctologies." D.L. Birchfield. *SAIL (Studies in American Indian Literatures)* 10.3 (Fall 1998): 94-96.
Hilden, Patricia Penn. "Readings from the Red Zone: Cultural Studies, History, Anthropology." *American Literary History* 10.3 (Fall 1998): 524-543.
Womack, Craig S. *Red on Red: Native American Literary Separatism*. Minneapolis: University of Minnesota Press, 1999.

Susan Bernardin's publications include articles on early and contemporary American Indian writers. She is also co-author of *Empire of the Lens: Anglo-American Women, American Indians, and Photography*, forthcoming (2001) from Rutgers University Press.

Review of *The Voice of the Dawn: An Autohistory of the Abenaki Nation*

Andrew Denson
Butler University

The Voice of the Dawn: An Autohistory of the Abenaki Nation. Frederick Matthew Wiseman. Hanover, N. H.: University Press of New England, 2001. 305 pages.

In the early 1970s, Abenakis in Vermont began the long process of trying to secure recognition as an Indian tribe. In doing so, they first had to convince their neighbors that there were Native American communities in Vermont at all. According to a widely held assumption, Indians had "disappeared" from the state sometime in the early nineteenth century, Abenakis having moved to Canada or faded into the non-Indian population. Although Vermont Abenakis succeeded eventually in establishing their indigenous pedigree, today many non-Indians reject the idea that this proven native ancestry entitles contemporary Abenakis to claim tribal status and rights. The Abenakis themselves may not have disappeared, but their rights as members of a First Nation somehow did. In essence, Vermont Abenakis have gained the right to call themselves Native American, but they have been unable to convince non-Indians (and more importantly state and federal governments) that they possess a direct political and cultural connection to the Abenakis of the colonial era.

The recognition fight takes up only a small portion of Frederick Matthew Wiseman's sweeping tribal history, but it profoundly shapes the manner in which Wiseman recounts the Abenaki past. Contemporary Abenakis, Wiseman argues, are the "heirs in a legal sense, not merely the descendents, of their ancestors" (2). Never having signed away their lands or relinquished their tribal status, they possess an uninterrupted history of sovereignty. Moreover, Wiseman suggests, Abenakis remaining in Vermont have passed down certain ethical values over many generations, along with knowledge of the natural world. That inheritance, he feels, represents an expression of cultural self-determination stretching from the pre-colonial era to the present. Thus, while Abenakis in Vermont may have stayed out of sight from the early nineteenth century until recent decades, their history as a people has continued without disruption. It is that unbroken history of the Abenakis, a history that will serve the contemporary struggle for recognition and sovereignty, that Wiseman seeks to transmit.

It is hard to imagine someone more qualified to undertake this project than Wiseman. An Abenaki raised in Vermont and an academic trained in archeology, he is able to provide both an insider's view of Abenaki life and a scholarly assessment of the archeological and ethnohistorical record. Moreover, since 1988 he has participated in Abenaki politics and activism, making him one of the few writers qualified to describe the Vermont tribe's political resurgence. At the present time Wiseman serves on the Abenaki tribal council and is the director of the Abenaki Tribal Museum in Swanton, Vermont.

Much of the book concerns the period prior to 1800, the best material coming in Wiseman's deft reconstruction of his people's subsistence activities and material culture over a very long period of time. What is truly fascinating about this section is Wiseman's effort to reinterpret elements of the archeological record in light of his commitment to Abenaki sovereignty and what he terms his Abenaki "chauvinism." Wiseman believes that ancient Abenakis were more advanced technologically than scholars have typically assumed, and he believes that the Abenaki homeland has always belonged to his people. Those two principles lead him to challenge some of the standard archeological wisdom on the Northeast. He is particularly eager to dispute archeological models that suggest the Abenaki country was colonized by Iroquoian peoples. While his hypotheses will no doubt be challenged in their turn, they are valuable at the very least because they demonstrate how a small shift in scholarly assumptions can lead to broad changes in the interpretation of a given collection of evidence.

The most interesting material, however, appears not in Wiseman's description of ancient or colonial times but in his relatively brief discussion of Abenaki life after conquest. In the late seventeenth century Vermont Abenakis began to migrate to Quebec, where they joined what became the modern Abenaki band at Odanak (St. Francis), a community recognized by the Canadian government. Those who remained in Vermont, Wiseman explains, went "underground." They retreated to lands unwanted by Anglo-Americans or formed communities of "River Rats" on the margins of non-Indian Vermont. In later years, some made a living selling splint-ash baskets to tourists or guiding Anglo-American sportsmen. Outsiders did not necessarily think of them as Indian; they were French-Canadians or "Gypsies." But they maintained a material culture, some subsistence activities, and a body of knowledge about their environment that Wiseman argues were distinctly Abenaki. Thus, while Vermont Abenakis today may lack the kind of documentary evidence that federal officials like to see in petitions for tribal recognition, there is a record of Abenaki existence even for this era of inconspicuous living.

Having made his case for Abenaki survival after 1800, Wiseman concludes his account with the story of the Vermont Abenakis' reemergence and renaissance in the last three decades. Spurred by the Civil Rights Movement and Red Power, various families in the early 1970s began to form themselves into a band capable of reintroducing Vermont to its native population.

Although Abenakis traditionally had lived in semiautonomous family groups, they decided at this time to adopt a more centralized form of government consistent with the Indian Reorganization Act (1934). As Wiseman explains, this proved useful to the Abenakis in presenting themselves to non-Indian authorities, but it also caused considerable problems. Leadership of this new government became a point of contention among Abenaki families, which in turn led to the development of bitter factional disputes and ultimately to the creation of rival organizations. Today there are a number of different bands of Vermont Abenakis. Wiseman feels that this multiplicity of groups is in keeping with his people's tradition of dispersed authority, but he regrets that factionalism has helped state and federal officials dismiss Abenaki sovereignty claims. The splintering of bands has allowed hostile politicians and the media to portray the Abenakis as too chaotic to merit recognition as a tribe. Wiseman suggests that a solution to this problem may lie in rediscovering the political methods of the pre-colonial era, when Abenakis maintained a decentralized political structure but met in councils to discuss issues affecting the entire tribe.

On the whole, *The Voice of the Dawn* is a success. Wiseman conveys a powerful sense of Abenaki persistence, and he ably dismantles the schizophrenic logic whereby Abenakis can be celebrated as part of Vermont's cultural heritage but denied the rights and sovereignty of a First Nation. A more thorough discussion of the twentieth century, however, would have improved Wiseman's account greatly. In the chapter on the Abenaki renaissance, for example, the descriptions of shifting factions and organizations are difficult to follow if one is not already familiar with Vermont Native American politics. Likewise, most readers will be left wanting more information on the Abenakis' "underground" years. The survival of unrecognized native communities after conquest is a fascinating and crucial topic. The state of Abenaki research, however, allows Wiseman to provide only a glimpse of that process, his information coming from material culture and his own family's experience. Hopefully *The Voice of the Dawn* will compel further investigation of these vital subjects, and Wiseman's account will become the foundation of a full literature exploring his people's history of hidden persistence and modern renewal.

Andrew Denson recently completed a Ph.D. in Native American history at Indiana University, and is currently teaching in the History Department at Butler University.

Review of *The Rock Island Hiking Club: Poems by Ray A. Young Bear*

Robert F. Gish
*Visiting Scholar/Writer, University of New Mexico;
Emeritus Professor of English and University Distinguished Scholar,
University of Northern Iowa.*

The Rock Island Hiking Club. Ray A. Young Bear. Iowa City: University of Iowa Press, 2001. 68 pages. ISBN: 0-87745-770-0. $24.95, cloth.

> To read/inscription without knowing/equals the point where night/introduces daybreak through/the ecstatic songs of circling/ geese. —Ray A. Young Bear

    Reading the poetry of Ray A. Young Bear is always a trip worth taking. It was so with Young Bear's first book of poetry, *Winter of the Salamander* (New York, 1980). It was true with his second poetry book, *The Invisible Musician* (Duluth, 1990). And it's three times true with Young Bear's third book of poems, *The Rock Island Hiking Club*. If viewed as installments, which in a sense they are, these three books represent a journey of thirty years. Oh what a marvelous, breath taking trip it is, bringing new meaning to "booking" travel with one of America's leading contemporary poets who happens to be Meskwaki, happens to have been born in Iowa, but in another sense is quintessentially "Indian."

    Ostensibly it's a "real time" trip of three decades. Actually it's an epic quest by a Janus-faced, genie-genius who takes the reader on the most magical of time travels: encounters seen not so much from a rocking, clattering Rock Island rail car, or a swooshing carpet invoked either by means of wand (at least in the pre-Palm Pilot sense), lamp, or bottle, but stimulated by the surreal peripatetic peregrinations and Lazy-Boy enchantments of a blindfolded visionary.

    Although Young Bear writes about his life and times in and around the Meskwaki Settlement in the heart of the heartland in the most personal and intimate way, mediating the many worlds in which he lives (e.g., American Indian and Anglo, oral and written, serene and angry, Settlement leader and marginalized citizen, etc.), read one of his poems (if you who can stop at one) and you will see what Blake calls the eternity of the imagination opening up before you. Young Bear's time and place, our moment as contemporaries, simultaneously kin and *other*, become merely a platform, an observation point, a station for what is past, passing, and to come—a perspective which is at once synchronic and diachronic, modern and atavistic, sophisticated and indigenous.

It's a transcendent universality—the essence of what one finds in Young Bear's poems and his many voices, personae, and analogs—that invigorates and reaffirms the spirit with the power of poetry's insight into the very same "shadow of a magnitude" which Keats and Coleridge knew and expressed. Any reader sensitive to the efficacy and sacrality of not only the poetic but the philosophic mind will sense in Young Bear's art what Blake and Keats and their great, gifted company of Romantics tried to express about the marvel and magic of the creative imagination. Call it scop or shaman power, here too another new poetry planet swims into our ken.

There have been other word ways than poetry for Young Bear over the years, although his novels and essays display the eternal music, rhythms, and resonance of poetry. In this larger, *The Rock Island Hiking Club* lends itself to an allusive reading of recent narratives, part of the author's continuing Sauk and Fox saga such as *Black Eagle Child: The Facepaint Narratives* (New York, 1992) and *Remnants of the First Earth* (New York, 1996). Young Bear's work has always been autobiographical, deeply grounded in the history and heritage of the Red Earth peoples, especially the lessons and legacies of his grandparents, his parents, his wife, his relatives, his friends—and the harassments and trespasses of his enemies and the larger oppressions of the dominant white culture of Iowa and of America.

The Rock Island Hiking Club is, of course, provocative, profound, and inscrutably beautiful on its own terms. It also evidences, however, Young Bear's proclivity, a completeness now becoming more and more recognizable, to merge the encompassing narrative forms and modes of fiction, memoir, and poetry, so as to function not so much in a performance of what W.C. Williams ironically identified with being a "literary guy," as it is the calling of a keeper of the word, a conduit for the myths, the histories, stories, memories and dreams of both individual self and collective culture—old converging with new, the indigenous blending with post-modern, "popular," technological culture. It's a tall essentially futuristic order but an ancient one too, one associated with poet as scribe and prophet. One senses in Young Bear's poetry that here is both art and artifact, something of immense value to us, but also to the future and whatever chronicles or canticles our new millennium and others' even newer ones might bring.

Now the Rock Island Line is a mighty good line, known—at least in song—more for pig iron than for passengers and poets. Here, however, the hike and the hikers, in the most fundamental sense, are manifestations and representations of Young Bear's misadventures, eulogies, and epiphanies along the Rock Island tracks that run near his Settlement home, nearby Tama and Marshalltown, and other various and sundry farm-lighted bergs in north-central Iowa. It's a rough railway, the Rock Island, one burdened with personal and family tragedies for Young Bear, playing off the genocidal routes and byways of the archetypal Iron Horse of industrialism and Manifest Destiny.

Young Bear and his "hiking club" (real and imagined) both resent and relish the walk, for who wants, really, to hop a freight or even toot the engineer's whistle whether in old or new days of the Settlement, land owned and purchased by Young Bear's own ancestors. Why ride the rails at all now when casino cash might buy back rights of way, engines, cars, and cabooses?

Young Bear dramatizes the hurt and happiness of incidental Rock Island crossings and intrusions always protecting the names of the guilty by positing an imaginary but oh so real Black Eagle Child Settlement. A Weeping Willow Elementary School class roster, accompanied by the alter-ego, choral voicings of Edgar Bear Child and his troop of human and ghostly not-so-merry walkers, human allies and galactic aliens, known too in *Black Eagle Child* and *Remnants*: Pat "Dirty" Red Hat, lovely Selene, Javier Buffalo Husband, and a host of ancestors seen and revivified through the resurrection of old photographs and ancestral archival records. It's a genealogical portrait of the community, the "club," as noted in the opening line of the volume's title poem: "Symbolically, they stand close together/as they have done throughout their lives...."

Readers, ever ready for vicarious commiseration, are invited to tag along, sometimes seeing, seldom really comprehending, at least not in the way the *bona fide* blooded club members see and know, the sights and events pointed out, "explained" in English and in Meskwaki. Walter Mitty's "ta-pocata, pocata" inscrutability has nothing on "call him hey, call him Ray, but call him to supper, Young Bear."

His twenty-three poem league boots—really one pair of dress and one pair of hike-about Reeboks—stride across the woodlands with the gait and swagger of an Indian Superman. Thus spake Zarathustra. Thus speaks Edgar and his war-hero, Potato Cousin relatives Willy Potato and his cousin Jason Scarmark, grandfather Victor Bearchild, Mary Two Red Foot, Robert No Body, Doreen Half Elk, *et alli*.

The real *nobodies* of this assembly of poems are the *others*, the "white men in neckties," seen ironically, intuitively by Mary Two Red Foot's baby grandson "No Body" who "looks down at the men/who are nearly transparent in the hot July 15, 1932, sun." But it is the whites, pale-faced at the virtuoso performance in front of them, that should be ever so grateful for these poems, especially for the ethnic and ecological insights gleaned from them.

As such, *Hiking Club* is a dream come true for the raw, wild, and warring instincts in us all, our passion to care, care about nature, care about each other, care about humanity over the usurpations of technology and the misguided impositions of the puny power struggles and relentless social and spiritual holocausts humanity faces.

Ah that we all could claim "Our Bird Aegis" in the totemistic sense of the word, rather than as sonar and missile defense systems. As part of the solidarity of the "club," standing like Doreen Half Elk with our "base in the earth," we witness a young black eagle shape shifting into a massive bear, talons turning into claws, *Me kwi so ta*, and as such he "looms against the last spring blizzard" testing the sutures of his vulnerability to "physical wounds and human tragedy." As aegis too he tells us so and mourns the loss of a younger brother specific and special to the speaker, a black eagle child himself. It is a strong albeit suppressed lament for not just one brother's mortality, but for all brotherhood, the brotherhood we have with each other and with the earth itself, a connection, alas, which we are disposed to ignore.

Our meddling with nature has not only its elegiac dimensions but also its absurdist potential, a time when eagles walk rather than fly, a time when not just the parking lots of our just desserts are concrete but our trees are too. "There exists a future when green trees will be extinct./In our ingenuity artificial tree factories—ATFs—/will flourish." The once fertile garden, now stupidly mechanistic, lost for sure. Progress arrived at through the *reductio ad absurdum* of our hardly "wildest" fabricated, replicated dreams, the tree of knowledge turned against itself, against all gardens become deserts, concrete trees incapable of fooling even the most naïve of engineers, but surely not fooling the seers, the clairvoyant ones, those who feel authenticity in the very blood of their covered red-eyed blindness:

> Far ahead I see myself walking under one,
> And I grow uneasy at the thought of chunks
> of painted concrete swaying in the man-made
> breeze from bark-textured iron rods.
>
> Don't worry, says the regional safety inspector,
> they can withstand mega-knot winds
> Plus they've got internal warning mechanisms
> with stress signals linked to monolithic fans
> in the western part of the state. Should a fracture
> occur, the fans are automatically programmed
> to slow down. ("Summer Tripe Dreams and Concrete Leaves")

Our leader knows the proper response, and we say with him "Bullshit," cursing the "false wind," and the "white dust and chips of paint" stippling his and our "indolent" faces.

Young Bear's various personae, erstwhile psychic voyagers, see also into the hidden and horrible worlds of death and mayhem, the victims of crimes across the continent, from the north in Alaska, to his Midwest Meskwaki homeland, via a common "Lazy-Boy," man and chair, become an enchanted, "hovercraft" seat to bizarre and disturbing sights, icy window etchings of amazing revelation, one long ache for the loss of a haunting younger brother, the love and zest of life become nada y nada da da da da: "No red wagon/ with three round-/faced children coming up/the muddy driveway/nearly toppling/No massiveness/No eternity/in 1955."

From time to time Young Bear's phrasing, almost apart from its meaning, raises up and socks the reader into head-shaking, "hot damn" oblivion—the very titles to these poems at once prologue and poem in themselves. Witness: "January Gifts from the Ground Squirrel Entity" (a homage to the reciprocal gifts or acorns for peanuts, paybacks from grateful chipmunks, or maybe a larger power, one who could penetrate a metal suitcase with tasty supernatural tidbits). Or take the Woody Allen wit of this invocation: "Joseph Campbell, punch 'Esc'." Ubiquitous Joe there when you need him. And speaking of hitting not just the escape button but the funny bone of linguistic pun and prank, enter "A Season of Provocations and Other Ethnic Dreams" and marvel at the range and wit of Young Bear's facility with not merely two languages but with the purest essence, the rarest presence of Language itself:

> English for Black Eagle Childs,
> Pat 'Dirty' Red Hat once noted,
> is saturated with linguistic pitfalls.
> For example, he once asked
> a coy waitress at an old German-
> style restaurant on Interstate 80,
> 'Do you serve alcoholics?'
> 'Yes, we do,' he was told
> that Sunday morning. At a Sears
> auto garage the manager peace-
> signed when Pat asked about
> 'hallucinogenic' rather than
> halogen headlights. And at
> the Youth Services Facility
> co-workers oft-reflected when
> he 'applied a Heineken' on
> a muskmelon pulp-choking
> girl. That singular misapplication
> had more notice than the turbulent
> adolescence saved. But no one quipped
> at the line given when he mis-dressed
> himself: 'I am completely reverse
> of what I am.' Because that term
> could fit anyone, ethnic—
> or otherwise. ("A Season of Provocations and Other Ethnic Dreams")

Virtuosity you say. Yes, but not so simple. Poetry inherently packs a wallop, always offering more bounce to the ounce. So much so in this instance that the "thinness" of Young Bear's *Hiking Club* has the punch of a whole bottle of nitro glycerin, the heft of the biggest of big Rock Island rails.

One personal favorite of this unabashedly partisan reader, is "Moon-like Craters on My Legs." In part it is because of the intimate knowledge I sense I have of this poem, a sense, no doubt mystical and superstitious in nature, of having read it and known it, maybe even lived it before..., the *déjà-vu*-all-over-again factor. But that's the fun, the adventure, and the reward of a trek with the *Rock Island Hiking Club*, the exhilaration of the expedition through the wonderment of this splendid, soul-snagging collection of beautiful, true poems. In them we see the Other as ourselves, the magnitude of our own shadow looming long and large out of and into the eternity of the imagination, a trip of a never ending never ever landscape of literature *in extremus*.

Robert F. Gish teaches English and Ethniic Studies, and is the author of *Beyond Bounds: Cross Cultural Essays on Anglo, American Indian, and Chicano Literature*, among other works.

Review of *Louise Erdrich, A Critical Companion*

Carol Miller
University of Minnesota

Louise Erdrich, A Critical Companion. Lorena L. Stookey. Westport, Connecticut: Greenwood Press, 1999. ISBN 0-313-30612-5. 184 pages, $29.95.

    It is in some sense disconcerting for an American Indian scholar to discover Louise Erdrich fitted snugly among approximately thirty other writers, including Tom Clancy, Dean Koontz, and Anne Rice, all subjects of this Critical Companions series. The editor's foreword, however, makes clear both the series' selection criteria and its objectives. "Best selling" writers have been chosen by an advisory board of high school English teachers and high school and public librarians, and the resulting critical analysis of their work is designed for the broadest appeal—to general readers, "fans," and students. The scholars who produce the volumes in the series are intended to bring to the work their "particular expertise in analyzing popular fiction" (x), rather than in, say, American Indian or African American literature more particularly. And there is as well an organizational template for each volume: an initial biographical chapter, a chapter on how the writer's work is contextualized within literary history and genre, and then separate interpretations of each of the writer's "most important, most popular, and most recent novels" (x). These chapters too conform to an internally consistent pattern, each organized around plot, character, and theme, with additional attention to "generic conventions" such as point of view, symbol and language, social context, etc. Finally, each chapter about an individual text provides an added-on "alternative" analysis, meant to familiarize the audience with a variety of critical methodologies. In the case of Erdrich's critical companion, for example, a psychoanalytical analysis is applied to *The Bingo Palace.* Other texts are treated from feminist, Freudian, reader-response, and multicultural critical approaches.

    The strengths and the weaknesses of this formulaic process of addressing texts are key to determining the effectiveness of this critical companion overall. The mutual "best seller" character of the advisory board's rationale for including writers in the series functionally breaks down the conventional artificial distinctions between "high" and "low" literary production: it is perfectly plausible that legions of readers—and teachers and students—will find readerly companions to the work of Erich Segal or Michael Crichton just as useful as ones examining the works of Toni Morrison or Anne Tyler.

And it is certainly a convenience to discover much of the entire body of the narrative writing produced by a prolific writer like Erdrich treated in one centralized analytical location.

Another issue is the balance of critical breadth and depth. The challenge, however, is not only whether an insightful critic of popular literature such as, in this case, Lorena L. Stookey, who has also authored for this series a critical companion to the works of Robin Cook, avoids a superficial gloss—the Cliff's Notes phenomenon. Indeed, Stookey's close readings and substantial bibliography produce overall a usefully comprehensive analysis which succeeds in attaining what the book jacket claims forthrightly as its primary objective—helping "students and lovers of fine literature approach Erdrich's work with greater appreciation for her bold narrative style." In fact, Stookey strives for admirably more, attempting from the first and throughout to establish the central features, themes, and narrative choices which create coherence within the whole of Erdrich's body of work. The facts of the biographical sketch, for example—her mixed blood background, literary marriage, regional sensibilities—are presented to account for Erdrich's interest in the "told" story" and the strong identification with family and community that consistently connect her narrative voice to older communal and cultural storytelling traditions. Stookey also finds a delicate and at least tentatively resolving way to deal with the disturbing 1997 suicide of Michael Dorris, Erdrich's husband, agent, and sometime collaborator.

A more complicated question, however, than general considerations of thoroughness is whether Erdrich, or, say, Morrison or Maya Angelou lend themselves to such a formulaic interpretive approach in quite so facile a manner as Segal or Cook might. More particularly, what effortful positioning of the critic herself in relation to the cultural/ethnic/racial dimensions of the work of such writers may be necessary to locate, for example, Erdrich's narratives not only within the mainstream of American fiction, but—crucially—in their primary relevance to the fast-expanding current of American Indian fiction as well?

In the overview analysis of chapter two, Stookey, casting Erdrich as a "citizen" of two nations, covers a lot of ground in just a few pages, providing broad-stroke observations that effectively connect her fiction in apparently equal relationship to both Euro-American and Native American literary traditions. Erdrich's critical reception as a genre-stretcher; the features of her work that create resemblances with William Faulkner, Flannery O'Connor, and Toni Morrison, but also with several generations of Native authors; her depiction of the marvelous as a means of introducing ambiguity; her insistent intertexuality as a constructing principle working incrementally to create complicated story and novel sequences—these are very large ideas each treated in barely a paragraph or two. This is, perhaps, the nature of the critical companion bete noir, but Stookey does not always avoid a resulting unevenness in the pointedness of her observations. How useful is it, after all, to point out that, like Morrison and other contemporary women writers, Erdrich offers scenes of "childbirth, domestic activity, and family life" (14). Stookey's summing up of how ambiguity differentiates Erdrich's use of the magical from the conventional understandings of the magical realists is incisive and clarifying. But her metaphor of a Chinese box to explain Erdrich's stories within stories misses the richer resonance and greater accuracy of explanations grounded in indigenous storytelling practices which resist closure and prescription. A further sign of this weakness is represented by the three-page discussion of Erdrich's "Ojibwa tradition," which limits itself to noting the presence, but not much about the significance, of three archetypal entities: the manitou, the windigo, and the trickster. Yes, Erdrich employs these figures richly, but in what specific ways? And how much more of Anishinabe civilization and history are woven into her contemporary mosaic, and how much more complexly?

Though Stookey returns to cultural influence as a recursive thread of analysis throughout her readings of individual texts, that influence is marked merely as one of many such threads. I am reminded of Paula Gunn Allen's wonderful essay, "Kochinnenako in Academe," (*The Sacred Hoop*) which lays out such a strong argument for nuanced critical readings privileging the perspective of tribal/cultural understandings. It isn't that this volume ignores the critical infusion of culture in Erdrich's fiction; it is that its author does not seem prepared to mine as deeply as they deserve the matter, the manner, and the significance of that infusion. Such an informed and tenacious recovery may be necessary for a fully functional critical analysis of Erdrich's work. If this is a critical manqué, it is in part attributable to the constrictions of the analytical formula: the overlay of an "alternative criticism" such as reader-response theory may be interesting and productive in its application to *Love Medicine* when it raises issues of intended audience; a generalized psychoanalytic gloss of some of the characters' motivations in *The Bingo Palace* seems less justified or enlightening.

Even when all this is said, this text fundamentally fulfills the goals set for it by its advisory board and its hard-working author, providing companionable access to a preparative wealth of information about Erdrich as a writer and about the products of her gifted imagination. Stookey's is a constrained analysis, but it opens paths to additional critiques and cultural sensibilities which can lead readers more deeply into the terrain of American Indian fiction.

Works Cited

Allen, Paula Gunn. *The Sacred Hoop: Recovering the Feminine in American Indian Traditions.* Boston: Beacon Press, 1986.

Carol Miller is an associate professor in the Program in American Studies and the Department of American Indian Studies at the University of Minnesota, Twin Cities. She has published on representations of "urbanity" in American Indian fiction, on issues of mediation in the work of Mourning Dove and Ella Deloria, and on Scott Momaday's and Leslie Silko's fictive uses of World War II. She is currently at work on a book-length study: *Shifting Shapes: The "Efficacious" Literary Tradition of American Indian Women's Fiction.*

Review of
Coyote Kills John Wayne: Postmodernism and Contemporary Fictions of the Transcultural Frontier

Jace Weaver
Yale University

Coyote Kills John Wayne: Postmodernism and Contemporary Fictions of the Transcultural Frontier. Carlton Smith. Hanover: Dartmouth/University Press of New England, 2000. ISBN: 0-58465-019-2, $45.00 (cloth); 0-58465-020-6,167pgs. $17.95 (paper).

In the years following the American Civil War, "waiting for the word from the West" gripped an anxious and worried nation. Never mind that the majority of soldiers on the frontier never even saw an Indian, let alone fought one. In the East, rumors fed rumors, and fools and murderers (or both) became the stuff of legend. Fetterman and Fort Phil Kearny, Forsyth and Beecher's Island, Custer and the Washita and Little Big Horn fueled hysteria among the genteel folk of Boston band New York. Dime novels and an ever-eager press made romantic heroes of Buffalo Bill, Black Bart, Jesse James, and Billy the Kid.

Carlton Smith, assistant professor of literature at Palomar College in California, makes clear that the West is a place both haunted and haunting. It is a place of ghost towns where one still expects to encounter Butch Cassidy or Samuel Maverick or Soapy Smith upon deserted and dusty streets. And it is a place that still exercises a terrific tug upon the American Mind (if indeed it can be called a geographic location at all and not merely a region of the collective psyche) through story, literature, and film.

Such observations are commonplace, even trite. Though hardly holding new revelation, they become in Smith's sure hand somehow interesting enough to capture renewed attention. Using the deconstructive tools of postmodern critical theory, he unpacks the West and Frederick Jackson Turner's articulation of the frontier afresh in eight erudite essays.

Smith is to be congratulated in bringing together both Native and European visions of pieces of this imaginary space. He examines texts as wide-ranging as William Vollmann's *The Rifles* and Thomas McGuane's *Deadrock* novels on the one hand, and novels by Native authors like Mourning Dove, Louise Erdrich, Thomas King, and Leslie Silko on the other. Bridging the two, he provides an impressive reading of Italian director Sergio Leone's spaghetti westerns, starring Clint Eastwood as the "man with no name" (the best single piece in the volume).

Yet just as the West itself slips elusively through the fingers of most who try to grab hold of it in the 21st century, so, ultimately, does it pour through Smith's fingers like the dry sands of Death Valley or the waters of some desert oasis forever unable to slake any thirst, though unquestionably able to whet a pre-existing appetite.

So intent is Smith upon driving home the haunted/haunting aspect of the West that the word itself (in its various forms) is grossly overused. If one adds the deployment of synonyms like "chimerical," the point is crystalline to the point of cracking under its own fragile clarity. It seems that Coyote, the by-now-cliché trickster of western Native American mythology who slays the archetypal cowboy hero of movies like John Ford's seminal *The Searchers* in Smith's title, has evaded the author's grasp entirely—taking a significant portion of "the West" with him.

Particularly in discussing Native American texts, Smith avers that he has been influenced by contemporary Native literary criticism. Yet his reading seems curiously shallow. He cites only Louis Owens, Gerald Vizenor, and an anthology by Arnold Krupat. As significant as those to whom he makes reference are, such a winnowing lacks depth and distorts the rich discourse currently afoot among Native critics. He ignores the work of critics like Robert Warrior, Craig Womack—or even, me. Though he discusses the Columbian Exposition of 1893, he does not take up or discuss the important analysis of Yup'ik scholar Shari Huhndorf of the subject. Likewise, with the exception of his preliminary discussion of *Cogewea* by Mourning Dove, he deals only with Native writers that are among the handful who have garnered the most critical attention—Silko, King, Erdrich, and Vizenor.

Though he writes with considerable verve about transcultural spaces and identities and transhistorical realities, the West he depicts is curiously close to that of transmitted tradition. It is largely (though by no means exclusively) an ethnically cleansed landscape where Whites are free to pursue their designs unmolested. It remains an Amer-European view. Even so, Smith does a credible job of deconstructing some of these images and the power they still exercise (albeit in ever-weakening fashion as they fast recede in time). A basic problem, however, is Smith's own erudition. In his postmodern play, his writing is often as recondite as some of the images he unpacks. For instance, I confess that I am unfamiliar with William T. Vollmann's novel *The Rifles*. And after reading Smith's hyper-articulate chapter on the book, I still have no idea what the book is about or why I should care.

All of this is simply to say that *Coyote Kills John Wayne* is not a perfect book. It is not to say that the effort is not worthwhile. More discourse is better discourse. Smith serves up an interesting and witty display that proves, ultimately, the truth at the end of John Ford's *The Man Who Shot Liberty Valance*, when James Stewart is told, "This is the West, sir. When the legend becomes fact, print the legend."

Jace Weaver is associate professor of American Studies, Religious Studies, and Law at Yale University, specializing in Native American Studies. He is the author of numerous books and articles on Native literature and culture, including *That the People Might Live: Native American Literatures and Native American Community* (Oxford, 1997) and the forthcoming *Other Words: American Indian Essays on Literature, Law, and Culture* (University of Oklahoma Press). He is currently working on a monograph on Native eschatology and apocalyptic messianism.